Contemporary Issues in Cultural Heritage Tourism

The perceived quality of a destination's cultural offering has long been a significant factor in determining tourist choices of destination. More recently, the need to present touristic offerings that include cultural experiences and heritage has become widely recognised, that this aspect of the tourism experience is an important differentiator of destinations, as well as being amongst the most manageable. This has also led to an increase in the management of such experiences through special exhibitions, events and festivals, as well as through ensuring more routine and controlled access to heritage sites.

Reflecting the increasing application of cultural heritage as a driver for tourism and development, this book provides for the first time a cohesive volume on the subject that is theoretically rich, practically applied and empirically grounded. Written by expert scholars and practitioners in the field, the book covers a broad range of theoretical perspectives of cultural heritage tourism: regeneration, policy, stakeholders, marketing, socio-economic development, impacts, sustainability, volunteering and ICT. It takes a broad view, integrating international examples of sites, monuments as well as intangible cultural heritage, motor vehicle heritage events and modern art museums.

This significant book furthers knowledge of the theory and application of tourism within the context of cultural heritage and will be of interest to students, researchers and practitioners in a range of disciplines.

Jaime Kaminski is a Lecturer and Research Fellow at the University of Brighton Business School (UK) where he specialises in the study of the socio-economic impact of heritage. He has a long-standing research interest in all aspects of the management of heritage sites, and their social, economic and environmental impact. Other research interests include the impact of social enterprise. He is head of heritage research at the Cultural Business Research Group at Brighton Business School, a Fellow of the Royal Geographical Society with IBG and an advisor to numerous heritage organisations, sites and projects.

Angela M. Benson is a Principal Lecturer in Tourism at the School of Service Management, University of Brighton. Angela has published over 20 articles and chapters in the areas of Volunteer Tourism, Best Value, Sustainability and Research Methods.

David Arnold is Director of Research Initiatives and Dean of the Brighton Doctoral College at the University of Brighton, UK. He has been involved in over 40 years of research in the design of interactive computer graphics systems and their application in architecture, engineering, cartography, scientific visualisation, dentistry and health and over the past 15 years on cultural heritage and tourism.

Contemporary Geographies of Leisure, Tourism and Mobility

Series Editor: C. Michael Hall

Professor at the Department of Management, College of Business and Economics, University of Canterbury, Christchurch, New Zealand

The aim of this series is to explore and communicate the intersections and relationships between leisure, tourism and human mobility within the social sciences.

It will incorporate both traditional and new perspectives on leisure and tourism from contemporary geography, e.g. notions of identity, representation and culture, while also providing for perspectives from cognate areas such as anthropology, cultural studies, gastronomy and food studies, marketing, policy studies and political economy, regional and urban planning, and sociology, within the development of an integrated field of leisure and tourism studies.

Also, increasingly, tourism and leisure are regarded as steps in a continuum of human mobility. Inclusion of mobility in the series offers the prospect to examine the relationship between tourism and migration, the sojourner, educational travel, and second home and retirement travel phenomena.

The series comprises two strands:

Contemporary Geographies of Leisure, Tourism and Mobility aims to address the needs of students and academics, and the titles will be published in hardback and paperback. Titles include:

1 **The Moralisation of Tourism**
Sun, sand ... and saving the world?
Jim Butcher

2 **The Ethics of Tourism Development**
Mick Smith and Rosaleen Duffy

3 **Tourism in the Caribbean**
Trends, development, prospects
Edited by David Timothy Duval

4 **Qualitative Research in Tourism**
Ontologies, epistemologies and methodologies
Edited by Jenny Phillimore and Lisa Goodson

5 **The Media and the Tourist Imagination**
Converging cultures
Edited by David Crouch, Rhona Jackson and Felix Thompson

Routledge Studies in Contemporary Geographies of Leisure, Tourism and Mobility is a forum for innovative new research intended for research students and academics, and the titles will be available in hardback only. Titles include:

Forthcoming:

Contemporary Issues in Cultural Heritage Tourism

**Edited by Jaime Kaminski,
Angela M. Benson and David Arnold**

Routledge
Taylor & Francis Group

LONDON AND NEW YORK

First published 2014
by Routledge
2 Park Square, Milton Park, Abingdon, Oxon OX14 4RN

Simultaneously published in the USA and Canada
by Routledge
711 Third Avenue, New York, NY 10017

Routledge is an imprint of the Taylor & Francis Group, an informa business

British Library Cataloguing in Publication Data
A catalogue record for this book is available from the British Library

Library of Congress Cataloging in Publication Data
Contemporary issues in cultural heritage tourism / [edited by] Jamie
Kaminski, Angela M Benson, David Arnold.
    pages cm. – (Contemporary geographies of leisure, tourism and
    mobility)
    Includes bibliographical references and index.
    1. Heritage tourism. I. Kaminski, Jamie. II. Benson, Angela M.
    III. Arnold, David.
    G156.5.H47C66 2014
    338.4'791–dc23
                                                          2013022045

ISBN: 978-0-415-81772-1 (hbk)
ISBN: 978-0-203-58368-5 (ebk)

Typeset in Times New Roman
by Wearset Ltd, Boldon, Tyne and Wear

For Valentina

Contents

Figures

Tables

Contributors

David Arnold is Director of Research Initiatives and Dean of the Brighton Doctoral College at the University of Brighton, UK. He has been involved in over 40 years of research in the design of interactive computer graphics systems and their application in architecture, engineering, cartography, scientific visualisation, dentistry and health and over the past 15 years on cultural heritage and tourism. He was coordinator of the EPOCH Network of Excellence under the EU's Framework 6 programme (FP6), involving 95 partners. More recently he coordinated 3D-COFORM, a large-scale integrating research project under FP7. He was the founding Editor-in-Chief of the ACM *Journal on Computing and Cultural Heritage* and is a past Chair of the European Association for Computer Graphics. David was educated at the University of Cambridge and has an MA in Engineering and Computer Science and a PhD in Architecture.

Apinya Baggelaar Arrunnapaporn is a Lecturer in Cultural Management at the College of Innovation, Thammasat University, Bangkok, Thailand. Her PhD in Architectural Heritage Management and Tourism, from Silpakorn University in association with Deakin University, Melbourne (2007) considered the 'Interpretation of Atrocity Heritage, the Case Study of the "Death Railway" of the River Kwai and Its Associations'. She also has an MA in Museology from the Reinwardt Academie, University of Amsterdam, the Netherlands (2000) and a BA in Anthropology, from the Faculty of Archaeology, Silpakorn University, Bangkok (1992). Dr Arrunnapaporn has worked in museum and art institutes for several years in the Netherlands. She is a Visiting Lecturer in Museum Studies and Cultural Management at several universities in Thailand. She has also been a consultant on heritage preservation projects and academic coordinator for international exchange programmes. She is a member of ICOMOS Thailand and is Chairman of Interpretation and Conservation for the International Committee for Interpretation and Presentation (ICIP).

Gregory Ashworth was educated at St John's College, Cambridge (BA), University of Reading (MPhil) and Birkbeck College, University of London (PhD). He has taught at the University of Wales, the University of Portsmouth and the University of Groningen. Since 1994, Gregory has held the position of Professor of Heritage Management and Urban Tourism in the Department of Planning, Rijksuniversiteit Groningen, the Netherlands. His main academic interests revolve around heritage management, a topic on which he has published extensively. His publications include: *The City in West Europe* (Wiley, 1981), *The Tourist-Historic City* (Wiley, 1990), *Heritage Planning* (Geopers, 1992), *Building a New Heritage: Tourism, Culture and Identity in the New Europe* (Routledge, 1994), *Dissonant Heritage* (Wiley, 1996), *European Heritage Planning and Management* (Intellect, 2001), *A Geography of Heritage* (Arnold, 2001), *Senses of Place: Senses of Time* (Ashgate, 2005), *Marketing Tourism Places* (Routledge, 1990), *Tourism and Spatial Transformation* (CABI, 1996) and *Place Marketing 'Selling the City'* (Wiley, 1990).

Angela M. Benson is a Principal Lecturer in Tourism at the School of Service Management, University of Brighton where she has been since January 2004, having previously held the position of Senior Lecturer at the Southampton SOLENT University (1995–2004). Due to the research undertaken with Australian colleagues on examining the motivations and legacy of volunteers at the Olympics (2010 and 2012), Angela was made an Adjunct Associate Professor of the University of Canberra, Australia in 2009. Prior to her career as an academic, she worked for 13 years in leisure and recreation, managing a range of facilities and events. Angela has published over 20 articles and chapters in the areas of volunteering (tourism and mega events), best value, sustainability and research methods. She is the Founding Chair of the Association for Tourism and Leisure Education (ATLAS) Volunteer Tourism Research Group, Fellow of the Royal Geographical Society with IBG and a Fellow of the Higher Education Academy.

Stephen Bird is Head of Heritage Services at Bath & North East Somerset Council. He has worked in museums and heritage management in Bath for many years. Stephen established Heritage Services as a business unit within the Council and, in recent years, conceived the Roman Baths Development Plan to transform the site's accessibility and retain its position as a leading visitor attraction. Stephen is a past president of the South Western Federation of Museums & Art Galleries and, until 2009, served on the South West Board of the Museums Libraries and Archives Council. He is a Fellow of the Museums Association and a Member of the Chartered Management Institute. Locally, Stephen sits on the Bath Abbey Development Board and the World Heritage Steering Group. He lectures on a variety of academic and heritage management subjects, sits on the Advisory Board of the Alexander Keiller Museum Avebury, is a Trustee of Glastonbury Abbey and a professional mentor with the Museums Association.

Tiziana Cuccia is Professor of Economic Policy at the University of Catania, Italy. She obtained a Laurea (BA) in Economics (1991) and a Doctorate in

'Technology and Economics of Production for the Environmental Safeguard' at the University of Catania (1995), and a Masters in 'Environmental and Resource Economics' at University College London (1993). Her scientific interests concern the economic evaluation of public goods, issues in cultural economics, with particular reference to artists' market labour, and tourism economics, especially the role of cultural heritage in fostering tourism. Her publications have appeared in international journals and books. Among her administrative duties, she was member of Academic Senate of the University of Catania (2005–2010); appointed in 2007, she was a member of the Ministerial Commission for the study and promotion of creativity in Italy.

Elke Ennen has been an Associate Professor of Visitor Studies since January 2006 at the Applied University of Breda (the Netherlands). She specialised in visitors connected to heritage. Elke studied human geography at the University of Groningen where she specialised in urban planning. Dr Ennen has a PhD in the field of urban planning from the same university. Her dissertation titled 'Heritage in Fragments: The Meaning of Pasts for City Center Residents' was presented in 1999. Until 2006 she worked as a Lecturer at the Faculty of Spatial Sciences at the University of Utrecht, in the field of heritage planning, planning of public spaces and city marketing. Elke is also Editor of the journal *Leisure Studies*, which considers research findings and policy plans in various sub-fields of leisure, including sports, recreation, tourism, media, volunteer work, use of space and time.

Wael Salah Fahmi was trained as an architect at Cairo University and received his PhD in Planning and Landscape from the University of Manchester (UK). He currently teaches architecture and urban design as a Professor of Urbanism at the Architecture Department of Helwan University in Cairo. He is also a visiting academic at the University of Manchester. Dr Fahmi has conducted research on Greater Cairo's urban growth problems and housing crisis (published in *Cities*). Further research focuses on the rehabilitation of historical Cairo (published in *Habitat International and International Development Planning Review*), the cemetery informal settlements (published in *Arab World Geographer*) and the garbage collectors community (*Environment and Urbanization* and *Habitat International*). Other recent publications include street movements within Cairo's public spaces (*Environment and Urbanization*) and Cairo's European Quarter (*International Development Planning Review*).

M.K. Flynn is currently a Research Fellow at the Archbishop Desmond Tutu Centre for War and Peace Studies at Liverpool Hope University. Previously, she was a Senior Lecturer in Politics at the University of the West of England (UWE), Bristol, and an Honorary University Fellow at the Exeter Centre for Ethno-Political Studies at the University of Exeter. Her research interests are in the areas of ethnic conflict, transitional justice, peace-building, democratisation, heritage and public policy. She has a double BA in English

Literature and Political Science (High Departmental Distinction). After then completing doctoral studies at St Antony's College, Oxford, she worked at universities in Israel and Ukraine before taking up her post at UWE. In 2001 she moved to Johannesburg, South Africa, for two years to assist in the starting up of a new offshore campus for Monash University, Australia, before returning to UWE. She is on the editorial board for the journal *Ethnic and Racial Studies* and at UWE convened the University Peace and Conflict Research Cluster.

Benjamin Hruska serves as the Historian for the US Department of Defense's US Court of Appeals for the Armed Forces in Washington, DC. Hruska's duties include the launching of a new oral history project at the Courthouse and managing public programmes. He recently received his PhD in Public History from Arizona State University and his dissertation covered the sinking of an American aircraft carrier in World War II. Before returning to graduate school, Hruska served as the Director of the Block Island Historical Society located on Block Island, Rhode Island. His duties there included operating the house museum, public programmes and the annual House and Garden Tour. Hruska has also earned an MA in Public History from Wichita State University.

Jaime Kaminski is a Lecturer and Research Fellow at the University of Brighton Business School (UK) where he specialises in the study of the socio-economic impact of heritage. He began his career as an archaeologist and has a PhD in archaeology from the University of Reading (1995). He has a long-standing research interest in all aspects of the management of heritage sites, and their social, economic and environmental impact. Additionally, his work for the university's Cultural Informatics Research Group covers aspects as diverse as heritage tourism, the sustainability of heritage sites and the impact of information and communication technologies in heritage. Other research interests include the impact of social enterprise. He is head of heritage research at the Cultural Business Research Group at Brighton Business School, a Fellow of the Royal Geographical Society with IBG, a Fellow of the Society of Antiquaries and an advisor to numerous heritage organizations, sites and projects.

Devi Roza Kausar graduated from the Faculty of Economics, Padjadjaran University, Bandung, Indonesia, where she majored in Marketing Management in 1998. She obtained her Master's degree in Tourism Management in 2002 from the Curtin University of Technology, Perth, Australia. Upon her return to Indonesia in 2003, Devi worked in the Indonesian Ecotourism Network Foundation (INDECON), an NGO working in the field of ecotourism. In 2007, she left for Nagoya, Japan, to pursue a doctoral degree in the Graduate School of International Development, Nagoya University. She obtained a PhD in International Development in 2010 after defending her dissertation on the socio-economic impacts of World Heritage tourism in rural areas in view of the management aspects of World Heritage Sites, using the case of Borobudur World Heritage Site. She is now a Lecturer at the Faculty of Tourism, Pancasila University, Jakarta, Indonesia.

Tony King was Associate Lecturer and Research Fellow in Politics at the University of the West of England (UWE), Bristol. His research expertise is in colonial history and politics of southern Africa, apartheid and post-apartheid South Africa, heritage and transitional justice. He studied at the University of Liverpool and the Institute of Commonwealth Studies before undertaking doctoral work at the University of Oxford (St Antony's College). Following his DPhil, he worked for a policy advocacy NGO in Johannesburg and Monash University. He has published extensively in journals and edited collections. He has worked with Dr M.K. Flynn on the Nuffield Foundation-funded project 'Post-Conflict Settlement, Heritage and Urban Regeneration in South Africa and Northern Ireland: the Redevelopment of the Old Fort and Long Kesh/Maze Prisons' (2007–2008) and UWE's EU/EuropeAid project 'Reconciliation and Peace Economics in Cyprus' (2010–2012).

Duangjai Lorthanavanich is Assistant Professor at the Integrated Bachelor's and Master's Degree Programme, Thammasat Business School, Bangkok, Thailand. She gained her PhD in the Integrated Sciences from the College of Interdisciplinary Studies, Thammasat University in 2010. Her PhD addressed issues of state, capital and the community in tourism management in Okinawa, Japan and in Mae Hong Son, Thailand. Her research is the integration of sociology, anthropology, Japanese studies and tourism to investigate and clarify community tourism management in Japan and Thailand. She has long-term research interests in Japanese studies, heritage management and tourism development, and community tourism management in Japan and Thailand. Her current research interest is heritage tourism management in South East Asia and South Asia. Dr Duangjai has coordinated the planning of the Thailand Tourism Master Plan 2008–2011, conducting a survey on heritage management for cultural tourism development in Northeast Thailand focusing on the Khmer heritage in Nakorn Rachasrima and Burirum province.

Eugenio van Maanen is a Senior Lecturer and Researcher in Heritage and Tourism at the NHTV Breda University of Applied Sciences. He is affiliated with the Academy of Tourism and the professorship of Visitor Studies. Eugenio studied human geography with a specialisation in international development studies at Utrecht University. He pursued a PhD at the University of Groningen, the Netherlands, on 'Colonial Heritage and Ethnic Pluralism: its Socio-psychological Meaning in a Multiethnic Society'. His research and teaching expertise include tourism product development and planning; heritage and tourism; uses and meanings of heritage; human resource development and tourism in developing countries; tourism research methods and techniques; and sustainability in tourism. At NHTV, he teaches courses in Tourism

Management and Heritage Tourism. He also teaches in the scientific BSc/MA programme Tourism, a cooperative venture between NHTV and Wageningen University.

Carlo Perelli is a Researcher at CRENoS, University of Cagliari and University of Sassari, Italy. After an inter-disciplinary MA in Mediterranean Studies conducted between Venice, Montpellier and Madrid, he received his PhD from the School for Advanced Studies in Venice, for a thesis on the implementation of sustainability policies in mass tourism coastal destinations. His interests are in tourism geography, planning for tourism, Integrated Coastal Zone Management (ICZM) and Tourism Carrying Capacity Assessment (TCCA), mainly in Sardinia (Italy), Morocco and Tunisia.

Ilde Rizzo is Professor of Public Finance at the University of Catania and former director of the Postgraduate Master on the Economics of Cultural Sector held by the Scuola Superiore of the University of Catania. She received a Doctor of Science *honoris causa* from the University of Buckingham, UK. She was Pro Vice-Chancellor at the University of Catania (1994–1999), member of the Italian National Public Works Authority (1999–2004) and also member of the Public Finance Advisory Committee at the Italian Treasury (2007–2008). She is currently President of the national independent Commission for Evaluation, Transparency, Integrity of Public Administration (CiVIT). She has published in many fields of public finance (cultural economics, performance measurement, efficiency of public expenditure, economics of procurement, health economics), including monographs, edited books and articles in professional journals and several other papers.

Begoña Sánchez Royo has a PhD 'Sobresaliente Cum Laude' and 'Doctor Europeus' from the Polytechnic University of Valencia, which focused on the impact of intangible cultural heritage. She has a degree in Economics from the University of Valencia, and is an accredited economist. Dr Royo has a Diploma in Business Administration from the University of Valencia Business School, a Masters in Agricultural Economics from the Polytechnic University of Valencia and a BA in Commerce from Dundee Abertay University (UK). She is also Assistant Lecturer at the University of Valencia in Master's courses related to Cultural and Sustainable Tourism. She has conducted socio-economic impact studies across Spain, including La Palma, the Province of Alicante and Valencia. Dr Royo is an advisor for the City of Valencia's nomination proposal for the 'Cultural Space of the Valencian Fallas Festival', which is to be considered for inclusion on UNESCO's Intangible World Heritage List.

Giovanni Sistu is Professor of Geography at the Faculty of Political Science, University of Cagliari, Italy. He graduated with honours in Geological Sciences at the University of Cagliari in 1985. Professor Sistu received his PhD in Mineral Prospecting at the Faculty of Engineering at the University of Cagliari. He worked for the Centre for Geo-mining and Mineralogical Studies of the CNR (Italian National Research Council). He was Junior Lecturer of Political and Economic Geography and Environmental Policies at the Faculty of Political Science, University of Cagliari, between 1995 and 2005. His main research interests are in environmental policies and local development; cultural tourism and geography in the Maghreb; and water and waste management in the Mediterranean region.

Geoffrey Smith is the Vice-President of the Federation of British Historic Vehicle Clubs (FBHVC) and Co-founder and Director of the Historic Vehicle Research Institute. Geoff's past career in the motor industry began as a training manager. A natural progression was to a role in human resources management, nationally and internationally, his career culminating at Jaguar Cars. After retirement, he became Chairman of the Federation of British Historic Vehicle Clubs for five years and Vice-President of the Federation Internationale Vehicules Anciens for eight years, a role involved with strategy and legislation. He initiated the first economic, employment, environment and cultural study into the UK heritage vehicle movement in 1997 and a similar European-wide study in 2006.

Dallen J. Timothy is Professor of Community Resources and Development at Arizona State University, USA. He is also Senior Sustainability Scientist and Director of the Tourism Development and Management Programme at the same university. In addition, Dr Timothy holds visiting professorships at the Universiti Teknologi Mara in Selangor, Malaysia and Indiana University, USA. He is also on the Scientific Advisory Board for La Rochelle Business School's tourism programme in France. He has published widely on many different aspects of tourism and heritage. He serves on the editorial boards of 11 international scholarly journals, as Editor in Chief of the *Journal of Heritage Tourism*, and as a Co-commissioning Editor of the *Aspects of Tourism* book series by Channel View Publications. Professor Timothy is currently working on projects in Europe, Asia, North America and the Middle East related to religious tourism, intangible heritage, heritage cuisines, heritage trails, geopolitics and tourism, and cross-border cooperation.

John E. Tunbridge is a graduate of St John's College, Cambridge and received his PhD from Bristol University. He joined Carleton University, Canada in 1969 and has since taught in Australia, the UK and South Africa. He is co-author of *The Tourist-Historic City* (Elsevier, London, 2000), *Dissonant Heritage* (Wiley, Chichester, 1996) and *A Geography of Heritage: Power, Culture, Economy* (Arnold, London, 2000). His research is concerned with the various dimensions of the geography of heritage, including tourist-historic cities, the geography of heritage and managing tourism in cities. Professor Tunbridge is a Visiting Professor at the University of Brighton Business School and Curtin University School of Marketing in Perth, Australia; since retirement from Carleton (as Emeritus) in 2008.

Preface

This edited book is the product of three research groups at the University of Brighton coming together. The Cultural Informatics Research Group has run two very large European projects in the ten years since it was founded at Brighton in 2002. The first of these was the EPOCH Network of Excellence in Open Cultural Heritage, which included elements of socio-economic impact analysis and cultural heritage tourism applications of information and communication technologies (ICTs). The Cubist Research Group (Cultural Business – Impact, Strategy and Technology) was founded to deliver the socio-economic impact evaluation methods within EPOCH from a base in the Brighton Business School. Since 2005 CUBIST has delivered six international symposia on socio-economic impact and strategies for change in cultural heritage in a series called 'Heritage Impact'. Similarly, the Tourism Research Group based in the School of Service Management has held seven symposia on tourism themes since 2001. Furthermore, associates of the Tourism Research Group are members of the Association for Tourism and Leisure Education (ATLAS) and have actively supported the organisation through committee membership and chairing special interest groups. This relationship led to the hosting of the ATLAS 2008 annual conference, which provided the three research groups with the opportunity to deliver a joint research agenda on issues related to cultural heritage tourism.

The concept and subsequent development of this edited book came some time after this event, in that a number of presenters, keynote speakers, academics and practitioners of the research groups' networks were encouraged by the debates that emanated from the event and continued beyond it. These discussions led to the proposal to draw together the range of material in this edited book, which is the result of contributions from academics and practitioners with whom the editing authors have networked for over a decade. The book includes a broad range of contributions, including theoretical perspectives, wide-ranging global case studies, practitioner perspectives and novel viewpoints on under-researched areas.

The audience for this book is twofold: first, the academic community as it is intended to provide a contribution to the literature on cultural heritage tourism. Undergraduates, postgraduates and PhD students, academic staff and researchers with a specific interest in cultural heritage tourism will find this book a useful resource for both mainstream topics and novel viewpoints on under-researched areas. However, the authors see this book also being used across a broader range of curriculum areas which includes tourism studies and management; heritage studies and management; cultural studies and management; cultural geography; volunteer studies and management; and technology and cultural heritage. The second audience is non-academic, which includes practitioners, NGOs, policy makers and governments. It is anticipated that this book will act as a useful source for this audience to develop knowledge and understanding of this global phenomenon and will impact on their future decision-making. The practitioner's contributions in this book demonstrate a 'closing-of-the-gap' between these two audiences.

Jaime Kaminski, Angela M. Benson and David Arnold
Brighton, April 2013

Acknowledgements

The combined efforts of a large number of people and organisations have made it possible for this book to be completed:

The Centre for Tourism Policy Studies combined with the Cultural Informatics Research Group to host the Association for Tourism and Leisure Education (ATLAS) 2008 annual conference under the title of 'Selling or telling? Paradoxes in tourism, culture and heritage', assisted by the Cubist Research Group, all at the University of Brighton. This event provided the catalyst for researchers on cultural heritage tourism to work together and eventually led to the proposal to co-edit this book. The editors are grateful to others who helped to make the 2008 conference successful, owing much to Professor Peter Burns and Dr Marina Novelli (of the School of Service Management), and to Jim McLoughlin and Babak Sodagar of the Brighton Business School.

Further, the keynote speakers from this conference, Professor Gregory Ashworth and Professor John E. Tunbridge, deserve special mention for continued support in the evolution and execution of the book.

This book would not have been possible without the hard work and continuing support of the participants from the Heritage Impact series of conferences, the participants at the ATLAS annual conference and in particular those that contributed a chapter: Apinya Baggelaar Arrunnapaporn, Gregory Ashworth, Stephen Bird, Tiziana Cuccia, Elke Ennen, Wael Salah Fahmi, M.K. Flynn, Benjamin Hruska, Devi Roza Kausar, Tony King, Duangjai Lorthanavanich, Eugenio van Maanen, Carlo Perelli, Ilde Rizzo, Begoña Sánchez Royo, Giovanni Sistu, Geoffrey Smith, Dallen Timothy and John Tunbridge. Your support and professionalism throughout the process was greatly appreciated.

We would like to thank the editorial team at Routledge for all their support and patience, throughout the publication process – start to finish.

We would also like to thank the management and colleagues at the University of Brighton for their continued support.

Last but not least, we would like to thank partners, family and friends who supported us continually during the development of this book.

Jaime Kaminski, Angela M. Benson and David Arnold
Brighton, April 2013

Part 1
Theoretical issues

1   Introduction

*Jaime Kaminski, Angela M. Benson and
David Arnold*

Introduction

During the summer of AD 19, the Roman general Germanicus Julius Caesar set
out for Egypt to tour its antiquities (Tacitus, Annals Book 2: 59).[1] While Germanicus's motives for his Egyptian visit may have been more politically driven
than simply visiting what, even by then, were the country's ancient sites, he
could do so because there was already a well-established tourist trail (Milne,
1916).[2] Even before the Romans, the Greeks had visited Egypt in order to absorb
its culture and history. As early as the mid-fifth century BC, the Greek writer
Herodotus ventured up the Nile as far as Elephantine (Herodotus, The Histories,
Book 2: 5–99).[3] Germanicus was not the first and would certainly not be the last
tourist to visit the antiquities of another culture. Heritage tourism has a long
history.

Clearly in the intervening two millennia the profile of the heritage tourist has
changed considerably. Over most of this period the capacity and the desire to
travel specifically to view the culture and antiquities of other societies was primarily the remit of those who had the financial means to afford to travel and the
education to appreciate what they saw. These pre-conditions typified the cultural
heritage tourist long after the Grand Tour had ceased to be part of the normal
education of European nobility. The huge growth of the middle classes spurred
by the industrial revolution created an emergent consumer base with disposable
income and increasing educational attainment, which created a demand for travel
and consumption of cultural and heritage products of all sorts (Towner, 1985).
However, disposable income and at least an interest in historically based narratives remain characteristics of the clientele to whom cultural heritage tourism
offerings will appeal. The demand from this consumer base led to a huge
increase in both the availability and the variety of cultural products during the
twentieth century, which Toffler (1964) called the 'cultural explosion'.

Driven by cheaper air travel, increased disposable income and leisure time,
tourism is now one of the largest industries in the world. Today, cultural heritage
and tourism are inextricably linked to a global industry of significant propor-
tions, with the perceived quality of a destination's cultural offering being a significant factor in determining tourist choices of destination. The need to present

touristic offerings that include cultural experiences and heritage has become widely recognized, with market surveys demonstrating unambiguously that this aspect of the tourism experience is an important differentiator of destinations, as well as being amongst the most manageable. Noticeably, the influence does not rely entirely upon the actual use of cultural heritage offerings by tourists. The cultural offering appears to influence consumer choice even when the consumer does not make the most of the opportunities and cultural heritage assets on offer. Furthermore, with the current growth in heritage tourism, there is increasing awareness of a number of critical issues in the sector. Many of these impacts are witnessed more widely in the tourism sector, but the differentiator with cultural heritage tourism is that the assets are essentially a non-renewable resource. If damaged, those resources cannot simply be replaced.

Cultural heritage tourism has the potential to generate both positive and negative impacts (Popescu and Corbos, 2010). These include economic (Mazzanti, 2002, 2003) benefits, such as employment opportunities, and the direct and indirect benefits of visitor expenditure. These sought-after economic benefits are often complemented by social benefits, such as community building and the enhancement of community identity, pride and stability, along with environmental benefits, such as the resources and imperative to preserve and maintain cultural and historic sites. The comparatively small number of cultural heritage tourists with their potential empathy for the local population is also seen as potentially beneficial (Smith, 1989). As such, when planned and managed effectively, cultural heritage tourism can be a driver for positive change. Conversely, when poorly managed, cultural heritage tourism can have a detrimental impact on communities. Cultural commoditization, gentrification and the undermining of local traditions and ways of life can be compounded by physical damage to heritage sites caused by inappropriate treatment and uncontrolled visitation.[4]

Cultural heritage tourism

The terms 'cultural heritage' and 'cultural heritage tourism' eponymously combine 'culture', 'heritage' and 'tourism'. Culture is one of the more problematic words in the English language (Bennett *et al.*, 2013: 63–8), heritage is little better, while only tourism can at least claim to have some superficial degree of standardization. This is further complicated by the differing perspectives from which cultural heritage tourism is viewed, including academic, public, scientific, official, governmental, legal and individual, to name but a few. These alternative perspectives sometimes overlap, sometimes conflict and sometimes run in parallel. Moreover, there is rarely a standard definition for each perspective, such as academia or the public. The combination of these value-laden words and the different perspectives goes some way to explaining why 'cultural heritage tourism' has generated such a plethora of definitions.

Cultural heritage

All societies have, and have had, a relationship with their past. Consequently, individuals and societies have always had their own definitions of cultural heritage. It is, therefore, unsurprising that the diversity of definitions for cultural heritage is enormous and the meaning has changed over time (cf. Jokilehto, 2005). As UNESCO notes, 'Originally, it referred only to masterpieces of artistic and historic value; now it is used more broadly and covers everything that has a particular significance to people' (UNESCO and IFT, 2007, Unit 1: 3). Moreover, this process of evolution continues to this day. The creation of (cultural) heritage does not stop. Hence the definition(s) will continue to evolve.

Heritage has been broadly defined as 'something that has been inherited from the past and which can be passed on to future generations' (UNESCO and IFT, 2007, Unit 1: 3). Although this definition highlights the potential of heritage to be passed on to successive generations, as Fairclough (2005: 30) notes, heritage is not just restricted to those things that 'we wish to pass on', but is 'everything that we have inherited', whether or not it is passed on to future generations. Refining this further, Ashworth (2009) has described heritage as 'the significance of the past to the present'.

Of course, in the public consciousness, this nebulous 'something from the past' is widely associated with buildings, monuments and artefacts. These are often to be found at some point during the heritage tourist's journey; however, as Dolff-Bonekämper (2005: 70) has noted, heritage is more than just an object, it is 'a societal relationship, an attribution of meaning and value to an object'. Moreover, this meaning is plural (e.g. values, beliefs, traditions) (Fairclough, 2005: 37). The Faro convention[5] articulates such a definition of cultural heritage in more detail:

> Cultural heritage is a group of resources inherited from the past which people identify, independently of ownership, as a reflection and expression of their constantly evolving values, beliefs, knowledge and traditions. It includes all aspects of the environment resulting from the interaction between people and places through time.
>
> (Faro Convention, Section 1, Article 2)

The variety of definitions and imprecise current usage means that any attempt at a more precise interpretation will nevertheless be interpreted more broadly. It remains possible that more precision may prompt more clarity of thinking and discourse over time, and so we note in passing that adopting Ashworth's distinction between heritage and history would mean that cultural heritage would be defined as 'that of society's current culture that is located and underpinned by tangible evidence of the past'.

Tourism

The World Tourism Organization (WTO) definition of tourism includes 'the activities of persons during their travel and stay in a place outside their usual place of residence, for a continuous period of less than one year, for leisure, business or other purposes' (World Tourism Organization, 1993). The WTO also makes a distinction between 'excursionists', who travel for less than 24 hours, and 'tourists', who stay at least 24 hours at their destination. Although this definition is well established, there are differences in the way that tourist flows are measured across the globe.

Cultural heritage tourism

The convergence between (cultural) heritage and tourism[6] has caused profound changes to both the production and the consumption patterns of cultural heritage tourism (Urry, 1990; Silberberg, 1995; Jolliffe and Smith, 2001). It is clear that the distinctive characteristics of cultural heritage resources allow them to play an unparalleled role in tourism development (Puczko and Ratz, 2007). The OECD (2009) views this as a basis to increase the tourism attractiveness and cultural supply offered by local communities. For example, the USA's National Trust for Historic Preservation defines cultural heritage tourism from a practitioner focus as:

> travelling to experience the places, artifacts, and activities that authentically represent the stories and people of the past and present. It includes cultural, historic and natural resources. Good cultural heritage tourism improves the quality of life for residents as well as serving visitors.
>
> (National Trust for Historic Preservation, 2013: n.p.)

In essence, the focus of most definitions of cultural heritage tourism is upon tourists visiting what could loosely be termed 'heritage places'. In some cases, an element of learning or education is also included as part of the definition; for others an element of the 'personal' is attached to the visit. This may also include aspects like diaspora, genealogy (Basu, 2007) and/or legacy tourism (McCain and Ray, 2003). Furthermore, Timothy (2011: 6) suggests that 'cultural heritage tourism encompasses built patrimony, living lifestyles, ancient artifacts and modern art and culture'. Using our new definition of cultural heritage above, we might encourage the definition that 'cultural heritage tourism involves travelling to experience the current narrative of the tangible evidence of the past and its relevance today'. Changing interpretations, as well as changing contexts for interpretation, mean that under this definition the cultural heritage tourism offerings are dynamic and evolving. Since such offerings are constantly being refreshed, their significance will also change over time.

Cultural tourism

Cultural heritage tourism is often viewed as a subset of cultural tourism. As with cultural heritage tourism, there has been a plethora of definitions. Some have focused on attempting to describe the different attractions visited by cultural tourists (a technical definition), while others have attempted a more conceptual approach by describing the motives and meanings associated with cultural tourism. ATLAS provides both a technical and a conceptual definition:

> Technical definition: All movements of persons to specific cultural attractions, such as heritage sites, artistic and cultural manifestations, arts and drama outside their normal place of residence.

> Conceptual definition: The movement of persons to cultural attractions away from their normal place of residence, with the intention to gather new information and experiences to satisfy their cultural needs.
>
> (Richards, 1996: 24)

Cultural heritage tourism literature and sustainability

According to the Centre International de Recherches et d'Etudes Touristiques (CIRET), there are 1,977 documents on the themes of heritage enhancement and culture (CIRET, 2013) linked to tourism, about a third of the number of documents on sustainability.[7] Many of these articles are to be found in the plethora of journals in the arena of culture, heritage and tourism. Whilst some of the journals are found in the tourism domain (*Journal of Heritage Tourism*, commenced 2006), others are more generic in their outlook: *International Journal of Cultural Studies* (commenced 1998); *International Journal of Heritage Studies* (commenced 1994); *International Journal of Cultural Heritage* (commenced 2000); *Journal of Computing and Cultural Heritage* (commenced 2008) and more recently the *Journal of Cultural Heritage Management and Sustainable Development* (commenced 2011). However, even a cursory search within the generic journals reveals that tourism-related articles comprise a significant component. What is also evident when examining the literature is the extent to which the writing is fragmented across a range of themes and over numerous individual case studies (Ashworth and Tunbridge develop this further in terms of heritage tourism studies as an academic discipline in chapter 2 of this volume). Loulanski and Loulanski (2011) undertook a meta-analysis of 483 studies in order to identify groupings that linked cultural heritage and tourism together within the broader concept of sustainability. After synthesizing the findings, they produced a representative set of 15 factors, as outlined in Figure 1.1.

   With the growing trend towards sustainability in all aspects of our daily lives, it is therefore pertinent that we engage in a brief discussion of sustainability and cultural heritage tourism. The most commonly cited definition of sustainable development is: development that 'meets the needs of the present without

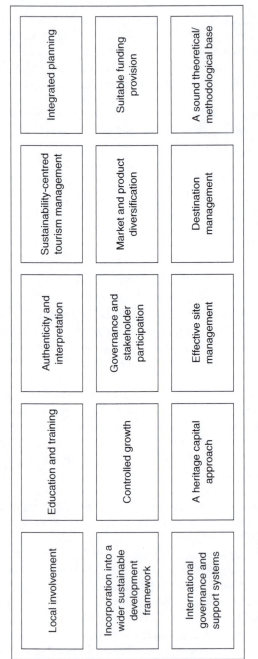

Figure 1.1 Cultural heritage and tourism groupings from a meta-analysis of cultural heritage tourism and sustainability (source: Loulanski and Loulanski, 2011).

Local involvement	Education and training	Authenticity and interpretation	Sustainability-centred tourism management	Integrated planning
Incorporation into a wider sustainable development framework	Controlled growth	Governance and stakeholder participation	Market and product diversification	Suitable funding provision
International governance and support systems	A heritage capital approach	Effective site management	Destination management	A sound theoretical/ methodological base

compromising the ability of future generations to meet their own needs' (World Commission on Environment and Development, 1987: 15). There is a comprehensive theoretical framework associated with the concept of sustainable development and there is no doubt that the tourism sector embraces sustainability as a principle. However, it is also evident that the implementation of sustainability has been much slower to come to fruition. DuCros (2001) viewed the rhetoric around cultural heritage tourism and sustainability as one of the main research issues in terms of what is the most appropriate way for cultural heritage tourism to be developed. In the last decade, there has been an increase of activity, primarily led by the global institutions, in order to deliver a coordinated agenda on cultural heritage tourism and sustainability. For example, the Council of Europe invited the European Association of Historic Towns and Regions (EAHTR, 2006) to develop a set of guidelines to outline how cultural heritage tourism can be developed to realize its economic and social potential in a more sustainable way. UNESCO and the Institute for Tourism Studies, Macau, China (IFT), jointly developed the 'Cultural Heritage Specialist Guide Training and Certification Programme' for UNESCO World Heritage Sites. In 2011, the International Union for Conservation of Nature (IUCN) commissioned a report to examine world heritage and sustainable tourism, with a view to establishing a list of priorities for action (Borges *et al.*, 2011). Moreover, UNESCO developed the World Heritage and Sustainable Tourism Programme around the same time (World Heritage Centre, 2013), with the following vision statement: 'World Heritage and tourism stakeholders share responsibility for conservation of our common cultural and natural heritage of Outstanding Universal Value and for sustainable development through appropriate tourism management' (UNESCO, 2013b: n.p).

In addition, the World Bank through its Urban Development Series has supported a number of publications (Ebbe *et al.*, 2011; Licciardi and Amirtahmasebi, 2012) to engage in the discourse around cultural heritage tourism and sustainability. As such, much of the rhetoric, initiatives and advice offered are still in their infancy and it is therefore too soon to tell the extent of stakeholders' engagement and consequently whether coherent implementation will happen.

Global trends

In 2011, international tourist arrivals worldwide were 983 million (an increase of 4.6 per cent on the previous year – 940 million), with international tourism receipts reaching a record US$1,030 billion (€740 billion) (UNWTO, 2011a, 2011b). There is no doubt that tourism is big business. However, establishing the extent of the market in terms of cultural heritage is problematic because different countries are using many alternative classifications and definitions and there appears to be no operational framework for international comparative measurement of the cultural heritage sector (Arnold and Geser, 2008). Despite this, there are disparate indications of the size of the market and this section will outline some of the data available.

The UNWTO (OECD, 2009: 21) reported that cultural tourism accounted for 40 per cent (359 million) of all international tourism, up from 37 per cent (199 million) in 1995. As part of the World Tourism Day 2010, themed 'Tourism – Linking Cultures', the UNWTO (2011c) press release announced that '940 million tourists travelled to a different country, coming into direct contact with tangible – art, monuments – and intangible – music, food traditions – culture' (n.p.); thereby, inferring that all tourists are cultural heritage tourists! The problem with this is that it is not consistent with creating a distinctive niche in an already crowded marketplace.

The ATLAS surveys[8] of 1997–2007 indicate growth in the proportion of tourists on a cultural holiday from 17 to 32 per cent (OECD, 2009). The last report by the ATLAS Cultural Tourism Project (Richards, 2007) indicates that 53 per cent of visitors were women (similar to previous years); 30 per cent of respondents were aged between 20 and 29 (higher than previous studies); and 70 per cent had a degree or higher degree – this was reflected in the 70 per cent who indicated they are managers and professionals. Approximately 30 per cent are engaged in occupations linked to culture. The top motivation was 'lots of interesting things to see'. The types of attractions visited were museums, at 64 per cent, being the most popular, followed by historic sites (51 per cent), monuments (58 per cent) and religious attractions (42 per cent); these were some way ahead of the next category, art galleries, at 22 per cent. Pop concerts, world music and dance events were the three lowest, all at approximately 3 per cent. Rome was the favourite cultural destination, with Florence ranked third and Venice ranked sixth, out of a total of 33 cities. This is not surprising when examining Table 1.2, which shows that Italy has the greatest number of World Heritage Sites listed, alongside a strong country brand that attracted 46.1 million tourists in 2011, ranking fifth on the International Tourists Arrivals (UNWTO, 2011a).

The US market is an important source of outbound cultural heritage tourists. Mintel (2010) found that 29 per cent of US international tourists travel to cultural, historical or religious destinations. This desire for cultural heritage products brings Americans to Europe, in particular the UK, France, Italy and Germany, accounting for 76 per cent of all arrivals to Europe in 2008. Research from the European Commission (EC) (EC Flash Eurobarometer, fl_258, 2009) suggests that 24 per cent of Europeans, when choosing a holiday destination, consider cultural heritage to be an influencing factor. It also indicates that Denmark, Ireland and the UK markets are the top three and the Eastern European markets are the least interested, with Bulgaria, Poland and Hungary being the last three on the country list. Further, Britain has used culture and heritage as a key offering in its tourism portfolio for decades. In a recent visitor survey, 57 per cent of respondents from 20 countries agreed that history and culture are strong influences on their choice of holiday destination. VisitBritain (2010) estimates this market attracts £4.5 billion worth of spending by inbound visitors annually, which underpins more than 100,000 jobs across the country.

The cultural heritage tourist has grown more sophisticated in their travel tastes. The OECD (2009) suggests this is a move away from 'sightseeing' to 'lifeseeing'; as such, this implies a shift from tangible cultural heritage (historic sites, monuments and museums) to intangible cultural heritage (arts, languages, music, festivals and pageants). The relationship between tourism and intangible cultural heritage has not yet been widely studied by the academic community (UNWTO, 2012: 12).

Whilst cultural heritage tourism is a global phenomenon, the influence of UNESCO's heritage list cannot be overlooked as the properties listed are often a major pull for tourists visiting destinations. By 2012, there were 962 properties listed; of these, 745 are cultural, 188 natural and the remaining 29 are on both lists. Since the turn of the millennium, 276 have been added, with two properties being delisted. In addition, state parties are encouraged to submit properties to the World Heritage Tentative List. These are properties which are considered to be suitable for inscription on to the World Heritage List if nominated at a future date. Currently, there are 1,579 tentative list sites in over 171 countries. Table 1.1 outlines World Heritage properties by region; just under half of the properties (48 per cent) are located within Europe and North America, with Europe holding the greater share (44 per cent). Of course, the predominance of UNESCO World Heritage Sites in Europe and North America does not immediately imply that there are more sites of outstanding cultural or natural importance to the common heritage of humanity in Europe compared to elsewhere. It merely underlines the fact that these countries have been fortunate enough to be located in a region that has had a fundamental role in instigating and running the convention (leading to greater awareness), and they have had the resources to undertake the application process.

Table 1.2 shows that, of the 157 countries where the 962 sites are situated, 25 of the countries have more than ten sites listed. These 25 countries account for 553 of the sites, whilst the remaining 409 sites are scattered over 132 countries.

Ascribing a property to the World Heritage List does not ensure its preservation or survival. In 2012, there were 38 sites on the list of World Heritage in Danger. This list is designed to raise awareness of the threats to the characteristics for which the property was inscribed onto the World Heritage List and,

Table 1.1 World Heritage Sites according to region

Regions	Cultural	Natural	Mixed	Total	%	State parties with inscribed properties
Africa	47	35	4	86	9	32
Arab States	67	4	2	73	8	17
Asia and the Pacific	148	55	10	213*	22	32
Europe and North America	393	59	10	462*	48	50
Latin America and the Caribbean	90	35	3	128	13	26
Total	745	188	29	962	100	157

Source: UNESCO (2013a).

Table 1.2 Number of World Heritage properties inscribed by each state party

Country (total 157)	No of sites (total of 962)
1 Italy	47
2 Spain	44
3 China	43
4 France	38
5 Germany	37
6 Mexico	31
7 India	29
8 United Kingdom of Great Britain and Northern Ireland	28
9 Russian Federation	25
10 United States of America	21
11 Australia	19
12 Brazil	19
13 Greece	17
14 Canada	16
15 Japan	16
16 Iran (Islamic Republic of)	15
17 Sweden	15
18 Portugal	14
19 Poland	13
20 Czech Republic	12
21 Belgium	11
22 Peru	11
23 Switzerland	11
24 Turkey	11
25 Korea, Republic of	10
Other (less than ten sites) 132	409

Source: Adapted from UNESCO (2013b).

therefore, corrective action is urgently needed. The threats to property come in many guises – armed conflict, natural disasters, pollution, urban sprawl and unchecked tourist development. Table 1.3 summarizes the list of World Heritage in Danger by region. The majority of the properties (42 per cent) are located within the African region.

Table 1.3 World Heritage in Danger by region

Regions	Cultural	Natural	Mixed	Total	%
Africa	4	12	0	16	42
Arab States	6	0	0	6	16
Asia and the Pacific	3	1	0	4	11
Europe and North America	4	1	0	5	13
Latin America and the Caribbean	4	3	0	7	18
Total	21	17	0	38	100

Source: UNESCO (2013a).

Contemporary issues in cultural heritage tourism

This edited book takes a broader perspective on the concept of cultural heritage tourism. Consequently, this collection of 20 chapters from expert scholars and practitioners in the field of cultural heritage tourism takes an in-depth look at both the theory and the application of tourism within the context of cultural heritage. The book's primary themes are: theoretical perspectives of cultural heritage tourism, regeneration, policy, stakeholders, marketing, socio-economic development, impacts, sustainability, volunteering and ICT, with many of the chapters drawing on case study data from around the globe: Malta, Gibraltar and Bermuda (chapter 5); Tunisia (chapter 6); Japan (chapter 7); South Africa (chapter 8); Egypt (chapter 9); USA (chapter 10); Thailand (chapter 11); France (chapter 12); Spain (chapter 12 and 16); Sicily (chapter 13); Java, Indonesia (chapter 14); and the United Kingdom (chapters 15 and 18).

The book consists of four parts. The first part of the book focuses on 'Theoretical issues' and consists of four chapters (1–4). This chapter (chapter 1), written by the editing authors, Kaminski, Benson and Arnold, provides a general introduction to cultural heritage tourism in terms of definition, sustainability, the scope of academic literature available and global trends. Furthermore, as follows, this chapter offers an insight into each of the following chapters. Chapter 2 by Ashworth and Tunbridge offers a discussion on theoretical underpinning for heritage tourism. They contend that, whilst it might be desirable to use ideas and techniques from other disciplines, without a structuring paradigm which includes a core set of concepts and terms, a collective knowledge is difficult to achieve. Chapter 3, by Timothy, examines vernacular heritage through the lens of the 'ordinary past'. He believes heritage consumers have shifting interests and a desire to see how the common person lived in the past. The final chapter in this section (chapter 4) is by Ennen and van Maanen. They focus on visitor flows and management in a multicultural context. They believe that 'identity' is becoming an increasingly important criterion in urban development.

The second part, consisting of chapters 5–12, is dedicated to 'Tensions and dissonance'. In chapter 5, Tunbridge provides 'a cautionary tale' using case studies of former Royal Navy bases. He suggests that the examples outlined are illustrations of more complex issues at all levels and are intended to guide public and professional discourses. Chapter 6 (Perelli and Sistu) discuss how tourism strategies have been central to the 'new Tunisia' by examining the links between heritage sites and mass tourism development and the extent to which the heritage narrative has changed course over the decades. Chapter 7 by Lorthanavanich outlines how in Japan the centralized policies of the 1960s began to meet with resistance from local communities. Two case studies are used to demonstrate the different arguments and functions of heritage and the role of interest groups in cultural heritage management. King and Flynn, in chapter 8, use the Old Fort prison complex, Johannesburg, as an example of heritage development for urban regeneration. Whilst the development is not complete, they believe it is still too early to judge this as failure as it stands as a visual anchor for post-apartheid aspiration. Chapter 9 by Fahmi examines the contested spatiality within Cairo's European Quarter. In his conclusion, he clearly outlines six key points that have destabilized heritage tourism development. In chapter 10, Hruska, through the lens of a public historian, investigates the 're-discovery' of an island's forgotten heritage and the extent to which re-constructing the past has been influenced by genealogy tourism and by a group of dedicated local volunteers. Chapter 11 is by Arrunnapaporn, who explores the controversy caused by poor interpretation and commodification of the 'Death Railway' in Thailand. The chapter is contextualized by the Second World War and the concept of atrocity heritage tourism. The final chapter in this section (chapter 12), by Kaminski, considers how escalating visitor numbers to the decorated Ice Age caves of France and Spain are having a detrimental effect on the cave art. The chapter examines the options available that allow the public to appreciate decorated caves in a sustainable manner, and considers the role that virtual solutions can play.

Part 3, 'Economics and impact', consists of chapters 13–16. The first chapter in this section (chapter 13) is by Cuccia and Rizzo, who investigate how seasonality is affected by cultural tourism supply and demand, using UNESCO World Heritage Sites in Sicily. Their findings suggest that UNESCO inscription is not effective in its own right in fostering cultural heritage tourism or overcoming the issue of seasonality. Clearer direction is required by local policy makers and other stakeholders to overcome the vertical and horizontal fragmentation. In chapter 14, Kausar offers an analysis of the socio-economic impact of the district surrounding the Borobudur World Heritage Site, Java, Indonesia – one of the largest Buddhist monuments in the world, but whose local community is predominantly Muslim. Findings suggest that, while the temple has little relevance in respect of religion for the local population, it influences the socio-economic development of the area, particularly though tourism-related activities. A partnership between the University of Brighton (Kaminski) and the Federation of British Historic Vehicle Clubs (Smith) has enabled a rare glimpse at 'motor vehicle heritage' in chapter 15. This chapter includes three economic impact assessments from UK case studies – the London to Brighton veteran car run, the Beaulieu International Autojumble and the Goodwood Revival Festival. Sánchez Royo, in chapter 16, discusses the value of intangible cultural heritage using the case of the Fallas Festival in Valencia, Spain. She describes a methodology for assessing the participants' value of the festival.

Part 4 draws together the final four chapters (17–20) by examining 'Future directions'. Arnold and Kaminski (chapter 17) explore the impact that technology is having on the nature of cultural heritage tourism. They examine the opportunities offered by the combination of the physical and virtual worlds and the relationship to past uses of simulated cultural artefacts. They conclude that, while there are many potential future avenues for technology in cultural heritage tourism, the barriers to adoption have probably more to do with philosophy, politics and economics than computer science or engineering. In chapter 18, Bird offers a practitioner's view of strategic planning for sustainability in respect of the Roman Baths in Bath. The chapter outlines the successive crises which have affected visitor behaviour and how managers in a local authority have used a number of measures to mitigate them. Volunteers are in many countries a key component of delivering cultural heritage tourism; Benson and Kaminski, in chapter 19, examine the role of both domestic and international volunteers and the extent to which these boundaries are becoming blurred. The final chapter of the book (chapter 20) is by the editing authors (Kaminski, Arnold and Benson) and offers an assessment of the global trends which are most likely to affect cultural heritage tourism in the coming decades. They see changes in population, the economy, environment and society as having being the biggest potential influence on cultural heritage tourism.

Notes

1 '59. M. Silano L. Norbano consulibus Germanicus Aegyptum proficiscitur cognoscendae antiquitatis....'. See http://classics.mit.edu/Tacitus/annals.2.ii.html for a translation.
2 Another well-known traveller of the Augustan era was Diodorus Siculus (i. 44.1; 83.9).
3 For more on Herodotus as a tourist, see Redfield (1985); for the origins of tourism, see Feifer (1985). See also http://classics.mit.edu/Herodotus/history.2.ii.html.
4 The lack of longitudinal studies of the impact of cultural tourism is seen by some commentators as problematic. In the absence of time depth, there can be a tendency to ascribe all negative impact to tourism (Wilson, 1993).
5 The 'Council of Europe Framework Convention on the Value of Cultural Heritage for Society' 2005.
6 The nuances between the terms 'heritage tourism' and 'cultural heritage tourism' are sufficiently slight that the terms have often been used interchangeably. As Timothy (2011: 6) notes, 'the differences, if they exist at all, are rather subtle'.
7 These statistics compare to 530 on wine tourism (CIRET, 2012) and 84 documents on corporate social responsibility (CIRET, 2013).
8 These are based on the ATLAS Cultural Tourism Project, which commenced in 1991. The project has focused on the collection of data on the motivations and behaviour of cultural tourists in destinations and cultural sites around the world (Richards, 2011).

References

Arnold, D. and Geser, G. (2008) *The EPOCH research agenda for the applications of ICTs to cultural heritage*, Budapest: Archaeolingua. Also available online at www.epoch.eu.
Ashworth, G. J. (2009) 'Do tourists destroy the heritage they have come to experience?', *Tourism Recreation Research*, 34(1): 79–83.
Basu, P. (2007) *Highland homecomings: Genealogy and heritage tourism in the Scottish Diaspora*, Abingdon: Routledge.
Bennett, T., Grossberg, L. and Morris, M. (2013) *New keywords: A revised vocabulary of culture and society*, Oxford: Blackwell.
Borges, M. A., Carbone, G., Bushell, R. and Jaeger, T. (2011) *Sustainable tourism and natural World Heritage – priorities for action*, Gland, Switzerland: IUCN.
CIRET (2012) Personal communication with Rene Baretje-Keller, President and Emeritus Member of the International Academy for the Study of Tourism. Aix en Provence, France: Centre International de Recherches et d'Etudes Touristiques (www.ciret-tourism.com).

CIRET (2013) Personal communication with Rene Baretje-Keller, President and Emeritus Member of the International Academy for the Study of Tourism, Aix en Provence, France: Centre International de Recherches et d'Etudes Touristiques (ww.ciret-tourism. com).

Dolff-Bonekämper, G. (2005) 'The social and spatial frameworks of heritage – What is new in the Faro Convention?', in Council of Europe (ed.) *Heritage and beyond*, Strasbourg: Council of Europe, 69–74.

DuCros, H. (2001) 'A new model to assist in planning for sustainable cultural heritage tourism', *International Journal of Tourism Research*, 3(2): 165–70.

Ebbe, K., Licciardi, G. and Baeumler, A. (2011) *Conserving the past as a foundation for the future: China-World Bank Partnership on Cultural Heritage Conservation*, Urban Development Series: Knowledge Papers. No. 12. World Bank and Urban Development & Local Government.

European Association of Historic Towns and Regions (EAHTR) (2006) *Guidelines: Sustainable cultural tourism in historic towns and cities*, Norwich: EAHTR.

European Commission (EC) (2009) 'Europeans and tourism – Autumn 2009', *Flash Eurobarometer 281*.

Fairclough, G. (2005) 'New heritage frontiers', in Council of Europe (ed.) *Heritage and beyond*, Strasbourg: Council of Europe, 29–42.

Feifer, M. (1985) *Tourism in history: From Imperial Rome to the present*, New York: Stein and Day.

ICOMOS (1976) 'Charter of cultural tourism', accessed in April 2013 at www.icomos. org/tourism/tourism_charter.html.

Institute for Tourism Studies (2013) 'Cultural heritage specialist guide training', accessed in April 2013 at www.ift.edu.mo/EN/Specialist_Guide/Home/Index/271.

Jokilehto, J. (2005) *Definition of cultural heritage: References to documents in history*, originally for ICCROM, 1990 and revised for CIF, 15 January 2005 on behalf of the Heritage and Society Working Group within the ICCROM Strategic Planning Process, accessed in March 2013 at http://cif.icomos.org/pdf_docs/Documents%20on%20line/Heritage%20definitions.pdf.

Jolliffe, L. and Smith, R. (2001) 'Heritage tourism and museums: The case of the North Atlantic Islands of Skype, Scotland and Prince Edward's Island, Canada', *International Journal of Heritage Studies*, 7(2): 144–9.

Licciardi, G. and Amirtahmasebi, R. (eds.) (2012) *The economics of uniqueness: Investing in historic city cores and cultural heritage assets for sustainable development*, Washington: The World Bank.

Loulanski, T. and Loulanski, V. (2011) 'The sustainable integration of cultural heritage and tourism: a meta-study', *Journal of Sustainable Tourism*, 19(7): 837–62.

Mazzanti, M. (2002) 'Cultural heritage as multi-dimensional, multi-value and multi-attribute economic good: Toward a new framework for economic analysis and valuation', *Journal of Socio-Economics*, 31(5): 529–58.

Mazzanti, M. (2003) 'Valuing cultural heritage in a multi-attribute framework: Microeconomic perspectives and policy implications', *Journal of Socio-Economics*, 32(5): 549–69.

McCain, G. and Ray, M. N. (2003) 'Legacy tourism: The search for personal meaning in heritage travel', *Tourism Management*, 24(6): 713–17.

Milne, J. G. (1916) 'Greek and Roman tourists in Egypt', *The Journal of Egyptian Archaeology*, 3(2/3): 76–80.

Mintel (2010) *Cultural and heritage tourism – International*, May 2010.

National Trust for Historic Preservation (2013) 'Historic preservation issues affecting you', accessed in March 2013 at www.preservationnation.org/issues/.

Organisation for Economic Cooperation and Development (OECD) (2009) *The impact of culture on tourism*, Paris: OECD Publishing.

Popescu, R. I. and Corbos, R. A. (2010) 'The role of urban tourism in the strategic development of Brasovarea', *Theoretical and Empirical Researches in Urban Management*, 7(16): 69–85.

Puczko, L. and Ratz, T. (2007) 'Trailing Goethe, Humbert and Ulysses tourism: Cultural routes in tourism', in G. Richards (ed.), *Cultural tourism: Global and local perspectives*, London: Routledge, 131–48.

Redfield, J. (1985) 'Herodotus the tourist', *Classical Philology*, 80(2): 97–118.

Richards, G. (1996) *Cultural tourism in Europe*, Wallingford: CABI.

Richards, G. (2007) *ATLAS cultural tourism survey: Summary report 2007*, accessed in March 2013 at www.tran-research.com/atlas.

Richards, G (2011) *Annual review of activities 2011*, accessed in March 2013 at www.atlas-euro.org/sig_cultural.aspx#2010.

Silberberg, T (1995) 'Cultural tourism and business opportunities for museums and heritage sites', *Tourism Management*, 16: 361–5.

Smith, V. L. (1989) *Hosts and guests: The anthropology of tourism* (2nd edition), Oxford: Blackwell.

Timothy, D. J. (2011) *Cultural heritage and tourism: An introduction*, Bristol: Channel View Publications.

Toffler, A. (1964) *The culture consumers: A study of art and affluence in America*, New York: St. Martin's Press.

Towner, J. (1985) 'The Grand Tour: A key phase in the history of tourism', *Annals of Tourism Research*, 12: 297–333.

United Nations Educational, Scientific and Cultural Organization (UNESCO) and Institute for Tourism Studies (IFT), Macao SAR (4th edition, 2007) *Tourism at cultural heritage sites in Asia, Cultural heritage, specialist guide training and certification programme for UNESCO World Heritage Sites, A training manual for heritage guides*, Macao: UNESCO and IFT.

United Nations Educational, Scientific and Cultural Organization (UNESCO). (2013a) *World Heritage List statistics*, accessed in June 2013 at http://whc.unesco.org/en/list/stat#s1.

United Nations Educational, Scientific and Cultural Organization (UNESCO). (2013b) *World Heritage and Sustainable Tourism Programme*, accessed in March 2013 at http://whc.unesco.org/en/tourism/.

United Nations World Tourism Organization (UNWTO) (2011a) *Tourism highlights*, Madrid, Spain: UN World Tourism Organization.

United Nations World Tourism Organization (UNWTO) (2011b) *UNWTO World Tourism Barometer*, Madrid: UNWTO.

United Nations World Tourism Organization (UNWTO) (2011c) *Tourism – Linking cultures: UNWTO launches World Tourism Day 2011*, PR No 11054, Madrid, 20 Jun 2011, accessed in March 2013 at http://media.unwto.org/en/press-release/2011–06–20/tourism-linking-cultures-unwto-launches-world-tourism-day-2011.

United Nations World Tourism Organization (UNWTO) (2012) *Tourism and intangible cultural heritage*, Madrid: UNWTO.

Urry, J. (1990) *The tourist gaze: Leisure and travel in contemporary societies*, London: Sage.

VisitBritain (2010) *Culture and heritage: Topic profile*, accessed in March 2013 at www. visitbritain.org/Images/Culture%20%26%20Heritage%20Topic%20Profile%20Full_ tcm29-14711.pdf.

Wilson, D. (1993) 'Time and tides in the anthropology of tourism', in M. Hitchcock, V. T. King and M. J. G. Parnwell (eds.) *Tourism in South East Asia*, London: Routledge, 32–47.

World Commission on Environment and Development (1987) *Our common future*, Oxford: Oxford University Press.

World Heritage Centre (2013) *World Heritage and Sustainable Tourism Programme*, accessed in April 2013 at http://whc.unesco.org/en/tourism/.

World Tourism Organization (1993) *Recommendations on tourism statistics*, Madrid: WTO.

2 Heritage and tourism

Between practice and theory?

Gregory Ashworth and John E. Tunbridge

Introduction

Interest in, concern about and a wish to experience the past, its relict structures, artefacts, sites, associations and narratives evolved over a period of about 150 years largely without any perceived need for philosophical justification, logically grounded concepts or even agreed terminology. It was a pragmatic activity engaged first in saving, protecting and storing and then in presenting, interpreting and using the past in the present to satisfy diverse contemporary cultural, political, social and economic needs. It was driven by necessity and opportunity, sets of pragmatic compromises driven by the possibilities of technology, political convenience, financial costs and benefits and socio-cultural fashion, not by theoretical reflection by those active in the field on what they were doing or why they were doing it. Its relationship to, indeed stimulus from, tourism is often traced back to the 'Grand Tour' of the Georgian aristocracy.

The deepening and widening of interest in heritage and especially its role as a resource in the now major economic enterprise of tourism (see Timothy and Boyd, 2003; Ashworth and Tunbridge, 2005) has disturbed and challenged this sometimes complacent, conceptually latitudinarian, pragmatism. Victory in Lowenthal's 'heritage crusade' (1996) has replaced the uncomplicated imperative to save and protect an individual historical resource for its own sake with the compelling necessity for selection and therefore non-selection from a much broader stock of potential resources. The burgeoning tourism demands discovered heritage resources as a largely freely accessible, flexible and, to the visitor, often zero-cost public good. The unavoidable questions, now posed of heritage and of the many demands upon it, must be what, whose, on what criteria, for what purposes and for whom? Answers to these can only be found within a theoretical framework. In addition, the attraction of scholars and practitioners from an increasingly varied range of scientific fields and applied practices has compounded the problem as each has imported the assumptions, concepts, paradigms and even terminology from their particular mother discipline. Multi- or inter-disciplinarity may bring a refreshing variety of approaches but it also can result in imprecision, confusion and contradiction or just isolation in mutual solitudes (Tunbridge *et al.*, 2013; Howard, 2013).

Heritage, as the study of the contemporary uses of imagined pasts, and heritage tourism, as the discretionary consumption of such pasts, are not unique in the inherent tensions between the many that are doing it and the few that are thinking about the significance of doing it, but the growing importance of the activity sharpens the debate.

This chapter poses and attempts to answer, even if such answers are paradoxical, such questions as 'in what senses does a study of heritage and specifically heritage tourism exist?' and 'does the practice need theory?' If so, will this be an amalgam or synthesis of existing theoretical frameworks derived from existing disciplines and practices or does heritage, and heritage tourism as a major use, need its own distinctive theory? In this respect, the needs of academics and practitioners, whether in the cultural, political or commercial arenas, may well differ radically. Academics need theory to construct academic disciplines, which are no more than a body of individuals who professionally associate with each other through the exchange and evaluation of ideas, using a mutually intelligible terminology, thus shaping the possibility of building upon each other's work so that knowledge is advanced. Conversely, such theory allows a disassociation from other disciplines. An agreed subject-centred theory could be viewed as a defence in a competitive struggle for institutional survival if heritage studies, ideally in supportive alliance with tourism studies, is to be viewed as an academic discipline in this sense. However, if it is not to be so viewed, can we live with and hopefully profit from, a fissiparous theoretical diversity, reaping the advantages of an eclecticism in which you use whatever theory you need from anywhere whenever you need it, with the only criterion being that it delivers the structural guidance needed in a particular task? However, the absence of a paradigm, core set of concepts or even an agreed common language or forums in which to express and debate these may condemn the study and practice of this activity to being no more than an intellectually shallow, continuously recurring set of pragmatic reactions to problem and place-specific requirements.

Is theory needed?

This is not the place to raise the wide discussion of the nature of theory. Suffice it to state for our purposes that theory (from the Greek θεωρια) is at its simplest no more than contemplation in contrast to action (πράξίς). Although contemplation is a solitary activity, theorizing is a social activity in so far as the results of individual contemplation are shared and tested in a social arena. This requires a basic collective understanding of what we are doing, which includes a common acceptance of terminology and a coherent group of tested general propositions, commonly regarded as correct, that can be used as principles of explanation and prediction for a class of phenomena. The question therefore is does the study of the uses of the past in the present have, or should it have, a theoretical foundation to structure such contemplation?

Heritage, viewed in this way as a field of intellectual endeavour, has characteristics different from most academic pursuits. First, it is a relative newcomer on the academic scene. Although there have been around 150 years of intellectual discussion of many of the key issues, these debates did not pose the fundamental questions of purpose and motivation. At an institutional level, novelty imposes the necessity to establish a disciplinary identity if only to stake a claim to a particular field of knowledge and expertise in competition with the established disciplines.

Second, most of those working professionally in the broad field of the uses of heritage are pursuing practical tasks. For more than 90 per cent of its practitioners, it is a practical activity involving techniques of material preservation, systems of storage and retrieval, expertise in presentation and interpretation, or the management and marketing of the consumer experience as notably in tourism. Reflection seems an irrelevant distraction from tasks that are clearly self-validating and cannot afford such distraction if they are to compete successfully for funding resources and commercial profit.

Third, and stemming from both of the above characteristics, the study of heritage tends to be case-study driven. General issues have typically arisen from quite specific events and cases. It was the flooding of the temples of Abu Simbel for the Aswan High Dam in 1968 that forced a debate on the implications of global ownership, leading to the World Heritage Convention of 1972. It was the increasing occurrence of flooding in the Venice lagoon from the mid-1960s that prompted the debate on priorities to be accorded to monument protection and its economic return through tourism and the industrial and navigational necessities for keeping the lagoon open to the sea. It was the continuing contradictory claims of Greece and Macedonia (Former Yugoslav Republic of Macedonia – FYROM) to Hellenistic heritage that initiated the debate on the questions of the nationalization of the past and thus which 'nation' should possess it and presumably profit from it. The destruction of the Buddhas of Bamyan in 2001 led to soul searching about the limits of the global claim. From the discovery of Ötzi the iceman in the Austrian/ Italian Ötztal Alps in 1991 to 'Kennewick Man' in Washington State in 1996, and subsequent cases beyond, it was specific, largely fortuitous events that prompted debate of the wider issues of value, meaning, ownership and priority of use.

Fourth, and a consequence specifically of novelty, theoretical reflection has to be retrofitted to an already existing stock of preserved and interpreted objects and events and their range of possible meanings. Although it might appear more logical in the performance of any task to first decide what is wanted and subsequently do it, the reverse has happened in heritage, with most of the memorialized events, objects, sites and areas being already in existence, along with both their officially authorized interpretations and popular mythologies, reinforced by established patterns of tourism marketing, before such questions of theory had begun to be posed.

These characteristics are not unique to either heritage or tourism studies but are shared with many other fields of practical endeavour, including management/ business studies – all activities dominated by practitioners and validated by practical indicators of success, with an absence of intrinsic or home grown theory, an absence which is frequently lamented.

Was the historical evolution of the study of heritage driven by theory?

In the century and a half of active concern for the contribution of the past to the present through its physical relics, historical narratives or memories, there certainly existed various paradigms, based upon assumptions that amounted to *post hoc* justifications for actions already performed. Whether these amount to an overarching theory or are just ways of dealing with the world around us is questionable.

The preservation paradigm that was dominant through most of the period, and is still prevalent among many practitioners concerned with heritage resources, makes assumptions about values and purposes. The clear, obvious and unchallenged imperative is expressed in the word 'save'. The main unquestioned assumption is that the past is real, it actually existed, and it can be preserved through its sites, monuments, memories and historical narratives for the self-evident benefit of the present and bequeathed intact to an assumed grateful future. The internecine issue among preservationists did not question the imperative to save but revolved around the application of the action. Some, notably Ruskin (1849), would save 'as found', after time and circumstance had impacted upon the relic. Others, notably Viollet le Duc (cf. *Entretiens sur l'architecture*, 1863, 1872), would not only save what existed but 're-establish a building in its finished state, which may in fact never have existed'. The word 'renovation' was the dividing shibboleth (Denslagen, 1994, 2009). It is notable that the word 'use' did not enter into these discussions. This might be considered strange as the idea of visiting the objects and sites so preserved was well established. The previously noted 'Grand Tour' (Towner, 1985; Trease, 1991), whereby an albeit small elite visited the physical relics of past civilizations as a necessary culmination of their education, was beginning to widen its popularity and provide an increasing credence to the preservationists' argument. However visitors were, at best, tolerated if they did not interfere with the objective of preservation and, at worst, seen as a potential enemy if they did.

What has been called the conservation paradigm was developed in place planning and management as a series of pragmatic compromises, largely to accommodate the results of the success of preservation and the increasing uses of the resources preserved. The focus shifted to include not only individual buildings (the 'monument') but also ensembles (the 'historic' or 'heritage' district). This in turn compelled a wider approach, if only because a single building could be treated as an art object in itself regardless of its contemporary use but a whole urban historic district or rural landscape could not. Function had to be added to form, which inevitably involved the planners and managers of place functions in both public and private sectors, in the interest of both the public good and of private profit. Thus what had been largely the preserve of architects and art historians now became linked to public policy objectives and commercial enterprises, wider than the building, site or narrative itself, which became an element in more extensive schemes of local area renovation, revitalization, renewal and regeneration. Larkham's book (1996), entitled *Conservation and the City*, which is structured by local area policy objectives rather than the historic characteristics of the buildings and areas in which they are applied, chronicled these changes in the United Kingdom. The phrase 'adaptive reuse' became a mantra in planning departments of local authorities throughout Western Europe and North America (Tiesdell *et al.*, 1996). The commercial use of the past became Hewison's '*Heritage Industry*' (1987). The critical difference between preservation and conservation, however, was not so much in the actions themselves as in the methods, attitudes and goals of those who were performing them. The decision to save is linked with the intention to use, often for purposes much wider than any cultural or aesthetic benefit derived from the objects themselves. However, the question remains, does 'adaptive reuse' amount to a theory or just a practical necessity to fill otherwise vacant structures and spaces or to capitalize upon what existed by commodifying it?

It was only with the development of a heritage paradigm that the focus shifted decisively from objects, sites or events to their purpose in contemporary uses and their outcomes. Structures, sites and places are seen as vehicles for the transmission of historicity, contributing to many contemporary social, political and economic needs. It is the fashioning of some representation, a key word, of a past in the present from selected relics, memories and histories. The purpose is thus not to save anything from the past but to use the past in the present: the use determines and, in that sense, creates the resource rather than use being a subsequent action for something already preserved. As Lowenthal (1985) put it, 'heritage is about creating something not about preserving anything'. In the heritage, in contrast to preservation, paradigm, all values are extrinsic and ascribed to the object by those who experience it. Such values are thus neither universal nor immutable, as different people at different times will ascribe different values. The value, and thus the heritage itself, is in this sense created by the current users in fulfilment of their contemporary needs. Tourists therefore create their own heritage; they do not expropriate someone else's (Ashworth, 2009). Heritage is thus a cultural creation of the present and, as with all culture, is fashion-driven. This is most evident in tourism where new presents will constantly imagine new pasts to satisfy rapidly changing needs, none of which are necessarily aligned with the values and needs of local populations.

This way of viewing the relics, memories and narratives of the past has a number of implications. If the process is demand-driven then, at least in theory, resources will be activated as contemporary needs require and thus are mutable, ubiquitous and infinite. It still remains taboo in many circles to even pose questions such as how much or how many (monumental buildings, sacralized sites, heritage towns and the like) does the present actually need or will the future require? Have we enough of these and how would we know when we have enough? In a preservationist perspective, tourism is viewed as the consumption of a finite resource in danger of depletion or exhaustion, whereas in a heritage perspective the resources consumed in tourism are, at least in theory, infinite. Even to suggest that we should attempt to construct comparative frameworks of supply and demand within which heritage and non-heritage objects and uses could be evaluated, including posing the question 'how much is it worth?', thereby aiding selection or non-selection, is to risk being dismissed as a cultural barbarian. Certainly the question of 'enough' appears to be anathema to such august collectors of monumental buildings as the UK National Trusts and their equivalents elsewhere, their often creative role in heritage tourism notwithstanding.

Does any of the above amount to 'theory' or just a series of ad hoc guidelines developed in response to specific practical situations?

Does heritage tourism need its own theory?

A glance through a house journal or website of a professional agency engaged in aspects of heritage (such as the English Heritage publication *Conservation* or the US National Parks Service *Journal of Heritage Stewardship*) does not reveal an absence of theory but on the contrary its over-abundance with many theories being applied in heritage situations or to heritage resources. However, these are theories and techniques derived from cognate or contributory disciplines. The preservation techniques of physical and biotic objects are derived from the natural sciences of chemistry, physics, biology, etc. or the preservation of 'intangibles' such as language, folklores, traditions and skills are drawn from anthropology, ethnology and the like. Techniques of marketing and managing the consumption of the past as product draw upon marketing and business studies and of course associated tourism studies. Although these, and many more, are used in heritage situations, they do not collectively constitute heritage theory.

Imported theoretical concepts are not only found in activities related to the heritage resources, they are also very evident in work on the explanation and understanding of heritage processes and outcomes. The study of heritage is dominated by concepts drawn from economics (including environmental economics, externalities/internalities and pricing/valuation systems), marketing (imaging, promotional techniques and consumer choice models), sociology (cultural capital, group identification and socialization), psychology (personal constructs, cognitive dissonance, memory and personality), history/art history (chronology, cause and effect, provenance and authenticity), political science (legitimation and nation-building) and not least, geography (space, scale, hierarchy, place-making, spatial diffusion and interaction). All of these and many more scientific disciplines have made, and continue to make, substantial and significant contributions within studies of the tourism uses of heritage, quite apart from cognate inter-disciplinary/post-disciplinary fields such as cultural or business studies, which have evolved despite the complications discussed below. There have been discernible changes over time in the preferred disciplines to quarry for concepts and ideas useful in heritage, among both those working with resources (architects, archaeologists, museologists and the like) and those working on application of these (planning, management, marketing, consumer behaviour, etc.).

The contribution of such imported and transposed theory is undeniable and, without it, thinking about the uses of the past would not have developed at all, but it brings with it its own problems. Concepts developed for one type of phenomenon are applied to another, sometimes with scant concern for differences in the contexts. Terminology and even technique may well be imported but divorced from the assumptions that originally underpinned them. Notorious in this respect is the import and use of terminology derived from business studies and marketing without an understanding of the full processes and concepts being applied (Kavaratzis and Ashworth, 2005).

There are also tensions stemming not only from the imported ideas but also from those producing them. The multidisciplinary nature of this field brings together individuals whose academic background but also institutional commitment is quite different. In higher education in particular there are considerable pressures to produce knowledge within specified disciplinary boundaries. The allocation of research funding, the evaluation of research productivity and the hierarchy of position, remuneration and esteem all prioritize efforts that converge with the mainstream of ideas of a particular discipline and discourage cross-disciplinary divergence. Thus many of those from diverse academic disciplines with an interest in either heritage or tourism matters nevertheless have a primary affiliation and responsibility to their 'mother' discipline.

Do heritage tourism studies exist as an academic discipline?

The question therefore becomes, in the context of this chapter: is heritage tourism as a study an academic discipline or could it become such? An academic discipline is a group of individuals who associate with each other, using a mutually intelligible terminology to exchange ideas and collectively develop a body of new knowledge for transmission to others. Equally such association implies a disassociation from other disciplines. There are also practical and political advantages of internal cohesion and external separation. Staking a claim to an area of knowledge and expertise, and promoting its educational and social importance, is an essential weapon in the continuing competitive struggle with other disciplines for resources of money, curriculum space and public recognition and esteem (Kuhn, 1962).

This raises the question, in what sense does such a disciplinary community exist that can be labelled 'heritage studies' or, more specifically here, 'heritage tourism studies' and the answer, as so often, is ambiguous. In the formation and maintenance of any such community, a crucial role is played by the usually interrelated trio of journals, conferences and academic associations and networks.

There are a limited number of journals with the word 'heritage' in their title, although this does not guarantee that the content will reflect heritage as defined here. One of the longest established (since 1969) is the US-based *Journal of Cultural Heritage* but its purpose and content was, and remains, the technology of preservation, using techniques from the natural sciences. Similarly there are journals serving particular elements of or approaches to heritage, whether specified or not, such as landscape history (*Journal of Landscape Studies* since 1979), property law (*International Journal of Cultural Property* since 1992), architectural and building history (*International Journal of Architectural Heritage* since 2005), anthropology (*Journal of Material Culture* since 1996). There are also the house journals of institutions and professional associations, amongst the oldest being the *Journal of Heritage Stewardship* of the United States National Parks Service, which includes federally designated heritage sites as well as national parks, and *Conservation* from English Heritage. However, the establishment of the *International Journal of Heritage Studies* in 1994 provided the first journal with a specific and comprehensive focus exclusively upon heritage studies, including uses. There have since been others, including *Future Anterior* (since 2004), with a stated mission to cover historic preservation, history theory and criticism, *Heritage Management* (since 2008) later renamed *Heritage and Society* in 2011 and the *Journal of Cultural Heritage Management and Sustainable Development* (since 2010), which emerged as an outlet for papers from the regular conferences organized on heritage themes by the Greenlines Institute for Sustainable Development.

Conversely, the scarcity of 'heritage' journals is matched by a plethora of tourism journals often specializing in specific disciplinary approaches (economic, sociological, cultural), techniques of analysis, types or settings of tourism activities. Such variety is paralleled by the variety and source of the theoretical ideas presented. Notably the *Journal of Heritage Tourism* (since 2006) brings in focus this specific use of heritage. Its content is dominated by studies either of tourist impact upon heritage sites and resources or of the tourism potential of heritage sites and areas. The theory underlying each is generally quite different. The *South Asian Journal of Tourism and Heritage* (since 2008) accepts articles in either field rather than those combining the two.

However, although there are a growing number of academic journals bringing together the work of scholars and practitioners of heritage tourism from many different intellectual backgrounds, it probably still remains the case that more work on heritage tourism topics and cases is published in the 'home discipline' journals (urban studies, tourism studies, area development studies, historical and cultural geography, place marketing, etc.) than in synoptic journals with the words 'heritage tourism' in their title or mission statement.

Conferences and seminars with heritage as the theme and tourism as a possible use or with tourism as the theme and heritage as a possible resource have increased dramatically in number and range of backgrounds of participants. Most usually such general themes are linked to some policy objective, such as economic development, environmental sustainability or the shaping and management of place image, identity or brand. Presentations and publications often derived from such gatherings have proliferated. A major disadvantage of the heterogeneity of potential heritage resources and academic approaches to them is that it is too easy to insert the word 'heritage', often replacing 'history', and present or publish a case description of a no doubt interesting historical event, site or building, leaving the reader to deduce the heritage meanings for contemporary societies and any potential for tourism development.

At the moment, there are no formal comprehensive heritage studies associations, although the Association of Critical Heritage Studies was established in 2012. However, there are many professional and academic associations, official and unofficial, concerned with specific heritage resources, their maintenance, interpretation or uses. Furthermore, various semi-academic organizations, such as the Naval Dockyards Society, are also concerned with specific historical resources and their heritage tourism significance for particular localities, such as Portsmouth, UK, in this case.

The existence of higher education courses awarding degrees or diplomas with heritage in the title, as noun or more often adjective, could be both an indicator of, and a stimulus to, the existence of a heritage studies academic community. A glance through lists of higher education courses reveals the existence of many such courses in most countries at undergraduate and more commonly postgraduate levels. In the UK in 2011, 45 such courses could be readily identified, predominantly as one-year postgraduate level, of which ten were offered by archaeology or history departments, eight by arts/cultural studies departments, four by geography or planning and two by tourism, but many were coordinated by multiple departments or were difficult to specify. There are many more courses in tourism, generally offered by 'professional' rather than 'scientific' educational institutions, where such a binary distinction in higher education is either explicit (for example, in Germany, Netherlands or Belgium) or implicit (UK). A few of these even offer a specialty or an option in heritage tourism.

Such courses tend to fall into two distinct categories. There are those that are clearly linked to specific careers, and may, in whole or in part, provide the entry qualification to a profession (town and country planning, museum studies, heritage tourism management and above all the hospitality industry in its many manifestations, are the most obvious in most countries). However, there are also those courses that may seem to have no clearly defined career path and contribute to a broad liberal studies education, most usually in departments of history or cultural studies.

Fragmentation or unity?

If the whole heritage tourism process is considered in three stages then the first, resource preservation and assembly, and last, heritage outcomes, are inherently fragmented and it is only in the critical middle stage of heritage creation that the idea of a commonly agreed overarching theory, an academic paradigm in Kuhn's (1962) sense, is both possible and desirable. The first stage of heritage resource preservation, maintenance and storage requires a variety of different expertise. This is inevitable because heritage activities and experiences can be constructed from an enormously varied range of physical objects, sites, events, personalities, memories and cultural expressions. The skills required in the shaping, maintenance and presentation of such diverse categories of resource are themselves quite diverse. The tasks of a museum curator, an administrator of a cultural performance or manager of a natural landscape or physical phenomenon just require different skill-sets.

Similarly, in the third stage, the outcomes of the heritage tourism process are also used in pursuit of a wide variety of quite different objectives, which necessitates being an integral part of many quite different activities, whether individual or collective, within commercial enterprises or public agencies. As a commercial profit-seeking activity, it is part of much wider hospitality, transport and business structures. As a public/collective activity, it is embedded in wider policy and place management interests and objectives. Public bodies, throughout the jurisdictional hierarchy, are highly unlikely to combine heritage and tourism in their responsibilities. The former is most usually found in cultural agencies alongside museums and archives; the latter is commonly assigned to economic development or business management agencies. This split may even be exacerbated by the allocation of place marketing, branding and promotion as the responsibility of a separate department of communication and information. Such separation may reflect the historical evolution of public involvement in these fields but is consolidated by differences of background, expertise and working methods of those involved. This point is illustrated by departmental and agency structures devolving from the ultimate pinnacle of political responsibility, the national ministry. The allocation of this responsibility and its nomenclature changes rapidly with political change in the priorities of national administrations, reflecting the significance and roles allocated by governments to heritage and to tourism and to various combinations of these.

Only a minority of countries has a separate ministry of heritage and, of those that do, some identify the specific national interest: both Pakistan and Sri Lanka have a *Ministry of National Heritage* and Canada a *Department of Canadian Heritage*. Most usually heritage is combined explicitly or implicitly with culture more generally (New Zealand, Kenya, Oman and many others). Ministries of culture are mainly tasked with the distribution of state subsidies, thus posing the question of what culture is it in the interests of the state to encourage and conversely what not. Sometimes again there is explicit mention of the national claim as in Poland's *Ministry of Culture and National Heritage*. Among the variants on this combination are Italy's *Ministry of Heritage and Cultural Activities* and Qatar's *Ministry of Culture, Arts and Heritage*. If not included under culture then heritage may be found with education, implicitly socialization, often together with many other assorted activities, as in Fiji's *Ministry of Education, National Heritage, Culture and Arts*. Similarly only a minority of countries has a separate ministry of tourism, some of which are large states (India, Brazil, Malaysia) and many others are small states with a notable economic dependence on tourism (Bahamas). More usually, tourism is allocated to either ministries of economic affairs, business and development (Colombia, Iceland, Burma, Netherlands, Peru) or to ministries of culture and the arts, with the implicit idea of combining cultural resource and tourism use (Pakistan, South Korea, Turkey, Ethiopia, Indonesia). As with culture, ministerial responsibility for tourism can be combined with other not obviously related activities, as with youth (Albania), transport, (Japan), recreation/leisure (Mauritius), regional development (Romania), natural resources (Tanzania) or sport (Thailand). If, as is common, neither heritage nor tourism receives any separate ministerial title then either is usually subsumed into ministries with a wide and diverse portfolio of culture, the arts or education and sometimes under just *Home Affairs* (Singapore), including tourism, parks, sports, or media and many others. It is notable that heritage is very rarely included in its entirety under ministries of environment, planning, urban affairs or economic development, although frequently different tasks related to heritage are distributed to different ministries, thus furthering the fragmentation of outcomes.

If fragmentation of expertise and objectives dominates the first and last stages of the process then only in the middle stage where the resources are transformed into heritage tourism products and experiences through selection, interpretation and packaging, ready for uses by others and leading to outcomes well beyond the study of heritage tourism itself, does it become possible and arguably necessary to attempt to focus the study around an approach to theory. It can of course be argued that there are many advantages of eclecticism. The ease of taking whatever idea or technique you need from anywhere, when you need it, with the only criterion being that it delivers what is required for that task, is superficially attractive. However seductive, such a siren-call should be resisted. Heritage and associated tourism studies must involve more than all and any bits of the commodified past that happen to be valued in some way, by some tourists, for some educational or entertainment purpose in the present. Eclecticism is no justification for a conceptual void and an imprecision in terminology and the thinking behind it. Without a structuring paradigm, and its core set of concepts and terms, collective intellectual effort directed towards increasing understanding is impossible and is replaced by a continuous fruitless reiteration.

A paradox of heritage in any such 'middle stage' core integration will be the need to recognize its plurality, as a central tenet of theory building. Not only are its resources and its uses plural, so too is its conceptual identity. Embedded in this plurality lies one or more strands of its inherent dissonance, a long-established concept which could fairly claim to be the founding tenet of any agreed heritage theory that might evolve. All this has implications, of course, for heritage tourism.

The adjective 'critical' has been recently added to the noun heritage (Smith, 2006). An attempted paradigm shift is frequently signalled by prefixing an existing study with a qualifier such as 'post' or 'new', signifying a moving on from existing theory. Words like 'alternative' or 'critical' signify not just a new approach but also one that counters in some way the old. The word critical might either mean crucially important or imply scepticism and disagreement. Both meanings could be argued to apply to all scientific endeavours. 'Critical' as a descriptor of theory has been used by literary studies to focus on the underlying meanings of texts (as in the 'Leavis School' of literary criticism) and by social studies to reveal the underlying structural faults of society with a view to remedying them (as in the 'Frankfurt School' of Marxist analysis). Thus a critical approach to heritage contains the idea of such a study being apart from, and thus critical of, a mainstream, which in this case can be assumed to be the end users, whether official agencies or commercial enterprises, their conventional assumptions, approaches and practices. The result therefore of an attempt to move beyond the practical world in which the study of heritage was born has led back to the world of practice, if only as a questioning, reflective mirror on the contemporary world. Again, this inevitably has implications for heritage tourism.

Thus it may be possible to combine an eclectic diversity in the management of resources and in the uses to which these are put with a focused theoretical framework, a common paradigm and a common terminology stemming from this, in the creation of a more securely grounded conception of heritage and thus a more soundly based heritage tourism. The increasingly apparent gap between academic theorizing and practical applications can best be bridged, not by academics being more aware of, or sympathetic to, the pragmatic difficulties of the many worlds of practice, but by more, better thought-out theory. Simply, academia can most effectively offer assistance to practice, if indeed that is its task, which is not self-evident, by clarifying what we are actually doing, and the consequences of doing it, by grounding such thoughts in unequivocal theory. Only in this way can there be an academic study of heritage, thus of heritage tourism, that has any meaning or, more important, possibility of the development of ideas through a convergence that will transcend the existing intellectual solitudes of scholarship, as well as bridge the yawning gap between theory and practice. Thus theory will enable the enormous practical potential unleashed by the harnessing of heritage to so many contemporary objectives to be realized. Whether or not we subscribe to the 'critical' perspective, we must be content with that.

References

Ashworth, G. J. (2009) 'Do tourists destroy the heritage they have come to experience?', *Tourism Recreation Research*, 34(1): 79–83.

Ashworth, G. J. and Tunbridge, J. E. (2005) 'Move out of the sun and into the past. The blue-grey transition and its implications for tourism infrastructure in Malta', *Journal of Hospitality and Tourism*, 3(1): 19–32.

Denslagen, W. (1994) *Architectural restoration in Western Europe: Controversy and continuity*, Amsterdam: A&NP.

Denslagen, W. (2009) *Romantic modernism: Nostalgia in the world of conservation*. Amsterdam: Amsterdam University Press.

Hewison, R. (1987) *The heritage industry: Britain in a climate of decline*, London: Methuen.

Howard, P. (2013) 'A geographer in heritage. Responding to "decennial reflections"'. A response to Tunbridge *et al.* (2013). *International Journal of Heritage Studies*, 19(4): 373–76.

Kavaratzis, M. and Ashworth, G. J. (2005) 'City branding: An effective assertion of place identity or a transitory marketing trick', *Tijdschrift voor Economische en Sociale Geografie*, 96(5): 506–14.

Kuhn, T. (1962) *The structure of scientific revolution*, Chicago: University of Chicago Press.

Larkham, P. (1996) *Conservation and the city*, London: Routledge.

Lowenthal, D. (1985) *The past is a foreign country*, Cambridge: Cambridge University Press.

Lowenthal, D. (1996) *The heritage crusade and the spoils of history*, Cambridge: Cambridge University Press.

Ruskin, J. (1849) *The seven lamps of architecture*, London: John Wiley.

Smith, L. (2006) *The uses of heritage*, London: Routledge.

Tiesdell, S., Oc, T. and Heath, T. (1996) *Revitalising historic urban quarters*, Oxford: Architectural Press.

Timothy D. J. and Boyd, S. W. (2003) *Heritage tourism*, Harlow: Pearson Education.

Towner, J. (1985) 'The Grand Tour, a key phase in the history of tourism', *Annals of Tourism Research*, 12(3): 297–333.

Trease, G. (1991) *The Grand Tour*, Yale: Yale University Press.

Tunbridge, J. E., Ashworth, G. J. and Graham, B. (2013) 'Decennial reflections on a "Geography of Heritage" (2000)', *International Journal of Heritage Studies*, 19(4): 365–72.

Viollet le Duc, E-E. (1863) *Entretiens sur l'architecture*, Vol. 1 (A. Morel & Cie, Éditeurs), Paris: Imprimerie de L. Martinet.

Viollet le Duc, E-E. (1872) *Entretiens sur l'architecture*, Vol. 2 (A. Morel & Cie, Libraires, Éditeurs), Paris: Imprimerie de L. Martinet.

3 Views of the vernacular

Tourism and heritage of the ordinary

Dallen J. Timothy

Introduction

For thousands of years, people have travelled in search of the glorious past. Even ancient sojourners travelled to historic sites that were already world renowned. Likewise, the focus of most modern-day mass tourism, besides beaches and waterfront resorts, has been the grand built heritage of bygone eras. For many years, the emphasis of heritage conservation and tourism has been the luxurious and distinguished elements of the built environment, most of which were known throughout the world with international allure. Cultural sites that commemorated the upper classes of society have long been the focus of heritage tourism, owing to their extravagance, their durability, their owners' ability to preserve and market them, and the political authority of the gentry in power – those who have always determined which heritages are most important and which ones deserve to be protected and passed down to future generations (Timothy and Boyd, 2003).

From the perspective of heritage tourism, architectural wonders such as cathedrals, government buildings, ancient monuments, castles, palaces, and fortresses are the most traditional and desirable attractions for tourists. Many destinations have based their tourism images and brands on world-famous archaeological sites or historic buildings in an effort to appeal to the masses, who desire to visit imposing places such as the Egyptian Pyramids, Westminster Abbey, Machu Picchu, or the Taj Mahal. While most tourists still aspire to see these most impressive sites, there is change in the air as increasing numbers of people desire more unique and authentic experiences that reveal more about the everyday life of common folk. This chapter takes a largely supply-side perspective to looking at how the heritage of the everyday, or ordinary past, is being more exploited and developed as an instrument for tourism development.

Heritage and the ordinary past

As already noted, people in positions of power throughout history have decided which heritages will be preserved, interpreted, and sold. This discriminatory selection process emphasized the most prominent elements of the built environment. In the very process of selecting the heritage of the aristocracy, the proletariat inheritance was displaced with symbols and structures that had direct relevance to only a small minority of the population. Thus, many 'less important' heritages and representations of some people's historical identity are 'disinherited' simultaneously while others are elevated to the highest and most visible positions (Ashworth, 2003; Tunbridge and Ashworth, 1996). This process and condition of societal amnesia, or the deliberate overlooking of certain parts of the past, may occur as society is uncomfortable with certain elements of its history (e.g. prostitution or slavery) or because controlling what heritage is portrayed can help the powerful elites achieve ideological or political aspirations. Often these actions have xenophobic undercurrents that validate the superciliousness of the ruling classes (Frost, 2008; Gable and Handler, 1996; Harrison, 2009; Timothy, 2011).

As a result of centuries of power manipulation, or in some cases simply imbalanced prioritizing, the most striking and outstanding objects of the past have been preserved and spotlighted for their economic and socio-political potential, often at the expense of the lesser-known 'inessential', or less lucrative heritage. Cities are home to many of the world's greatest monuments, although the subtler features of the urban milieu (e.g. sewers, cemeteries, brothels, and bars) have been ignored for a very long time in the overall heritage and tourism discourse. Likewise, tourists have long visited the imposing buildings of the countryside (Aalen *et al.*, 1997), almost entirely ignoring the more commonplace rural vernacular landscapes that surround them. Even UNESCO's initial efforts to call attention to the world's built environment via the World Heritage List have perpetuated this predicament because it too focused overwhelmingly on grandiose and tangible artefacts of bygone eras, ignoring the remnants of the everyday life of everyday people.

Change is on the horizon, however. In 1993, UNESCO's Nara Document on Authenticity acknowledged the importance of both tangible and intangible heritage. Later, in 2003, the UNESCO Convention for the Safeguarding of Intangible Cultural Heritage emphasized the critical state of many of the world's intangible heritages and set out to offer assistance in documenting and protecting these immaterial elements of culture (Blake, 2009; Leimgruber, 2010; Ruggles and Silverman, 2009). This realignment by UNESCO paved the way for a worldwide heritage organization to begin focusing on cultural elements beyond the magnificent built environment. It also helped reiterate the idea that not all cultural heritage is monumental, or even built, from a global or local perspective.

Although this convention was pivotal in causing national governments and the world community to think concertedly about the value of immaterial and ordinary heritage, scholars have been serious about it for much longer. For decades, anthropologists and cultural geographers have been interested in the landscapes and objects of the common man and woman (Bender 2006; Cosgrove 1990). Interpreting the ordinary landscape has been a favourite activity of geographers since the mid-twentieth century (Jackson, 1984; Lewis, 1979). Assessing components of the vernacular landscape was believed to reveal a great deal of information about how people adapt to, and place imprints upon, their natural environments. As well, such analyses disclosed important evidence of social relations and cultural evolutions (Cosgrove, 1990; Hough, 1990; Kilpinen, 1994).

Early recognition of the importance of vernacular heritage is evidenced in the works of many cultural geographers. Some of the most common elements of the ordinary environment are barns and storage sheds (Auer, 1989; Ennals, 1972; Gaskell and Tanner, 1998; Gritzner, 1990; Hart, 1994; Kaups, 1989; Noble, 1993), vernacular house architecture (Brandhorst, 1981; Jackson, 1990), rural agricultural landscapes and irrigation systems (Crook and Jones, 1999), rural fences (Murray-Wooley and Raitz, 1992; Pickard, 2007) and outhouses (Bollinger, 2005; McCarthy, 2007), to name only a few. Most rural regions have struggled to preserve these landscape features because there has been little economic rationale to do so. The most notable exceptions are commonplace features included in the territory of national parks or other protected cultural areas.

In addition to a lack of political will and unbalanced power relations, as already noted, there are several other constraints to conserving the ordinary heritage. These are particularly pronounced in the less-developed portions of the world, although they exist everywhere to some degree. Foremost among these constraints is the lack of economic rationale for preserving ordinary cultural heritage (Timothy and Nyaupane, 2009). This takes on many forms, including small budgets and a dearth of public funds, but perhaps even more profound is the fact that there is too much heritage to protect. In some places, remnants of the cultural past are everywhere, and not all of it can be saved, especially given budgetary and staff constraints. Therefore, the heritage focus tends to be placed on the grandiose rather than the ordinary and, in this process, the ordinary becomes extraneous, unconservable, and unsellable (Timothy, 2011).

Also lying in the way of the heritagization of the vernacular landscape are three common misconceptions about cultural heritage: that it has to be old, it has to be outstanding, and it has to be tangible. Heritage is, in fact, whatever society inherits from the past and utilizes in the present (Tunbridge and Ashworth, 1996). There are no age limits, requirements of tangibility, or level of notoriety required for something to have heritage value. Thus, a native dwelling abandoned in the 1970s is as much heritage as is one abandoned in the 1700s, although the latter will most certainly be more highly prioritized because it is older and has a higher scarcity value in most modern societies (Timothy, 2011).

Likewise, myths, beliefs, languages, music, folklore, foodways, social structures, smells, sounds, and tastes are as much heritage as are tangible features such as buildings, pottery, or furniture (Ruggles and Silverman, 2009; Schofield and Szymanski, 2011; Smith and Akagawa, 2009). In the words of Schofield and Szymanski (2011: 2), '...special things need not always be tangible'. And, as this chapter is attempting to highlight, fences, barns, cemeteries, roadside markers, and farmscapes are just as much heritage as the bigger and more famous icons of the world. Fairclough (2009b: 127) noted how much heritage 'is of everyday significance that will never reach national or regional lists and registers of protected or classified buildings'. Kavoura and Bitsani (2013) call attention to how much urban heritage there is in Athens beyond the Acropolis, and they submit that Greece would do well to recognize other measures of the Athenian past that have not heretofore been the focus of Athens' tourism industry.

A third constraint is the social disregard for what is considered by society to be old. This is a particularly acute problem in parts of Asia and Africa. In many societies, old is undesirable because it is the antithesis of development or socio-economic 'progress' (Timothy, 1999; Timothy and Boyd, 2003). As a result, the normative philosophy 'old is bad, new is good' often permeates urban planning and development. In the western world, old buildings, even ordinary ones, are often recognized as important heritage, and efforts are made to preserve them or reuse them for modern purposes while preserving some aspects of their histor-ical integrity. In some regions, however, old buildings are more commonly razed to make way for modern housing and rebuilding (Esposito and Gaulis, 2010; Timothy, 1999). Ordinary heritage is sometimes seen as disgraceful and back-ward. From many a developing-world perspective, new and ornate buildings are instead a hallmark of a truly modern society (Timothy and Nyaupane, 2009).

Unfortunately, it is only when the built heritage is gone that society in some locations begins to value it most earnestly, and the valuation process often has to be initiated by foreign interests (Esposito and Gaulis, 2010). This reflects Thompson's (1979) 'rubbish theory', which suggests that the value of things increases when those things become rubbish, suggesting the scarcity value noted earlier. Esposito and Gaulis (2010: 17–18) note that 'rescue is possible when those objects become so scarce that their value dramatically increases'. They use historic shop houses in Singapore as an example:

> shop houses in South-east Asia are sometimes considered as heritage when they are seriously deteriorated and when most of them have been destroyed. For example, Singapore was full of shop houses but most of them were destroyed. The few that survived were recently revaluated and restored...
>
> (Esposito and Gaulis, 2010: 18)

Teo and Huang (1995: 589) also discussed this concept in Singapore and indicated that 'tourists were attracted by the façades of old colonial buildings that have been carefully restored. In contrast, Singaporeans attach a great deal more to activities and lifestyles ... that have since been removed or have disappeared...'.

From a tourism perspective, there is evidence to suggest that increasing numbers of people are becoming more dissatisfied with the ways in which her-itage has for generations been presented to the public. In most cases, this is reflected in an increased desire to see and learn about the lives and 'houses of ordinary people' (Ehrentraut, 1993: 274). This reflects a discontent with the imbalance in the official heritage narrative that has favoured the aristocracy and their lives of glamour, versus chronicling how the bourgeoisie struggled to eke out a living and survive devastating socio-economic conditions such as slavery, poverty, disease, ethnic conflict, war, and high infant mortality (Timothy, 2011).

As well, travellers are increasingly more sophisticated now than they have been in the past and are starting to shun traditional 'McDisneyized' cultural attractions (Ritzer and Liska, 1997) that are predictable and staged specifically (and usually superficially) for tourists. Travellers are also better educated, and although they want to see the most world-famous heritage sites, they are becoming more interested in visiting off-the-beaten-path destinations and attractions 'because of their past association with the private lives of ordinary people' (Schofield, 1996: 335), rather than only those ostentatious ones that have long been included in most tour itineraries geared towards the masses (Boyd, 2008; Knudsen and Greer, 2008; Kruse, 2005; Sears, 1989; Teo and Yeoh, 1997; Timothy and Boyd, 2006). Clifford (2011: 14) said it well in suggesting that 'It is not the castle, cathedral, or cuckoo pound ... that separately defines the significance of a place, but a messy mingling of things tangible and intangible, fixed and transient, big and small, ordinary and special'.

Ehrentraut (1993) examined the growing importance of the ordinary rural farmhouse and its outbuildings for domestic tourism in Japan because the Japanese market desires to see how life was for ordinary Japanese in bygone eras. Arthure (2012) and Howie (2000) noted the importance of drawing attention to themes which local communities feel strongly about – things that give the community its sense of identity, including its stories, people, and places. Similarly Schofield and Szymanski (2011: 2) observe that ordinary heritage involves the sounds, smells, tastes, events, and people that make places special, unique, and significant. In their words, the 'cultural significance' of the vernacular heritage is comprised of the 'ordinary, mundane, everyday places, the commonplace in national terms, but deeply ingrained with local significance and special to those who live there'. Fairclough (2009a: 38) noted the same sentiment when local, ordinary heritage structures 'tended to be overlooked even though these were the buildings that gave the patina of age and a sense of local distinctiveness to a place, the qualities that seem to be most valued by people'. Fairclough (2009a) argues further that the modern approach to heritage is more inclusive and context-specific. Heritage is also, he suggests, more determined by whatever the people value and is often 'marginal' and mundane.

Heritage tourism has long been a tool for the ideological framing of history and identity, wherein 'glossier' versions of the past have been presented to tourists and other visitors (Johnson, 1999). According to Huxtable (1992: 24–25), cultural attractions have commonly replaced reality with fantasy because visitors have tended to prefer 'sanitized ... versions of the past' that ignore 'the gritty accumulations of the best and worst we have produced'. Growing numbers of scholars, however, have acknowledged the need to tell a less sterile version of history in the visitor setting, even if it means revealing uncomfortable parts of the past, 'warts and all', which governments, interest groups, and the public might rather keep hidden from the general tourist gaze (Atkinson and Laurier, 1998; Crooke, 2007; Hardy, 1988; Logan, 2009; Nagle, 2010). This, too, has encouraged the development of an ordinary, mundane, or even troubled heritage, beyond the sanitized versions that have traditionally been produced for tourists.

Such efforts to de-sanitize the past truly epitomize the democratization of local heritage for tourists and other consumers.

Many destination regions are beginning to realize a shift in demand and are expanding their heritage products to include sites beyond the well-worn tourist circuits. Even places without globally known cultural attractions are interested in becoming involved in heritage tourism for its possible economic implications. Çela *et al.* (2009) examined such a case in the US Midwest where commonplace agricultural heritage (e.g. silos, vineyards, tractor factories, and dairy farms) is being promoted to enhance community pride, identity, and employment. Derrett and St Vincent Welch (2008: 73) evaluated the worth of farm sheds to the rural heritage that represents the 'spirit of the Australian outback'. They concluded that there was a general sense of reverence among urban Australians for these farm outbuildings as part of the vernacular landscape, which helps solidify a sense of value for Australia's settler past. Such ordinary heritage, they argue, could play an important role in the aesthetics of a scenic drive and rural tourism development.

Individual vernacular landscape elements will typically not draw significant tourist attention by themselves. However, when linked together into themed cultural routes or heritage trails, a sufficient critical mass can be created to appeal to large numbers of sightseers. Prideaux (2002) provides an example of the Queensland Heritage Trails Network, which aimed to develop secondary cultural attraction-based routes that would draw visitors beyond the most popular coastal destinations into the rural hinterland to visit and appreciate the ordinary landscapes of the outback.

Related trends in the heritagization of the ordinary

Landscapes are visible manifestations of material culture and the ways in which humans modify the environment. Lowenthal (1997) acknowledged the crucial role of tourism in helping to protect vernacular landscapes, particularly rural agricultural settings and their physical features. O'Hare (1997) emphasized the importance of place distinctiveness in terms of cultural landscapes in Australia for tourism. As indicated above, features of the vernacular landscape individually and collectively are beginning to play a more prominent role in tourism development and regional marketing. Bridges, prisons, jails, mines, docks, boats, fish shacks, gardens, fences, barns and many more banal characteristics are being featured more commonly in online and printed marketing materials as destination management organizations come to appreciate heritage's promotional potential.

For example, the Cornwall Council (2011) recently began to stress the value of Cornwall's everyday heritage, including fish sheds, lime kilns, and boathouses. The council believes these features work together to create a place-based cultural product with tourism potential. These physical manifestations of the ordinary past illustrate the importance of local heritage coming out of the shadows of the bigger and better-known tangible patrimony.

Besides the heritagization of ordinary landscape elements as noted above, there are many ways in which heritage is becoming more democratized in a tourism context (e.g. religious tourism/pilgrimage, dark tourism, diasporic return travel, and genealogy/roots tourism). However, this section briefly highlights only a small selection of these trends, including agritourism, heritage cuisines, indigenous culture, and industrial heritage, all of which demonstrate a multiplicity of characteristics associated with ordinary heritage as a tourism product.

Agritourism, or the use of agriculture, its products, processes, and places for tourism purposes, is becoming an increasingly popular niche (Sznajder *et al.*, 2009). Participating in farming practices (e.g. planting, watering, fertilizing, and harvesting), touring plantations, staying on farms and ranches, eating fresh food, helping to harvest animal products, and purchasing locally grown produce are all functions of agritourism. Involvement in agronomy-based tourism fulfils many people's desires and satiates their interests. For some people, these activities are critical in reliving their own agrarian pasts, creating nostalgic experiences they remember with fondness or desire to pass on to their own children (Timothy and Ron, 2009). Other people participate because they are curious about how foods are produced or are interested in seeing exotic plants and animals. While there are many reasons people participate in agritourism, these activities reflect bygone times and rural places when life was simpler, purer and 'more wholesome' (Willits, 1993). Agritourism is the classic meeting of heritage and agriculture, for it relies upon the farming patrimony of places. The crops produced, methods used to harvest, farm buildings and tools, and land use patterns all form an important rural heritage that reflects the values and customs of ordinary people living ordinary lives.

Related to agricultural heritage is the notion of heritage cuisines and foodways. Food is a blend of tangible and intangible elements that not only define people's struggles with nature but also illuminates human relations, available resources, familial and religious traditions, tastes, and smells. Like other important markers of culture (e.g. languages, spiritual beliefs, folklore, social mores, and ethnicity), cuisines are an important part of cultural and national identity (Timothy and Ron, 2013) and help sustain a sense of communal solidarity (Cusack, 2000; Cwiertka, 2006). Most worldwide cuisines started out as 'peasant food' and evolved as recipes and ingredients were refined and supplanted with introduced materials from the outside. Ethnic gastronomy and foodways are replete with cultural heritage indicators that attest to the everyday struggles of everyday people, trying to survive harsh environments, colonialism, forced migration, or other external forces. Foodways are also important in helping migrant communities preserve memories of their homelands and support diasporic identities.

The heritage of indigenous peoples has always been on the cultural travel itinerary and tour circuit, largely because of the differentness associated with natives, their traditions (e.g. dress, music, and dance), and their built environment (Butler and Hinch, 2007). Traditionally, indigenous heritage was conserved and their stories told from an outsider perspective. It was the conquerors and colonialists who interpreted their own Eurocentric past, usually with only tangential reference to the lives and struggles of the natives. As well, in countries such as Australia, Canada, the United States, South Africa, and other colonial states, the ways in which the indigenes were vanquished, killed, and subjugated became the official heritage narrative that glorified the European incursion.

Now, however, more balanced and authentic representations of the native past have begun to be presented to tourists. With more serious demand for cultural knowledge and experiences among the travelling public, more balanced narratives are being told (Hueneke *et al.*, 2009; Johnston, 2003) as many of the world's developed countries have recognized the injustices of past colonial actions (Ardren, 2004). The increase in political, social, and economic empowerment among many native groups attests to changing attitudes and shifting heritage narratives that have begun to pervade tourism. In the twenty-first century, it is more commonplace for indigenous peoples to own stewardship of their heritage and interpret it for tourism (Timothy, 2011).

One additional manifestation of the heritagization of ordinary places is the ascendance of the industrial past (industrial archaeology) into the ranks of worthy places and artefacts to preserve. With the shift from manufacturing and extractive economies to more post-Fordist service economies in the mid-twentieth century, many assembly plants, factories, shipyards, mines, timber camps, fish processing plants, and other industrial works began to shut their doors. This had a number of serious consequences. First, economies failed and many jobs were lost to the people who had long depended on heavy-industry jobs. In small communities, this resulted in high levels of out-migration to other areas where work could be found. Second, buildings and industrial infrastructures sat derelict for years, creating not only aesthetic problems for many communities and areas, but also health and environmental hazards. Third, these dilapidated places were often slotted for demolition, which created unusable brownfields in many cities and suburban areas, and obliterated a conspicuous part of the historical identity of places and its tangible expressions.

In an era of rapid de-industrialization, an equally rapid movement arose to try to protect the industrial past. The movement was strong because of manufacturing's importance as a heritage phenomenon that not only defined place identities (Ruiz Ballesteros and Hernández Ramírez, 2007), it was in fact the raison d'être of many of these very same communities. The lobby to protect industrial archaeology began in earnest in the 1950s in the UK and spread rapidly to other developed countries. It gained tremendous momentum between the 1960s and the first decade of the new millennium. Even UNESCO began to underscore the pertinence of the industrial past in inscribing the Røros Mining Town (Norway) in 1980 on the World Heritage List. This was followed by other manufacturing and extractive sites, such as Engelsberg Ironworks, Sweden (1993), Völklingen Ironworks, Germany (1994), Verla Groundwood and Board Mill, Finland (1996), and Wieliczka Salt Mine, Poland (2008). Adding these and other industrial sites to the World Heritage List also called international attention to this important part of the heritage of the ordinary working class.

During the same time period, industrial relics and places became important tourist attractions (Alfrey and Putnam, 1992; Conlin and Jolliffe, 2010; Jolliffe, 2013). Guidebooks were published in the 1980s and 1990s to direct people to the most illustrious manufacturing and mining heritage attractions (see Falconer, 1980; McDonald, 1996), and visitation increased a great deal to the point where even functioning mines, shipyards, factories, power plants, and other industrial places initiated visitor programmes to help generate additional revenue through entrance fees, guided tours, museums, and souvenir shops (Timothy, 2011; Xie, 2006). Tourism also became an important public relations tool for operational sites because it gave companies an opportunity to build goodwill with surrounding communities (Alonso *et al.*, 2010; Rudd and Davis, 1998) and highlight their role in the local heritage of the working classes.

Conclusions

This chapter examined the shifting interests among some heritage consumers and within tourist destinations from a desire to see, experience, and display only the grandiose heritage of the world's aristocracy to a deeper appreciation of how the common person lived in the past. Vernacular landscapes have developed through human history via the everyday activities of common folk, including peasants, farmers, slaves, traders, and indigenous populations.

As western societies become increasingly unsettled in the modern world, and as tourists have become over-satiated with the spectacular elements of the built environment, there is an increasing awareness of the heritage of the ordinary people of society and the ordinary landscapes they have created (e.g. villages, agricultural patterns, barns, fences, hospitals, plantations, jails, schools, native cultures, cemeteries, industrial sites). This has translated into increased visitation to view vernacular landscapes that tell of the historical struggles of life among the proletariat, the downtrodden, and the powerless minorities in society. This chapter examined these issues as part of a more balanced heritage narrative in the post-modern world and utilized empirical examples to highlight how the landscapes of the ordinary are becoming a more common element of heritage tourism and what destinations are doing to highlight this element of the past as an important part of their heritage product.

There are many forms of tourism and attraction types that highlight the heritage of the ordinary, including agritourism, industrial tourism, indigenous cultures, and heritage cuisines. As well, there are many changes occurring in the heritage arena that have begun decentralizing and democratizing the past from an elitist domain and unbalanced chronicle to a more decentralized and inclusive account of history. This chapter has only scratched the surface in calling attention to this possibility. However, there is evidence to suggest that, in the realm of tourism, the commonplace and mundane parts of the past are becoming an increasingly important part of visitors' expectations and interests, and destinations are beginning to respond.

References

Aalen, F. H. A., Whelan, K., and Stout, M. (eds.) (1997) *Atlas of the Irish rural landscape*. Cork: Cork University Press.

Alfrey, J. and Putnam, T. (1992) *The industrial heritage: Managing resources and uses*. London: Routledge.

Alonso, A. D., O'Neill, M. A., and Kim, K. (2010) 'In search of authenticity: a case examination of the transformation of Alabama's Langdale Cotton Mill into an industrial heritage tourism attraction', *Journal of Heritage Tourism*, 5(1): 33–48.

Ardren, T. (2004) 'Where are the Maya in ancient Maya archaeological tourism? Advertising and the appropriation of culture', in Y. Rowan and U. Baram (eds.) *Marketing heritage: Archaeology and the consumption of the past*, 103–113. Walnut Creek, CA: AltaMira Press.

Arthure, S. (2012) *'Not just a small place': Marion cultural heritage survey*. Unpublished student report, Department of Archaeology, Flinders University, Australia.

Ashworth, G. J. (2003) 'Heritage, identity and places: For tourists and host communities', in S. Singh, D. J. Timothy and R. K. Dowling (eds.) *Tourism and destination communities*, 79–98. Wallingford, UK: CAB International.

Atkinson, D. and Laurier, E. (1998) 'A sanitised city? Social exclusion at Bristol's 1996 International Festival of the Sea'. *Geoforum*, 29(2): 199–206.

Auer, M. (1989) *The preservation of historic barns*. Washington, DC: US National Park Service.

Bender, B. (2006) 'Place and landscape', in C. Tilley, W. Keane, S. Küchler, M. Rowlands, and P. Spyer (eds.) *Handbook of material culture*, 303–314. London: Sage.

Blake, J. (2009) 'UNESCO's 2003 Convention on intangible cultural heritage: The implications of community involvement in "safeguarding"', in L. Smith and N. Akagawa (eds.) *Intangible Heritage*, 45–73. London: Routledge.

Bollinger, H. (2005) *Outhouses*. St Paul, MN: MBI Publishing.

Boyd, S. W. (2008) 'Marketing challenges and opportunities for heritage tourism', in A. Fyall, B. Garrod, A. Leask, and S. Wanhill (eds.) *Managing visitor attractions: New directions*, 283–294. Oxford: Butterworth Heinemann.

Brandhorst, L. C. (1981) 'Limestone houses in central Kansas', *Journal of Cultural Geography*, 2(1): 70–81.

Butler, R. W. and Hinch, T. (eds.) (2007) *Tourism and indigenous peoples: Issues and implications*. Oxford: Butterworth Heinemann.

Çela, A., Lankford, S., and Knowles-Lankford, J. (2009) 'Visitor spending and economic impacts of heritage tourism: A case study of the Silos and Smokestacks National Heritage Area', *Journal of Heritage Tourism*, 4(3): 245–256.

Clifford, S. (2011) 'Local distinctiveness: Everyday places and how to find them', in J. Schofield and R. Szymanski (eds.) *Local heritage, global context: Cultural perspectives on sense of place*, 13–32. Farnham: Ashgate.

Conlin, M. and Jolliffe, L. (eds.) (2010) *Mining heritage and tourism: A global synthesis*. London: Taylor and Francis.

Cornwall Council (2011) 'West Portholland "fish sheds"'. Available at www.cornwall. gov.uk/default.aspx?page=19897 (accessed December 1, 2012).

Cosgrove, D. (1990) 'Landscape studies in geography and cognate fields of the humanities and social sciences', *Landscape Research*, 15(3): 1–6.

Crook, D. S. and Jones, A. M. (1999) 'Traditional irrigation and its importance to the tourist landscape of Valais, Switzerland', *Landscape Research*, 24(1): 49–65.

Crooke, E. (2007) 'Museums, communities and the politics of heritage in Northern Ireland', in S. Watson (ed.) *Museums and their communities*, 300–312. London: Routledge.

Cusack, I. (2000) 'African cuisines: Recipes for nationbuilding?', *Journal of African Cultural Studies*, 13(2): 207–225.

Cwiertka, K. J. (2006) *Modern Japanese cuisine: Food, power and national identity.* London: Reaktion Books.

Derrett, R. and St Vincent Welch, J. (2008) '40 sheds and 40 kilometers: Agricultural sheds as heritage tourism opportunities', in B. Prideaux, D. J. Timothy and K. S. Chon (eds.) *Cultural and heritage tourism in Asia and the Pacific*, 73–83. London: Routledge.

Ehrentraut, A. (1993) 'Heritage authenticity and domestic tourism in Japan', *Annals of Tourism Research*, 20(2): 262–278.

Ennals, P. M. (1972) 'Nineteenth-century barns in Southern Ontario', *Canadian Geographer*, 16(3): 256–270.

Esposito, A. and Gaulis, I. (2010) *The cultural heritages of Asia and Europe: Global challenges and local initiatives.* Amsterdam: Asia-Europe Foundation.

Fairclough, G. (2009a) 'New heritage frontiers', in D. Thérond (ed.) *Heritage and beyond*, 29–41. Strasbourg: Council of Europe.

Fairclough, G. (2009b) 'The cultural context of sustainability – Heritage and living', in D. Thérond (ed.) *Heritage and beyond*, 125–128. Strasbourg: Council of Europe.

Falconer, K. (1980) *Guide to England's industrial heritage.* New York: Holmes & Meier.

Frost, W. (2008) 'Heritage tourism on Australia's Asian shore: A case study of Pearl Luggers, Broome', in B. Prideaux, D. J. Timothy and K. S. Chon (eds.) *Cultural and heritage tourism in Asia and the Pacific*, 305–314. London: Routledge.

Gable, E. and Handler, R. (1996) 'After authenticity at an American heritage site', *American Anthropologist*, 98(3): 568–578.

Gaskell, P. and Tanner, M. (1998) 'Landscape conservation policy and traditional farm buildings: A case study of field barns in the Yorkshire Dales National Park', *Landscape Research*, 23(3): 289–307.

Gritzner, C. F. (1990) 'Log barns of Hispanic New Mexico', *Journal of Cultural Geography*, 10(2): 21–34.

Hardy, D. (1988) 'Historical geography and heritage studies', *Area*, 20: 333–338.

Harrison, R. (2009) *Understanding the politics of heritage.* Manchester: Manchester University Press.

Hart, J. F. (1994) 'On the classification of barns', *Material Culture*, 26(3): 37–46.

Hough, M. (1990) *Out of place: Restoring identity to the regional landscape.* New Haven: Yale University Press.

Howie, F. (2000) 'Establishing the common ground: Tourism, ordinary places, grey-areas and environmental quality in Edinburgh, Scotland', in G. Richards and D. Hall (eds.) *Tourism and sustainable community development*, 101–118. New York: Routledge.

Hueneke, H., Baker, R., Davies, J., and Holcombe, S. (2009) 'Tourist behaviour, local values, and interpretation at Uluru: "The sacred deed at Australia's mighty heart"', *GeoJournal*, 74(5): 477–490.

Huxtable, A. L. (1992) 'Inventing American reality', *New York Review of Books*, 39(20): 24–29.

Jackson, J. B. (1984) *Discovering the vernacular landscape.* New Haven, CT: Yale University Press.

Jackson, J. B. (1990) 'The house in the vernacular landscape', in M. P. Conzen (ed.) *The making of the American landscape*, 355–369. London: Routledge.

Johnson, N. C. (1999) 'Framing the past: time, space and the politics of heritage tourism in Ireland', *Political Geography*, 18(2): 187–207.

Johnston, A. M. (2003) 'Self-determination: Exercising indigenous rights in tourism', in S. Singh, D. J. Timothy, and R. K. Dowling (eds.) *Tourism in destination communities*, 115–134. Wallingford: CAB International.

Jolliffe, L. (ed.) (2013) *Sugar heritage and tourism in transition*. Bristol: Channel View.

Kaups, M. E. (1989) 'Finnish meadow-hay barns in the Lake Superior region', *Journal of Cultural Geography*, 10(1): 1–18.

Kavoura, A. and Bitsani, E. (2013) 'Managing the World Heritage Site of the Acropolis, Greece', *International Journal of Culture, Tourism and Hospitality Research*, 7(1): 58–67.

Kilpinen, J. T. (1994) 'Finnish cultural landscapes in the Pacific Northwest', *Pacific Northwest Quarterly*, 86(1): 25–34.

Knudsen, D. C. and Greer, C. E. (2008) 'Heritage tourism, heritage landscapes and wilderness preservation: The case of National Park Thy', *Journal of Heritage Tourism*, 3(1): 18–35.

Kruse, R. J. (2005) 'The Beatles as place makers: Narrated landscapes in Liverpool, England', *Journal of Cultural Geography*, 22(2): 87–114.

Leimgruber, W. (2010) 'Switzerland and the UNESCO Convention on Intangible Cultural Heritage', *Journal of Folklore Research*, 47(1–2): 161–196.

Lewis, P. K. (1979) 'Axioms for reading the landscape: Some guides to the American Scene', in D. W. Meinig (ed.) *The interpretation of ordinary landscapes: Geographical essays*, 11–31. New York: Oxford University Press.

Logan, W. (2009) 'Hoa Lo Museum, Hanoi: Changing attitudes to a Vietnamese place of pain and shame', in W. Logan and K. Reeves (eds.) *Places of pain and shame: Dealing with 'difficult heritage'*, 182–197. London: Routledge.

Lowenthal, D. (1997) 'European landscape transformations: The rural residue', in P. Groth and T. W. Bress (eds.) *Understanding ordinary landscapes*, 180–188. New Haven: Yale University Press.

McCarthy, K. (2007) *Florida outhouses: An ode to the shack in the back*. Charleston, SC: The History Press.

McDonald, M. R. (1996) *A guide to Scottish industrial heritage*. Edinburgh: Scottish Industrial Heritage Society.

Murray-Wooley, C. and Raitz, K. (1992) *Rock fences of the Bluegrass*. Lexington: University Press of Kentucky.

Nagle, J. (2010) 'Between trauma and healing: Tourism and neoliberal peace-building in divided societies', *Journeys*, 11(1): 29–49.

Noble, A. G. (1993) 'Barn entry porches, pent roofs, and decorated doors of the eastern Midwest', *Journal of Cultural Geography*, 14(1): 21–34.

O'Hare, D. (1997) 'Interpreting the cultural landscape for tourism development', *Urban Design International*, 2(1): 33–54.

Pickard, J. (2007) 'Australian rural fences: heritage challenges for conserving the unconservable', *International Journal of Heritage Studies*, 13(6): 489–510.

Prideaux, B. (2002) 'Creating rural heritage visitor attractions – the Queensland Heritage Trails Project', *International Journal of Tourism Research*, 4: 313–323.

Ritzer, G. and Liska, A. (1997) ' "McDisneyization" and "post-tourism": Complementary perspectives in contemporary tourism', in C. Rojek and J. Urry (eds.) *Touring cultures: Transformations of travel and theory*, 96–109. London: Routledge.

Rudd, M. A. and Davis, J. A. (1998) 'Industrial heritage tourism at the Bingham Canyon Copper Mine', *Journal of Travel Research*, 36(3): 85–89.

Ruggles, D. F. and Silverman, H. (eds.) (2009) *Intangible heritage embodied*. Dordrecht: Springer.

Ruiz Ballesteros, E. and Hernández Ramírez, M. (2007) 'Identity and community: Reflections on the development of mining heritage in southern Spain', *Tourism Management*, 28(3): 677–687.

Sears, J. F. (1989) *Sacred places: American tourist attractions in the nineteenth century*. Boston: Oxford University Press.

Schofield, J. and Szymanski, R. (2011) 'Sense of place in a changing world', in J. Schofield and R. Szymanski (eds.) *Local heritage, global context: Cultural perspectives on sense of place*, 1–11. Farnham: Ashgate.

Schofield, P. (1996) 'Cinematographic images of a city: Alternative heritage tourism in Manchester', *Tourism Management*, 17(5): 333–340.

Smith, L. and Akagawa, N. (eds.) (2009) *Intangible heritage*. London: Routledge.

Sznajder, M., Przezbórska, L., and Scrimgeour, F. (2009) *Agritourism*. Wallingford: CAB International.

Teo, P. and Huang, S. (1995) 'Tourism and heritage conservation in Singapore', *Annals of Tourism Research*, 22(3): 589–615.

Teo, P. and Yeoh, B. S. A. (1997) 'Remaking local heritage for tourism', *Annals of Tourism Research*, 24(1): 192–213.

Thompson, M. (1979) *Rubbish theory: The creation and destruction of value*. Oxford: Oxford University Press.

Timothy, D. J. (1999) 'Built heritage, tourism and conservation in developing countries: Challenges and opportunities', *Journal of Tourism*, 4: 5–17.

Timothy, D. J. (2011) *Cultural heritage and tourism: An introduction*. Bristol: Channel View.

Timothy, D. J. and Boyd, S. W. (2003) *Heritage tourism*. Harlow: Prentice Hall.

Timothy, D. J. and Boyd, S. W. (2006) 'Heritage tourism in the 21st century: Valued traditions and new perspectives', *Journal of Heritage Tourism*, 1(1): 1–16.

Timothy, D. J. and Nyaupane, G. (eds.) (2009) *Cultural heritage and tourism in the developing world: A regional perspective*. London: Routledge.

Timothy, D. J. and Ron, A. S. (2009) 'Farmers for a day: Agricultural heritage and nostalgia in rural Israel', Paper presented at the annual conference of the Association of American Geographers, Las Vegas, Nevada, March 26.

Timothy, D. J. and Ron, A. S. (2013) 'Heritage cuisines, regional identity and sustainable tourism', in C. M. Hall and S. Gössling (eds.) *Sustainable culinary systems: Local foods, innovation, and tourism & hospitality*, 275–290. London: Routledge.

Tunbridge, J. E. and Ashworth, G. J. (1996) *Dissonant heritage: The management of the past as a resource in conflict*. Chichester: Wiley.

Willits, F. K. (1993) 'The rural mystique and tourism development: Data from Pennsylvania', *Journal of the Community Development Society*, 24(2): 159–174.

Xie, F. F. P. (2006) 'Developing industrial heritage tourism: A case study of the proposed Jeep Museum in Toledo, Ohio', *Tourism Management*, 27(6): 1321–1330.

4 Telling the truth or selling an image?

Communicating heritage as an instrument in place marketing

Elke Ennen and Eugenio van Maanen

Introduction

The number of visitors to many historical sites is increasing. Cities and sites like Bath, Venice, Carcassonne or Mont St Michel are at times overwhelmed by visitors and their effects. This has created numerous paradoxes and conflicts in the management of such cities and sites (see also Ennen, 2006).

A dilemma that can occur in the urban development process by planners is to ensure a balance of interests. Problems can occur when the triangular balance between the destination, its stakeholders and visitors is disturbed because the development initiatives are not in the interest of all parties involved. Often it is the stakeholders, especially the residents, who do not see their interests reflected in these policies, planning and decision processes. Consequently, the need for management of visitor flows has become more prominent. Since each destination has its own unique characteristics – thus rendering standard solutions impractical – such management has to take a multi-faceted approach. These issues become even more complex in a multicultural context.

A discussion about contested interests and possibly conflicts is especially applicable in situations where the population of a destination is culturally and ethnically diverse. In these instances, 'what to preserve', 'whose heritage' and 'for whom' become highly pertinent questions. Different stakeholders may very well give different answers to these questions, which can in turn lead to conflicting interests in terms of using the same resources at the same place and same time. In the context of heritage and its function within place marketing, several scenarios can be distinguished, regarding the recognition, identification, support and selection of heritage. These scenarios are analysed to determine the extent to which heritage is a manifestation of the dominant group in the attempt to safeguard values, standards, identity and history. Most of the time, these processes leave little room for those members of society who are not in influential positions – for instance, minority groups and the lower classes. However, it is questionable if it could ever be possible for heritage to reflect a colourful and rich diversity that covers all the multicultural and ethnic interests of its population.

This is especially relevant for colonial heritage because it is based on external resources. Therefore, the function, acceptance and recognition of imported colonial heritage in a multicultural and ethnic context need to be considered. Although the discussion and analysis of heritage within a plural cultural and ethnic society is underway (recently emphasized by Van Maanen, 2011; Ashworth *et al.*, 2007), it is still not an overworked area of research.

However, in an era of globalization in which societies are becoming increasingly plural in terms of culture and ethnicity, it is important to obtain a better understanding of the function and selection of heritage in these societies. The process of urban development and the role of heritage will be successful when the various cultural and ethnic components of society are involved and taken into account in the planning and development process. In order to better understand how people from different cultural and ethnic backgrounds value heritage, planning and management strategies need to take account of this in an open process. The purpose of such policies is to enhance the support, participation and acceptance in society with respect to the consequences that occur when heritage is used as an instrument in place marketing and urban development strategies to attract increasing visitor numbers.

This chapter seeks to contribute to the theory and discussion around heritage selection, visitor flows and management in a multicultural context. It is structured as follows. The next section starts with an introduction that relates the ideas of heritage and visitor flows to urban development. The third section considers heritage as an instrument in urban planning. The fourth section outlines a plural ethnic context that focuses on identity and sense of place in the contribution to the interpretation of colonial heritage to illustrate how difficult questions in multicultural destinations can be answered. The final section draws conclusions and opens the debate on the attitude regarding the reality of communicating heritage as an instrument in place marketing regardless of the choice between telling the truth and just selling the image.

Heritage, flows of visitors and urban development

> History is a form within which we fight, and many have fought before us. For the past is not just dead, inert, confining; it carries signs and evidences also of creative resources, which can sustain the present and prefigure possibility.
>
> (Sardar and Van Loon, 1997: 34)

Heritage, as an interpretation of resources, is receiving increased attention in policies regarding planning and management strategies in urban development processes (see, for instance, Tiesdell *et al.*, 1996). The aim of these policies is to increase the attractiveness of cities, communicated through place marketing, as destinations, especially for visitors. In many cases, local agencies focus on issues such as how to increase the number of visitors to a destination or attraction and how to put such places on mental maps. In general, economic motivations such as employment and revenue generation through inward investment underlie these perspectives. Urban development plans concentrate on product development, improvements of infrastructural services and accessibility. As a part of product development, heritage is coming to assume a key role.

Tunbridge and Ashworth (1996) describe the commodification process as one in which a resource is transformed into a marketable product. They see landscapes, symbols, pasts and stories as resources for commodification. In developing an attractive product, a clear selection is made from the whole range of available resources in order to create visitor destinations (see Figure 4.1). By selecting a resource to commodify as a visitor destination, this resource is in effect being interpreted. Certain meanings are being ascribed to the resource and connotations associated with it are being valued, cherished and chosen above others in order to transform it into an appealing and marketable product. In the selection of resources to commodify, the quality and substance of the resources is subject to competition and conflict. So, what is ultimately 'manufactured' as a visitor destination can be explained by selection processes influenced by political will and financial resources to conserve rather than the intrinsic importance of the artefacts themselves. This commodification of heritage is clearly illustrated, for instance, in studies by Tunbridge and Ashworth (1996), Ennen (1999) and Van Diepen and Ennen (2008).

Heritage is not 'what is preserved and conserved by an institutionalized process of selection' (Ashworth, 1991: 3), nor is it 'everything an individual or society inherited', but heritage is an individual or collective interpretation of elements of the past. However, what is real? And who decides what is real? Historical information is interpreted and experienced differently. Historical information can include elements as diverse as: historical periods, like eighteenth-century Bath (UK) or Delft (the Netherlands); historical events, like World War Two; the way of life of residents, such as the Amish or Mennonites in Pennsylvania; original functions like cathedrals and mills; political history, like statues of local heroes; or architecture such as Art Nouveau in Brussels (Ennen, 1999). Elements from the past become heritage when they have meanings for individuals or groups in the present; in this way, heritage is created.

Evidently, attention paid to heritage in urban development is related to processes of change in society. In 1985, Chapin and Kaiser (1985) noted that in addition to the organization of activities, urban quality is the most important determinant when it comes to choices of locations made by people and organizations. In this process, quality not only refers to the quality of life, but also to the quality of the possibilities for work and recreation:

> Although land use planning does not touch directly on all qualities that users consider to be important, for example, the amount of indoor space and its

Selection	Target group	
Resources ⟶ **Interpretation** ⟶ **Products**		

Figure 4.1 The commodification process (source: adapted from Tunbridge and Ashworth, 1996: 7).

arrangement, it facilitates the urban planner's task of evaluating factors related to land use planning to know the relative importance attached to each of the whole range of qualities the user considers to be important.

(Chapin and Kaiser, 1985: 199)

In urban development 'romantic architecture', 'retro-architecture' or 'new-urbanism' are increasingly commonplace (see also Dogterom *et al.*, 1997). New urbanism is a reaction to the anonymity and uniformity of American suburbs and denotes that a 'we-feeling' can be encouraged by means of town planning and architecture. What these concepts have in common is the attention paid to the past in renewed meanings. There are, for instance, the newly created cities of Lelystad and Almere in the Netherlands where the cities have been planned around a specific past. Lelystad presents itself as Batavia-city and emphasizes a colonial past of the Golden Age, whereas Almere tries to give itself a 'historical identity' by means of the construction of a full-size replica of Belgium's Jemeppe Castle, also known as Hargimont Castle, which dates from the thirteenth century.[1] Newly constructed housing areas are increasingly furnished with a 'historical identity'. Dutch examples include the archaeological 'silence-areas' in the Leidsche Rijn housing estate in Utrecht and the development of Brandevoort, a Dutch 'nostalgic' housing development with historical elements in Helmond. Designing such projects adds an immaterial layer referring to certain pasts. This layer is a collage of myths and narratives and fits the nostalgic desire for past times.

Heritage destinations, either preserved or created, are popular and the number of visitors is growing. Visitor flows at heritage sites can be analysed quantitatively as well as qualitatively (see Figure 4.2). In terms of quantity, one might think of a situation where a destination has (too) many, enough or (too) few visitors. When the destination has enough visitors, there are few, if any, problems. However, when there are too many or too few visitors, problems may occur. A historical site with too many visitors may be attractive from an economic point of view. The downside, however, is the potential negative effects such as nuisance, increased traffic, erosion or other damage to heritage sites and objects. On the other hand, when historical sites attract too few visitors, the commercial viability or even the long-term survival of the site may be at risk (Ennen, 2007).

Quality, on the other hand, may involve desired and/or undesired effects resulting from visitor flows. Visitors may be sought, for instance, for their positive attitude towards heritage assets or their expenditure at the site and the related economic benefits. Alternatively visitors may not be wanted because they seek experiences other than those offered at the sites, which could be in conflict with other visitors and users seeking to use resources at the same time.

However, it is often difficult to identify the 'desired' or 'undesired' status and it largely depends on the purposes one wishes to achieve with the heritage destination. After all, visitor destinations like heritage sites rarely achieve the number of visitors they wish for. Too few desired and/or too many undesired visitors are what cause most of the problems. After an analysis of the impacts,

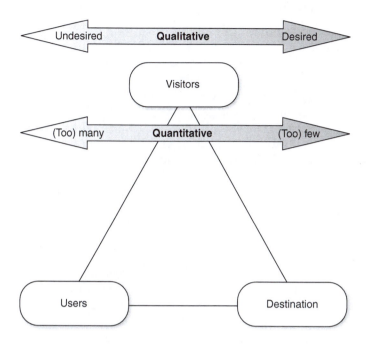

Figure 4.2 Visitors: quantitative and qualitative approach.

the next stage is to determine how to deal with these; in effect, maximize the positive and minimize the negatives.

Heritage as an instrument in urban planning

The multicultural nature of a society must form part of the discussion of the role of heritage as an instrument in urban planning and development. A multicultural context makes the interpretation of heritage and the use of it in urban planning and development a multifaceted phenomenon, especially because the value attached to heritage is extremely diverse and contributes in many ways to a sense of place and identity. Moreover, if the resources that are available for interpretation originate from a colonial period, it becomes pertinent to ask: in what way and to what extent do different population groups in a plural ethnic society contribute to the socio-psychological meaning of colonial heritage?

An understanding of the attitude of the different stakeholder groups associated with colonial heritage is necessary. As such, the aim of this is to achieve wider support and empathy for the previously described impacts, among the various local stakeholder groups.

Sense of place and place identities

In essence 'sense of place' is about assigning an affinity to a particular place, described by Carter *et al.* (1993) as a 'place or space to which meaning has been ascribed'. These meanings stem from human experiences and can be individual as well as collective. Place identities are generally created on the basis of the sense of belonging that individuals or societies attach to places. Consequently, it is not a static phenomenon. Just like heritage, it is created by individuals, making it dynamic, unique and changeable through time. According to Ashworth and Graham (2005), 'senses of place are the products of the creative imagination of the individual and of society, while identities are not passively received but are ascribed to places by people'.

Place identities are created, which suggests that they do not come about haphazardly. Again, as with heritage, it is about who decides, about inclusion or exclusion, what is it used for and for what purposes? In other words, it focuses on the relationship between senses of place, being expressed in place identities, and senses of time. The processes that contribute to creating a sense of place are especially determined by the social, cultural and economic context in which they occur. These aspects are subject to changes over time and can influence and alter the place identities. These changes can be the result of economic transformation, shifts in policy and power structures, social alterations or changes in the meanings and values people attach to cultural expressions or artefacts.

The attribution of identities to places is an evolutionary process. This is determined by elements such as changing actors with their changing goals, ideas and purposes and the changing characteristics of a place identity over time. Therefore, according to Huigen and Meijering (2005), place identities are constructed and reconstructed. The evolutionary process of a current place identity has its origin in its past and constitutes the foundation for its future identity. It makes place identity a multidimensional phenomenon with plural characteristics based on concepts such as ethnicity, culture and society. In this way, it is comparable to the discussion, definition and position of heritage in almost every respect.

With this in mind, it is interesting to consider the colonial past – and the heritage produced by this past – in the processes that create this sense of place and place identities and the possible changes herein. Heritage is a key mechanism in the process of how people remember their pasts, how they interpret the past and how they use it to create their own sense of place and time, and finally transform it into place identities. Bearing this in mind, 'different identities might be allocated to the same region at the same point in time, and for that reason, we should not speak of "the" identity of a region but of identities in the plural' (Simon, 2005).

One example of a plural ethnic society that has been ruled for more than 300 years as a colony is Surinam (see also Van Maanen, 2011). Surinam's immense cultural diversity is manifested in the composition of its population comprising a variety of ethnic groups. While the East Indian and Afro-Surinamese (Creole) dominate the population, accounting for 33 per cent and 30 per cent, respectively, there are sizeable groups of Javanese (17 per cent of the total population) and 8 per cent Maroons (Bush Negroes). The indigenous Amerindian population makes up a further 3 per cent of the population in Surinam, while Chinese, Lebanese, Jews, Europeans and others constitute 9 per cent (ABS, 2006). The historic city centre of Paramaribo as an example of colonial heritage was inscribed on UNESCO's World Heritage List in 2002. Paramaribo is described as an exceptional example of the gradual fusion of European architecture and construction techniques with indigenous South American materials and crafts to create a new architectural idiom. Furthermore, it is a unique example of the contact between the European culture of the Netherlands and the indigenous cultures and environment of South America in the years of intensive colonization of this region in the sixteenth and seventeenth centuries (UNESCO World Heritage Centre website) (UNESCO, n.d.).

However, collective interests are not always in accordance with individual interests; every individual has unique experiences that are uniquely valued and transformed into senses of places and identities that differ from collective ones. Many of these tensions and conflicts can be traced back to how decisions are made. In other words, what official governmental agencies are involved, who decides, what, how and in what way do these decision processes take place? Does the decision or policy reflect the feelings of the majority within a society or is it supported by just a small elite group? Regardless of which approach is chosen, a top-down or bottom-up approach, people, individuals or collectives will always be included or excluded. Described by Rose (1995) as 'identifying with' in the case of belonging to a group, or as 'identifying against', meaning not belonging to the other groups, it is about the exclusion or inclusion of people, communities and groups that are placed in its multidimensional context, making identity a complex, relational phenomenon.

Several studies (Van Hoven *et al.*, 2005; Ashworth, 2005; Kuipers, 2005) emphasize the consequences of inclusion and exclusion of certain groups in the creation of places and identities. Another dilemma is the association between the sense of place as an expression of an official position with that of a popular one. Heritage plays an important role in this respect. The consequence of obtaining heritage status alters the potential and position of, for instance, an area or building and influences the sense of place accordingly. The position of heritage in these processes contributes in various ways – for example, through narratives, imaginations and representations.

Particularly in colonized nations such as Surinam, in which the original population groups have been widely suppressed by colonial rulers, it is rather difficult to deal with this legacy and to find a way to raise a voice in the selection process of heritage and thus the creation of an identity. This drastic integration between heritage and identity is supported by the fact that a World Heritage Site has to be nominated by the national governments of the state parties that ratified the 1972 World Heritage Convention. According to Lowenthal (1998), this implies that these national icons expressed in heritage are an expression of a national identity and therefore determined by those who select them.

Telling the truth by selling an image versus telling the truth or selling an image? A call for discussion

In urban development, identity is becoming an increasingly important criterion. It is inevitable to connect urban policy more closely to the experiences of people. For instance, cultural diversity in large cities is increasing. Different population groups need to be given the opportunity to express their own identity and preferences in terms of space. Moreover, urban policy is in need of a new social basis. Citizens need to be involved more in urban planning and all its attendant problems. Therefore, the problems need to be addressed in their different roles in society. Although attaching a meaning to something is in essence an individual matter, social interaction will lead to collective interpretations. This implies that a cultural identity of space, expressed in a place, is in fact a social construct based on mutual interpretation.

To what extent and in what way a society is set up, in relation to its ethnic composition, its mutual willingness to adapt to other ethnic (dominant or majority) groups, acceptance and support of ethnic minority groups within one society, are leading in the proportion and need for creating an own identity and sense of place. The political context and use of (colonial) heritage is strongly determined by the extent to which a society is willing to accept its ethnic diversity and consider this as valuable for the community as a whole.

Figure 4.3 is based on the process of commodification of heritage and shows a simplified model to express the relations between the position in society, colonial heritage, sense of place and identity. The commodification of colonial

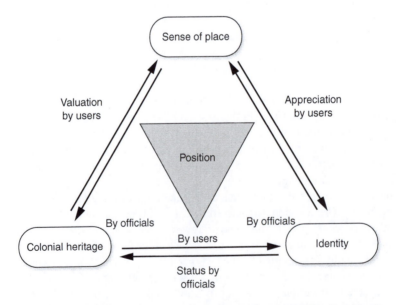

Figure 4.3 The relationship between the position in society and colonial heritage, sense of place and identity (source: adapted from Kuipers, 2005).

history and its resources can be approached from two different but related perspectives. First, that of the official agencies that purposively and consciously 'produce' colonial heritage in a top-down way, based on their interpretation and motivation, which is valuation, status and appreciation of 'their' colonial history that needs to be remembered for future generations. Second, that of its users, typified as 'consumers', approaching their colonial history bottom-up with no explicit ends of their own. This bottom-up approach in place identity is more about how and to what extent a place reminds users of their past and how they appreciate it.

The triangle in the centre represents the position of individuals or groups in society. This position is a balance determined by political, cultural and economic dominance in society, depicted by power and voice, among other things. The position influences the strength and relation of the valuation, status and appreciation between colonial heritage, sense of place and identity. A distinction is made between users (residents, consumers and visitors) and officials (governmental agencies, heritage experts, NGOs).

Clearly, the model consists of mutual relations. For instance, sense of place contributes to the creation of colonial heritage, as does colonial heritage to sense of place. The same can be said about the relation between colonial heritage and identity, and sense of place and identity. The actors involved determine the direction of these relations. It explains that 'officials' and 'users' value colonial heritage simultaneously but from opposite directions. The arrows in this model symbolize the impact direction, not the direction of the relationship. It is this reciprocity, between valuation and appreciation in combination with officials and users, that finally determines the lifespan of colonial heritage, sense of place and identity.

Applied to, for instance, the situation of Surinam's capital city, Paramaribo, one may wonder whether perhaps its colonial past and the transformation into the preservation and conservation of built colonial heritage could be a top-down approach imposed by official, governmental agencies based on economic, cultural, ethnic or political considerations. Or is it supported by its users and do they consider this colonial history and its remaining resources a part of their own history that they value and appreciate to such an extent that it is important for them to conserve and preserve it for future generations? In a multi-ethnic society such as Paramaribo, this is an interesting issue. A recent study conducted in Paramaribo by Van Maanen (2011) showed that it is unfounded to assume that built colonial heritage connects different ethnic population groups constructively. For government policy, it implies that the use of built heritage as a consciously chosen instrument to create a common national identity and feeling of mutual solidarity is of little benefit or entirely ineffective. Therefore, how realistic, feasible and desirable is (colonial) heritage as an instrument in a process of urban development and place marketing? As we have seen, within this complex of factors, a multicultural context adds an extra and more complicated dimension. After all, how do you manage and plan the functionality of heritage in an urban development process within a multicultural context? A multicultural society implies the existence of plural heritage, identities and senses of place. In other words, to what extent does the use of (colonial) heritage in urban development do justice to the community as a whole and to what extent does it contribute to an increasing need of having identities in a multicultural setting? Very probably, the functionality of heritage in urban development will benefit only a small, selective and influential group, because those who are in the position to select and decide are the ones who determine the function of heritage.

This will be expressed in how, where, for whom and for what purpose place marketing is effected, which means that the selection of heritage and its functionality is not about telling the truth, but about creating and selling a desired image.

Note

1 Construction of the building started in 2000 but was never finished and at present it is a modern ruin.

References

ABS (2006) *Statistisch Jaarboek 2005*. Paramaribo: Algemeen Bureau van de Statistiek.

Ashworth, G. J. (1991) *Heritage planning*. Groningen: Geo Press.

Ashworth, G. J. (2005) 'Imagining Newfoundlands', in Ashworth, G. J. and Graham, B. (eds.) *Senses of place: Senses of time*. Aldershot: Ashgate, 177–191.

Ashworth, G. J. and Graham, B. (2005) 'Senses of place: Senses of time and heritage', in Ashworth, G. J. and Graham, B. (eds.) *Senses of place: Senses of time*. Aldershot: Ashgate, 3–12.

Ashworth, G. J., Graham, B. and Tunbridge, J. E. (2007) *Pluralising pasts: Heritage, identity and place in multicultural societies*. London: Pluto Press.

Carter, E., Carter, J. and Squires, D. J. (1993) *Space and place: Theories of identity and location*. London: Lawrence and Wishart.

Chapin, F. S. J. and Kaiser, E. J. (1985) *Urban land use planning*. Chicago: University of Illinois Press.

Dogterom, J. C., Ponec, I. E., Van Den Heiligenberg, E. and Rutten, J. (1997) *Verlangen naar romantische architectuur*. Amsterdam: SFB Vastgoed en bpf-bouw.

Ennen, E. (1999) *Heritage in fragments*. Groningen: Faculteit der Ruimtelijke Wetenschappen Rijksuniversiteit Groningen.

Ennen, E. (2006) *Bindingen, belevingen en verleidingen*. Breda: NHTV Academic Studies.

Ennen, E (2007) *Dillemma's in bezoekersstromenland; wat gaan we (nu weer) beleven?*, Breda: NHTV Academic Essays no. 1.

Huigen, P. P. P. and Meijering, L. (2005) 'Making places: A story of De Venen', in Ashworth, G. J. and Graham, B. (Eds.) *Senses of place: Senses of time*. Aldershot: Ashgate, 19–30.

Kuipers, M. J. (2005) 'The creation of identities by government designation: A case study of the Korreweg District, Groningen, NL', in Ashworth, G. J. and Graham, B. (eds.) *Senses of place: Senses of time*. Aldershot: Ashgate, 205–219.

Lowenthal, D. (1998) *The heritage crusade and the spoils of history*. Cambridge: Cambridge University Press.

Rose, G. (1995) 'Place and identity: A sense of place', in Massey, D. and Jess, P. (eds.) *A place in the world?* Oxford: Oxford University Press, 87–132.

Sardar, Z. and Van Loon, B. (1997) *Cultural studies for beginners.* Cambridge: Icon Books.

Simon, C. (2005) 'Commodification of regional identities: The "selling" of waterland', in Ashworth, G. J. and Graham, B. (eds.) *Senses of place: Senses of time.* Aldershot: Ashgate, 31–45.

Tiesdell, T., Oc, T. and Heath, T. (1996) *Revitalizing historic urban quarters.* Oxford: Architectural Press.

Tunbridge, J. E. and Ashworth, G. J. (1996) *Dissonant heritage: The management of the past as a resource in conflict*, Chichester: John Wiley and Sons.

United Nations Educational, Scientific and Cultural Organization (UNESCO). (n.d.) *Historic Inner City of Paramaribo.* Available at http://whc.unesco.org/en/list/940/ (accessed June 2013).

Van Diepen, A. and Ennen, E. (2008) De bestemming als identiteitsverschaffer. Symbolische betekenissen voor bestemmingen en bezoekers. *Vrijetijds Studies*, 26.

Van Hoven, B., Meijering, L. and Huigen, P. P. P. (2005) 'Escaping times and places: An artist community in Germany', in Ashworth, G. J. and Graham, B. (eds.) *Senses of place: Senses of time.* Aldershot: Ashgate, 155–164.

Van Maanen, E. G. O. M., (2011) *Colonial heritage and ethnic pluralism: Its sociopsychological meaning in a multiethnic society.* Breda: NRIT Media.

Part 2
Tensions and dissonance

5   Problems in selling heritage for tourism

A cautionary tale, with insights from Europe's (pen)insular margins

John E. Tunbridge

Introduction

Heritage has arguably generated the most remarkable growth industry of the late twentieth century, continuing now well into the twenty-first. Its commercial impact, upon tourism especially, is too easily discussed in straightforward economic terms. However, there are problems with this: those who manage relevant jurisdictions are not necessarily positive to heritage – or to particular heritages – when heritages are in competition with one another or with alternative tourism or other planning objectives. This chapter discusses the cases of three small jurisdictions in warm (pen)insular locations, in all of which official perspectives on heritage – specifically of former Royal Navy bases – are significantly at variance with those of non-governmental organizations dedicated to heritage resource conservation and related tourism promotion. The discussion is a salutary reminder, with greater resonance for larger and more complex societies, that the course of heritage development – and ultimately of its impact assessment – does not necessarily 'run smooth'.

This chapter is not intended to 'rain on heritage's parade'; merely to insert a note of caution into the conventional wisdoms, even hubris, that at times permeate public and professional discourse on heritage and its promotion for tourism.

Forty years ago, 'heritage' was emerging into the public consciousness. It was a time of growing environmental concern, for many reasons, sharply accented by the energy crisis of 1973 – which became a catalyst for the conservation of old buildings, widely equated with 'heritage' at the time. These developments were particularly marked in North America, where the notion of a historical inheritance outside of Boston, Quebec and a few other places came as a revelation; the currency of 'heritage' and related terminology in public discourse then diffused across the Atlantic, where its use had hitherto been more incidental in environments routinely regarded as historical.

In Canada, all this had particular resonance in the wake of its 1967 Centennial, for which the capital, Ottawa, had led communities across the country into the discovery that they did, in fact, have a past – and its legacy might have sociopolitical and economic significance for the present and indeed the future. As a young urban geographer at Carleton University in Ottawa, bearing the imprint of a European background, I had the temerity to suggest that the heritage phenomenon had geographical significance, most obviously for the changing valuation of different areas in the city. Unwittingly perhaps, the Canadian heritage awakening, and my own pioneer geographical contribution to it, was adding a significant strand to the international zeitgeist, which was building heritage on kindred ideas relating to the importance of urban morphology, city image and sense of place.

Now formally retired from a career spent in heritage studies, I have the opportunity for reflection on the progress of a concept and phenomenon. In 1973, one might shoehorn a heritage paper into a broader disciplinary conference; now there is a profusion of heritage conferences and publications at every turn, and the word has become one of the busiest in the English language. The dream of 1973, indeed! But could it become the nightmare of, say, 2023?

There are concerns, at least; with distinct generational overtones. Heritage may become discredited, particularly in the minds of the young, by the fatigue, 'glocalised' homogenization and above all dissonance of which many of us have written from time to time (Ashworth and Tunbridge, 2004; Tunbridge and Ashworth, 1996). It may be perceived as out of touch with evolving social and economic priorities (Quinn and Wiebe, 2012) or it may simply be deemed an unaffordable luxury. Locally, there may be other problems; in Canadian small-town Main Streets, notably, when heritage has seen you through the summer tourism season to the Santa Claus parade, will it keep you warm (and out of the shopping malls) through four months of bitter winter? As Ashworth has noted, heritage is a variously contentious concept and cannot be bequeathed to a future with a mind of its own (Ashworth, 1991). We might well ask: if heritage becomes discredited, who will pay for the future nurturing of the historical resources upon which it is widely interpreted to depend? Heritage may be flexibly manageable, but will it remain so in this scenario?

Behind these concerns lies a broader malaise over the perception of heritage in different disciplines which operate as solitudes with respect to one another. Indeed the basic interpretation of the term itself oscillates between some writers (often active conservationists) who equate 'heritage' with historical resources, be they tangible or intangible, and others (arguably the more ivory-tower academics) who equate it with the contemporary meanings – typically plural – which are selectively mined from such historical resources. These solitudes and distinctions have recently been a discussion focus in the literature, unsurprisingly with dissent among those involved as to what, if anything, might be done about it (Tunbridge *et al.*, 2012).

In terms of practical contemporary involvement with heritage, I have recently noticed both a congestion in the time/space organization of conferences and a diminishing grasp among their potential participants as to what is scheduled when and where – and, no doubt, what can be funded. In part, of course, this reflects the mutual solitudes noted above between disciplines which have staked out a heritage interest but which are liable to stage their conferences without reference to each other. I suggest, however, that we go forward, in pursuit of our heritage impact, regeneration, identity and other praiseworthy concerns, with a degree of circumspection as to their possible repetition, future risks to their viability, and strategies for their management into possibly less friendly posterities.

Against this background of future heritage uncertainties, it may be instructive to relate here a 'cautionary tale' regarding heritage tourism, from my recent research insights. As is widely recognized when realism prevails, many variables may impair the capacity of heritage to fulfil our expectations. My tale concerns Malta, Gibraltar and Bermuda: three small, densely populated resort jurisdictions with limited resources for 'blue' (marine) tourism and accordingly similar needs to generate 'grey', heritage, tourism (Ashworth and Tunbridge, 2005). Despite the mutual proximity and broadly common interest of the concerned parties in such small places, even they illustrate a range of constraining government attitudes and stakeholder tensions over the development of heritage tourism. The issue is seen from the perspective of my research on naval heritage, which is long-standing but has recently been undertaken in association with the Naval Dockyards Society. All three locations are former major British naval bases, offering now a range of heritage resources, within larger military heritages and, to a greater or lesser extent, within larger heritage tourism industries.

I should note that all three cases are simplified, from more detailed studies published or in progress elsewhere (in particular, Tunbridge, 2008), in order to bring key points into focus. These points are sufficient, however, to corroborate Mike Robinson's (2008) comment that 'heritage is messy'. Indeed, heritage tourism is messy.

Malta

In the case of the Republic of Malta, there is undoubted government support for heritage tourism, via the Malta Tourism Authority. But, there are simply too many built heritage resources for the means of their restoration.

There is a cultural 'stratigraphy' of successive influences, invasions and occupations in this highly strategic centre of the Mediterranean, spanning some 5000 years. These are notably Neolithic, Phoenician, Roman, Byzantine, Arab, Norman, Knights of St. John, French and British. Among these, the Neolithic and Knights periods provide the favoured heritage tourism products, associated with a series of World Heritage Sites, along with the ancient capital Mdina, which is of composite creation.

Malta's early megalithic structures have naturally attracted attention because of their status as some of the oldest free-standing monuments in the world (Cilia, 2004). The Hal Saflieni Hypogeum and seven other megalithic temples on Malta were inscribed on the UNESCO World Heritage List in 1980. Correspondingly, the 275 years when Malta was the preserve of the Knights Hospitaller of St. John of Jerusalem would witness tumultuous events such as the Great Siege (1565), and an immense investment by the Knights in infrastructure and art on the islands, prompting UNESCO recognition of the capital, Valletta, as world heritage also. This palimpsest of ancient and early historical activity is complemented by a huge legacy of more recent military heritage. Malta's Grand and Marsamxett harbours are two of the best anchorages in the Mediterranean. This, in conjunction with the nodal location of the islands approximately equidistant between Gibraltar and Alexandria, and between Sicily and North Africa, has made them attractive to military powers through the centuries. The completion of the Suez Canal in 1869 rendered Malta the most important British naval base in the Mediterranean. Today Malta has one of the highest concentrations of military fortifications and associated structures anywhere in the world. With these fortifications comes a long-standing narrative of sieges and Empires.

The legacy of the past two centuries has been relatively neglected, however, even where based upon earlier foundations. Yet Malta was the premier overseas naval base of the British Empire, this was the basis of the Maltese socio-economy for some 175 years and it produced in the Axis Siege of 1940–3 the most stirring narrative in Malta's history – a story of successful resistance and hair's-breadth survival outweighing the much-vaunted Great Siege of 1565, when the Knights repelled a Turkish invasion (on the Axis Siege, see notably Elliott, 1980 and Smith, 1970). In the competition for restoration resources, the British period is however too recent, too awkwardly post-colonial (despite wartime Anglo-Maltese comradeship) and too potentially dissonant to a now substantially German and Italian – i.e. former enemy – international heritage market.

However, government involvement in restoration of Dockyard Creek on Grand Harbour, the heart of the former naval base, has recently been increasing,

Figure 5.1 Malta: Grand Harbour, Valletta, and Dockyard Creek and vicinity (source: author).

spurred by the need for an elite marina, revitalization of the now depressed area and diversification of heritage tourism in light of international competition; and motivated particularly by the remaining legacy of the Knights' base upon which the British was superimposed (Bonnici and Cassar, 1994; MacDougall, 2007; Tunbridge, 2008). Meanwhile, although there is public recognition of the wartime heritage in the War Museum, Siege Memorial and elsewhere, it has been left to non-government agencies, notably the Malta Heritage Trust, to take the initiative in marketing the British military and the wartime heritage to tourism. This it does with some panache, however, having reinstituted the British noonday gun on the bastions of Valletta overlooking the former naval base and transporting tourists thence to its Malta at War Museum overlooking Dockyard Creek (based upon a restored rock-hewn air-raid shelter) and Fort Rinella, which guarded Grand Harbour in the Victorian era (with interpretation of its 100-ton Armstrong gun). Nevertheless, in the restoration of these 'recent' heritage resources, Malta's basic financial limitations are still compounded by some official diffidence and poor inter-agency coordination involving government and NGOs, and among these I have encountered tensions with official perspectives and complaints of inadequate government support. Moreover there is a geographical problem of access to Dockyard Creek: most hotels are in the 'blue' tourism environment well removed on the far side of Grand Harbour; and water transport across it effectively died with the naval base and has yet to be adequately reinstituted, leaving circuitous road transport around the harbour as a time-consuming alternative (Ashworth and Tunbridge, 2005). Whether recent EU accession will help ameliorate the shortfalls of heritage tourism, when economic conditions allow, is an interesting question: an EU initiative has already assisted in the production of historical plaques which have been installed around and near Dockyard Creek in recent years (Tunbridge, 2008).

The above observations primarily reflect fieldwork undertaken at the close of 2007. They still applied five years later, when the slow pace of restoration on Dockyard Creek was evident. However, the closer one looks, the more apparent becomes the under-exploited visitor-attractive potential of naval/military heritage resources in its vicinity. A noteworthy case is the Capuccini naval cemetery in Kalkara, close to Dockyard Creek and carefully maintained by the Commonwealth War Graves Commission, a place which speaks eloquently of Malta's military past but equally of the relative inaccessibility of some of its heritage resources; in this case, tucked away in the back streets lacking effective land or water transport to Valletta (Tunbridge, 2011).

Gibraltar

In the case of Gibraltar, government is again broadly supportive of heritage tourism, but development pressure is too great for heritage to be generally prioritized. Heritage tourism resources include the legacy of Neanderthal remains from caves and quarries across Gibraltar (Finlayson, 2010). These represent the densest concentration of Neanderthal/Mousterian sites in Europe. Such is their scientific importance, because of Gibraltar's status as the last known refuge of Neanderthals in Europe, that world heritage status is being sought (for the Gorham's Cave Complex) and even a Neanderthal/early human themed park has been mooted (Mascarenhas, 2012). But until such developments materialize, these assets are not likely to be a major driver for inbound tourism.

The majority of heritage assets are related to the military function which Gibraltar's control of Mediterranean access has all but dictated for its successive Moorish, Spanish and British occupiers. Despite the palimpsest of ancient and historical activity on Gibraltar, the legacy of sieges and armed conflict combined with urban growth on a small footprint means that much of the surviving historical fabric dates from the last three centuries of British control. A few notable exceptions include the remains of the Moorish Castle and Tower of Homage, which overlook the Bay of Gibraltar, and the Moorish baths, which have been excavated beneath the Gibraltar Museum. Spanish architecture survives in some defensive structures, such as the Charles V Wall, and the Cathedral of St Mary the Crowned and the Franciscan Convent, which is now the official residence of the Governor of Gibraltar. The current British military association with Gibraltar began on 4 August 1704 when Admiral Sir George Rooke, commanding an Anglo-Dutch force, captured the town from its incumbent Spanish garrison and established a military base. Under the terms of the Treaty of Utrecht in 1713, Gibraltar was ceded to Britain in perpetuity. Spain unsuccessfully attempted to wrest control in the siege of 1727 and again during the Great Siege of Gibraltar (1779–83). Like Malta, Gibraltar became an important British Royal Navy base and because of its strategic location played a key role in the run-up to the Battle of Trafalgar and during the Crimean War. Gibraltar became a Crown Colony in 1830 and over time became increasingly aligned with both British military and commercial interests. The opening of the Suez Canal only increased its strategic value and the later nineteenth century saw major investments in both the fortifications and the port. During the Second World War, the strategic location of Gibraltar once again played a crucial role in the Allied war effort, particularly in the landings in North Africa in 1942 (Hills, 1974; Harvey, 2001; Rose, 2001). Over 300 years of British military activity on Gibraltar has generated a plethora of heritage assets and, as with Malta, Gibraltar is a contender for one of the most heavily fortified regions in the world.

Where these military resources have an established functional priority, as in the Trafalgar Cemetery, wartime tunnels in the Rock, and Casemates Square, which has been refurbished for heritage-tourism retailing as the northern anchor of the main street, their future appears safe enough. Furthermore the town's nomenclature is laden with military/naval associations; there are also naval memorials, notably one built by the United States following the First World War and commemorating Anglo-US naval cooperation in that conflict. Otherwise, however, new and usually high-rise residential and related development clearly takes precedence. Despite the efforts of the Gibraltar Heritage Trust and its local and overseas allies (notably the Naval Dockyards Society), the waterfront heritage resources are being eroded, particularly around Rosia Bay south of the dockyard, which is reputedly where Nelson's body was brought after Trafalgar. There a preserved 100-ton Armstrong gun, unique outside of Malta, is being overshadowed; the nearby naval cottages, villas and Victualling Yard are visibly threatened; and the naval water tanks, of exceptional architectural interest, have been destroyed in recent years, by development and its associated parking needs. There is, moreover, an access problem to the naval heritage. All three of our cases have good bus systems, which cannot, however, negate the road congestion resulting from dense populations which persist in driving too many cars. Like Malta, Gibraltar presently lacks the water transport which might circumvent this. However, the Gibraltar Heritage Trust has recently proposed (2008) a water link from the town centre south via the harbour to Rosia Bay and beyond, serving tourist and local needs, and accessing a suggested floating maritime museum (in a converted vessel) which could be moored on its itinerary. Whether this would boost heritage tourism sufficiently in government's view to arrest the attrition of its existing resources by extraneous development remains to be seen; one positive factor is the goodwill extended by the private operator (Cammell Laird) of the former naval dockyard, which would be a prominent point of interest along such a water route.

No action had been taken to this effect by 2013, however. Meanwhile the high-rise development behind the naval cottages and Victualling Yard inexorably advances; it would take considerable optimism to expect them to withstand indefinitely the stresses thereby placed upon them, particularly as they obstruct the sea view for some of the high-rise occupants. Ultimately, the former naval

Figure 5.2 Gibraltar: naval heritage locations relative to the town and Rock (source: author).

waterfront could be left with no more than a pair of isolated forts as tourist attractions, in locations too specific to their function to be challenged by alternative development.

Bermuda

In the case of Bermuda, government is yet again broadly supportive of heritage tourism. But there is a sense, from its literature and from other stakeholders' comments, of cultural-political bias towards the Afro-Bermudian/American facet of its heritage tourism. This has been apparent for some years and remained so on my most recent visit in 2012 (however, the government has changed since).

Bermuda's first capital, St George, was settled in 1612 and is the oldest continually inhabited English town in the New World. However, prior to the American Revolution, Bermuda had been largely left to its own devices by the British government. With no significant landmass or natural resources, Bermuda's early economy relied on agriculture, salt production, ship building and maritime pursuits. Many of these activities were supported by a slave economy until slavery was formally abolished with the enactment of the Emancipation of Slavery Act in 1834.

It was the loss of the American colonies that began a radical shift in the social and economic underpinning of Bermuda. The strategic value of the islands did not go unnoticed, and in 1795 the Royal Navy created a permanent base and began acquiring land around the archipelago for the development of a naval base and dockyard. The harbours were improved and the archipelago fortified, while a substantial 'Bermuda Garrison' defended the islands. By 1818, the Royal Navy's North American Station was moved from Halifax in Nova Scotia to Bermuda, which was better positioned to counter threats from the United States and guard the western Atlantic shipping lanes (Craven, 1990).

Sometimes referred to as 'Fortress Bermuda' or 'the Gibraltar of the West', defence had become the foundation of the Bermudian economy. Despite the decline in military expenditure on the islands from the 1870s, Bermuda would prove to be vital to the Allied war effort during both world wars. More than two centuries of military investment in the islands have created a huge resource of heritage assets, which contributed to St George (and its related fortifications) achieving UNESCO World Heritage status in 2000.

Bermuda has one of the oldest 'blue' tourism economies, dating from the Victorian era and based primarily on its proximity to the east coast market of North America; however, its limited resources and high costs have increasingly marginalized it in competition with the warmer Caribbean destinations. Thus it needs heritage tourism and has successfully developed an elite market for its distinctive, picturesque limestone version of an early North American built environment, which its recent four-hundredth anniversary of settlement (2009) gave it a particular opportunity to showcase; more generally it markets itself as a 'mirror' of US history, in which it has always been involved, and the African dimension of this is undoubtedly a legitimate recent growth area. Furthermore, it has developed its major military heritage resource, the Royal Naval Dockyard,

Figure 5.3 Bermuda: Royal Naval Dockyard, overlooking Hamilton and western Bermuda (source: author).

around the initial focus of the Bermuda Maritime Museum located in its impressive Keep; the Dockyard was historically aimed at the US, effectively closed in the 1950s, but now in its northwestern peninsula location provides an additional cruise-ship and yachting destination complete with 'festival marketplace' accoutrements (Tunbridge, 2002).

However, Bermuda is (like Malta) festooned with fortifications and related structures from many eras, the more prominent of which were built to defend the access channel through the coral reef to the Dockyard and which are an essential adjunct to its heritage (Harris, 1997). Yet whilst some of these are just manicured remnants lacking interpretive connection, others are completely ruinous and even inaccessible, abandoned to vandals and hurricanes. Fort Cunningham is a rare steel-fronted Victorian fort which guarded access to St George, thus the Dockyard, from nearby Paget Island; this is now abandoned (along with some rare guns) to natural regeneration. However, it is unsafe and inaccessible without special permission and is quite unknown – indeed unknowable – to the mass of potential heritage tourists. Since St George and its immediate fortifications are a World Heritage Site, the failure to restore the wider fortification system and connect the whole as an integrated World Heritage Site with the Dockyard, the defence of which was latterly its central purpose, causes frustration at the Bermuda Maritime Museum upon which the interpretation task effectively devolves. Indeed the initiative to complete restoration of the Dockyard itself, notably Casemates Barracks, has been left (by its government-controlled development company) to the Bermuda Maritime Museum and its volunteer sup-porters. The Bermuda Maritime Museum executive has protested government failure to espouse comprehensive conservation, not only regarding the ubiquitous military heritage but a variety of others, in the capital Hamilton and elsewhere. By 2012, its status had been elevated by redesignation as the National Museum of Bermuda, but its officials remain concerned to engender a more fully articu-lated government policy towards heritage tourism in general and Bermuda's rare assemblage of naval/military resources in particular. There is, however, a current growth in underwater archaeology (cf. Bojakowski, 2011; Bojakowski and Boja-kowski, 2011), favoured in government tourism policy and based on the many shipwrecks on Bermuda's offshore reef system, together with the museum's spe-cialist artefact preservation facilities.

In contrast to the situations reported above for Malta and Gibraltar, Bermuda has developed an excellent water transport system to ease its land congestion, serving Hamilton and linking St George by way of the Dockyard. It is also exceptionally well supplied with vessels for hire, for diving as well as water sports. These assets for heritage tourism access are facilitated by its protective coral reef and thus cannot be simply replicated in its peers discussed above, despite their considerable development of marine tourism resources.

The Bermuda Maritime Museum, in its new guise as the National Museum of Bermuda, hosted a conference of the Naval Dockyards Society in 2012 (com-memorating the War of 1812) in the Dockyard, for which purpose its high profile and water accessibility were key prerequisites. The possible impact of the con-ference upon government perspectives and policy remain to be seen.

There is a very significant addendum to the naval/military heritage resources of Bermuda which requires comment. The most recent installations were the US bases agreed between Churchill and Roosevelt in 1940 and finally vacated in 1995. They constitute a major land and facility resource with significant heritage overtones (Harris, 1997; Tunbridge, 2004), but current discourse concerning them centres upon redevelopment priorities and environmental contaminants rather than heritage tourism potential, setting them somewhat apart from the argument of this paper, at least in the perspective of 2012.

Conclusions

My 'cautionary tale' is not intended to denigrate the heritage tourism enterprise of Malta, Gibraltar or Bermuda; indeed I would not wish to offend or embarrass my friends and colleagues in these fascinating places by over-emphasizing any shortcomings within their jurisdictions. My point is essentially a salutary reminder: the value of promotion, impact measurement and the various dimen-sions of heritage is contingent upon the relative place of heritage, and of specific heritages, in public policy; and the degree to which this accords or is at odds with the views of other heritage agencies. The cases briefly discussed here are small illustrations of a much more complex issue in larger jurisdictions, where governments and their priorities operate in hierarchies, with inter-agency divergences at and between each level; some of the resultant heritage outcomes being anathema to concerned agencies in the voluntary sector.

There is one very particular point of concern in all this. Heritage has been credibly claimed and widely accepted to be inherently dissonant, either actually or potentially (Tunbridge and Ashworth, 1996). This is because it is widely regarded as a matter of meanings, as noted above, rather than of the historical resources from which those meanings can be variously derived (Tunbridge *et al.*, 2012). Some of those meanings – innately always intangible – will inevitably be dissonant to someone or other, sooner or later. All heritage interpretations at sites of historical interest should therefore be alert to dissonances. But if you are the director of a historical site or museum, and your principal preoccupation is fundraising from diffident government (or private) sources, it is possible that you will seek to deflect or even suppress dissonant interpretations which could undermine government (or private) willingness to offer financial support. I have encountered at least one such concerned reaction to dissonance in my dealings with embattled conservation NGOs in the jurisdictions I have discussed.

It is evident that we need to remember that conservation, marketing, impact measurement and all else that concerns our resources in the heritage field are hostages to divergent agency/stakeholder perspectives, priorities and quite possibly anxieties. Whether or not we seek to change this is, of course, an issue in itself. Whether or not, I suggest that a key research issue regarding heritage tourism outcomes should be the dynamic between governments and non-governmental organizations in the field.

To return to my concerns expressed earlier for the future of heritage (nightmare or not): the muddier the heritage waters, the clearer the risk, to my mind at least. Heritage and its tourism are messy businesses; we cannot avoid this, indeed we have more to say because of it. The better we recognize the problems of heritage, however, and seek to ameliorate them as appropriate, surely the greater the credibility, thus long-term funding worthiness and consequent survivability, of our professional field.

Acknowledgements

Thanks are due to numerous heritage colleagues, primarily representing heritage NGOs, in the three places discussed; and especially to Mario Farrugia, Executive Director of the Malta Heritage Trust, and John Ebejer, architect formerly of the Malta Tourism Authority; and Edward Harris, Executive Director, and Charlotte Andrews, Advisory Curator, of the National Museum of Bermuda. As always, responsibility for the perspectives expressed above rests with the author.

References

Ashworth, G. J. (1991) *Heritage planning.* Groningen: Geo Press.

Ashworth, G. J. and Tunbridge, J. E. (2004) 'Whose tourist-historic city? Localizing the global and globalizing the local', in Lew, A. A., Hall, C. M. and Williams, A. M. (eds.) *A companion to tourism.* Oxford: Blackwell, 210–22.

Ashworth, G. J. and Tunbridge, J. E. (2005) 'Moving from blue to grey tourism: Reinventing Malta'. *Tourism Recreation Research*, 30(1): 45–54.

Bojakowski, P. (2011) 'The Western Ledge Reef Wreck: Continuing research on the late 16th-/early 17th-century Iberian shipwreck from Bermuda'. *Post-Medieval Archaeology*, 45(1): 18–40.

Bojakowski, P. and Bojakowski, K. C. (2011) 'The Warwick: results of the survey of an early 17th-century Virginia Company ship'. *Post-Medieval Archaeology*, 45(1): 41–53.

Bonnici, J. and Cassar, M. (1994) *The Malta Grand Harbour and its dockyard*. Malta: Bonnici & Cassar.

Cilia, D. (ed.), (2004) *Malta before history: The world's oldest free-standing stone architecture*. Valletta: Miranda Books.

Craven, W. F. (1990) *An introduction to the history of Bermuda*. Somerset: Bermuda Maritime Museum.

Elliott, P. (1980) *The cross and the ensign: A naval history of Malta, 1798–1979*. Cambridge: Patrick Stephens.

Finlayson, C. (2010) *The humans who went extinct: Why Neanderthals died out and we survived*. Oxford: Oxford University Press.

Harris, E. C. (1997) *Bermuda forts: 1612–1957*. Somerset: Bermuda Maritime Museum Press.

Harvey, M. (2001) *Gibraltar: A history*. Stroud: The History Press.

Hills, G. (1974) *Rock of contention: A history of Gibraltar*. London: Robert Hale.

MacDougall, P. (2007) 'The naval arsenals of the Knights of St. John'. *Transactions of the Naval Dockyards Society*, 3: 65–74.

Mascarenhas, A. (2012) 'Gibraltar plans Neanderthal themed park', *Gibraltar Chronicle*, 14 September 2012.

Quinn, C. and Wiebe, C. (2012) 'Heritage redux: New directions for the movement'. *Heritage*, 15(3): 4–10.

Robinson, M. (2008) 'Culture beyond heritage: The experiences of cultural tourism'. Paper presented at the ATLAS (Association for Tourism and Leisure Education) annual conference on 'Selling or telling? Paradoxes in tourism culture and heritage', Brighton, July 2008.

Rose, E. P. F. (2001) 'Military engineering on the Rock of Gibraltar and its geoenvironmental legacy', in Ehlen, J. and Harmon, R. S. (eds.) *The environmental legacy of military operations*. Boulder, CO: Geological Society of America, 95–121.

Smith, P. C. (1970) *Pedestal: The convoy that saved Malta*. London: William Kimber.

Tunbridge, J. E. (2002) 'Large heritage waterfronts on small tourist islands: The case of the Royal Naval Dockyard, Bermuda'. *International Journal of Heritage Studies*, 8(1): 41–51.

Tunbridge, J. E. (2004) 'The Churchill-Roosevelt bases of 1940: The question of heritage in their adaptive reuse'. *International Journal of Heritage Studies*, 10(3): 229–51.

Tunbridge, J. E. (2008) 'Malta: Reclaiming the naval heritage?' *International Journal of Heritage Studies*, 14(5): 449–65.

Tunbridge, J. E. (2011) 'The Capuccini Naval Cemetery, Malta'. *Dockyards (The Naval Dockyards Society)*, 16(1): 14–16.

Tunbridge, J. E. and Ashworth, G. J. (1996) *Dissonant heritage: The management of the past as a resource in conflict*. Chichester: Wiley.

Tunbridge, J. E., Ashworth, G. J. and Graham, B. J. (2013) 'Decennial reflections on a "Geography of Heritage" (2000)'. *International Journal of Heritage Studies*, 19(4): 365–400.

6 Jasmines for tourists

Heritage policies in Tunisia

Carlo Perelli and Giovanni Sistu

Introduction

Tourism has been one of the pillars of Tunisia's economy under both Bourguiba's and, from 1987, Ben Ali's regimes. The contemporary transition towards a 'new Tunisia' offers an opportunity to describe how tourism strategies have been central to Tunisian development and the links between heritage sites and mass tourism development. This chapter will investigate how Tunisia embraced tourism as a mechanism for supporting economic growth, the State's control over society and integration with the global economy. National heritage strategies, heritage site selection, conservation practices and Tunisian identity discourses have been shaped coherently with this developmental approach.

The Tunisian experience after independence in 1956 provides a clear example of how governing regimes can use tourism and heritage to build and legitimate national identity and to encourage nationalism in the building process of a *new* State. Much consideration has been given to the link between heritage, tourism and national identity (Ashworth, 1994; Palmer, 1999; Apostolakis, 2003; Altinay and Bowen, 2006; Burns, 2008). Several authors have shown how national memory building in Tunisia was largely founded on mythological heritage and how tourism was inextricably part of this process (Ennabli, 1998; Abbassi, 2005; Hazbun, 2008; Saidi, 2008; Gutron, 2010). Carthage, for instance, symbolised the success of the dominant discourse of a Mediterranean and African identity over the Arab-Islamic, symbolised by the city of Kairouan. Glorification of the Carthaginian past and of its heroes Hannibal and Dido allowed both Bourguiba and Ben Ali to legitimate their leadership through a mythological past of dominion over the Mediterranean. Carthage's Presidential Palace is, in the eyes of Tunisians, the place where power has been exerted since 1956. A year after the revolutionary events, Tunisia's new President, Marzouki, chose to continue using the Presidential Palace after his election in December 2011. The same Presidential Palace is today part of the new narrative of Tunisian history and, in December 2011, students visited it for the first time in post-independence Tunisia. As Saidi (2008, 2011) clearly describes, Ben Ali adopted Carthage and its symbols in national and international tourism promotion strategies. In this sense, tourism has been a central factor in the production, development and preservation of the *official* local culture. This process supported a discourse of national identity in two ways. First, in relation to the Tunisian community, the separation between local and tourist spaces has been rapidly diminishing. As in many other mass tourism destinations, tourists and locals share the same spaces of consumption and this contributes to the dissemination and support of national heritage values between Tunisian people. The guided tours of the medina of Tunis, for instance, are mainly frequented by the Tunisian middle and upper classes (Saidi, 2012). Second, the selection of heritage sites in mass tourism areas helped reinforce the message for the international community.

At present, day-by-day evolution of the political system in Tunisia is questioning this consolidated framework and issues of social and economic equity, political-religious identity and attributions of meaning to heritage sites. The chapter focuses on four cases that have been empirically investigated by the authors. The case studies are either mass tourism destinations supporting some heritage policies or important heritage sites. The cases are: Carthage as a nationalist symbol; Djerba, a mass tourism destination characterised by a multicultural heritage; Uthina, an ancient Roman colony that provides an insight into the role heritage sites played in the regime as a welfare tool; and finally the crisis affecting the traditional pottery sector in Cap Bon, the leading tourist region in Tunisia (see Figure 6.1). Starting from these cases, the chapter considers the role of heritage in incorporating territories into the global tourism market, in developing a national mythological past, and provides some suggestions on how heritage strategies can be influenced by the recent revolutionary events in Tunisia.

Methodology

Field research has been conducted from 1999 until the present day and has been integrated with secondary data and literature in English, French and Italian. Field research activities in Djerba and Uthina included interviews, participant observation, insights from informal discussions and interactions with local residents and administrators. In Uthina, semi-structured interviews with 110 workers at the site were conducted in May 2006. Interviews explored the perception of economic and social benefits and of issues associated with the presence of the site. Interviews were conducted with the support of a local translator in Arabic. In Djerba, 20 semi-structured interviews with hotel managers, academics, local administrators and representatives of NGOs were conducted in 2009. Interviews focused on tourism development and impacts on the local community. We interviewed key stakeholders in French. In Nabeul, data have been provided by the local Chamber of Commerce.

Tourism, development and the good scholar

Since the 1960s, tourism planning in Tunisia has been part of a national development strategy adopted through National Development Plans every five years. Tunisia adopted the twelfth plan for 2010–2014 just before the explosion of

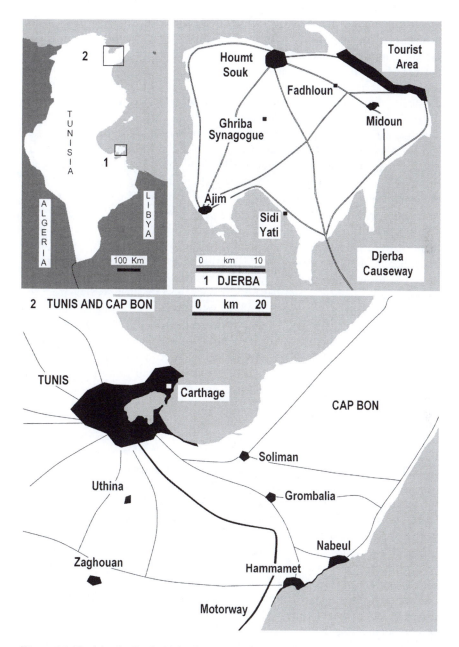

Figure 6.1 Tunisia, the Tunis–Nabeul area and Djerba.

revolutionary events that lead to a regime change. Tourism development has been traditionally oriented through a top-down planning approach with the specification of quantitative (and optimistic) objectives for investment and growth. In the last plan, for instance, a GDP growth rate of 5.5 per cent was predicted over the period 2010–2014, with a contribution from the services sector fixed at around 70 per cent of the total (Republic of Tunisia, 2010). In the same period, the direct contribution of tourism to GDP's growth is expected to be 5.1 per cent (from 2007 to 2009, it was 2.4 per cent).

In the early days of mass tourism, the political system had one leading man and one leading party, which led to a nearly limitless role for the State as tourism planner, marketer, owner and manager. Initially tourism was developed by the State, which financed basic infrastructure and incentives for entrepreneurs. Furthermore, between 1960 and 1965, the State developed pioneering tourism resorts and provided around 40 per cent of bed capacity (De Kadt, 1979). By the 1970s, nearly all new tourism resorts were developed by the private sector or by mixed private and government initiatives, but the tourism sector continued to be controlled by the State. After 1987, Ben Ali's extended family controlled much of the tourism business and a large share of the market. Unsurprisingly, this privatisation process was supported by economic liberalisation starting from the 1987–1991 development plan. In the twenty-first century, mass tourism in Tunisia has seen low growth leading to stagnation (Khlif, 2004; IACE, 2011) and inevitably during revolutionary 2011 international tourism revenues decreased by 40–50 per cent according to the Ministry of Tourism.

To counteract this, from May 2012 citizens from Gulf Cooperation Council states were no longer required to have a visa to enter Tunisia. During the last decade, heritage site visitation has clearly followed the annual seasonality and inter-annual variations seen in international tourist visitation. In this sense, heritage tourism can be considered as subordinate to mass tourism (Ministère de l'Environnement, 2010).

In Tunisia, reformism provided the conceptual framework to legitimate the call for urban elites, a strong man and a State capable of making the transition towards modernity. Reformism is one of the key principles with which to understand Tunisian politics and, consequently, its impact on tourism and heritage strategies (Hibou, 2010a, 2010b, 2011). Hibou's hypothesis is that 'the Tunisian political *imaginaire* is structured around reformism' (2010a: 14). Political reformism in Tunisia is strongly relational, readjusted according to the evolution of Tunisia's relations with western societies and the international community. The recent history of EU–Tunisian relations shows how Ben Ali profited from the ambiguity of the reformism concept and of the EU understanding of Tunisian reality mainly through democratization, modernity and westernisation narratives (Camau and Geisser, 2003). From a western perspective, the conceptual opposition between reformism and revolution led to unquestioned support of the Tunisian regime's reformism, which was underpinned by the EU's fear of a (mainly Islamic) revolution. The contradictions between the reformist principles and the regime's practices have been evident to more critical observers who have used neologisms like 'authoritarian reformism', 'authoritarian liberalism' or 'modern administrative dictatorship' to define the Tunisian regime (Hibou, 2010a). Nevertheless, Tunisia has been designated by international development agencies as a model country in the MENA (Middle East and North Africa) region to foster economic and political reforms. During the last 25 years, Tunisia experienced a partial erosion of national economic sovereignty because of the influence of the International Monetary Fund (IMF) and the World Bank. Evidence from the late 1980s shows little economic need for loan programmes and some observers consider that the economic restructuring by means of liberalisation and reforms was a way to bring MENA countries under western economic influence (Harrigan *et al.*, 2006).

Similarly the political dimension of tourism clearly emerges in the strategic heritage projects supported by international agencies (Bianchi, 2005; Samuels, 2009). Heritage tourism has been used as a tool to propagate selected images of national identities just like sport (Abbassi, 2007b), education (Abdennaceur, 2005; Abbassi, 2007a) or mass media (Hammond, 2005; Haugbølle and Cavatorta, 2011). The heritage tourists experienced and consumed powerful icons of national identity, which contributed to legitimate the official narrative of *Tunisianess*. An emerging 'right to tourism', discourse, directed at the local and Maghreb middle classes in order to support domestic tourism, reinforces the bridge between the tourist experience and the definition of national identity. Despite the internal opposition attempts to support counter memories and spaces of resistance by means of different representations of national history, it seems evident that Ben Ali's regime has been largely successful in silencing alternative narratives of the past (Larguèche, 2008).

Cultural production has used and reinterpreted this strategy in different ways. The book *The Return of Hannibal or the Rebirth of an Era* is an ideological manifesto written in 1997 by Sadok Chaâbane (one of the leaders of Ben Ali's own Constitutional Democratic Rally party). Here Hannibal is a reference point and an inspiration for the citizens, a symbol of the imagined leading role of modern Tunisia under Ben Ali's guide (Abbassi, 2007a). In a more ironic way, the novelist Abdelaziz Belkhodja in *Le retour de l'éléphant* ('the return of the elephant') imagines a future when Tunisia will change its name to the Republic of Carthage and will become one of the world's leading nations. The core assets of this future Tunisia will be cultural tourism and national heritage that will supersede sandy beaches, which will no longer be tourist attractions (Saidi, 2008; Pieprzak, 2010).

The evolution of the State's governance architecture in the heritage sector can aid the understanding of how cultural *patrimoine* like tourism have been integrated into the general reformist narrative together with nationalism's and global heritage's policy elements. In contrast to the French protectorate, the Tunisian elites in the first decades of independence underestimated the political potential of 'creating' heritage sites. Heritage was initially perceived as an academic subject. From 1966, heritage came under the supervision of the INAA (Institut National d'Archéologie et d'Art). The INAA helped to integrate popular culture in the official national heritage but the lack of heritage management led to deficits in conservation and exploitation policies. This attitude was related to two different strategic approaches. On the one hand, the new republic wanted to mark a break in the memory-making process of the French protectorate. But, most importantly, the pillars of Bourguiba's modernisation process were technological and scientific advance. With the exception of the Ribat of Monastir, no new sites were added to the national heritage list between 1956 and 1985. In 1977, the Centre for the Study of the National Movement's History (Institut Supérieur de l'Histoire du Mouvement National) was created. Active from 1983, the centre focused on the historical analysis of the controversial independence transition. This led to the creation of the AMVP in 1988 (Agence Nationale de Mise en Valeur et d'Exploitation du Patrimoine Archéologique et Historique). This was an institution with clear commercial priorities to support heritage conservation and tourism. In parallel, the INAA was transformed into the National Institute for Heritage, INP (Institut National du Patrimoine), in 1993, with a stronger link with the nationalist policies of Ben Ali's regime and the official narrative of *Tunisianess*. In 1994, the Cultural Heritage Code confirmed the nationalist character of the Tunisian notion of heritage but simultaneously integrated in law the universal vision of heritage as a global value supported by the international organizations. The leading role of the State in the definition of heritage and cultural policies was validated and increased by the reform of the AMVP as the executive agency for the regime's cultural and historical heritage policies called AMVPPC (Agence de Mise en Valeur du Patrimoine et de Promotion Culturelle) from 1997 (Bacha, 2008).

Tunis and Carthage in the early years of national heritage development

One of the key elements in the selection process of Tunisian national cultural heritage has been the support for tourism's integration in the global economy and the link between coastal tourism and heritage sites (De Cesari, 2010). During the 1970s, several researchers started to highlight the effects of mass tourism development on Tunisian culture. De Kadt's *Tourism: Passport to Development?* considers the link between development, local society and equity issues in Tunisia (De Kadt, 1979). In Groupe Huit's eyes, the museumisation and banalisation of traditional heritage was evident from the first stages of tourism development (Groupe Huit, 1979). They reported the results of a survey of perceptions of the spatial environment of Sousse city in which high-school and university students were asked to rank five buildings or structures in order of importance. They chose airports and hotels as the most important and they generally rated tourism-related buildings over any example of local architecture. Boudhiba's analysis (1976) parallels Groupe Huit's observations. He delineates the traumatic effects of the tourism acculturation process, especially concerning values. The emphasis is placed on an Orientalist discourse and consumerism: 'When one thinks about it there is something diabolical about this constant temptation and this invitation to taste these extravagant and still forbidden fruits of the consumer society. There is a tremendous temptation to imitate and emulate the tourist' (Boudhiba, 1976: 12).

Governing regimes were not concerned by the emerging academics' (slightly anti-tourism) analysis. The consistent promotion of tourism development in coastal zones led to increased regional inequalities; however, positive and negative impacts on Tunisian society have been underestimated (Sethom, 1979; Poirier, 1995; Zaiane, 2006; Hazbun, 2008; Miossec and Bourgou, 2010). Spatial inequalities and planning policies, competition for water, integration with other productive sectors, low-skill workers and more generally the opportunity costs of a tourism-based strategy and its real effects on local communities' wellbeing have been largely ignored. Outside coastal destinations, heritage and culture policies followed the regime's reformist ideology even more strictly.

Medinas are the traditional Arab old cities which are generally clearly separate from the colonial or modern neighbourhoods. All over North Africa, medinas have been the subject of heritage policies, with Tunis Medina being a key example (Bigio and Licciardi, 2010). The first formal initiative considering Arab-Islamic urban heritage conservation dates to 1912 when around 20 sites in the Medina of Tunis were declared historical monuments and protected by colonial law (Khanoussi, 2009). After independence, the demographic changes in the Medina of Tunis led to an adaptation and banalisation of the medina's heritage to cater for the needs of new residents arriving from the countryside (Van der Meerschen, 1972; Micaud, 1978). Bourguiba's ideology of modernisation denigrated traditional Arab urban planning. For example, the proposed Tunis planning scheme in 1957 aimed to clear parts of the ancient medina (McGuinness, 1997). Medinas were being abandoned by the traditional residents who wanted to follow a modern lifestyle, but they were also becoming the focus for various associations. One of the first being the *Association de Sauvegarde de la Médina de Tunis*, which was set up in 1967. Medinas have become a stage for hegemonic struggles between local elites and in some ways a contested space. The medinas' associations, especially in Tunis, have been the framework where national history, memory-building practices and national identity were negotiated (Larguèche, 2008). In the early 1970s, the Medina of Tunis Association sought UNESCO help to save the medina and to rehabilitate the houses in the Hafsia neighbourhood. The government used the opportunity to reorganise the interventions under the lens of a developmental vision of heritage. The law no. 74–89 in 1974 was the formal act of adhesion to the UNESCO conservation system and both the medina of Tunis and Carthage were consequently inscribed in the World Heritage List in 1979, together with El Jem amphitheatre. Urban regeneration projects led by the State included the bulldozing of shanty areas within the ancient cities. Unsurprisingly, in most cases the rationale behind the regeneration interventions was inspired by gentrification strategies (Escher and Schepers, 2008). In the case of the medina associations of Tunis and Kairouan, the role of technical consultancy to municipalities resulted in the exercise of an effective political role of mediation and in the control of budgets

(Akrout-Yaïche, 2002). In both cases, the associations acted in coordination with international bodies like UNESCO and national authorities like INP (INP, 2008). The Tunisian Third Urban Development Project (1982–1993) instigated by the World Bank focused primarily on the rehabilitation of medinas and provided the financial basis to legitimate the heritagised version of ancient Arab-Islamic urban settlements as veritable (and consumable) icons of national identity. Tourism developers are obviously aware of this process, as seen in the *Medina Mediterranea* centre located in Yasmine Hammamet (Hazbun, 2008). Covering 11 hectares, it is presented as a real medina inspired by Arab-Andalusian heritage and mixing elements from Mahdia, Kairouan, Sousse, Sidi Bou Saïd and Seville. The centre hosts hotels, shops, meeting centres, amphitheatres and a theme park, which is inevitably called Carthageland.

Another turning point was UNESCO's Save Carthage project. This was driven by the rapid urban sprawl of Tunis and the pressure of hotels on the Carthage peninsula. The project was born after a direct appeal for help from the government and the INAA to UNESCO in 1972. This brought together a large group of international specialists from ten countries planning around 15 actions (Greene, 1999). UNESCO supported the creation of a research centre called the *Centre d'etude et documentation archeologique de la conservation de Carthage* (CEDAC). UNESCO required foreign archaeological units to provide the excavated sites with all infrastructure required for tourist visits. For the first time, the project integrated large-scale archaeology in the heritage valorisation process. Continuous fundraising activities targeting international donors were used throughout the project (1972 to 1984). From the beginning of the project, however, local elites and government tried to occupy and privatise portions of the protected area, challenging the conservation project and showing that INAA's conservation mission was largely limited by the regime's private interests. At the end of the Save Carthage project in 1985, the Tunisian government formally created the *Parc archéologique national de Carthage – Sidi Bou Said*, under law no. 85–1246. Parts of the planned archaeological area were gradually privatised or even formally reclassified as urban areas, especially around the ancient port. Under international pressure, two ministerial committees chaired by Ben Ali discussed the archaeological park in 1991. Both a UNESCO preoperational plan (Lesage, 1995) in 1995 and a UNESCO mission in 1999 yielded no effective results. Ben Ali's regime constantly gave verbal support for conservation aimed at UNESCO but in practice privatised protected areas. Carthage is the most visited heritage site in Tunisia, with more than 800,000 visitors in 2007. Following the revolutionary events in January 2011, new initiatives have been undertaken by academics and opinion makers to save the reclassified areas and the physical remains in an effective archaeological park.

The heritage narrative in practice outside Tunis: Djerba, Uthina and Nabeul

The principal heritage project implemented by the Tunisian government during the last decade was the Tunisia Cultural Heritage project. Financed by the World Bank with €19.2 million in 2001, the project received three funding extensions until December 2011. The philosophy of the project was to reinforce the developmental vision of heritage, including six main pilot sites in a broad capacity-building effort in order to support cultural tourism. The choice of pilot sites (two archaeological sites in Carthage and Uthina; two medinas at Kairouan and Sousse; museums like the Bardo National Museum in Tunis, the Sousse Archaeological Museum and the Djerba Arts and Traditions Museum) confirmed and reinforced the hierarchy between *official* heritage sites. At the same time, the project aimed to reinforce the centralised structures of heritage management by means of institutional capacity-building programmes for the INP and the AMVPPC.

In Djerba,[1] the Tunisia Cultural Heritage Project focused mainly on conservation and an extension to the Arts and Traditions Museum in Houmt Souk. Other museum projects supported by private sources are more integrated with mass tourism circuits. Tourism is now so deeply ingrained in the island's heritage that even the Arabic transcription of the name Jerba has been substituted by law with the colonial form Djerba to protect an important trademark in the international tourism market (Bourgou and Kassah, 2008). The link between identity, heritage and tourism in the island has a long history. In 1924, the French protectorate placed restrictions on the choice of house colours during the first wave of urban heritage policies in the country. However, the protectorate also used Djerba as an open internment camp for the leaders of the Tunisian opposition during the 1950s. In the early years of mass tourism development, Djerba fitted the needs of the industry. Club Med established one of its pioneering resorts (*la Fidèle*) on the island in 1954, four years after opening. In his speech on the island in November 1966, Bourguiba described the progressive abandonment of traditional ways on the island for tourism as being inevitable. In 1973, the government instituted through law no. 73–162 the first 'Zones Touristiques' selected to host State structural interventions and included Djerba, which at this time had around 7,500 hotel beds. In this phase, the coastal areas had been expropriated by the State in the name of *public interest* to benefit tourism developers. Local people were partially indemnified with allocations of recently nationalised collective lands. In reality, Djerba's local heritage has been completely neglected unless compatible with a developmental discourse. The cultural heritage in Djerba is mainly the result of the adaptation to water scarcity caused by the arid climate. Settlement on the island was traditionally organised on a *menzel* system, of small subsistence communities integrating agriculture and small-scale breeding. Fishing was the other traditional economic activity. Tourism has caused constant population growth, but while towns and cities are growing, the traditional rural economy is nearly disappearing. Today the *menzel* system is the backdrop of coastal tourism and is almost abandoned except when preserved for tourism or residential functions. Today the island is one of the leading international mass tourism destinations in Tunisia. Around 99 per cent of overnight tourist stays are concentrated in the municipalities of Houmt Souk and Midoun, on the island's east coast.

Over the centuries, Djerba has been home to Berber, Ibadite Islamic and Jewish communities. The Jewish community on the island is one of the most important in North Africa (Tessler and Hawkins, 1980; Udovitch and Valensi, 1980) and has maintained very good relations with former regimes. Under Ben Ali's regime, Jewish neighbourhoods on the island were heavily protected by the local police. Today Djerba hosts around 1,600 people, which is the majority of the Tunisian Jewish community. The annual pilgrimage to the Ghriba synagogue is the most famous heritage event in the island. The Ghriba synagogue in the village of Er-Riadh probably dates from the first century. The spring pilgrimage to the synagogue attracts people from all over the country but also from Europe. Apart from the religious aspects, the event became a tourist attraction and a festival is organised during the event week. During the former regime, the festival represented a powerful symbol of Tunisia's religious tolerance and a tool for tourism promotion (Carpenter-Latiri, 2010). The festival has twice been the target of attacks. The first, in 1985, caused the death of three people. In 2002, 14 Germans, five Tunisians and two French citizens were killed in a bomb attack on the synagogue. Al Qaeda claimed responsibility for the bombing, but the regime attempted to conceal the real nature of the attack by talking of an accident (Hibou and Hulsey, 2006) so as not to legitimise Al Qaeda's role in Tunisia and to not compromise the country's reputation as a safe tourist destination.

The year 2011 was marked by disorder in the management and conservation of the heritage sites on the island. The NGO *Association pour la Sauvegarde de l'île de Djerba* and the *Institut National du Patrimoine* were the only institutions who attempted to limit the depredations, in the power vacuum. Mosques and other sacred buildings traditionally resisted tourism speculation and played an important role in both local memory and history. Several local mosques were damaged, palm trees were destroyed and illegal building increased during 2011. Moreover, important archaeological sites such as the Phoenician mausoleum of Henchir Bourgou built in the fourth century BC have been under speculative attack. Furthermore, the absence of State control has allowed Salafist groups, which were heavily repressed by Ben Ali, to emerge once more. In Djerba and northern Tunisia (e.g. in Le Kef city), groups of Salafists have damaged or occupied local mosques, restricting access to local people. Locals are mainly followers of the more tolerant Ibadite Islam and venerate the wise men or saints buried in mausoleums, but Salafists consider this to be heretical. In Djerba, the Sidi Yati's mosque built in the tenth century and restored in 1995 was desecrated in absence of official protection from State authorities and local institutions. The violent appropriation of religious sites also affects heritage tourism because the Salafists who occupy the sites prevent the access of both representatives of the INP (the National Heritage Institution) and visitors. The most significant conflict has been at the Fadhloun mosque in Midoun, an impressive fortified site restored in the 1990s by the INP and the AMVPPC and part of the tourism circuit of the island. One week after Ben Ali's fall, Salafists occupied the site, ejected those responsible for the site's maintenance and only allowed access to Muslims.[2] The AMVPPC received no help from Tunis and could do nothing. Meanwhile, Salafists are redefining the site's meanings. They have removed the tourist merchandising stalls surrounding the mosque, legitimated the new religious functions by asking for the authorisation of the Ministry of Religious Affairs and initiated a petition to the AMVPPC to devote the space exclusively to religion. At the moment, an agreement has been reached limiting visits to the morning, but the absence of decisions from State institutions clearly expose this site and other heritage in Djerba to considerable uncertainty.

Poverty reduction has become one of the keywords of heritage tourism promotion. In Tunisia, former regimes have been quick to adopt the keywords of the international community's debate and poverty reduction priorities suddenly entered into Ben Ali's official rhetoric in the 1990s. In the late1990s, the World Bank integrated the cultural dimension of development into its priorities and since has been one of the principal supporters of the adoption of poverty reduction strategies based on heritage exploitation in MENA regions (Cernea, 2001; Hawkins and Mann, 2007; Samuels, 2009). Of course adopting the same keywords does not imply that they share the same meanings. Poverty reduction policies in Tunisia followed the personalistic and clientelist behaviour that defined the regime's networks.

The archaeological site of Uthina[3] is located 30 km south of Tunis near modern Oudna and has been excavated intermittently since 1892. Uthina became an example for archaeological site management in Tunisia, promoting the idea of archaeological heritage management over simple archaeological practice. But analysis of the site's economic impacts reveals that it creates mainly welfare effects. Although Uthina is close to the Tunis urban area and one of the main development axes of the country, the site is rarely frequented by locals and poorly integrated into the main tourist circuits. Nearly 90 per cent of the tourists visiting the region arrive by bus and leave without visiting the site. The economic leakages from heritage tourism take place continuously. The incomes from the entrance fees have benefited the AMVPPC rather than local communities (Sistu, 2007). Because of the lack of real interest from coastal mass tourism, the Uthina excavations have ended up only having a moderate socioeconomic impact, apart from employment. In fact, the large number of low-skill jobs created (110 at the time of our interviews in 2006, rising to a maximum of around 150 in some periods) has benefited the surrounding communities. In the project area, unemployment is a major problem but the absence of technical skills development and vocational training for the site workforce limits occupations to low-skilled activities. Around 85 per cent of the workforce were illiterate or were only educated to primary school level. More than 95 per cent were married with children and 96 per cent lived in houses without a toilet. The average monthly salary was 180 Tunisian dinars (around 100 euros in 2006).

Nearly half of the workers came from the building sector and the rest were from agriculture and small commerce. One in five had never worked before. The majority of people working in the site had secondary occupations in traditional sectors. Many workers disliked the excavation and conservation jobs and nearly 70 per cent of them would have quit if possible. The workers were positive about future transformation of the site into a consolidated tourism attraction because of a possible stable future occupation in tourism services. In contrast to other localities in Tunisia, Uthina has been imagined as a space for research and tourism-oriented entertainment. Uthina has been the backdrop of several Italian TV series. This is probably the best attempt to integrate the welfare function of the site with Uthina's international marketing image. After the revolutionary events of 2011, Uthina has been included in a list of 46 new sites selected by the Tunisian government to be proposed for nomination to the World Heritage List. Because of the crisis of coastal tourism, supporting cultural tourism is generally perceived in Tunisia as an inescapable choice. The positive effects of this choice, especially over poverty reduction, are questionable. The regional disequilibrium in the access to resources has been considerable, as revealed by the draft of the last State budget before the end of Ben Ali's regime, forecasting 82 per cent of total resources to coastal areas and only 18 per cent inland (Hibou *et al.*, 2011). The Uthina region, like others hosting heritage sites, lacks support for any economic activity related to tourism services from commerce to food and drink, from transport to accommodation. Occupation is reduced to low-skill jobs and vocational training is absent. The informal sector is the only one to benefit from heritage sites in the short term and really to involve local people, but it is paradoxically discouraged as not being consistent with the vision of tidy, contemporary tourism.

Tunisia has a rich heritage of pottery production. Tunis, Djerba, Kairouan and some Berber villages are the traditional centres of production. In the Cap Bon region, Nabeul[4] is the most important centre for ceramics, with over two millennia of heritage. According to the last data available from the Chamber of Commerce, in 2008, Nabeul hosted around 710 craftsmen in the pottery and stone sector, over 60 per cent of the regional total. The local high-quality clays have attracted many different cultures, including the colonial French, who have helped shape the contemporary Tunisian pottery style (Loviconi and Loviconi, 1994). Both everyday pottery and artistic ceramics are produced, although the first faces competition from plastic and glass objects, while artistic pottery depends heavily on the tourist market (ONA, 2009). Tourism has affected the pottery sector in Nabeul in different ways. The artisans use international tourism networks and facilities to commercialise abroad. In the general framework of liberalisation of the Tunisian economy, the World Bank financed an export promotion programme called the Export Development Project (EDP) between 2000 and 2009. From 2005 to 2009 the project founded the FAMEX (Export Market Access Fund) programme, which focused on capacity building for professional organisations and professional consultants but also on co-financing investments related to foreign market access. In the FAMEX period, the Nabeul Governorate obtained 908 million dinars, nearly one third of the total amount of the funding for the craftworks sector. Furthermore, tourism opened new commercial channels to craftsman aiming to diversify their production. The tourism industry in the Nabeul Governorate is localised along the southern coastline between Hammamet and Nabeul. Tourism seasonality impacts on the organisation of production and on cost management. What emerges from the Chamber of Commerce evaluations is that the roughly 350 production centres in Nabeul today face different problems, notably with regard to commercialisation (local products in an international market; traditional design preservation), production (quality of raw materials used for mass production; labour costs) and market protection from international competition. Strong dependence on tourism led to a decrease in mass production because of the 2011 crisis.

And after revolution?

After travelling in Tunisia during recent years, we are reminded of some vivid souvenirs. The overwhelming presence of Ben Ali's portraits in public spaces and the police women's smile in Avenue Bourguiba, Tunis' main tourist boulevard. The jasmines sold on street corners and the giant Labib statues, a cartoon-style fennec symbol of the National Programme 'Boulevards de l'Environnement', covering each municipality in Tunisia. Such images spanned the country to show how the dominant (reformist/Orientalist) narratives of identity and culture brought together the coastal tourism front stage with the rest of the country (Saidi, 2006). There is the tale of a welcoming modern country, led by a wise and strong leader, but open to the world and sharing the same globalised values. A year after Ben Ali's resignation on 14 January 2011, some elements of innovation in the public debate on heritage and practices are emerging while Tunisia is trying to create new spaces of mediation between different narratives of the present and future national identity.

Cultural associations for heritage conservation, medina regeneration or cultural production are present in Tunisia. The *Touraht* Association, launched in 2010, supports the diffusion of heritage's private patronage in Tunisia and the creation of international networks in order to attract private funding. The association supports the creation of theme resorts, both inland and on the coast, inspired by local civilisations and integrating culture, craftwork and tourism.

Cultural NGOs can be also be used to protect the unclassified Tunisian heritage sites in the absence of effective State control. Damage to sites and the construction of illegal buildings are increasingly evident in tourist areas like Djerba but also in inland regions, such as around the Roman aqueduct at Zaghouan or Le Kef mosque. On the other hand, the 46 new sites selected by the government as candidates for the World Heritage List tell of the anxious attempt to revitalise the tourist economy with the certified UNESCO label. How heritage sites of *Outstanding Universal Value* can help marginalised Tunisian regions overcome contemporary inequalities remains controversial. Some doubts emerge also with regard to the diffusion of museum projects in the country. Museums can offer an interesting opportunity to provide spaces and forms to alternative narratives of the past which are now neglected. But other signals are controversial, such as the trial of Nessma TV, charged with attacks against morality and public order. The TV channel aired *Persepolis*, a film containing an image of God, and was accused of blasphemy. Protests in Tunis led to violent confrontations with police in October 2011. Salafist occupations of religious heritage sites, and the Public University of Manouba in Tunis symbolically replacing the Tunisian flag with the black Salafist one in March 2012, raise more questions. It is a critical point, and concurrent memory-building processes certainly will result in conflicting narratives challenging the Tunisian community's collective tolerance.

Notes

1 During recent years, we have been involved in several research activities in Djerba. From 2008 to 2010, we worked on a project funded by the Sardinia Region to support the improvement of environmental standards in hotel management. From January 2010 to June 2012, we worked on the TOURMEDEAU project, aiming to improve tertiary waste water treatment in coastal tourism destinations (EU programme CIUDAD, funded by the European Neighbourhood Partnership Instrument, www.tourmedeau.eu).
2 *La Presse de Tunisie*, 18 July 2011.
3 We worked at the Uthina excavations between 1999 and 2006. The results reported in the text are drawn from direct interviews in the excavation site involving 110 workers in May 2006.
4 From February 2007 to the close of 2009, we worked on the Destinations project, promoting tourism planning and tourism management strategies in the coastal zones of the southern Mediterranean. From January 2010 to June 2012, we worked on the South-East Archeritage project, aiming to promote tourism strategies, tourism planning and the valorisation of Roman archaeological sites (part of the EU CIUDAD programme).

References

Abbassi, D. (2005) *Entre Bourguiba et Hannibal. Identité tunisienne et histoire depuis l'indépendance*, Aix-en-Provence, Paris: IREMAM-Karthala.

Abbassi, D. (2007a) 'Modèles identitaires proposés aux jeunes dans la Tunisie postcoloniale (1956–2006): Entre nationalisme arabe et imaginaire méditerranéen', *3èmes Rencontre Jeunes & Sociétés en Europe et autour de la Méditerranée*, 24, 25, 26 Octobre 2007, Marseille: Céreq.

Abbassi, D. (2007b) 'Sport et usages politiques du passé dans la Tunisie des débuts du XXIe siècle', *Politique et sociétés*, 26(2–3): 125–142.

Abdennaceur, J. (2005) 'Les élèves, l'histoire et l'identité acceptée. Quête identitaire et visées institutionnelles: cas de la Tunisie', *Carrefours de l'éducation*, 2(20): 159–174.

Akrout-Yaïche, S. (2002) 'Local involvement in urban management: the experience of the City of Tunis', *International Social Science Journal*, 54: 247–252.

Altinay, L. and Bowen, D. (2006) 'Politics and tourism interface: The case of Cyprus', *Annals of Tourism Research*, 33(4): 939–956.

Apostolakis, A. (2003) 'The convergence process in heritage tourism', *Annals of Tourism Research*, 30(4): 795–812.

Ashworth, G. (1994) 'From history to heritage – from heritage to identity: In search of concepts and models', in Ashworth, G. and Larkham, P. J. (eds.), *Building a new heritage, tourism, culture and identity in the new Europe*, London: Routledge, 13–29.

Bacha, M. (2008) 'La construction patrimoniale tunisienne à travers la législation et le journal officiel, 1881–2003: De la complexité des rapports entre le politique et le scientifique', in *L'Année du Maghreb, IV, 2008, 'La fabrique de la mémoire: Variations maghrébines'*, Paris: CNRS Éditions: 99–122.

Bianchi, R. (2005) 'Euro-Med heritage: Culture, capital and trade liberalisation – implications for the Mediterranean city', *Journal of Mediterranean Studies*, 15(2): 283–318.

Bigio, A. G. and Licciardi, G. (2010) 'The urban rehabilitation of medinas. The World Bank experience in the Middle East and North Africa', *World Bank, Urban Development Series*, May 2010, No. 9.

Boudhiba, A. (1976) 'The impact of tourism on traditional values and beliefs in Tunisia', *Joint UNESCO-IBRD Seminar on the Social and Cultural Impacts of Tourism*, Washington, 8–10 December, 1976.

Bourgou, M. and Kassah, A. (2008) *L'Île de Djerba. Tourisme, environnement, patrimoine*, Cérès: Tunis.

Burns, P. (2008) 'Tourism, political discourse and post-colonialism', *Tourism and Hospitality Planning and Development*, 6: 61–73.

Camau, M. and Geisser, V. (2003) *Le Syndrome autoritaire. Politique en Tunisie de Bourguiba à Ben Ali*, Paris: Presses de Sciences Po.

Carpenter-Latiri, D. (2010) 'The Jewish pilgrimage of the Ghriba in the Island of Jerba and The semantics of otherness', in Ahlbäck, T. and Dahla, B. (eds.) *Pilgrimages today*, series Scripta Instituti Donneriani Aboensis, Vol. 22, Donner Institute: Turku, 38–55.

Cernea, M. M. (2001) *Cultural heritage and development: A framework for action in the Middle East and North Africa*, Washington D.C.: World Bank.

De Cesari, C. (2010) 'World Heritage and mosaic universalism: A view from Palestine', *Journal of Social Archaeology*, 10(3): 299–324.

De Kadt, E. (1979) *Tourism: Passport to development? Perspectives on the social and cultural effects of tourism in developing countries*, Oxford: Oxford University Press.

Ennabli, A. (1998) 'The museum of Carthage: A living history lesson', *Museum International*, 198, 50(2): 23–32.

Escher, A. and Schepers, M. (2008) 'Revitalizing the medina of Tunis as a national symbol', *Erdkunde*, 62(2): 129–141.

Greene, J. A. (1999) 'Preserving which past for whose future? The dilemma of cultural resource management in case studies from Tunisia, Cyprus and Jordan', *Conservation and Management of Archaeological Sites*, 1(2): 43–60.

Groupe Huit (1979) 'The sociocultural effects of tourism in Tunisia: A case study of Sousse', in De Kadt, E. (ed.) *Tourism: Passport to development? Perspectives on the social and cultural effects of tourism in developing countries*, Oxford: Oxford University Press: 285–304.

Gutron, C. (2010) *L'archéologie en Tunisie (XIXe-XXe siècles). Jeux généalogiques sur l'Antiquité*, Paris: Karthala-IRMC.

Hammond, A. (2005) *Pop culture Arab world! Media, arts, and lifestyle*, Santa Barbara, CA: ABC-CLIO.

Harrigan, J., Wang, C. and El-Said, H. (2006) 'The politics of IMF and World Bank lending: Will It backfire in the Middle East and North Africa?', in Paloni, A. and Zanardi, M. (eds.) *The IMF World Bank and policy reform*, London: Routledge: 64–99.

Haugbølle, R. and Cavatorta, F. (2011) 'Vive la grande famille des médias tunisiens:

Media reform, authoritarian resilience and societal responses in Tunisia', *Journal of North African Studies*, 17(1): 97–112.

Hawkins, D. E. and Mann S. (2007) 'The World Bank's role in tourism development', *Annals of Tourism Research*, 34(2): 348–363.

Hazbun, W. (2008) *Beaches, ruins, resorts: The politics of tourism in the Arab World*, Chicago, IL: University of Minnesota Press.

Hibou, B. (2010a) 'Discipline and reform – I, Sociétés politiques comparées', *Revue européenne d'analyse des sociétés politiques*, No. 22, February.

Hibou, B. (2010b) 'Discipline and reform – II, Sociétés politiques comparées', *Revue européenne d'analyse des sociétés politiques*, No. 22, March.

Hibou, B. (2011) *The force of obedience: Political economy of repression in Tunisia*, Cambridge: Polity Press.

Hibou, B. and Hulsey, J. (2006)'Domination and control in Tunisia: Economic levers for the exercise of authoritarian power', *North Africa: Power, Politics & Promise, Review of African Political Economy*, 33(108): 185–206.

Hibou, B., Meddeb, H. and Hamdi, M. (2011) *Tunisia after 14 January and its social and political economy: The issues at stake in a reconfiguration of European policy*, Copenhagen: Euro-Mediterranean Human Rights Network (EMHRN).

IACE (2011) *Le tourisme en Tunisie: Constat du secteur, défis et perspectives*, Tunis: Institut Arabe des Chefs d'Entreprises.

INP (2008) *Réhabilitation et tourisme durable à Kairouan, Tunisie. La tradition, les habitants et le tourisme*, Tunis: Institut National du Patrimoine, Tunisie and Consortium Rehabimed.

Khanoussi, M. (2009) *Gestion et conservation du patrimoine culturel immobilier dans les pays du Maghreb – la Tunisie*, Rabat: UNESCO.

Khlif, W. (2004) 'L'hôtellerie tunisienne: Radioscopie d'un secteur en crise', in *L'Année du Maghreb, I, 2004, L'Espace Euro-Maghrébin*, Paris: CNRS Éditions: 375–394.

Larguèche, A. (2008) 'l'histoire à l'épreuve du patrimoine', in *L'Année du Maghreb, IV, 2008, 'La fabrique de la mémoire: Variations maghrébines'*, Paris: CNRS Éditions: 191–200.

Lesage, D. (1995) *Etude de perfectibilité pour la création du Parc National de Carthage Sidi Bou Saïd*, Tunis: UNESCO Centre du Patrimoine Mondial.

Loviconi, A. and Loviconi, D. (1994) *Les faïences de Tunisie: Qallaline and Nabeul*, *Edisud*, Paris: Cérès and Institut du Monde Arabe.

McGuinness, J. (1997) 'Political context and professional ideologies: French urban conservation planning transferred to the Médina of Tunis', *Journal of North African Studies*, 2(2): 34–56.

Micaud, E. C. (1978) 'Urbanization, urbanism, and the Medina of Tunis', *International Journal of Middle East Studies*, 9(4): 431–447.

Ministère de l'Environnement (2010) *Indicateurs du tourisme durable en Tunisie*, Edition 2010, Tunis: Ministère de l'Environnement.

Miossec, J. M. and Bourgou, M. (2010) *Les littoraux: Enjeux et dynamiques*, Paris: PUF.

ONA (Office National de l'Artisanat) (2009) *Monographie des activités de la Céramique traditionnelle en Tunisie, République Tunisienne*, Tunis: Ministère du Commerce et de l'Artisanat.

Palmer, C. (1999) 'Tourism and the symbols of identity', *Tourism Management*, 20(3): 313–321.

Pieprzak, K. (2010) *Imagined museums: Art and modernity in postcolonial Morocco*, Minneapolis: University of Minnesota Press.

Poirier, R. A. (1995) 'Tourism and development in Tunisia', *Annals of Tourism Research*, 22(1): 157–171.

Republic of Tunisia (2010) *Economic and social development in Tunisia, 2010–2014: Towards an innovation and creation based growth*, Tunis: Republic of Tunisia.

Saidi, H. (2006) 'Vadrouilleurs, Dervishes and tourists: Going between frontstage and backstage in Tunisia', *Journal of North African Studies*, 11(4): 409–420.

Saidi, H. (2008) 'When the past poses beside the present: Aestheticising politics and nationalising modernity in a postcolonial time', *Journal of Tourism and Cultural Change*, 6(2): 101–119.

Saidi, H. (2012) 'Capital cities as open-air museums: A look at Québec City and Tunis', *Current Issues in Tourism*, 15(1–2): 75–88.

Samuels, K. L. (2009) 'Trajectories of development: International heritage management of archaeology in the Middle East and North Africa', *Archaeologies, the Journal of the World Archaeological Congress*, 5(1): 68–91.

Sethom, H. (1979) 'Les tentatives de remodelage de l'espace tunisien depuis l'indépendance', *Méditerranée*, 35: 119–125.

Sistu, G., (ed.) (2007) *Immaginario collettivo e identità locale: la valorizzazione turistica del patrimonio culturale fra Tunisia e Sardegna*, Milan: Franco Angeli.

Tessler, M. A. and Hawkins L. (1980) 'The political culture of Jews in Tunisia and Morocco', *International Journal of Middle East Studies*, 11(1): 59–86.

Udovitch, A. L. and Valensi, L. (1980) 'Communautés juives en pays d'Islam: identité et communication à Djerba', Annales. Économies, Sociétés, Civilisations, 35e année, No 3–4: 764–783.

Van der Meerschen M. (1972) 'La médina de Sfax, enquête préliminaire à sa régénéra-tion', *Moumentum*, VIII, UNESCO-ICOMOS: 5–32.

Zaiane, S. (2006) 'Heritage tourism in Tunisia: Development one-way choice', *Tourism Review*, 61(3): 26–31.

7 Heritage regeneration and development in Okinawa, Japan

Taketomi Village and Shuri Castle

Duangjai Lorthanavanich

Introduction

Japan is facing a population decline. With an aging society and local industries moving to invest overseas, an increasing number of towns and cities need to be revitalized. To resolve these problems, local governments have tried to re-create heritage, thereby improving the quality of the environment for residents and also to attract tourists for economic benefits. Consequently, since the 1990s the Japanese government has been actively engaged in promoting cultural and natural heritage at the local level and intervening to support the establishment of culture as the core of local development. This revitalization of interest in heritage is particularly dynamic today at local and regional levels. The rebuilding of communal ties in local society has been identified as a key strategy in securing more meaningful lives for citizens.

Regeneration has featured regularly on the agenda of many governments in recent years, particularly in those countries that have suffered a significant level of economic or industrial decline. The Department for Culture, Media and Sport in the United Kingdom (DCMS) defined regeneration as 'the positive transformation of a place – whether residential, commercial or open space – that has previously displayed symptoms of physical, social and/or economic decline' (DCMS, 2004). This definition emphasizes that regeneration can only be applied to areas that are being re-developed after industrial decline, and does not necessarily apply to those that are in the first throes of industrial development. Thus the term has generally been used in the context of developed Western countries (Smith, 2007: xiii). Regeneration in Japan is covered by the concept of 'machi-zukuri' (town building and community development), which has been used to transform areas to enhance residents' quality of life. Within this framework, heritage regeneration is an important process for the revitalization of villages, towns, cities which have a unique culture but do not have much industrial or commercial infrastructure to create employment for local people. The local and central governments have been the major drivers in the development of such localities, using a combination of heritage regeneration and tourism development as mechanisms to develop regions such as Okinawa.

In Japan, revitalization projects and budgets are often channelled through Japanese Interest Groups. These interest groups are generally categorized into two types: the first includes protective, functional, and so-called business interest groups, whilst the second includes promotional groups which are concerned with issues that affect society. Japanese Interest Groups are different from the Western political concept, which are defined as 'the organizations which have an autonomy from government and political party which put effort to have influence in making decision the public policy'. After World War II, Japanese Interest Groups created stronger relations with political parties and bureaucracy and some are supported by the government. They get permission from the government to allow them to bid for government projects and they receive the budget allocated to follow such a procedure. These include the Construction Groups, Small Medium Business Groups, and Farmers' Groups.

What is particularly interesting in the case of Japan is the role the national government entrusts to provincial and local authorities in the management of World Heritage and national heritage properties and the local authorities' involvement in the formulation of legislative tests and recommendations. This chapter examines two case studies which allow us to consider the concept and roles of interest groups vis-à-vis cultural heritage management at two heritage sites, Shuri Castle and Taketomi Island Village, both within the Okinawa prefecture.

This chapter considers the legislative framework and different levels of governmental responsibilities for heritage management and the development of heritage tourism in Japan. This is then followed by sections considering the historical background of Okinawa province and the development of tourism in that province. Two case studies of heritage tourism 'products' are explored (Shuri Castle and Taketomi Island) and their different characteristics, as heritage sites, as tourism products and as political challenges, are considered. The conclusions then examine the issues arising from the case studies, such as whether local communities benefit from the investment in developing tourism offerings or in the resulting tourism sector growth.

Cultural heritage management in Japan

Heritage can be an important component in the shaping of quality environments and place images, deliberately projected with the aim of attracting inward commercial investment (Ashworth, 1992). Moreover, the integration of cultural and natural heritage ties in with the contemporary concept of sustainability, which not only encompasses the physical maintenance of the resource but also social and cultural relevance (Tunbridge and Ashworth, 1996: 17–18).

National strategies in Japan have encouraged the development and enhancement of a regionally diverse culture which is intended to foster civic pride and renew local cultural traditions. Two additional historical legacies – the influx of Western culture during the Meiji era (1868–1912) and the subsequent abandonment of many Japanese traditions, combined with the restrictive policies of the military regime that held power during the 1930s – have led to a modern-day Japan committed to open borders, cross-cultural exchange, and the preservation of historic and indigenous culture (Zemans, 1999: 46).

Japan has a long-standing heritage conservation and preservation tradition initiated by the national and local governments. This has led to the successful restoration and protection of local, prefectural, and national heritage (including World Heritage). By 2009, Japan had 85 listed historic buildings located in 73 towns, and 38 prefectures that were listed and managed by the local administrative authorities. Historic National Heritage is divided into six categories: village, ancient residential area, merchant's port and trading area, industrial transition area, temple and shrine area, tea shop and surrounding area. There are 12 agencies involved in preservation work. They are part of Historic National Heritage. In 2013, there were 17 World Heritage Sites in Japan (13 designated cultural, and four natural world heritage).

There is a long history of legislation to protect heritage sites in Japan. One of the earliest measures was the 'Ancient Temples and Shrines Preservation Law' of 1897. Numerous legislative measures were developed for the protection of cultural properties in the aftermath of the chaos of the Meiji restoration. These included: the 'Historical Sites, Places of Scenic Beauty, and Natural Monuments Preservation Law' of 1919, which was enacted in response to rapid changes in the natural environment; the 'National Treasures Preservation Law' of 1929, which extended protection to cultural properties other than temples and shrines; and the 'Law Regarding the Preservation of Important Works of Fine Arts' of 1933, which made it illegal to export important works overseas. In the wake of economic restoration in the post-World War II period, additional laws and regulations were instigated for the conservation of historical, cultural, and natural properties. These included the 'Cultural Properties Protection Law' of 1950, which defined cultural properties as historical buildings, art, sculpture, handicrafts, and other intangible cultural assets, such as theatrical plays and folk performance arts. A 'Law Concerning Special Measures for the Preservation of Ancient Cities' was enacted in 1966 designating ancient cities such as Kyoto, Nara, and Kamakura and preserving historic districts. Other legislation included the 'Natural Park Law' of 1957, the 'Nature Conservation Law' of 1972, the 'Landscape Law' of 2004, and the 'Eco-Tourism Promotion Law' of 2007 (UNESCO, 2004a: 32). The legal environment related to the conservation of historical, cultural, and natural properties is thus well developed in Japan.

In the years after World War II, the government was the main driver in the development of rural areas. However, in the late 1960s, this centralized policy began to meet with increased resistance from rural communities. People living in the countryside wanted more of a say in the management of cultural and natural resources in their locality. A civic movement for the preservation of historical sites and the conservation of the environment grew in strength and spread to all regions of Japan. The civic movement for the preservation of local cultural sites and the conservation of the natural environment in Taketomi Village discussed later in this chapter is regarded as the classical case in Japan. Taketomi Village in Okinawa was the first example of a village in Japan where a civic movement devoted to local heritage preservation managed to stem the tide of outside resort developers. It would become a good practice model showing how local communities could preserve their heritage. This encouraged other local communities in other areas of Japan to take action to preserve their local culture and natural resources. Objections were raised by local communities to government development plans for rural areas that could result in the exploitation of cultural and natural resources that were to the detriment of the needs of local people. This movement, coupled with a growing awareness among rural communities of the value of their traditions and heritage, forced the central government to reconsider its policies. Under legislation implemented in 1975, the Law for the Protection of Cultural Properties (Bunkazai Hogo Hou) saw a system set up to identify sites of historical or cultural significance which merited preservation.

Japanese government policies on tourism development during the 1970s and 1980s gave a huge boost to Japan's rural economy and the tourist-resort industry. A series of sweeping reforms in development policy for the Japanese archipelago entitled Nihon Rettou Kaizou Ron were implemented in order to boost infrastructure (Knight, 1996: 165–180). This was initiated by former Japanese Prime Minister Kakue Tanaka, whose term in office (1972–1974) coincided with the second national development plan (1969–1975). The ideology of Dokenya Shihon Shugi focused on state-initiated projects, with budgets being allocated to local administrative bodies to undertake construction and other infrastructure projects. As a result, the bureaucracy mushroomed and officials authorized to grant funds to local authorities became more powerful than many politicians. Also enacted around this time was the so-called 'Resort Law' of 1987 (Risootto Hou), which relaxed some of the regulations governing investment in tourist businesses (Kitagawa, 1999: 115).

In the 1980s, the government launched a policy of providing support for the preservation of local heritage and the promotion of rural community tourism. Under the slogan 'age of local community' (chiho no jidai), a variety of projects were initiated in response to local needs that were directed not only towards economic development but also towards cultural development. People in local areas have come to understand that the promotion of indigenous culture and the revival of tangible and intangible forms of tradition are essential for bringing their communities out of obscurity. As a result, new cultural facilities to serve local communities have been built, and cultural groups of all sorts have been formed. These efforts represent the pillars of townscape preservation and community development (machi nami hozon) campaigns in various parts of the country. Rural communities were encouraged to get involved in the revival, preservation, and management of sites of cultural value in order to attract tourists and stimulate the local economy.

Continuity in conserving and restoring towns, villages, and dwelling houses or surrounding areas of historic value has led to some locations being designated areas of preservation and later national heritage.

Then, in the 1990s, the concept of town building and community development (machi-tsukuri) became official government policy. This involves the revitalization of old towns and the preservation of their physical environments in order to improve the welfare and the general well-being of residents. This period of consolidation aimed to meet the expectations for international recognition. In 1989, Japan contributed to cultural heritage abroad by establishing the 'UNESCO-Japan Funds-in-Trust for the Conservation of Cultural Heritage'. In 1990, the Agency for Cultural Affairs incorporated projects for the conservation and restoration of cultural property buildings in the Asia-Pacific Region. Local authorities have a central role in Japanese World Heritage policy, especially in the case of nominations. Each local/provincial authority has its own tentative list and suggests potential sites of universal value (UNESCO, 2004b: 34).

Methodology

This research is based on longitudinal field surveys undertaken in April 1999, May 2001, and November 2006 in the Okinawa prefecture and, more specifically, in Naha City and Taketomi Island Village. Qualitative research methods were used by participatory observation and in-depth interviews with consultants, academics, local authority officials, local residents, and journalists from local media organizations. The study data are interpreted within the socio-cultural context of Japan.

The historical background of Okinawa prefecture

The Okinawa prefecture is the furthest southwest in Japan. It comprises 160 islands in a chain over 1,000 kilometres (620 miles) long, which extends from Kyūshū in the southwest to Taiwan. The population of approximately 1.31 million, or about 1 per cent of the total population of Japan, lives on 50 of these islands. The population of Okinawa Island alone is approximately 1.15 million, of which approximately 300,000 reside in the capital, Naha City. The entire prefecture is located within a subtropical climate zone.

Okinawa was originally an independent Ryukyu kingdom. In 1372, it became a tributary state of China's Ming dynasty and in the early seventeenth century also began paying tribute to the Japanese shogun. The Ryukyu Kingdom was a maritime nation that prospered through trade with Japan and other Asian nations. Through exchanges with these countries, Okinawa evolved a unique culture. The islands were formally annexed by the Japanese Empire in 1879 and were invaded by US and Allied forces in 1945.

After World War II, the Ryukyus, like the rest of Japan, were occupied by the US. The Americans maintained control of Okinawa even after the 1951 Treaty of San Francisco, which came into effect in 1952. Twenty years later, in 1972, the Ryukyus were returned to Japan but military bases continued to operate under the US–Japan Security Treaty, despite pleas from numerous Okinawan's for their removal. The US military presence remains an issue in local politics (Ota, 2000: 126–127).

Furthermore, perceived discrimination against Ryukyuans by mainland Japanese is a cause of additional resentment (Hogama, 1993: 19–23). The Ryukyuan culture, though closely related to Japanese culture, is nonetheless distinctive. Okinawa has received considerable cultural influence from China, Taiwan, and South East Asia, reflecting its long history of trade with these regions. As such it has developed its own distinctive political, cultural, and religious traditions. Okinawan is the most widely spoken Ryukyuan language and, although related to Japanese, it is unintelligible to many mainland Japanese. Notwithstanding, because of the standard use of Japanese in schools, on television, and in all print media in Okinawa, these cultural differences are often glossed over in Japanese society. Consequently, many Japanese consider Okinawans to be Japanese, sometimes ignoring their distinct cultural and historical heritage in insensitive ways, one example being the use of Japanese to rename places in Okinawa. Many Okinawans feel that the Japanese ignore their distinct ethnic identity, cultural and historical heritage, and natural environment. The inherent conflict between the Ryukyuan and Japanese identity has been used by community leaders to mobilize support among the locals for the preservation of natural and cultural resources, leading to mutual assistance, locally initiated development projects, and the fostering of a strong sense of belonging, what is often termed 'localism' (Hogama, 1993). Furthermore, this heightened sense of localism has led some Okinawans to call on the US government to return the land currently occupied by military bases. They have also demanded that the central government pay more attention to the people's quality of life, to environmental problems, and to heritage regeneration, instead of focusing solely on economic development.

Tourism development in the Okinawa prefecture

With the painful memories of the Okinawan people from World War II, the central government has treated Okinawa as a special case by providing a budget to support tourism development, with funds being channelled down to local government at the prefectural level, the municipality level, and even the village level.

After the central government launched the first Okinawa Development Plan (1976–1981), the local authorities began promoting tourism to the islands. However, the first Okinawa Tourism Plan emphasized infrastructure development (Hashimoto and Satoh, 2003: 93–96). The policies and plans for tourism development in this period were initiatives launched mainly by state entities, with follow-up by local administrative authorities. However, this policy attracted outside interest groups such as big tourist businesses and resort developers to come to invest in the tourism sector, which in turn led to a massive exploitation of Okinawa's natural resources. In Okinawa and other rural areas, this led to an influx of entrepreneurs and land developers from mainland Japan.

Guided by national development policies, the prefectural administration launched the Okinawa Tropical Resort Development Plan 1992–2001 (Office of the Okinawa Prefecture, 1992) and Okinawa was also given an image makeover.

It was no longer promoted as a former battlefield; instead Okinawa was re-imaged as a tropical destination, a resort island, and the location of several heritage sites, one of which was the Shuri Castle, in Naha City, which was renovated in 1992 and designated as an UNESCO World Heritage Site in 2000. This development plan also paved the way for another flood of outside business-men eager to invest in the tourism sector, a further exploitation of natural resources and the regeneration of cultural heritage only as a tourist commodity. However, Okinawa's infrastructure and living standards improved remarkably after the third ten-year development plan (1992–2001), with the tourism sector expanding about tenfold since the US administration returned control to Japan. The industry generated an income of almost 400 billion yen (US$5 billion), primarily due to private sector initiatives (Iwasa, 2004).

Under the fourth national development plan (2002–2011), the focus of the Okinawa Tourism Development Plan was further altered. Because of its geographical location, Okinawa was recognized as having an important role both politically and in terms of marine resources. The government designated the island as a strategic location in the 'Southern Sea', as a hub linking Japan and other Asian countries. It began actively promoting foreign tourism, especially from other parts of Asia, in order to boost the economic revival of rural areas (Hamashita, 2003: 7–25). A network of internal flight routes was launched to link inaccessible, would-be tourist destinations to urban centres, more legislation promoting international tourism was enacted, and systematic plans for attracting more visitors to Okinawa were prepared.

Tourism has been one of the principal mechanisms for development in Okinawa. Iwasa (2004) noted that Okinawa's development has been driven by the Okinawa Tourism Policy and the support of the government. Toguchi (2006) has pointed out that the reason why the tourist industry in Okinawa has grown at an average rate of 4.5 per cent per year since the 1970s is that the government has consistently funded promotional efforts and there has been considerable cooperation from the private sector and the media.

Cultural heritage management in Okinawa prefecture

The following case studies consider the function of heritage. At Shuri Castle, UNESCO World Heritage Site designation was used as the catalyst to attract regional development, including the creation of a cultural tourism offering (Allen, 2002). In Taketomi Island, the preservation of heritage became a weapon for local people to resist over development and exploitation of an area of heritage significance.

Shuri Castle – regeneration of cultural heritage as a tourist product

The central government allocated a budget of 23 billion yen (US$295 million) to be used over a five-year period to fund mega-projects that improved access, enhanced townscapes, and developed tourist facilities to an international standard in Naha City and other towns where the World Heritage properties are located. This included building a visitor centre, car parks, and tourist information office. The castles of Okinawa, known as 'gusuku' in the Okinawan language, are among the most significant monuments on the islands and testify to the unique cultural and historical heritage of the Ryukyu Kingdom. In December 2000, five castles and four related sites were designated as UNESCO World Heritage Sites under the collective title of the 'Stone-Fortress (Gusuku) Sites and Related Properties of the Kingdom of Ryukyu'. UNESCO justified World Heritage status because:

> The building and ruins are the products of an independent kingdom created through exchange with Japan, China and other countries in Southeast Asia, symbolizing the lost ancient Ryukyus. Stones were laid using distinct masonry techniques to create the walls and partitioning stone closures.
>
> (UNESCO, n.d.)

One of the Gusuku sites, Shuri Castle, in Naha City, was the traditional seat of the Ryukyuan kings, whose kingdom encompassed Okinawa, Miyako, Yaeyama, and the Amami Islands between 1406 and 1879. Originally built in the second half of the fourteenth century, it was the most important castle of the Ryukyu Kingdom, serving as both residence and seat of government of the ruling Shoo dynasty (Nakachi, 1999: 4–5). During World War II, it was used as a command post by Imperial Japanese forces and was almost completely destroyed by the US bombardment during the Battle of Okinawa in 1945. The site was later used as offices for the prefecture of Okinawa and subsequently for the University of the Ryukyus. When officials began promoting tourism to Okinawa, the university was relocated. Shuri Castle is the only castle in Okinawa that has been reconstructed. Since the completion of the reconstruction in 1992, it has become a major tourist attraction and has a park covering about 18 hectares surrounding it. In 2011, Shuri Castle attracted approximately 5.48 million tourists, of whom 5.19 million were Japanese, with the remaining 290,000 being foreign tourists (Office of the Okinawa Prefecture, 2011)

Furthermore, all sectors of the tourism industry, in conjunction with the media, were involved and the help of the media was enlisted to sell the prefecture as a tourist destination. As part of managing resources for tourism at the prefectural level, the central government and the media created an image for Okinawa which helped stimulate the tourist economy. Television is a highly influential medium for the Japanese and often sets trends by leading consumer behaviour. In 1993, a NHK (Japan Broadcasting Corporation) historical drama spurred interest in Okinawa's cultural history. This dovetailed with the prefecture's policies to promote study tours for Japanese students to learn more about Okinawan culture and history. Then, in 2001, another NHK drama, *Churasan*, which was broadcast until 2007, espoused a new virtuous image for Okinawan people, while TV programs simultaneously presented traditional

Okinawan cuisine as healthy food, which also attracted more visitors to the island. Thus, the central government, the Okinawan authorities, the media, and the tourism business network 'keiretsu' all played a key role in stimulating consumption and choosing which local resources to develop as tourist commodities.

These major initiatives and investment stimulated the economy and tourism in Okinawa, and the economy of the country as a whole. In this case, 'heritage' functioned as an instrument for economic and social regeneration. It was indeed used as a product of the commodification process.

Taketomi – heritage as an instrument in negotiations with the 'powers-that-be'

Taketomi is a small island in the archipelago, located six kilometres south of Ishigaki Island. It covers about 5.4 square kilometres and is home to 173 house-holds, totalling 337 individuals (Office of the Okinawa Prefecture, 2012). Seventy per cent of locals' income derives from tourism, the rest from rearing livestock, fish aquaculture, and harvesting sugarcane and seaweed. Some 416,438, mainly domestic, tourists visited Taketomi Island in 2005 (Office of the Okinawa Prefecture, 2006).

Historical and cultural values have been conserved to the present day because of the efforts of local people and NGOs who banded together to protect their land from resort speculators and developers, thereby successfully controlling their cultural heritage (National Diet Library, 1993; Nishiyama and Shinichi, 2006: 53–73). Local leadership enabled the 'Taketomi Island Charter' or the 'Taketomi Town Historical Scenery Area Preservation Act' in 1986 (National Diet Library, 1993) to be passed, resulting in Taketomi Island Village being selected as an 'Important Traditional Construction Preservation Area' by the Administration of Culture and National Heritage in 1987. The participation of local intellectuals, academics, and NPOs was an important factor in creating a well-rounded body of cultural knowledge and reviving the locals' pride in their community and an awareness of the value of their heritage; thus, enabling these leaders to negotiate with the powerful resort speculators and developers from a position of strength by utilizing heritage as an instrument to protect their local culture, natural resources, and the traditional landscape. Consequently, houses and other buildings have retained their local identity and traditional form. They are roofed with thick, orange, earthenware tiles (kawarabuki) and their walls are made from coral stone and rise to the height of the eaves. The roads on the island are covered with white sand and pebbles.

This very different and unusual scenario is one in which heritage was used as an instrument in negotiations with the 'powers-that-be' in the Taketomi town administration and the powerful resort speculators and developers. It prevented the incursion of outside entrepreneurs and helped to preserve the Okinawan res-idential landscape and traditional lifestyle. It is now seen as a good practice model of resource management in small islands. This sociological phenomenon was built on a solid foundation of community. The unique social history of a place, its memory, local identity, and strong beliefs in their respected ancestors became the basis for a general understanding between the village commission (*kou min kan*) and NPOs (Nishiyama and Shinichi, 2006).

Taketomi highlights what can be achieved when local people take charge of their own cultural heritage and tourism management. The social and cultural conditions at the village level helped to facilitate the management of resources. These conditions include: 1) respect for one's ancestors; 2) love of and pride in local culture; 3) the involvement of knowledgeable people; 4) local people's participation in planning and management; 5) perceivable benefits from tourism; and 6) capable local leaders in Taketomi. For example, in the 1970s, Mr Yoshinori Uesedo played a major role in leading the community against resort developers. He became the chairman of the Taketomi Community Centre. Such conditions can be found, too, in the management of tourist resources in other parts of rural Japan (Mizoo, 1994: 13, 16–19). Consequently, the community is able to contain tourism development within sustainable tourism limits to maintain and improve the quality of life for the local people. The concept of sustainable tourism development in Japan has five key conditions:

1   Local people's participation in planning and management in order to ensure benefits accrue directly and indirectly to the local community;
2   Perceivable benefits from tourism should be distributed to the local community equally and stimulate the local economy over the long term;
3   Local people should participate in the preservation and conservation of local culture and natural resources;
4   Tourist sites should have potential to attract tourists continuingly and increase tourism;
5   The local community defines the regulations to preserve and control resource utilization (Mizoo, 1994: 13–19; Ashiba, 1994: 243–248).

Conclusions

This study has found that there are a range of actors in developing tourism to stimulate the economy and generate heritage sites. These include the central government, local authorities, academics, policy-makers, city planners, non-profit organizations, the media, the private sector (especially airlines, tour operators, and hotel groups), and the local communities themselves.

Most tourism development in Japan involved the central government in association with the local authorities initiating a project which then pours money into building infrastructure and providing services and facilities for tourists. This investment stimulates the local and national economy. The central government has taken a rather capitalistic approach to economic development by investing in infrastructure such as museum buildings and utilizing heritage as a tourist product. For example, Shuri Castle was chosen to be the centre of development as a tourist product for the economic and social benefits and with the involvement of the interested stakeholders, but the interests of the local people were secondary. As Schouten (1995: 21) suggests, heritage is history processed into a commodity through mythology, ideology, nationalism, local pride, romantic vision, or just plain marketing. A point reinforced by Ashworth (2007: 50–53), who states that 'heritage' has acquired a multiplicity of quite different, frequently contradictory, meanings and expectations, ranging from idea to policy, to industry to education. The role of heritage mentioned in this study is not just a commodity but a means of protecting and regenerating the total quality of life of the local people, as Ashworth (2007) stressed in the current role of heritage in society. The regeneration of the Shuri Castle World Heritage Site can make a contribution to the local economy through increased visitor numbers and capital expenditures, while stimulating the national economy as well. Shuri Castle and the eight other Okinawan heritage sites are listed together on the World Heritage Site register as the *'Stone Fortress (Gusuku) Sites and Related Properties of the Kingdom of Ryukyu'*. Together they have had an impact on the growth of Okinawa tourism development and the stimulation of construction businesses in Japan but this occurred because the government allocated a huge budget for regenerating the cultural and environmental landscape surrounding the sites.

In contrast, the case of Taketomi Island Village is an expression of a powerful relationship between local identity, a strong sense of belonging, and shared beliefs, which contribute to preserving communal values and heritage at the local level. It was found that the attempt by locals and NPOs to preserve the town's historical heritage site utilized the legislation from the Town Historical Scenery Area Preservation Act as an instrument in their negotiations with the 'powers-that-be' and with private-sector developers in the 1970s. The strength of a society and strong sense of belonging come from the existence of a collective memory and common awareness among its members; that is, that all of them are ultimately part of the same community. This has unified the local people in their attempts to balance their ideas on conservation with national policies on rural tourism development in Okinawa.

The most important elements influencing the management of heritage attractions are the strong sense of belonging, the desire to preserve communal values and a unique shared heritage that have evolved in Okinawa. This has unified the locals in their attempts to balance their interests in the conservation of their communities with national policies on community-tourism development. The result has been the notable success enjoyed by locally managed heritage attractions (Lortanavanit, 2007).

The *Gusuku Sites and the Related Properties of the Kingdom of Ryukyu* were designated as World Heritage Sites in 2000. Shuri Castle, in Naha City, is an initiative launched by central government, prefectural government, and local administrative authorities. This significant heritage site was regenerated as a tourist product and placed on the global stage through designation as a World Heritage Site. The politics of heritage were crucial in deciding on economic investment for tourism development and in the re-imaging of rural tourism of

Okinawa. This example indicates the role and influence of vested interests and other stakeholders, who exercise real power in developing the national economy and stimulating local economy.

This study of the Okinawa prefecture, Japan, helps us to explore some of the different concepts affecting heritage management for tourism representing town regeneration. The two case studies have provided contrast in terms of the arguments and functions of heritage: that is, capitalism versus localism, and market-led developmentalism versus community-led conservationism.

Acknowledgements

I am most grateful to Yoshinori Uesedo, local leader in Taketomi Island Village, the Okinawa prefectural government officers Yoshiro Iwasa and Akira Toguchi, local journalist Tomoko Itokazu, and Professor Jim Elliotte for their academic support. I am also grateful to The Thailand Research Fund for providing a grant to conduct field research.

References

Allen, M. (2002) *Identity and resistance in Okinawa.* Lanham: Rowman & Littlefield.

Ashiba, H. (1994) *Shin kankougaku gairon (Introduction to new tourism).* Kyoto: Mineruva shobou.

Ashworth, G. J. (1992) 'Heritage and tourism: An argument, two problems and three solutions', in C. A. M. Fleischer van Rooijin (ed.) *Spatial implications of tourism.* Groningen: Geo Pers, 95–104.

Ashworth, G. J. (2007) 'On approaches, gaps and bridges in heritage', in J. McLoughlin, J. Kaminski, and B. Sodagar (eds.) *Perspectives on impact, technology and strategic management.* Budapest: Archaeolingua, 50–53.

DCMS (2004) *Culture at the heart of regeneration.* London: Department of Culture Media and Sport (DCMS).

Hamashita, T. (2003) *Introduction to Okinawa.* Tokyo: Chikuma shinsho.

Hashimoto, K. and Satoh, Y. (2003) *Kankou kaihatsu to bunka: minami kara no toikake (Tourism development and culture: Wind from the south).* Kyoto: Sekai shisou sha.

Hogama, S. (1993) *Okinawa no rekishi bunka (History and culture of Okinawa).* Okinawa: Chuukoo shinsho.

Iwasa, Y. (2004) 'Okinawa kankou no hatten to kankou gyousei no henkou' ('Okinawa tourism development and government tourism policy change'). *Proceedings of the Japanese Society of Tourism Conference,* December, 1–4.

Kitagawa, M. (1999) *Kankou shigen to kankyou: chiiki shigen no katsuyou to kankou shinkou (Tourism resource and environment: Use of local resources and tourism promotion).* Shiga: Sanraizu.

Knight, J. (1996) 'Competing hospitalities in Japanese rural tourism'. *Annals of Tourism Research,* 23(1): 165–185.

Lortanavanit, D. (2007) 'State, capital and the community in tourism management: The case study of Yomitan town in Okinawa province, Japan'. *Journal of Asian Review, Journal of Chulalongkorn University,* 28(2): 160–182.

Mizoo, Y. (1994) *Kankou jigyou to keiei (Tourism development and management)* (third edition). Tokyo: Touyoukeizai.

Nakachi, K. (1999) *Ryukyu Islands and Okinawans (Sightseeing and lifestyle)*. Okinawa: Okinawa Times.

National Diet Library (1993) *Shin chihou no jidai: rittai teki chiiki zukuri no doukou to chousa (New era of local movement: Direction of regional regeneration and survey)*. Tokyo: Survey Division of National Diet Library.

Nishiyama, N. and Shinichi, I. (2006) 'The possibility of cultural heritage management by the community: The measure of cultural heritage management type NPO in Take-tomi Island', in N. Nishiyama (ed.) *Cultural heritage management and sustainable tourism research*. Osaka: National Museum of Ethnology, 53–73.

Office of the Okinawa Prefecture (1992) *Seikai ni otozureru toropicaru rizooto airando: Okinawa no keisei wo mezashite (Preliminary tourism development plan in Okinawa: Building a tropical resort island)*. Japan: Office of Okinawa Prefecture.

Office of the Okinawa Prefecture (2006) 'Okinawa kankou no sugata: Okinawa Tourists Statistics in 2005', Naha: Office of Okinawa Prefecture.

Office of the Okinawa Prefecture (2011) *Okinawa kankou no sugata (Statistics on Okinawa tourism)*. Naha: Office of Okinawa Prefecture.

Office of the Okinawa Prefecture (2012) 'Population of the town of Taketomi by area (end of January 2012)'. Taketomi, Okinawa Prefecture: Town of Taketomi. Available at www.town.taketomi.lg.jp/uploads/fckeditor/uid000005_20121011095746f21712cb.pdf (accessed October 21, 2012).

Ota, M. (2000) *Okinawa kichi naki shima e no douhyou (Towards a future Okinawa without military bases)* (second edition). Tokyo: Shuuei sha shinsho.

Schouten, F. (1995) 'Heritage as historical reality', in D. T. Herbert (ed.) *Heritage, tourism and society*. London: Mansell, 21–31.

Smith, M. (2007) *Tourism, culture and regeneration*. Wallingford: CABI.

Toguchi, A. (2006) 'Okinawa kankou seichou no housoku' ('Conditions of Okinawa tourism growth'). Retrieved on August 1, 2006 from *Okinawa kankou to keizai (Okinawa tourism and economics)* No. 705: www.sokuhou.co.jp.

Tunbridge, J. E. and Ashworth, G. J. (1996) *Dissonant heritage: The management of the past as a resource in conflict*. Chichester: John Wiley.

UNESCO (2004a) 'Local involvement in the protection of World Heritage in Japan', *The World Heritage Report 12: The state of World Heritage in the Asia-Pacific region 2003*. Paris: UNESCO.

UNESCO (2004b) 'The state of World Heritage in the Asia-Pacific region 2003', *The World Heritage Report 12*. Paris: UNESCO World Heritage Centre.

United Nations Educational, Scientific and Cultural Organization (UNESCO) (n.d.) *Gusuku sites and related properties of the Kingdom of Ryukyu*. Available at http://whc.unesco.org/en/list/972 (accessed June 28, 2013).

Zemans, J. (1999) 'A comparative overview', in J. Zemans and A. Kliengartner (eds.) *Comparing cultural policy: A study of Japan and the United States*. London: SAGE Publications, 19–60.

8 Heritage as urban regeneration in post-apartheid Johannesburg

The case of Constitution Hill

Tony King and M.K. Flynn

Introduction

This chapter examines the revitalization of the Old Fort prison complex in central Johannesburg as Constitution Hill, an example of the use of heritage development as urban regeneration. Closed in 1983 after ninety years' operation, the site was redeveloped between 1998 and 2004 and is now the home of the new Constitutional Court, the highest court in South Africa. Intended as a multi-tasking example of post-apartheid urban regeneration, the Hill – as it is often referred to – is also a significant heritage site with an over-arching vision for a human rights campus, based around the Court, along with considerable scope for commercial development. This chapter discusses the Hill's two main purposes. First, its post-apartheid heritage is harnessed to emphasize the contrast with South Africa's authoritarian past, and it supports the post-apartheid order by hosting a number of institutions – the Constitutional Court being the most important – that underpin human rights and constitutional democracy. Second, it is being developed as a tourist destination and as a 'ripple-pond' development to kick-start improvement in Johannesburg's depressed north-eastern inner city (City of Johannesburg, 2004: 12). A strand that links these two purposes is Constitution Hill's role as a centre of public discourse on human rights in South Africa. Finally, the chapter discusses how Constitution Hill operates now and highlights its failures as well as successes.

Constitution Hill and South African heritage

Apartheid-era South African heritage focused, unsurprisingly, on the privileged white minority to the detriment of the majority, and heritage sites concentrated on dividing South Africans into various ethnic groups as defined by apartheid policies. On the establishment of democratic government after the transition from authoritarianism in 1994, the heritage sector was badly skewed. Post-apartheid South African heritage has, therefore, focused away from the divisive nature of apartheid heritage and on a new nationhood underpinned by new national values around human rights (King and Flynn, 2012: 69). The heritage of Constitution Hill, as the location of the Constitutional Court, introduces the notion of restoring justice to South African society, and places the institutions of the new democracy on the relics of the old order. Constitution Hill is part of the Legacy Projects, a series of high-profile emblematic monuments and cultural interventions commissioned by the South African government after the fall of apartheid and transition to democracy in 1994 (Department of Arts and Culture, 2013). Most were chosen for their significance in the struggle against apartheid. However, Constitution Hill is different in that its heritage is intended as an expression of post-apartheid national values rather than as a commemoration of a single person or event. In keeping with the manifestation of national values, Constitution Hill's past as an everyday urban prison becomes an umbrella for people of all backgrounds. Unlike the former prison on Robben Island off Cape Town, which charges R230 (US$26), Constitution Hill is free to access (only one part charges a small entrance fee), and largely eschews the great leader narrative. Although Robben Island is very high profile in international discourse, the unremarkable nature of the Old Fort prison complex is arguably more relevant to the average South African.

The Old Fort site's redevelopment is part of the creation of an urban 'emblematic landscape' in post-apartheid South Africa (Graham, 2002: 1008). This new heritage provides a sense of both a break with the authoritarian past and a linear narrative locating the institutions of the new South Africa on relics of the old (Graham, 2002: 1006). Constitution Hill's heritage as manifested by its redevelopment is therefore part of legitimizing the new South Africa, and especially its new democratic dispensation, as based on the constitutional rule of law, and is a clear example of how the South African government is using post-apartheid heritage as a nation-building tool.

The development of Constitution Hill's heritage is therefore intimately linked to the articulation of human rights as a new national narrative. The vision for the Hill is for it to become a centre for human rights based around the Constitutional Court and other state institutions supporting the young democracy (known as Chapter 9 bodies after the chapter in the constitution that established them), a sort of 'one-stop human rights protection and heritage centre'.[1] Two Chapter 9 bodies, the Public Protector's Gauteng office and Commission for Gender Equality, are already present, with hopes that some others will similarly relocate. In addition, the judges support the construction of both a jurists' college and a limited-service hotel for visiting lawyers and judges. While too much commercial development would be 'inappropriate', institutions and services closely related to the workings of the Court would be welcome.[2] Connected with these would be office space for relevant organizations and law firms, as well as a visitor attraction and new public space. Indeed, indication of the Hill's prestige is the fact that the Johannesburg Development Agency (JDA) is being constantly lobbied by law firms asking for office space on the Hill.[3] However, as discussed later, the Hill's western side along Joubert Street, where these developments are intended for, currently consists only of prepared spaces with foundation pillars and mothballed buildings.

The Old Fort and redevelopment as Constitution Hill

The Old Fort itself was built in 1896–9 by the South African Republic government to protect the Witwatersrand gold mines from British incursions and to police the unruly mining town of Johannesburg. It is one of the oldest structures in Johannesburg, itself founded only in 1886. Then on the highest point of the town, the Old Fort sat astride the gold-bearing reef whose wealth would shape South African history and society. On a clear day, the country's capital, Pretoria, is visible fifty kilometres to the north. The Old Fort was the end of the Johannesburg wagon route from Pretoria; passengers would alight at the livery stables, now the Constitution Hill visitors' centre, after a two-day journey and change to a two-horse trap for the short ride down into town.[4] When the British occupied Johannesburg in May 1900 during the South African War, they converted the Fort into a prison for white male prisoners and it housed a number of notable Boer commanders.

The Old Fort complex, later commonly known as Number Four after one of the prison buildings, subsequently became the main prison for central Johannesburg and, in addition to the original Fort, further structures were built between 1904 and 1928. In total, the penal buildings comprised the Old Fort (white male prisoners), the Women's Gaol (mixed race but segregated), Number Four (black male prisoners) and the Awaiting Trial Block (ATB) (black male prisoners). During the twentieth century until closure in 1983 the complex has held rebelling Afrikaner commanders in 1914, striking white miners in 1913 and 1922, and over time political prisoners of all races (including Nelson Mandela and Mahatma Gandhi), as well as hundreds of thousands of black Africans caught up in the web of racist laws that restricted everyday life under apartheid. As a site, therefore, some argue that the Old Fort complex carries meaning for South Africans of every background,[5] although it resonates most for black South Africans imprisoned in such large numbers. Upon closure and the transfer of inmates to Diepkloof Prison in Soweto, the Old Fort itself was taken over by the Rand Light Infantry for drill practice. The Women's Gaol was occupied by the city of Johannesburg's Security Department, some of whose members were in the Civil Cooperation Bureau, which was the apartheid state's dirty tricks unit (Constitution Hill, 2006: 45). Number Four and the ATB were left to decay.[6]

As Johannesburg grew, the Old Fort site (see Figure 8.1), once isolated on a hill, became squeezed between the office district of Braamfontein to the west, densely populated and now very deprived Hillbrow to the east and wealthy Parktown to the north. These different areas overspill onto the site visually and physically with both public and residential buildings adjoining and overlooking the prison structures. Directly next to Number Four, overlooking its courtyard where black male prisoners were stripped and humiliated, is the (white) nurses' home, which is now mothballed, connected to the then whites-only Queen Victoria women's hospital (also closed) at the site's north-west corner. Meanwhile, municipal offices of the Metro Centre loom over the courtyard of the Women's Gaol where black women were similarly humiliated. On the Hillbrow side, apartment

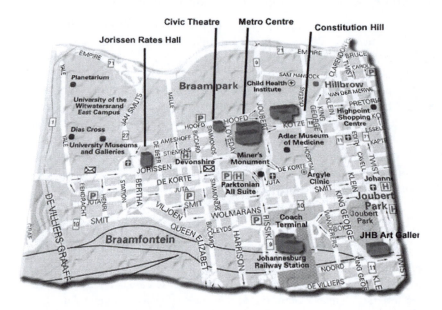

Figure 8.1 Constitution Hill in the context of the northern inner city. The railway station (Park Station) is a fifteen-minute walk away (source: City of Johannesburg, 2009, www.joburg.org.za).

blocks barely a hundred metres away look out over the Old Fort and a primary school abuts the site from Parktown to the north. The Old Fort prison complex was, therefore, an integral and familiar part of the cityscape.

When the new, post-apartheid Constitutional Court was established in 1995, it was temporarily housed in a non-descript office complex in Braampark opposite the Old Fort complex. However, for the Court's permanent location, the National Party (that codified apartheid in government after 1948) had favoured Bloemfontein, where the Supreme Court of Appeal sits, while the African National Congress (ANC – in power since 1994) instead proposed placing it in Soweto.[7] Pretoria and Midrand, just north of Johannesburg, also lobbied for the Court.

While the Court was looking for a permanent home, Judge Johan Kriegler, who as a lawyer had visited clients in the Old Fort, appreciated that the site could be turned to that purpose. The site is accessible in central Johannesburg due to its proximity to densely populated Hillbrow and the fact that thousands of pedestrians use Kotze Street on its south side. It is also close to bus and commuter minibus taxi routes. Kriegler believed it would be meaningful as a place of oppression and detention turned into a place of justice where 'hope should be in place of hopelessness'.[8] The site was in public hands already, so there would be no buying-out of private landowners, while moving from Braampark across the road to the new location would be logistically straightforward. For example, when the move happened, the Court's entire library was relocated in only two days.

The development of Constitution Hill was paid entirely from public funds. It was a partnership between the city of Johannesburg, which project-managed the development through the city's economic development agency, the Johannesburg Development Agency and the province of Gauteng, which channelled the great majority of the funds through its strategic development arm, Blue IQ. The national Department of Justice paid for the Court building itself. Gauteng, comprising Johannesburg, Tshwane (Pretoria) and the Vaal, is South Africa's smallest province, but is the country's economic engine with an economy larger than that of most African states. Over 80 per cent of the development costs, some R400 million (US$53 million), were paid by the province through Blue IQ.

Indeed, the Hill's original budget from the Department of Justice was so inadequate that Blue IQ's intervention proved crucial.[9] Broadly, Blue IQ's remit is to direct public investment into developing high-tech economic nodes, and to instigate urban regeneration through high-profile projects, some of which are based around a site's heritage value. As well as the funding of the development of Constitution Hill, the improvement of Newtown (on the western side of the inner city) has been largely successful, whereas that of Kliptown (where the Freedom Charter was signed in 1955 in Soweto) has attracted criticism for falling short. Nonetheless, such projects encourage both economic development and, crucially, the normalization of urban areas after decades of enforced segregation, hence intimately weaving heritage into the very fabric of the city.[10] As a result, Blue IQ, a provincial body, has remained an integral part of the development policy process around Constitution Hill even though the city, rather than the province, owns most of the site.

Heritage development at Constitution Hill

Despite the site's historical significance, the development of heritage spaces on the Constitution Hill site was a belated add-on to initial considerations about urban regeneration, which demonstrates the tensions between its two professed purposes. The architectural competition for the new Court building was won in 1998 by two firms of young South Africans, OMM Design and Urban Solutions. The brief was to build the Court and prepare the rest of the site for development, which involved designing and building a parking basement and preparing foundations for future development on the precinct's western side along Joubert Street, between the Women's Gaol and the former women's hospital.[11] Meanwhile, the Old Fort and Women's Gaol have readily been turned to their new uses as heritage areas and office space. Number Four – formerly the prison for black men – was turned into an interpretive space, especially as its design, with mass cells leading off a courtyard, did not lend itself to being used any other way (Gevisser, 2004: 512). However, the ATB was demolished with the Court now sitting on part of its footprint. Although it was the only structure to be pulled down, some believe that it was actually the most important building of the complex in heritage terms, since it housed most of the political prisoners and the visitors' block 'where "outside" met "inside"'. However, its dismantling was a condition of building the Court since the Court could not fit elsewhere on the site and the ATB's heritage value would be reflected in the museum spaces of Number Four (Gevisser, 2004: 516).

The design of the Court building and chamber are redolent with symbolism to sharply distinguish the new Court's protection of the constitution from South Africa's apartheid past, with the heritage of the Constitution Hill site residing in the fabric of the Court building itself. For example, bricks from the demolished ATB were used for the Great African Steps along the Court's western side, as well as part of the chamber wall itself. The four ATB stairwells were preserved, two as stand-alone structures in Constitution Square outside the Court and two integrated into the structure of the Court building. The judges themselves were extremely active in the building committee while the Court was planned and built.[12] Hence the design of the chamber re-states the right to fair trial as a basic constitutional right with advocates arguing their cases at the same eye-level as the judges (Le Roux, 2005: 312). Meanwhile, the public seating looks down onto the bench to demonstrate that the judges are not above the people, and, if a prisoner is in the Court, s/he wears civilian clothes and is not handcuffed.

The city of Johannesburg clearly draws on Constitution Hill's heritage for the opportunity to develop the north-eastern inner city, including Hillbrow.[13] Its 2004 Heritage Policy Framework states that: 'Heritage resources are viewed as positive instruments for growth and change and identified as major drivers of inner city revitalization' (Davie, 2007). Generally heritage developments, such as Constitution Hill, are considered valuable contributions, boosting the urban environment and resources, even if only a minority of inhabitants actually use them (Graham, 2002: 1015). As Brian Graham has commented, heritage sites do not necessarily pay for themselves, but such amenities are often an integral part of urban regeneration projects, a sentiment echoed by the city's own JDA that oversaw Constitution Hill's development (Graham, 2002: 1014).

In Johannesburg, Constitution Hill is the most obvious site at which tapping into heritage value is being used to create 'ripple-pond investment', whereby the upgrading of a site is intended to impact on the surrounding area (City of Johannesburg, 2004: 20–1). Indeed attaching economic and infrastructural development to heritage sites is taking place throughout South Africa, including places outside the main urban centres where development imperatives are at their starkest (Flynn and King, 2007). However, although the Old Fort's heritage value was obvious, heritage issues themselves were secondary to getting the Court built and working; the city 'supported this project not so much because they believe in the power of heritage, but because they are interested in inner-city regeneration' (Gevisser, 2004: 517). The question of how to develop the site's heritage and museum aspect was something of an afterthought.[14] Indeed, the Heritage, Education and Tourism (HET) team that organized museum spaces and accompanying narrative only became involved in September 2002 when the site was already under construction. Heritage spaces had not even been part of the architects' original brief, something that was the 'biggest mistake'[15] concerning planning for multi-purpose site use.

When the HET team began its work, it sought opinions from residents in Hillbrow and used small local companies, when possible, for catering, sound equipment and ad hoc support staffing. However, when funding was reduced from 2005 onwards, the links with Hillbrow were not properly maintained[16] and, as a consequence, the local community 'has not fully bought in to Constitution Hill as a site on their doorstep'.[17] However, Hillbrow itself is in a state of continual flux. As a key destination for both foreign and domestic migrants into central Johannesburg, the neighbourhood has a very high turnover of residents as well as ongoing issues grounded in social and economic deprivation. This dynamic mirrors the rest of the inner city, 90 per cent of whose residents did not live there ten years ago (Simone, 2008: 72). Therefore, the failure to create meaningful links with Hillbrow is, to an extent, a consequence of local demographics and not simply shortcomings on the part of Constitution Hill.

The heritage development of Constitution Hill attempts to include all the site's manifestations. It was best known as a prison, but also has a long, less-remembered history as a fort and military site.[18] Therefore, much restoration has highlighted its military past. The original guns from emplacements on the south-west and north-east corners were tracked down in KwaZulu Natal and returned to their original positions.[19] Meanwhile, another aspect of the site's forgotten history is being considered for renovation. There is a series of tunnels under the Fort that were originally part of the arsenal, and later used to move sensitive and political prisoners. Now these have been blocked off as a security measure for the Court, but there is scope to develop what is accessible as a tourist attraction.[20]

The HET team was crucial to the development of the Hill as a place both of memory and of nation-building; as one former team-member commented, 'the memory of the people is ... a public asset'.[21] Although Johannesburg is seeking to attract more overseas tourists, and Constitution Hill is a part of that, the Hill is primarily a significant site for South Africans as both a former prison and the home of the new constitution (Gevisser, 2004: 517). Therefore, although the domestic tourist market is less lucrative, 'it is important that as many South Africans as possible visit and make use of the site and see it as an important part of their lives' (Johannesburg Development Agency, 2002: 18). Heritage is crucial to the success and significance of the Hill, even though it is not a money-spinner. Indeed, Amos Masondo, the mayor of Johannesburg, will not relinquish the city's ownership of the site unless the integrity of the HET work is guaranteed.[22]

Economic considerations: tourism and urban regeneration

As well as a human rights campus, Constitution Hill is intended as a tourist attraction, since heritage 'is the most important single resource for international tourism' (Graham, 2002: 1006). The city of Johannesburg's 2001 Tourism Strategy indicated that Johannesburg stood out as the only South African destination with a high proportion of visitors from elsewhere in Africa who do not travel to other cities or provinces. It is also the only destination where travelling for the purpose of business was on a par with travelling for a holiday, which means a high proportion of visitors to Gauteng are on short-term (under a week) trips with perhaps no more than one day free for tourist activities. Meanwhile, in 1995, 80 per cent of Gauteng's tourists were domestic; this dropped to 60 per cent in 2000 with an increase in foreign tourism, both long-haul and from within Africa, and no decrease in the actual number in domestic tourists (City of Johannesburg, 2001). The 2001 Tourism Strategy did recognize that Johannesburg lacks natural advantages in competing for leisure tourism, although this is largely mitigated by its pre-eminence regarding conference and exhibition venues and its position as the business capital of sub-Saharan Africa. Indeed, inner-city hotels cater most of all for MICE (Meetings, Incentives, Conferences, Exhibitions) guests (Rogerson and Kaplan, 2007: 282). Because of this pattern of short-term, domestic and business visitors, Constitution Hill positions itself as a site that can be visited briefly as part of a day's tour of the inner city.[23]

Drawing together the heritage value of Constitution Hill, its intended function as a human rights campus and its development as a tourist site are the broader issues of post-apartheid urban regeneration, and specifically the improvement of Johannesburg's inner city. Indeed, it is significant that the Constitution Hill project was managed and funded by economic development and strategic investment agencies rather than heritage or education departments. Although the first democratic elections took place in 1994, Johannesburg has only been able to plan beyond the short-term since 2001. This was due to political uncertainty, fiscal problems and budgetary difficulties – in 1997 Johannesburg was surviving on a R200 million (US$26 million) overdraft.[24] In other words, the city has only been in a position to address its myriad problems for ten years. Although service delivery and managerial capacity remain problematic due to qualified personnel shortages and (until 2008) rapid economic growth outstripping existing infrastructure,[25] the emphasis in post-apartheid development remains the revival of urban areas as both living spaces and economic engines. In the case of Johannesburg, uplifting the city's built environment, erecting public art, taking over derelict buildings and regulating street traders benefits residents and businesses as much as it does tourists.

Hence Johannesburg is joining dozens of other cities worldwide seeking replacement industries when traditional ones have declined. In central Johannesburg's case, these are manufacturing and mining, which has been compounded by the relocation of much commerce to the northern suburbs. This leaves a number of derelict and disused sites in the inner city (Law, 1992: 600–1). For a city like Johannesburg, whose inner-city fabric is often typified as run-down and dangerous, tourism promotion brings the added benefits to residents of improved infrastructure, better security and usable leisure facilities (Rogerson and Kaplan, 2007: 267).

Central Johannesburg began to deteriorate in the late 1960s as many white residents and businesses moved out. As apartheid crumbled from the mid-1980s onwards, black Africans and other people of colour began to move in, and most white residents (and even more businesses) moved to the suburbs (Reid, 2005: 155). Although there was a racial element to the relocation in and out of the inner city, Johannesburg's decline is not unique and mirrors the hollowing out of many cities around the world during this time. Since 1994, the upper middle and middle classes have retreated even further into secure gated communities and shopping malls (Beall *et al.*, 2002: 175–85), turning Johannesburg into what Martin Murray has called 'a cocooned city of urban fortresses' (Murray, 2008b: 170), a pattern common in other cities worldwide (Atkinson, 2006: 823). Indeed, the most integrated parts of Johannesburg are its shopping malls and casinos (Mbembe, 2008: 63; Murray, 2008b: 152). In this respect, Constitution Hill is not just the redevelopment of a former prison site, but also part of normalizing Johannesburg by creating public spaces for everyone in a city defined more by barriers and division.

The revitalization of inner-city Johannesburg is of both national and international significance, and one of six Mayoral Priorities set out by the city's 'Joburg 2030' strategy to upgrade the city to world-city status by 2030 (City of Johannesburg, 2003: 6–7). Although most economic expansion is taking place to the north of the centre, most people live to the south. Therefore, the inner city and Central Business District (CBD) are a pivotal point for providing people with contact with and access to the formal economy. Despite high-profile development in nearby Sandton and Midrand, central Johannesburg remains 'the largest employment centre in metropolitan Johannesburg and a major economic generator and employment and service centre' (Reid, 2005: 157).

The inner city alone is the biggest contributor to Johannesburg's Gross Geographical Product (GGP) (City of Johannesburg, 2004: 6). It is home to over 200,000 people and up to 800,000 commuters pass through every day. It also has over double the A and B grade[26] office space of wealthy Sandton, many corporate headquarters have remained, and it is also a key entry-point for small, medium and micro enterprises (SMME) (City of Johannesburg, 2004: 6). Since around 2000, the inner city has begun to recover with the introduction of City Improvement Districts, better collection of rates and more security and infrastructural development. The recovery is apparent in the increase in attendance at cultural venues (Wessels, 2006: 16) and the partial reversal of the population flow outwards as popular perceptions as well as the material fabric of the inner city improve.[27] Although some commentators lament the perceived sanitization of the inner city (Murray, 2008a: 158), others argue that supposed lack of authenticity is a matter of taste rather than moral values, and that residents and businesses welcome a predictable environment in which to live and work (Christopherson, 1994: 412). The city's aim is, therefore, to link post-apartheid development with attracting more businesses, services and residents back to the inner city.

Constitution Hill now

Following the development of the Court and work to maintain and repair heritage areas, the Constitution Hill site comprises (Figure 8.2):

- the Constitutional Court and Constitution Square (an open space)
- museum, heritage and venue-hire spaces in:

  - Number Four
  - the Women's Gaol (including some office space for Chapter 9 bodies)
  - the Old Fort (including some office space)
  - the Round House (a plastic dome for venue-hire purposes)

- a basement parking garage with 1,700 bays
- spaces above the basement ready for development, which include:

  - the old nurses' home
  - the former women's hospital
  - several blocs with foundation pillars already in place.

The site's income derives from a number of sources. One is from visitors, including school groups, paying for tours. General admission visitor numbers per month

Figure 8.2 Constitution Hill looking south. From top left: 1. Old Fort; 2. Women's Gaol; 3. Cleared areas ready for building; 4. Nurses' home; 5. Women's Hospital; 6. Amphitheatres ('the kidneys' – one now covered by a dome); 7. Open ground; 8. Constitutional Court; 9. Number Four (source: Blue IQ).

of around 10–11,000 comfortably outstrip the target of 8,000. School groups regularly come for organized tours, and the Hill does local educational outreach, although the Hill's marketing manager admitted that 'not enough is being done to penetrate schools outside Johannesburg and Gauteng'.[28] Meanwhile, income from corporate events, film shoots and venue hire rises and falls, although the Round House, a plastic dome covering one of the amphitheatres and used for corporate and other functions, has increased occupancy and income.[29] Some office space in the Old Fort and Women's Gaol is rented by Chapter 9 bodies, providing a modest and steady income stream, while the site also hires out rooms and court-yards for functions and meetings, which, however, does not bring in steady or substantial income. Interestingly, the most lucrative source of income is the site's car-parking basement, since Nedbank (a major financial institution) and other companies at Braampark use it. However, despite income streams from a number of sources, the modest surplus is then paid back to the JDA to offset the JDA's support when Constitution Hill was running at a deficit.[30]

Consequently, Constitution Hill does not generate enough income at present to undertake additional major developments or projects. Its break-even figure is around R700,000 (US$79,000) per month, which was not achieved until the erection in June 2007 of the Round House. However, since this was built the Hill makes a surplus of between R180,000 and R300,000 (US$20,500–US$34,000) depending on how many functions take place that month. Thus the Hill can meet its daily needs, but there is little money left for capital expenditure, education programmes and other projects. Substantial donor funding received in 2004 was spent on public programmes, as well as general and operational expenditure. Meanwhile, a further donation from the Constitution Hill Trust, a not-for-profit advocacy group for the Hill, has not happened.[31]

One criticism of heritage development in post-apartheid South Africa is that, despite many programmes and the private sector's willingness to contribute money as part of corporate social responsibility, heritage has been, in effect, expected to sell itself, and relevant bodies did not develop marketing plans.[32] To offset this, Constitution Hill advertises to attract more business and tourist visi-tors. As of 2008, its marketing manager was interviewed on television and radio, while there were regular advertisements on the radio on Jozi FM, Radio Metro and Yfm. There were also four advertising billboards at strategic locations in Johannesburg: near the Orlando stadium in Soweto; by the Grayston offramp in Sandton; at Kempton Park near the airport; and at the Eastgate mall on the eastern approaches to the centre. Tying the marketing strategy and Constitution Hill's tourism outreach together was the 2010 soccer World Cup, which took place in South Africa.[33] There is also one type of event that 'sets Constitution Hill aside'[34] from other heritage sites in South Africa and consciously combines its past as a prison and present as home of the constitution. Once a year, as part of the rehabilitation process, there is an event for inmates about to be released; governors of three local prisons (Boksburg, Diepkloof and Leeuwkop) send these inmates to the Hill for a day dedicated to poetry, choir singing and inspira-tional talks.

Yet the Constitution Hill site is only partly developed. The Court has been built and is working, museum and heritage spaces have been established or refurbished, and some office space and venue hire are available. However, large gaps remain. There is only one place to eat, the coffee shop in the Old Fort, which cannot cater for more than a couple of dozen people at a time, and is inadequate if many people are attending the Court. Indeed, in March 2008, the Chief Justice apologized to counsel for ANC President Jacob Zuma, who was before the Court, because there was nowhere to have lunch on site that could cater for them all.[35] Meanwhile, almost half the site has not been developed beyond preparing foundations or mothballing existing buildings. The empty western side of the Hill along Joubert Street is intended for appropriate commercial development, but there are few signs of this happening.[36] This is indicative of current shortcomings; one judge referred to this as 'second thoughts and cold feet' (Law-Viljoen, 2006: 16).

Part of the problem regarding further site development is the question of ownership. The Hill is divided into two entities. The Constitutional Court itself is owned and run by the Department of Justice. The rest of the Hill is managed by the JDA, and most of the site outside the Court is owned by the city of Johannesburg, apart from a pocket of land around the former hospital, which belongs to the province of Gauteng. Indicative of a lack of long-term security is that Constitution Hill employees are on 12-month rolling contracts, and this is an improvement on the six-month contracts they had previously.[37]

There are too many owners and uncoordinated stakeholders, with one (Blue IQ) having paid to redevelop the site but without claim of ownership. This has caused inaction on the part of prospective developers that has serious consequences.[38] For example, the proposed Mandela Centre, to house Nelson Mandela's archive next to the Women's Gaol, cannot be developed yet due to this uncertainty and some believe it should have been included in the original architects' brief.[39] The JDA is running the Hill on behalf of the city, but this is only a temporary arrangement and capital projects are still on the drawing board. The province of Gauteng, through Blue IQ, paid the bulk of the development costs and would like to see some kind of return on the R400 million (US$45.5 million) paid out. Furthermore, the city does not have the money to develop the Hill itself, and its management and development experts are responsible for the whole city, not just this corner of the inner city.

In order to solve the problem of tenure on Constitution Hill, in 2007, the then Director General of Gauteng, Mogopodi Mokoena, suggested handing the entire site to the national Department of Public Works,[40] something that has not happened.[41] In February 2010, a ministerial and provincial committee was established to make decisions on the development of the site.[42] In mid-2011, some restoration work was undertaken to make safe and refurbish some areas that were falling into disrepair. Although the city and Blue IQ are joint shareholders in the Constitution Hill Development Company, which is intended to administer the site's further development, little has moved (O'Donnell, 2011).

There is also a lack of political will to finish the job now that the Court is up and running. While the original brief – to build the Court and prepare the site for further development – has been fulfilled,[43] money and attention from the city, province and national government have been directed elsewhere, especially since all spare resources were diverted to the 2010 World Cup that South Africa hosted. Political momentum also slowed down when President Thabo Mbeki resigned in September 2008. His successor, Jacob Zuma, was involved in court battles on corruption charges until early 2009, and service delivery slowed as key personnel were shifted following the April 2009 elections, again won by the ANC. Meanwhile, the province of Gauteng has been experiencing the same stasis as the national government – Premier Mbhazima Shilowa resigned in Mbeki's wake and the CEO of Blue IQ, Nomhle Canca, was suspended (Shoba, 2012), although she reached an out-of-court settlement. Shilowa's successor, Paul Mashatile, only lasted five months before he was moved to deputy minister in the Department of Arts and Culture. Therefore, until personnel at all levels of government are settled, no-one is making large-scale decisions. However, the vision for the Hill remains for a fully developed human rights complex centred around the Court, and the Chief Justice has a veto over what developments can take place on the Hill. Therefore, the prospect of inappropriate development next door to the Constitutional Court, such as a casino and theme park as is the case at the privately developed Apartheid Museum, is unlikely to happen.

Conclusion

Constitution Hill is one of the most high-profile heritage developments in post-apartheid South Africa. Although its heritage value is used primarily to encourage the upgrading of the Johannesburg's north-eastern inner city, the material heritage aspect of the Hill has been largely maintained and partly developed, despite not being part of the original redevelopment brief. Some parts of Constitution Hill's development have come to a standstill and the lack of progress in turning it into a human right campus, with the Court, Chapter 9 bodies and related organizations and law firms, points to a lost opportunity to fulfil the original vision. In some ways, it is incomplete, much like the redevelopment of the Johannesburg inner city itself.

However, it would be hasty to judge the Hill a failure because its development is incomplete. The various institutions of post-apartheid South Africa are only nineteen years old at most, and the new heritage competes with other public priorities, of which South Africa has many. The fact that the Court has been built, to great acclaim, and is fully operational is a positive note. But the Court is only one part of the Hill – albeit by far the most important one. The site's heritage use has been partly developed, and the number of daily visitors indicates that Constitution Hill is not empty, although education programmes and related activities are not as widespread as many would like. Nonetheless, more needs to be done to fulfil Constitution Hill's mandates, not only as a beacon of human rights,[44] but to encourage tourism and urban regeneration as well. The original vision was for the development of the site's western side to subsidize the rest of the Hill, as its office, residential, retail and hospitality rentals would bring in far more money than the heritage spaces. However, the lack of further development thus far militates against the Hill as a definitive centre for inner-city regeneration. While this does not indicate that what *has* been achieved is insignificant, it does mean that the further physical development of the Hill is currently on hold. But despite this, Constitution Hill, with its conjoined heritage and economic imperatives, will continue to stand as a visible reminder, articulation and anchor for post-apartheid aspirations in the South African cityscape.

Acknowledgements

The authors would like to thank the Nuffield Foundation for funding their 2007–8 project 'Post-Conflict Settlement, Heritage and Urban Regeneration in South Africa and Northern Ireland: the Redevelopment of the Old Fort and Long Kesh/Maze Prisons', from which this paper is drawn. They would also like to thank all the interviewees for generously giving up their time.

Notes

1　Interview, Yvonne Mokgoro (Constitutional Court Justice), 14 March 2008.
2　Interview, Yvonne Mokgoro.
3　Interview, Lebowa Letsoalo (Development Engineer, JDA); Interview, Kate O'Regan (Constitutional Court Justice).
4　Interview, Johan Kriegler (retired Constitutional Court Justice), 7 March 2008.
5　Interview, Johan Kriegler.
6　Interview, Ivan May (CEO, Constitution Hill Trust), 5 March 2008.
7　Interview, Arthur Chaskalson (retired Chief Justice), 7 March 2008.
8　Interview, Johan Kriegler.
9　Interview, Arthur Chaskalson.
10　Interview, Jameel Chand (Head: Group Marketing and Communications, Blue IQ), 14 March 2008.
11　Interview, Paul Wygers (CEO, Urban Solutions), 13 March 2008.
12　Interview, Paul Wygers.
13　Interview, Kate O'Regan, 4 March 2008, Interview, Lael Bethlehem (CEO, JDA).
14　Interview, Lauren Segal (CEO, Trace and former HET team leader), 5 March 2008.
15　Interview, Paul Wygers.
16　Interview, Lauren Segal.
17　Interview, Darryl Petersen (Site Manager, Constitution Hill), 12 March 2008.
18　Interview, Darryl Petersen.
19　Interview, Lebowa Letsoalo, 7 March 2008.
20　Interview, Lebowa Letsoalo.
21　Interview, Audrey Brown (BBC journalist, former HET team coordinator), 23 August 2008.
22　Interview, Lael Bethlehem.
23　Interview, Alice Moloto (Manager: Marketing, Sales and Administration, Constitution Hill), 12 March 2008.
24　Interview, Jameel Chand.
25　Interview, Simon Dagut (Research Manager, CDE), 10 March 2008.
26　There is no fixed definition of office space grades. 'A' grade refers to prime office space in desirable and prestigious locations, and attracts high rent. 'B' grade is the next grade down for businesses that want to pay average or just below average rent.

27 Interview, Neil Fraser.
28 Interview, Alice Moloto.
29 Interview, Alice Moloto.
30 Interview, Darryl Petersen.
31 Interview, Ivan May.
32 Interview, Narissa Ramdhani (CEO, Ifa Lethu Foundation), 12 March 2008.
33 Interview, Alice Moloto.
34 Interview, Alice Moloto.
35 Interview, Yvonno Mokgoro.
36 Interview, Ivan May.
37 Interview, Darryl Petersen.
38 Interview, Jameel Chand.
39 Interview, Lael Bethlehem; Interview, Paul Wygers.
40 Interview, Lael Bethlehem.
41 Interview, Darryl Petersen.
42 Pers. comm., Edwin Cameron (Constitutional Court Justice), 18 March 2010.
43 Interview, Paul Wygers.
44 Interview, Yvonne Mokgoro; Interview, Albie Sachs (Constitutional Court Justice), 21 January 2008.

References

Atkinson, R. (2006) 'Padding the bunker: Strategies of middle-class disaffiliation and colonisation in the city'. *Urban Studies* 43(4): 819–32.

Beall, J., Crankshaw, O. and Parnell, S. (2002) *Uniting a divided city: Governance and social exclusion in Johannesburg*. London: Earthscan.

Christopherson, S. (1994) 'The fortress city: Privatized space, consumer citizenship', in A. Amin (ed.) *Post-Fordism: A reader*. Oxford: Blackwell, 409–27.

City of Johannesburg (2001) *Tourism strategy 2001*. Available at www.joburg.org.za/index.php?option=com_content&id=1116&limitstart=1 (accessed September 7, 2013).

City of Johannesburg (2003) *Executive mayor's mid-term report*. City of Johannesburg. June 2003. Available at http://joburg-archive.co.za/2003/coj-report/CoJMidReport-EngExecSum.pdf (accessed April 28, 2008).

City of Johannesburg (2004) *Johannesburg inner city regeneration strategy business plan 2004–2007*. City of Johannesburg. March 10. Available at www.joburg-archive.co.za/udz/04.doc (accessed April 3, 2009).

City of Johannesburg (2009) 'Map of Constitution Hill'. Available at www.joburg.org.za/maps/braamfontein.html?bw=700&bh=700, n.d. (Accessed 10 August 2009).

Constitution Hill (2006) *Number Four: The making of Constitution Hill*. London: Penguin.

Davie, L. (2007) *Joburg has enviable heritage collection*. September 21, 2007. Available at www.joburg.org.za/index.php?option=com_content&task=view&id=1649&Itemid=168 (accessed September 7, 2013).

Department of Arts and Culture (2013) *Legacy projects*. South African Government. Available at www.dac.gov.za/aboutDAC/Arts%20and%20culture%20initiatives.htm (accessed March 26, 2013).

Flynn, M. K., and King, T. (2007) 'Symbolic reparation, heritage and political transition in South Africa's Eastern Cape'. *International Journal of Heritage Studies* 13(8): 462–77.

Gevisser, M. (2004) 'From the ruins: The Constitution Hill project'. *Public Culture* 16(3): 507–19.

Graham, B. (2002) 'Heritage as knowledge: Capital or culture?'. *Urban studies* 39(5–6): 1003–17.

Johannesburg Development Agency (2002) *HET Feasibility Study Report*. November. Available at www.jda.org.za/keydocs/conhill/het_feasibility_study.pdf (accessed September 18, 2013).

King, T. and Flynn, M. K. (2012) 'Heritage and the post-apartheid city: Constitution Hill, Johannesburg'. *International Journal of Heritage Studies* 18(1): 65–82.

Law, C. (1992) 'Urban tourism and its contribution to economic regeneration'. *Urban Studies* 29(3–4): 599–618.

Law-Viljoen, B. (2006) *Light on a hill: Building the Constitutional Court of South Africa*. Johannesburg: David Krut Publishing.

Le Roux, W. (2005) 'The right to a fair trial and the architectural design of court buildings'. *South African Law Journal* January: 308–18.

Mbembe, A. (2008) 'Aesthetics of superfluity', in S. Nuttall and A. Mbembe (eds.) *Johannesburg: The elusive metropolis*. London: Duke University Press: 37–67.

Murray, M. J. (2008a) *Taming the disorderly city: The spatial landscape of Johannesburg after Apartheid*. Ithaca, NY: Cornell University Press.

Murray, M. J. (2008b) 'The city in fragments: Kaleidoscopic Johannesburg after Apartheid', in G. Prakash and K. M. Kruse (eds.) *The spaces of the modern city: Imaginaries, politics and everyday life*. Princeton NJ: Princeton University Press: 144–78.

O'Donnell, M. A. (2011) 'Big new development plans for Constitution Hill precinct'. *Engineering News*, May 6. Available at www.engineeringnews.co.za/article/constitution-hill-upgrades-and-refurbishments-2011-05-06 (accessed December 1, 2011).

Reid, G. (2005) 'Reframing Johannesburg', in E. Charlesworth (ed.) *Cityedge: Case studies in contemporary urbanism*. London: Elsevier, 154–67.

Rogerson, C. M. and Kaplan, L. (2007) 'Tourism promotion in "difficult areas": The experience of Johannesburg inner city', in C. M. Rogerson and G. Visser (eds.) *Urban tourism in the developing world: The South African experience*. New Brunswick, NJ: Transaction Publishers: 265–91.

Shoba, S. (2012) 'Gauteng broadband project "faces axe"', *BDLive*, August 6. Available at www.bdlive.co.za/articles/2010/07/06/gauteng-broadband-project-faces-axe (accessed September 7, 2013)

Simone, A. (2008) 'People as infrastructure: Intersecting fragments in Johannesburg', in S. Nuttall and A. Mbembe (eds.) *Johannesburg: The elusive metropolis*. London: Duke University Press: 68–90.

Wessels, M. (2006) *Johannesburg inner city performance indicators 2006*. Johannesburg Development Agency. Available at www.jda.org.za/keydocs/indicator_report/inner_city2006.pdf (accessed September 7, 2013).

9 Contesting Cairo's European Quarter

Heritage tourism and the pedestrianization of the Stock Exchange Sector

Wael Salah Fahmi

Introduction

As contemporary cities increasingly turn to tourism as a means of economic development, and as gentrification expands in many cities, more critical accounts of the nexus of tourism and gentrification are needed. Indeed, tourism studies can contribute much to on-going debates of urban transformation, globalization and gentrification. Consequently, this chapter examines the contested spatiality within Cairo's European Quarter in relation to various heritage management policies, tourism development approaches and local people's interests. Further, it explores the restoration and rehabilitation within Cairo's downtown, which involved pedestrianization of public spaces and architectural conservation and adaptive reuse of Belle Époque buildings. The investigation of the Stock Exchange sector as a contested landscape takes up this challenge of broadening tourism analyses and in doing so contributes to a more critical urban sociology of gentrification.

After the introduction, the second section presents a theoretical review related to heritage tourism and the conservation, rehabilitation and gentrification of historical districts. The third section outlines the methods of the study. The fourth section explores Cairo's European Downtown district and the fifth section highlights the heritage management approaches in Cairo. The sixth section offers a historical and current perspective of the pedestrianization of the Stock Exchange. The seventh section discusses the findings of the primary stakeholders. The eighth section offers a critique of the Stock Exchange Sector Project and, finally, the ninth section concludes the chapter.

Heritage tourism and approaches to urban conservation and rehabilitation

Heritage tourism is defined by Kibby (2000) as tourism that engages with the cultural tradition of a particular location, including tangible remains of the past, culturally valued natural areas and intangible cultural assets (Ashworth, 2000; Poria *et al.*, 2003; Richards, 2000). The complex relationship between tourism and heritage has been analysed by Nuryanti (1996) in terms of marketing-built heritage, planning for heritage and the interdependencies between heritage tourism and the local community. This was later demonstrated in Daher's study (2005) of Jordan's Historic Old Salt Development Project, which attempts to understand the mechanisms, rationales, internal and external forces, actors and power networks that privileged a particular discourse on urban regeneration/heritage tourism projects

The prospects for cultural heritage management within historic environments have been discussed in terms of conservation planning options of restoration, renovation and rehabilitation, as illustrated in previous studies of Cairo's medieval (Islamic) city (Sutton and Fahmi, 2002; Fahmi and Sutton, 2003). Restoration of monuments focuses on certain individual significant listed edifices, potentially neglecting other historical buildings within the surrounding urban fabric, and thus resulting in a 'museum town', for tourists rather than for residents. In contrast, rehabilitation focuses on whole quarters or districts, with the cultural built environment heritage being considered part of the present population's everyday life. The rehabilitation of the built environment is related to the more general maintenance of the entire city and the enhancement of local activities and accessibility to heritage buildings through finding new uses for restored buildings. More importantly, rehabilitation within historical districts is closely related to environmentally and socially specific forms of sustainable tourism based upon the mainstream conservation-for-development perspective. Such a sustainable approach to tourism development aims to benefit the local population, economically and culturally, whilst giving incentives to protect cultural heritage with economically feasible urban strategies.

Within the context of planning in historic environments, a dichotomy exists between preserving the past for its intrinsic value and the need for development in response to changing societal values. Such a dichotomy arises from the new sense of historicity and a romantic nostalgia for the past in relation to heritage management (Ashworth, 2000). Nasser (2003) argues for a sustainable approach to planning heritage places based on a community and culture-led agenda. Her study presents the idea of sustainability as an overarching framework for managing tourism in heritage places based on the balance between socio-cultural needs, economic gain and the protection of the heritage resource. Closely relevant are D'Auria's (2001) suggestions for integrating sustainable development within spatial planning mechanisms, whilst encouraging local participation in preserving the cultural heritage. This was also recognized by Grimwade and Carter (2000), who considered social inclusion and sustainable conservation of heritage sites as providing socio-economic advantages for local communities. In addition, Bailey (2008) assesses the implications of re-using unique state-owned enterprises within Havana's central district to achieve improvements in its social and cultural fabric, with pressures for restructuring and commodification being moderated at the city level for the benefit of its residents. Yuen (2005) examines Singapore's development plans, which recognize people as active participants in the construction of place identity and take account of public opinion.

Since the 1980s, an increasing number of cities have developed pedestrianized city centre districts, creating new urban consumption spaces for public activities, as noted in Dokmeci *et al.*'s (2007) study, which investigates the pedestrianization of the main street of Beyoglu in Istanbul's central business district. The revitalization process was attributed to Beyoglu's distinguished architectural character and accessible central-city location. Similar to Cairo's European Quarter, Beyoglu's development reached a climax during the nineteenth century following increased European trade and cultural influence. Whilst the pedestrianization of Beyoglu's main street was based on public and private cooperation, afterwards it became a market-led restructuring with the opening of international retail outlet stores, thus contributing to the functional transformation and changed land prices within surrounding neighbourhoods.

Gotham (2005) highlights the broader social forces and critical issues that affect gentrification, such as urban restructuring, socio-cultural changes and actions of large corporate firms in redeveloping certain heritage spaces into spaces of entertainment and consumption (such as Cairo's Stock Exchange sector). According to Smith and DeFilippis:

> the frontier of gentrification is more than ever coordinated with the frontiers of global capital investment making the newest wave of gentrification in cities one part of a larger spatial restructuring of urban areas associated with the transformations of production, social reproduction and finance.
>
> (1999: 651)

Accordingly, gentrification and tourism are largely driven by mega-sized financial firms and entertainment corporations, which formed new institutional connections with traditional city boosters (chambers of commerce, city governments, service industries). As local elites use tourism as a strategy for economic revitalization, tourism services and facilities are incorporated into redevelopment zones and gentrifying areas. In this new urban landscape, gentrification and tourism amalgamate with other consumption-oriented activities such as shopping, restaurants, cultural facilities and entertainment venues, leading to an altered relationship between culture and economics in the production and consumption of urban space (Gotham, 2005).

As more attention is paid to the conservation of those areas of the historic city that are intensively used by tourism, this results in selectivity of land use, with upward inflationary pressure on local economies (Nasser, 2003). Land and property prices become neither affordable nor responsive to local needs. This will ultimately result in higher rent prices (to levels expected in Cairo's European Quarter). Moreover, if land is sold as freehold to the developers (as in the case of the Ismailia Real Estate Company's [IREC] acquisitions of various properties within Cairo's European Quarter), it means loss of sovereignty for the locals. Inflation caused by tourism pushes prices up beyond the reach of locals, thus restricting resources to foreign investors and tourists, which could cause resentment amongst locals. This is related to Chang's (2000) argument that urban areas are popularly viewed as sites of conflicts or contested landscapes between groups of people with divergent claims on the city.

The study methods

In early 2006, the author administered a small area survey within the Stock Exchange sector. The Stock Exchange scheme was chosen because of the following criteria:

- The project is the most recently renovated area in Cairo's downtown.
- The area covers a district of 60,000 square metres and includes 35 buildings dating from the 1920s and 1930s.
- The Stock Exchange lies close to the Egyptian Museum, a major heritage tourist attraction and to the main commercial circulation axes in Downtown Cairo.
- The area is regarded as the 'Golden Triangle district', characterized by architectural styles ranging from Baroque, Rococo and Neoclassical to Art Nouveau.

The sample of individual and organizational stakeholders was based on a random stratified selection of categories (primary and secondary) according to respondents' degree of involvement in the area. This was followed by a stratified sampling of representatives from each category (sub-groups). Accordingly, 90 primary stakeholders (30 local residents, 40 urban youth, ten shop owners and ten street vendors) were selected, in addition to 20 secondary stakeholders, including five Cairo municipality officials, five planners and five entrepreneurs, who expressed the official view, and five members of a local NGO (Egyptian Centre for Housing Rights), who provided a critical perspective regarding the lack of local participation and community involvement, the threat of eviction and property speculation activities. Stakeholders' attitudes and evaluation of the project were varied and dependent on socio-economic, political, institutional and cultural affiliations (see Table 9.1).

Ninety primary stakeholders were selected according to their degree of responsiveness and willingness to participate in the interviews. Focus group discussions and respondents' narratives provided a useful tool for investigating the interests, roles and responsibilities of different stakeholders and the impacts, negative or positive, of the pedestrianization project. Local residents, street vendors and shop owners expressed their attitudes towards environmental conditions within the area, in terms of landscape features, public spaces and services and their future expectations concerning security of tenure and the threat of eviction posed by gentrification and land speculation. Three topics were identified as guidelines for open-ended interviews and for focus group discussions:

- general attitudes with respect to the positive and negative impacts of the project;
- satisfaction with environmental conditions regarding landscape, open spaces, maintenance and management levels in the area;
- future expectations.

Cairo's European downtown district

Until the nineteenth century, Cairo's urban centre was located in the 'Islamic' city, elevated above the floodplain on the eastern side of the Nile Valley (El Kadi and Elkerdany, 2006). As dams were erected to control flooding, the Nile's wetlands were drained, which allowed a new city centre to be constructed on the eastern riverbank, adjacent to Islamic Cairo. This new nineteenth-century downtown was constructed according to the Parisian Haussmannian model, with wide boulevards and shopping arcades, for the emergent Egyptian landlord and merchant classes and for the European delegations during the reign of Khedive Ismail (Myntti, 1999). Consequently, the architecture of Cairo's new urban quarters was in part the creation of the new cosmopolitan bourgeoisie and European-based architects, with a variety of styles existing side by side – Baroque, Neoclassical, Art Nouveau, Art Deco, Rococo – thus producing an eclectic group of elegant buildings. There were French and English bookshops, tea rooms and sidewalk cafes, fashionable boutiques, art galleries and multi-story Parisian-styled commercial and residential buildings.

The transition from Islamic to European periods was symbolized by the transfer of political power from the Islamic Citadel to the Abdin Palace (constructed in 1863), thus shifting the city's centre of gravity westward with the development of 'European' Cairo (Abu Lughod, 1971). This led to the bifurcation of the city into two realms depicted as east/west or traditional/modern, each defined in stark contrast to one another (Stewart, 1999).

Between the 1950s and the 1970s, Cairo's downtown was subject to a process of gentrification and many Belle Époque buildings were confiscated and passed on to state-owned insurance companies and reused for public and commercial functions (Raafat, 2003). Much of the urban development associated with the new regime was focused around *Al-Tahrir Square*, with the construction of the headquarters for the newly founded Arab League and the *Mugamma*, the central administrative building that handles most civilian records (Stewart, 1999).

Since the 1980s, Cairo's downtown areas have been characterized by urban decay caused by rent freezes, the expansion of the tertiary sector, outflows of residents, increasing traffic congestion and air pollution, combined with a lack of maintenance and unplanned renovations. Consequently, European Cairo's 'shared colonial heritage' was added in 1998 by ICOMOS to the list of heritage at risk.

Located largely in Cairo's central business district and on the Nile frontage, Belle Époque buildings occupy prime real estate sites (Stewart, 2003). In addition to advertisement billboards and air-conditioning units that obscured exterior ornamentation, the construction of additional floors to the original buildings (with no effort to upgrade the original structure) has dramatically altered the architecture and building safety, endangering residents. With rent freeze laws being imposed from the 1960s, property owners have more interest in demolishing the old buildings and constructing new ones. However, for some homeless people, living on the rooftop of a Belle Époque building is a better alternative than sleeping on the street. Thousands of Egyptians who flooded into Cairo during the economic boom of the 1970s had no money to rent an apartment, and instead set up houses on the rooftops. Some roof-dwellers set up wooden shacks on the roofs, whilst others built permanent rooms with makeshift toilets, stand-pipes and even baths.

In addition, strict security surveillance was maintained, especially close to government buildings and recently in public squares and cafes, initially follow-ing street demonstrations between 2004 and 2006. Nevertheless, further col-lective actions took place during the 2011 Winter Uprising by protestors demanding democratic reform, who occupied *Al-Tahrir Square* and organized an 18 day sit-in. As a consequence of the international media broadcasting of the 2011 sit-in, *Al-Tahrir Square* became a tourist attraction and a symbol of mass non-violent resistance, whilst witnessing weekly civil mobilizations in the form of mass demonstrations, sit-ins and marches.

Heritage management approaches

El Kadi and Elkerdany (2006) have noted that, until recently, the criterion used to designate cultural objects in Cairo was based exclusively on visible markers of historic value, producing listings of built forms categorized solely from their outstanding external features. Such listing intended to ensure the preservation of heritage buildings and aimed to avoid the removal or modification of architectur-ally significant features. Field surveys identifying, listing and registering sites with various government authorities constituted the basis for a more scientific method for developing a conservation programme. Documentation was managed by CULTNAT (the National Centre for the Documentation of Cultural and Natural Heritage), which was created in 2000 by the Ministry of Communication and Information Technology (CULTNAT, 2007). However, the stringent protec-tion measures for Cairo's European architectural heritage implemented during the 1990s stopped neither their decay nor their demolition; one reason being that many palaces and villas were not officially registered as heritage because they were less than one hundred years old, and so did not fall under the mandate of the Supreme Council of Antiquities. The Law 117 of 1983 for the protection of antiquities defines heritage as:

> Any building or movable object produced by the arts, sciences, literature, religions, morals, etc., since the prehistoric era and up to 1883, is considered as heritage. And also any building or movable object discovered on Egyp-tian territory and produced by a foreign civilization having had relations with Egypt in one of the above mentioned periods.
>
> (Egyptian Antiquities Organization, 1985)

This law expanded the power of the Supreme Council of Antiquities, which is now the central institution responsible for managing the conservation, restoration and rehabilitation of Egypt's patrimony. The law allows the Supreme Council of Antiquities to expropriate property, to issue demolition and construction licenses and to protect monuments and their surroundings (El Kadi and Elkerdany, 2006), and it slowed down the demolition of villas and palaces. However, Stewart (2003) warns of a loophole whereby it is possible to demolish villas if they are uninhabitable. Official decrees between 1993 and 1998 banned the demolition of palaces and houses linked to key events or personalities, with the last decree prohibiting alterations of any architecturally outstanding palace, house or building used for administrative, educational or cultural activities. Nevertheless, the proliferation of official decrees, the engagement of different ministries of tourism, culture, housing and *awqaf* (religious endowments), and private- and public-sector enthusiasm have all contributed to the inadequacies of urban planning strategies and national-heritage management.

Since the 1980s, the Ministry of Culture has pursued a policy for safeguarding Cairo's European heritage through the reuse of restored houses and palaces for new cultural, educational, recreational and tourism-related activities, with two types of reuse being identified: permanent and occasional. Whilst registered palaces and houses have been permanently converted into hotels, museums and libraries, some Belle Époque buildings served as temporary venues for concerts and art exhibitions. Following the 1992 earthquake, the Cairo Governorate encouraged the restoration of selected nineteenth-century buildings. Fourteen conservation projects were implemented between 1982 and 2000 and managed by the Ministry of Culture. Most conservation projects were financed through national sources, although there are a few exceptions (El Kadi and Attia, 2002).

The restoration of these buildings was not part of an overall rehabilitation of the whole downtown area and hardly involved any community participation or any social investment. However, a new approach to the urban landscape was taken in the 1990s with attempts to pedestrianize certain downtown districts to preserve their built heritage. The upgrading of *El-Alfi Sector* (23,000 square metres) was initiated by Cairo Municipality in 1997, as part of a rehabilitation and pedestrianization project. This pilot scheme aimed at converting several downtown streets into pedestrian promenades. The project was financed by the Cairo Governorate (LE 3 million), which appointed the public sector-owned Arab Contractors Company to renovate infrastructure networks, to upgrade public utilities, to introduce street furniture, wooden benches and newly paved pedestrianized streets and to restore building frontages (as in Figures 9.1 and 9.2).

With the pedestrianization of *El-Alfi Area*, a commercial axis was emphasized by an open market and shops or stalls for street peddlers. A network of secondary streets was used for accessing services to the area, with parking spaces located on vacant land for local inhabitants and shop owners. No further rehabilitation efforts were developed after 1997, with the area being occupied by homeless people and street peddlers/vendors, whilst being used for parking at night.

Figure 9.1 Restored buildings and street furniture (source: author).

Figure 9.2 Street vendors and stalls (source: author).

Pedestrianization of the Stock Exchange sector

In 2001, the pedestrianization of the Stock Exchange sector was launched as a business-orientated initiative to revive the Stock Exchange and to promote the area as a tourist district. The project included the Stock Exchange and the Cosmopolitan Hotel, which were restored between 1990 and 1996. The Stock Exchange scheme, three times the size of *El-Alfi Area* project, was based on public–private partnership, focusing on the physical development of public space, with the renovation of infrastructure, pedestrianization of streets, installation of street furniture, landscaping and the restoration of building façades.

The project to rehabilitate the Stock Exchange district was initiated in 1999 by the Secretary of State for Governmental Affairs, with the aim to save the Stock Exchange, which needed both renovation because of underground water and technological networks equipment to facilitate financial and transactional trading operations. Whereas the government had initially supported a project of the New Cairo Financial Centre (Muqattam Towers), which would transfer the Stock Exchange to Cairo's southern suburbs in front of the historical Salah El-Din's Citadel, a group of investors strongly rejected this idea and offered to restore the old building. They started renovating the building, but then realized the urgent need to upgrade the surrounding area as well, since the district is regarded as the financial and commercial centre of the city, attracting foreign businessmen and brokers.

The rehabilitation process was implemented using private sector funding supplied by consulting firms and entrepreneurs. It involved the conversion of several streets into pedestrian areas, the installation of street furniture and landscaping, as well as the restoration of building façades (Figures 9.3 and 9.4). Dilapidated buildings were subject to thorough restoration and renovation, with façades being painted off-white to ensure harmony.

Stakeholder analysis of the Stock Exchange Scheme

Primary stakeholders (Table 9.1)

Local residents (30 respondents)

Most respondents mentioned the diversity of architectural and urban elements in buildings and public spaces, with emphasis being made on landscaping features (n=19 respondents), street furniture (n=17), decorative pavement and façade ornaments (n=22). They expressed support for landscaping open space (n=18), paving main streets (n=20) and reducing noise pollution (n=13). Environmental services such as the water supply were considered inadequate in some areas (n=8), with many utilities and services being urgently needed (n=15). Many were sceptical about the government's ability to deliver appropriate services (n=27). Most respondents wanted a proper garbage collection system (n=25) and an adequate sewage system (n=15). Whilst future urban improvements were

Figure 9.3 Urban landscape (source: author).

Figure 9.4 Restored buildings' façades (source: author).

considered the government's responsibility, expectations that services would improve with urban rehabilitation projects were often not met (n=30), probably because such schemes were aimed at tourists and business investors rather than local residents.

Although local residents recognized aspects of environmental improvement within the area, all respondents were concerned about their security of tenure and about the authorities' future proposals for the area.

Table 9.1 Field survey, February–March 2006 (based on Burton, 1999)

Stakeholder	Interests/expectations as expressed by respondents during in-depth interviews	Project impact* identified by respondents	Relative priorities of interest**
Primary stakeholders			
local residents (house owners/ tenants)	Infrastructural provision	(−)	1
	Security of housing tenure	(−)	
	Urban environmental conditions	(+/−)	
Retail shop owners	Service accessibility	(−)	1
	Increased income	(+)	
	Public facilities	(+)	
	International and local tourism potentials	(+/−)	
Street vendors	Security of tenure	(−)	1
	Economic opportunities	(−)	
	Accessibility	(−)	
	Local tourism	(+)	
Urban youth	Accessible public spaces	(+)	2
	Provision of socio-cultural activities	(+/−)	
Secondary stakeholders			
Cairo municipality staff	Buildings restoration	(+)	2
	Tourism potential	(+)	
	Service provision	(+)	
Project planners	Expansion of project to surrounding areas	(+/−)	2
	Landscape improvement	(+)	
	Heritage protection	(+)	
NGOs	Economic activities	(−)	3
	Security of tenure	(−)	
	Public facilities	(+/−)	
	Community involvement	(−)	
Entrepreneurs	Business opportunities	(+)	3
	Real estate investment	(+)	
	Tourism services	(+/−)	

Notes
* Potential project impact according to respondents.
** Relative priorities of interest in meeting respondents' needs.
(−) negative impact/negative response; (+) positive impact/positive response.
(+/−) more likely to have positive impact; (−/+) more likely to have negative impact.
1 highest priorities of interest.
2 intermediate priorities of interest.
3 least priorities of interest.

We are reluctant to give up our (spacious) downtown apartments because rent control has kept the monthly rent of our four-bedroom apartment fixed at LE50 for generations. The low rent also explains why landlords do not maintain the buildings. Every year a few buildings collapse when landlords, seeking to bypass rent control, add illegal extra storeys to their buildings.

(Interview with a local tenant)

Owners therefore preferred to withhold properties from the rental market or to seek high 'key money' payments before embarking on rental agreements. Rent control even permitted low-rent property to be handed down from one generation of tenants to the next. 1996 rent control laws allowed increases in rents and the cessation of this inheritance of tenancies, while the 2001 Mortgage Law provided for better financing of house purchase.

Retail shop owners (ten respondents)

The retail shop owners questioned were initially interested in the project and its potential for creating urban development activities (n=7 respondents). When they realized that this was not going to happen, many of the shop owners opposed the pedestrianization plan (n=10). They mentioned that one direct effect of the upgrading and pedestrianization project was the disruption of socioeconomic transactions as well as prospective markets (n=10). They now often express concern about its effects, as pedestrianization has affected vehicular access to storage areas (n=9). Generally respondents expressed the need for accessibility of vehicles and for pedestrian access to public spaces. Respondents (n=8) were concerned about the future of their retail shops as a result of the opening of new downtown shopping malls, such as the nearby Talaat Harb Shopping Centre. All expressed their worries concerning the non-affordability of their merchandise to many middle-class shoppers who prefer to buy from informal street vendors, another threat to their retail enterprises.

Street vendors (ten respondents)

The situation was more uncertain for those respondents who had set up informal enterprises, such as temporary stalls in the area. Street vendor respondents indicated that the project has contributed to their lack of security of tenure (n=10) because of harassment from retail shop owners in the area (n=8) and the local authority's reluctance in regulating the location of their enterprises (n=10). Such regulation involves a complex procedure full of bureaucratic delays and considerable expense. Despite the fact that some of the respondents (n=4) have obtained a legal stay order from the courts to halt the removal of their original stalls, this was not followed by a sustained campaign in support of them, thus leading to their eventual eviction.

Urban youth (40 respondents)

Despite their lack of involvement in the project, with no previous or current consultation, the urban youth expressed satisfaction with the improved environmental quality of the area (n=30 respondents). They mentioned the need to maintain mixed and diverse uses, including multi-functional layouts (n=20), both residential and commercial, in order to provide vital street socio-economic and cultural life (n=25), encompassing coffee shops (n=33), street markets (n=30) and public services (n=29). 'I believe that the Stock Exchange project has encouraged cultural reinvestment whilst sensitizing the public to the value of urban heritage' (interview with an urban youth).

During the spring of 2006, urban youth activists organized pro-democracy street rallies, demonstrations and sit-ins in *Al-Tahrir Square* and *Talaat Harb Square* close to the Stock Exchange sector, despite obstacles to collective action in terms of an emergency law in force which 'renders illegal a meeting of five people in public spaces without government permission' (Fahmi, 2009). Despite security forces' confrontations with demonstrators, urban youth activists regarded coffee shops and public spaces within the Stock Exchange sector as places for social encounters, political debates and campaigns.

Consequently, respondents (n=26) considered downtown pedestrianization projects as a governmental cover to establish security surveillance restrictions within public areas and street coffee shops where urban youth activists meet. This was confirmed by respondents (n=32), with the introduction of tight security measures and street surveillance after the pedestrianization.

Secondary stakeholders (Table 9.1)

Planners (five respondents)

Planners at the General Organization for Physical Planning (GOPP, 1997) indicated that the project had a positive impact in terms of heritage protection (n=5 respondents), urban environmental improvement (n=4), landscape development (n=3) and increased tourism facilities (n=2). Nevertheless, they were quite critical about the lack of a strategic dimension expanding the project to surrounding areas. They emphasized the need for official advocacy to generate awareness amongst primary stakeholders of the benefits of the rehabilitation and pedestrianization actions, so increasing people's influence.

Local municipality (five respondents)

The five officials pinpointed the positive impact of the project in terms of real estate investment opportunities as a result of upgrading residential stock, the development of vacant plots and better service provision. They considered that the project will eventually lead to the sustainable use of restored buildings and improved environmental quality standards.

> The pedestrianization of the Stock Exchange sector represents a tourist, commercial, cultural and recreational axis. The project is concerned with landscape and architectural characteristics of the area whilst establishing tourist services, constructing a multipurpose commercial and cultural hub, providing services in some of the vacant areas, and reusing existing buildings.
>
> (Interview with an official at Cairo's local municipality)

Entrepreneurs (five respondents)

All five respondents said that the pedestrianization project has increased business opportunities and provided a pollution-free environment, which would create a sustainable financial district. 'We formed a committee of businessmen, called the "Friends of the Exchange", to enforce building codes and follow-up maintenance and cleanliness at their own expense' (Interview with an entrepreneur).

Local NGO – Egyptian Centre for Housing Rights (five respondents)

A contradictory view was expressed by five members of a local NGO (Egyptian Centre for Housing Rights), who stressed the adverse consequences of the project. Respondents indicated that a lack of coordination between the local municipality and the community contributed to the project's failure to provide sufficient job opportunities and economic activities, whilst contributing to the lack of security of tenure. However, respondents stressed that heritage protection and additional public facilities were partially achieved.

> Recent official rehabilitation interventions since 2000 have favoured more technical aspects of restoration and infrastructural improvement and the development of degraded areas for future investment. This opens up the possibilities for increased land prices and more property speculation. The out-migration of local people, moving either voluntarily or compulsorily, will be paralleled by a reverse re-population by more professional and less artisan people bringing in craft workshops, galleries, and tourist accommodation which could replace housing for local residents in Cairo's European Quarters. This would amount to a form of gentrification.
>
> (Interview with a member of ECHR)

General critique of the Stock Exchange sector project

The Stock Exchange project raises questions regarding the meaning and significance of downtown European heritage and public spaces from different stakeholders' perspectives. The project's contested nature was conceived as:

- political and bureaucratic centre (by central government and state security officials);
- commercial centre (by shop owners and street vendors);
- architectural heritage area for tourism consumption (by planners and official municipality);
- residential stock (by long-term tenants, small hotel owners, professionals' private offices);
- central financial district (by business entrepreneurs and property speculators);
- public spaces (by urban youth).

Interviews revealed that the Stock Exchange project was oriented more towards business interests and was not part of an overall plan which would be replicated to include surrounding areas. This was attributed to various factors. First, as the Stock Exchange sector is located along the main commercial spine between *Al-Tahrir Square*, *Talaat Harb Square* and *Mostafa Kamel Square*, the project would have provided a basis for major rehabilitation and a car-free city centre, which would have improved the environment and tourism-related activities.

Second, the project was not part of a strategic master plan and focused more on business interests rather than socio-cultural development. There was a lack of coordination between various agencies (local, NGOs, municipality, planners), apart from that between business entrepreneurs, 'Friends of the Stock Exchange' and contractors implementing the restoration and landscaping operations.

Third, the scheme did not involve the local community and particularly tenants who were concerned about their security of tenure, especially with the introduction of the new rental law (with a five-year contract and higher monthly rents subject to a property market valuation), which would effectively end their 1960s low-rent contracts. The project's approach ignored the poor urban population as restrictions deterred street vendors and informal stalls in the pedestrianized zone.

Finally, against the main objective to create a financial centre to serve those business entrepreneurs who initiated and financed the scheme, the project achieved an un-anticipated success in creating (night time) public spaces and street coffee shops occupied by urban youth activists and street vendors. Consequently, more security measures were introduced to curb urban youths' street activities. The presence of security surveillance in the area since the 2006 street demonstrations led to various confrontations between security forces and urban youth gathered in street coffee shops. This probably discouraged the municipality from developing more public spaces with cafes and street markets.

Conclusions

The future of Cairo's downtown district

Since the launch of the Stock Exchange project in 2001, no similar major district development has occurred within downtown Cairo, except for individual façade decorations and street landscaping. Such initiatives are mainly administered by the National Organization for Urban Harmony (NOUH), which is affiliated to the Ministry of Culture. This might be attributed to various developments influencing the overall future of the area.

First, the situation within the Stock Exchange sector, with cafes turning into venues for political public dissent and street youth activism, has contributed to tightening security measures and setting up checkpoints after midnight for both late-night strollers and street vendors.

Second, as decrees prohibiting building demolitions were not applied, land and property speculation prevailed within the downtown area, especially for those buildings not recognized by the Supreme Council of Antiquities as heritage. The only obstacle to such speculative operations is the difficulty of evicting long-term tenants residing in some rundown apartment blocks, despite the new rental law.

Third, some owners of residential buildings intentionally vandalize their own properties in order to have them declared architecturally unsound. When this is proven and charges are pressed, these individuals are ordered to repair the damage they inflicted, but this is never done.

Fourth, property speculation was facilitated by the fact that the Military Decree no. 7 of 1998 was declared unconstitutional by the Supreme Council Court in January 2007, thus lifting the ban against demolishing old villas and historical buildings. There is no clear evidence about the impact of this resolution on property speculation activities, particularly since the 2011 Uprising. Recent security unrest and clashes between protestors and security forces have had more adverse effects on the maintenance of various Belle Époque buildings within the area surrounding *Al-Tahrir Square*.

Fifth, the government approved another law, in 2008, to govern the protection of architectural heritage. This law concerned property owners who had kept their villas and buildings despite the 1950s' nationalization laws. It appeared to provide owners with financial incentives, ranging from tax deductions to maintain and restore their buildings, to their use as bank collateral, the raising of rents above the 1960s rates and the trading of properties for plots of land in the city's periphery.

Finally, as decayed buildings are expected to be demolished, except for Belle Époque registered buildings, vacant plots will permit increased property speculation within the downtown area. Accordingly, a slow process of gentrification and land use change could occur within Cairo's European Quarter, which will encourage residents and merchants to move out to suburban districts. This will be paralleled by an upward filtering of some degraded housing stock through total renovation or renewal, or through conversion into up-market studios. This scenario could be related to recent speculative activities administered by the Ismailia Real Estate Company (IREC), which is affiliated with an offshore company. The IREC purchased some Belle Époque buildings, and modified their façades without coordination with the Supreme Council of Antiquities.

Sustainability of heritage management approaches

The issue of the restoration of individual Belle Époque edifices versus the rehabilitation of the whole urban environment is the central concern of this study. Similar to the medieval old city, it can be argued that the rehabilitation of Cairo's European Quarter should be socio-cultural in its orientation and not primarily economic-development orientated. The built environment context or fabric of the many significant Belle Époque buildings should be maintained and upgraded, together with some development of associated open spaces to better display them.

The pedestrianization of the Stock Exchange sector involved an upward filtering of some degraded housing stock. Total renovation or renewal would change the type of housing from 1920s' large, middle-class flats into up-market studios. The movement of a middle-class population into the upgraded downtown housing stock is being facilitated by new mortgage and rent control laws (Fahmi and Sutton, 2008). In addition, whilst the prohibition against adaptive reuse of some buildings was considered a major barrier to community participation, there remains a need to introduce local activities, commercial uses and tourist functions to help perpetuate the heritage inherent in the built environment, and thereby to avoid a second phase of dereliction. Previous studies of people as active participants in the making of place identity for conservation areas in Singapore (Yuen, 2005) and the cooperative movement of public and private sectors in revitalizing and pedestrianizing Beyoglu's main street in Istanbul (Dokmeci *et al.*, 2007) suggest that community involvement in the rehabilitation of Cairo's European Quarter can be maximized through reforms to establish conservation-orientated committees.

Whilst the issue of six decrees succeeded in avoiding the demolition of numerous architectural edifices, these decrees were not subsequently supplemented by regulatory measures to safeguard listed buildings and their environment. The lack of an integrative framework to give coherence to the range of public and private activities in Cairo's European districts is clearly reflected in the array of unrelated projects and ad hoc initiatives sponsored by diverse agencies. With no strategic plans for Cairo's European Quarter being developed by either the Ministry of Culture or the Supreme Council of Antiquities, each agency was responsible for one aspect of the built environment, whilst devising and implementing interventions based on its own objectives.

Accordingly, this study suggests an overall urban management approach and a strategic vision for the rehabilitation of heritage sites with better coordination between agencies regarding land use and building regulations, proper management mechanisms for restored monuments, maintenance of public spaces and decaying housing stock and public awareness campaigns disseminating information about the objectives of the heritage management projects. Following UNESCO's (2003) recommendations, which state that restoration of monuments is unsustainable if the socio-cultural and economic conditions of the surrounding urban context are not addressed, this study calls for a stakeholder approach to the heritage management of Cairo's European Quarter, involving public–private partnership and grass-roots cooperation between the local community, NGOs, heritage experts and local authorities.

References

Abu Lughod, J. (1971) *Cairo: 1001 years of the city victorious*, Princeton: Princeton University Press.

Ashworth, G. J. (2000) 'Heritage, tourism and places: A review', *Tourism Recreation Research*, 25(1): 19–29.

Bailey, N. (2008) 'The challenge and response to global tourism in the post-modern era: The commodification, reconfiguration and mutual transformation of Habana Vieja, Cuba', *Urban Studies*, 45(5–6): 1079–1096.

Burton, S. (1999) 'Evaluation of healthy city projects: Stakeholder analysis of two projects in Bangladesh', *Environment and Urbanization*, 11(1): 41–52.

Chang, T. C. (2000) 'Singapore's Little India: A tourist attraction as a contested landscape', *Urban Studies*, 37(2): 343–366.

CULTNAT – Centre for Documentation of Cultural and Natural Heritage (2007) *Cairo architectural heritage: 19th and 20th century architectural heritage of the downtown* (CD-ROM – second edition), Alexandria: Bibliotheca Alexandrina.

Daher, R. F. (2005) 'Urban regeneration/heritage tourism endeavours: The case of Salt, Jordan', *International Journal of Heritage Studies*, 11(4): 289–308.

D'Auria, A. J. (2001) 'City networks and sustainability – The role of knowledge and of cultural heritage in globalization', *International Journal of Sustainability in Higher Education*, 2(1): 38–47.

Dokmeci, V., Altunbas, U. and Yazgi, B. (2007) 'Revitalization of the Main Street of a distinguished old neighbourhood in Istanbul', *European Planning Studies*, 15(1): 153–166.

Egyptian Antiquities Organization (1985) *Law no. 117 of 1983*, Cairo: EAO.

El Kadi, G. and Attia, S. (eds.) (2002) 'Restoring Cairo', *Misr El Mahrousa, Impressions of Egypt*, 17: 1–128.

El Kadi, G. and Elkerdany, D. (2006) 'Belle-Époque Cairo: The politics of refurbishing the downtown business district', in D. Singerman and P. Amar (eds.) *Cairo cosmopolitan: Politics, culture, and urban space in the new globalized Middle East*, Cairo: The American University in Cairo Press, 345–371.

Fahmi, W. (2009) 'Bloggers' street movement and the right to the city: (Re)claiming Cairo's real and virtual spaces of freedom', *Environment and Urbanization*, 21(1): 89–107.

Fahmi, W. and Sutton, K. (2003) 'Reviving historical Cairo through pedestrianization: The Al-Azhar street axis', *International Development Planning Review*, 25(4): 407–431.

Fahmi, W. and Sutton, K. (2008) 'Greater Cairo's housing crisis: Contested spaces from inner city areas to new communities', *Cities*, 25(5): 272–297.

General Organization for Physical Planning (GOPP) (1997) *The upgrading of valuable districts in Greater Cairo*, unpublished report for the 'Project for the upgrading of urban environments of historic districts, terms of reference', Cairo.

Gotham, K. (2005) 'Tourism gentrification: The case of New Orleans, Vieux Carré (French Quarter)', *Urban Studies*, 42(7): 1099–1121.

Grimwade, G. and Carter, B. (2000) 'Managing small heritage sites with interpretation and community involvement', *International Journal of Heritage Studies*, 6(1): 33–48.

Kibby, M. (2000) 'Tourists on the mother road and the information superhighway', in M. Robinson, P. Long, N. Evans, R. Sharpley and J. Swarbrooke, (eds.) *Expressions of culture, identity, and meaning in tourism*, Sunderland: British Education Publishers, 139–150.

Myntti, C. (1999) *Paris along the Nile: Architecture in Cairo from the Belle Époque*, Cairo: The American University in Cairo Press.

Nasser, N. (2003) 'Planning for urban heritage places: Reconciling conservation, tourism, and sustainable development', *Journal of Planning Literature*, 17(4): 467–479.

Nuryanti, W. (1996) 'Heritage and postmodern tourism', *Annals of Tourism Research*, 23(2): 249–260.

Poria, Y., Butler, R. and Airey, D. (2003) 'The core of heritage tourism', *Annals of Tourism Research*, 30(1): 238–254.

Raafat, S. (2003) *Cairo, the glory years – Who built what, when, why and for whom*, Alexandria: Harpocrates Publishing.

Richards, G. (2000) 'Tourism and the world of culture and heritage', *Tourism Recreation Research*, 25(1): 9–17.

Smith, N. and DeFilippis, J. (1999) 'The reassertion of economics: 1990s gentrification in the Lower East Side', *International Journal of Urban and Regional Research*, 23(4): 638–653.

Stewart, D. (1999) 'Changing Cairo: The political economy of urban form', *International Journal of Urban and Regional Research*, 23(1): 103–127.

Stewart, D. (2003) 'Heritage planning in Cairo. Multiple heritages in a mega-city', *International Development Planning Review*, 25(2): 129–152.

Sutton, K. and Fahmi, W. (2002) 'The rehabilitation of Old Cairo', *Habitat International*, 26(1): 73–93.

UNESCO (2003) *World heritage papers: Identification and documentation of modern heritage*, Paris: UNESCO.

Yuen, B. (2005) 'Searching for place identity in Singapore', *Habitat International*, 29(2): 197–214.

10 Volunteering around the block

Revisiting Block Island's Manissean heritage

Benjamin Hruska

Introduction

In 1661, sixteen European families settled in the small New England island of Block Island, Rhode Island. Following the European settlement, the indigenous residents of the island, the Manisseans, experienced a rapid cultural decline. They were enslaved and inter-married with African-American slaves brought to the island. Over the generations, their descendants of mixed African and Manissean background lost the oral traditions and other aspects of their Manissean heritage.[1] By the nineteenth century, the leading historian on Block Island declared that only a handful of elderly residents held claim to any Manissean heritage (Livermore, 1877). In short, according to him, the Mannissean heritage would become extinct with their passing. Consequently, for the past thirty years, heritage volunteers on Block Island have sought to expand the current cultural heritage narratives to include the first pre-European inhabitants[2] and reclaim this lost Manissean heritage.

Volunteer residents led official efforts to explore this history with a funded archaeological excavation on the island in 1991 with a view to gathering physical evidence of the Manissean culture. Schwartz highlights that

> archaeologists have pieced together a possible Manissean population count of between 300–500 in 1636. But by 1774, some 140 years later, only 51 Manisseans remained, the rest having either died out or left the island. The last known Manissean, Issac Church, died unheralded at age 100 in 1886 – without anyone realizing the unique historical contribution the Manissean people had made.
>
> (Schwartz, 1990: n.p.)

Also, modern-day, internet-driven genealogical research is connecting descendants of the Manisseans to their history. Many of these individuals, some of whom were completely unaware of any non-European ancestry, are embracing this forgotten aspect of their family heritage.[3] Both of these stakeholder groups, volunteer residents acknowledging the Manissean story and those connected to the Manisseans by genealogy, gathered in the summer of 2011 on Block Island. Together, they dedicated a stone marker to the Manisseans, thus formally acknowledging the 'un-sung' heritage of a bygone era. In addition, there is also a growing appreciation by visiting tourists as the excavated material has been placed on display at the local museum to highlight the existence of human heritage before European arrival.[4]

Consequently, this chapter examines the 're-discovery' of Manisseans that has been led by volunteer residents of Block Island and, along with it, the family genealogy and tourist engagement of the human history of the island before 1661. This 're-discovery' resulted in the erection of a stone marker to the Manisseans, which became part of a larger tourist trail of stone markers located around the island. This system of heritage markers is accessible by visitors looking for points of interest that are walking, biking, or driving around the scenic environs of the island community. While the vast majority of these markers focus on European history, the addition of this Mannissean marker denotes a shift in heritage, a shift in which the history of the island embraces the heritage of human history before European settlement in 1661.

After the introduction, the chapter continues with a short section on the methods used to collect the data for this chapter; this is followed by twelve sections. The first two sections set the scene by examining 'Block Island' and 'Old Block'. The third section outlines the 'Complexity of heritage' and the fourth section introduces the 'Block Island Historical Society (BIHS)'. The fifth section outlines the use of 'Historical stone markers' that celebrate a selected history. The 'Challenges' are discussed in section six. The following five sections ('Towards legitimising heritage – the archaeological excavation'; 'Acknowledging Manissean heritage'; 'Seeking personal heritage through genealogy'; 'Chagum Pond'; 'Recognition of lost heritage – a stone marker') highlight the stages of a lost heritage finally being acknowledged. The final section concludes the chapter.

Methods

This chapter is written from the perspective of a public historian and, as such, two main approaches have been used. The first is archival research that focused on historic archival material and local history publications, such as books and pamphlets, on the island's history. Many of these mention the history of the Manisseans. These works are available for purchase at the Block Island Historical Society and at other island stores. In addition, fifteen qualitative interviews were undertaken. These interviews, conducted after the event, provided valuable background information on the island community and the nature of remembering the Manisseans. There were also semi-structured, face-to-face interviews, which were conducted on the day of the dedication of the event; these interviews granted a window into the perspective of those who were visiting the island for the dedication. Of the sixty-five descendants in attendance, contact information of five individuals was exchanged, which allowed for later interviews to be conducted by phone. When combined, these oral interviews and archival research present a level platform of analysis in examining the resurgence of the Manisseans's inclusion into the heritage of Block Island.

Block Island

Block Island in the State of Rhode Island is located fourteen miles off the southern coast of New England. The island is located on the eastern seaboard, ninety miles due south of Boston and just 150 miles east of New York City; as a result of this, the summer months see Block Island expand from the 1,000 year-round population to 15,000–20,000 as tourism becomes one of the main economic drivers of island life. While the ten weeks of summer represent the peak times of tourist activity, with visitors flocking to the island to visit the natural landscapes, spend time on the beach, engage in the many recreational sports on offer, and visit the attractions, such as Victorian-era buildings, the museum, and lighthouses, the less-populated shoulder seasons, spring and fall, have started to attract visitors with particular interest in Native American history and history of slavery in New England. Consequently, the island's museum is a focal point during this time, with staff being able to spend more time with visitors who are conducting research on their family history.[5]

One major issue that greatly affected the European development of the island was the fact that no natural harbour existed. The lack of a harbour gave rise to an economy based primarily on farming and fishing. Very little changed and very few new residents moved to the community outside of the descendants of the original sixteen European families that arrived in 1661.[6] This 200-year period of virtually uninterrupted residency by these sixteen original families produced a unique situation that now has a considerable influence on researchers of family history and genealogy. However, after the American Civil War (1861–1865), the Federal government greatly increased the amount of spending for infrastructure. This included the building of a new lighthouse on Block Island and the construction of a harbour. The harbour, completed in 1875, allowed for the docking of ferryboats, which brought summer tourists from eastern cities, and the island began its transformation from European farming and fishing settlement to New England tourist economy as hotels, restaurants, and other tourist businesses began to expand. In the 1950s, the local historian Ethel Colt Ritchie wrote, 'In the gay nineties period it was a fashionable watering spa and many doctors in Newport and Narragansett sent their patients across to the island to find renewed health' (Ritchie, 1955: 2). She continued, 'Then the town blossomed forth with several great hotels of Victorian architectural influence and flourished like the green bay tree for many decades' (Ritchie, 1955: 2). However, for those generations of islanders making their living off the land, this massive influx of tourism and the changes that followed it were not necessarily welcome. Ironically, this disruption in the farming and fishing community paled in comparison with what the original Manisseans experienced in the seventeenth century.

Old Block or Manisses (meaning Little God's Island)

Thirty years before the European settlement of the island in 1661, the Manisseans had an altercation with the English trader John Oldham, which resulted in his death. In retaliation, the following year the Massachusetts Bay Colony sent a military expedition to the island led by Captain John Endicott. This group landed in 1637 and demonstrated the overwhelming power the Native Americans faced in this new world. With flintlock firearms, the group quickly pushed back the Manissean warriors. The entire population of the island fled their homes and hid in the nearby forests and swamps. Endicott's men brought destruction to the Manissean villages and corn crops. Their wigwams and stockpiles of food were burned. The corn in the fields was destroyed and the dogs that remained behind were slaughtered (Ritchie, 1955: 70–73).

This painful lesson was not quickly forgotten, as evidenced just twenty-four years later. When the European families first landed in 1661, there were only thirty men; they were greatly outnumbered by the nearly 400 Manissean adult males (Livermore, 1877: 188–189). While some tensions certainly existed, open warfare never transpired. However, within a matter of years, the Manisseans' lifestyle was so altered that their cultural decline became quickly evident. By 1700, only 300 Manissean men, women, and children remained. This decline was the result of three main factors. First, they lost their land, which radically transformed their way of life. Second, many fled the island and joined the stronger allied tribes on the mainland and, finally, many of those that remained were enslaved or forced into some type of indentured servitude. In the decades ahead, these individuals would inter-marry with African-American slaves, who were brought to the island in the early 1700s.[7]

In short, the cultural destruction of the Manisseans was nearly total. In 1774, just 113 years after the landing of the Europeans, only fifty-one descendants from those estimated 1,000 Manisseans remained. In addition, the intermarriage with the African slaves complicated the story of their heritage. By the time of the American Revolution in 1776, just fifty remained and their population continued to decline steadily during the next century. Later, when the prominent historian of the island, the Reverend S. T. Livermore, published his *History of Block Island* in 1877, he wrote, 'A single remnant of the old aboriginal stock is living on the island' (Livermore, 1877: 64). While Livermore (1877) would consider this old resident as the end of the line in terms of Manissean heritage, generations born in the twentieth century would challenge Livermore's interpretation of heritage. The descendants of this one gentleman, along with descendants of others who found links to the Manissean story, would use modern genealogy to challenge and expand the notion of tribal heritage and in the process create a tourism niche.[8]

Complexity of heritage

The genealogical significance of Block Island is seen in the case of John Rathbone, one of the original European settlers of Block Island. Rathbone was born in Lancashire, England around 1628, emigrated to Massachusetts Bay Colony in 1655, and represented one of the sixteen families who landed on the island in 1661. With his wife, Margaret, he fathered eight children (Cooley, 1898). This couple illustrates the complexity of modern-day genealogy. If you lived over 300 years ago and had multiple children, you could have thousands of descendants. Today over 30,000 people are descended from John and Margaret Rathbone, including the vast majority of Americans alive today with the surnames Rathbone, Rathbun, and Rathburn (Cooley, 1898). This complexity was not limited to only the Rathbone family but is indicative of many European families who settled in North America before the year 1700. However, the majority of North American families' genealogy charts illustrate the nomadic nature of the American experience, with family members starting on the eastern seaboard and moving further west as time moved forward. Block Island served as a rare genealogical realm in New England, with multiple generations staying in one particular space. While certainly some individuals left, in comparison with the ebb and flow of Europeans on the mainland, Block Island had a relatively stable population for the first few generations after European settlement.[9]

Islanders with Manissean heritage are illustrated in the writing of Livermore, whose work functioned as a narrative recording the island history of landmarks and major historical events. One section included the history of the Manisseans as it was known at that time. Livermore also wrote about an island resident in his eighties named Isaac Church, whom he viewed as the last Manissean. Livermore wrote of Isaac's impact as a link to the original inhabitants to the island community. According to him, 'Uncle Isaac will be cherished by the children now living, who in mature years will speak of him as the last and worthy representative of the ancient Manissean lords of the soil, who will soon be known only in history' (Livermore, 1877: 65–66). Isaac informed Livermore that at the time of their interview he was eighty-eight years old. He stated he never knew his father, and grew up with his mother, but believed he was over half Manissean in terms of heritage. Livermore, in describing Isaac, wrote, 'If his father were not an Indian his mother was surely a full-breed, and vice versa, for his hair and features are thoroughly Manissean' (Livermore, 1877: 65). Both Isaac's personal feelings of heritage and Livermore's position as a historian making his observation demonstrate the nineteenth-century views on the meaning of heritage.

More importantly, the central historian of Block Island viewed Isaac as not a link in the chain of the past Manissean heritage, but rather a sad end of a people. Livermore concludes with his observation of Isaac as the end of heritage. He wrote, 'The descendants of Isaac Church are too far removed from aboriginal blood to be classed with Indians' (Livermore, 1877: 66). From his perspective as a nineteenth-century historian, the claim to any Manissean heritage ended with Isaac. Livermore's perspective concludes that Isaac's descendants possessed no rightful claim to the human heritage of Block Island before 1661.

Block Island Historical Society (BIHS)

In 1941, a prominent resident of the island, Lucretia Mott Ball, passed away and willed a collection of objects to a museum. With the island having no such institution to receive the objects and fearful the collection would go to an institution on the mainland, the residents founded the Block Island Historical Society (BIHS). This volunteer-based organisation was devoted to preserving the material and cultural heritage of the island community. Steps taken by the organisation included the purchase of a three-storey Victorian hotel formerly known as the Woonsocket House. Acquired in 1945, the Society transformed the hotel into a historic home that celebrated the history of the island (Ritchie, 1955: 25). While the first generation of volunteer leadership showed amazing organisational ability in the founding, management, and transformation of the hotel into a museum, their scope of heritage focused on the history of the island after European settlement. For the BIHS founders, history started in 1661 with sixteen European families landing on the island.

The BIHS early leadership did acknowledge the Manisseans' existence marginally; these members were born in the late nineteenth and early twentieth centuries. They grew up as children in a nation where women did not earn the right to vote until 1920 and Native Americans were not recognised as US citizens until 1924 (American Library Website, 2012). The point of view of this generation of history-minded islanders can be seen in the very first sentence of the island history of Ethel Colt Ritchie. She wrote, 'The earliest history of Block Island is found in the yellowed records of colonial New England' (Ritchie, 1955: 1). While later in her work, Ritchie writes of the then known facts of the Manisseans, these are again seen as something foreign, not quite understood. Thus, she epitomises the history-minded individuals volunteering on the island in the 1950s; while aware of the Manissean story, they did not fully embrace this heritage as an important aspect of the island history. This was reflected in the volunteer-based historic house museum that showed objects and exhibits related to the community history to the ever-growing number of tourists. As such, the BIHS celebrated a heritage that at best marginalised Manissean heritage.[10]

Historical stone markers

The BIHS selection and promotion of Euro-centric historical memory was not limited only to the historic house museum. From the group's very founding, it erected historical stone markers in the hopes of making both island residents and tourists more conscious of the island's history. These historical stone markers placed around the island noted the spot of a previous windmill, the location of a mass grave of victims of a maritime disaster, and geographical features of the island (Ritchie, 1955: 26). The central theme of all these was the exclusion of any mention of pre-1661 island history. For island visitors touring the island after World War II (1940s–1950s), these markers celebrated the original European settlers of this community and once again the Manissean history was marginalised. In contrast to these BIHS formal historical stone markers, local residents started to gather physical evidence of pre-European island inhabitants, such as pot chards and arrowheads that littered the ground and served as testaments to the existence of the Manisseans. One island resident, growing up in the 1950s and 1960s, collected these artefacts or heritage markers of Manissean heritage.

Gathered together, this collection of arrowheads and pot shards served as one of the first steps of this island community towards realising the depth of the island's human history (Block Island Historical Society, n.d.(a)) prior to 1661.

As the BIHS entered the 1980s, the institution's fourth decade of cultural service on the island, the next generation of voluntary Board Members joined the organisation. As younger volunteers who came of age in the 1960s and 1970s, these Board members held a more inclusive vision of what the historical narrative should include with the BIHS exhibits and activities. While they certainly respected the first generation for their leadership and acknowledging the accomplishments of founding the BIHS, these new volunteer members also sought to expand the historical narrative of the island community to look at the heritage of the human story of the island that predated the year 1661.

One of these new members was Pam Littlefield, who joined the Board in her early twenties in the early 1980s. Her lineage to the European heritage on the island is extensive, with the Littlefields arriving on the island in 1715, and her genealogy connects her to many of the original sixteen families. She is twelve generations removed from the European settlement in 1661 and her children represent the thirteenth generation to grow up in the island community. However, her interest in the island heritage included a subject not discussed openly with the first generation of leadership of the BIHS. This interest focused on residents living on the island who were in families that were rumoured to be descendants of the mixed culture of African/Manissean heritage. Littlefield's interest, and that of other new Board members, pushed to expand the heritage of this community to include the indigenous culture that had quickly succumbed to European domination.[11]

Challenges

Initial resistance to the story of the Manisseans was not limited to the original leadership of the BIHS. The majority of the year-round residents viewed the early inhabitants as insignificant to the island's history. One major factor was that no Manisseans remained in a recognisable form on the island. Unlike the western tribes of the US, where relatively large numbers of descendants live, and even in New England where smaller groups of descendants of eastern tribes can be found, no island residents clearly held the reins of the Manissean heritage. Due to the complex nature of island genealogy, many residents who claimed a connection to the original settlers were therefore also quite possibly descendants of the African slaves and Manisseans. However, in the nineteenth and early twentieth centuries, this was not something to be embraced culturally and claimed as personal heritage. As a result of this marginaliasation of the Manissean narrative, combined with relatively very little physical evidence, many rumours were believed as fact about the indigenous residents that stressed to doubt any claims of their legitimacy as the first settlers of the island.[12]

One such claim was that the Manisseans were not year-round residents of the island. This argument attempted to delegitimise the Manisseans by asserting that these Native Americans were only summer residents and that over the course of the year they resided on the mainland and that these were a sub-group of the larger nation of the Narragansett tribe. This claim suggested these individuals in the warmer months of summer and early fall used canoes to reach the island and take advantage of shell fishing and the ability to plant and grow corn. However, once the crops were harvested, these residents returned to the mainland for the majority of the year. Another claim was that the island was a place of exile for early Native American tribes. Again, this sought to confront the notion that, if year-round habitation did take place, it did not count due to the fact that the Manisseans were made up of undesirables from other tribes along the southern coast of, what became, New England.[13] Rumours such as these passed from generation to generation, and from resident to resident, and could only be confronted with actual facts. Physical evidence from the original Manisseans held the power to present an accurate picture of Manissean culture and life, and thus repudiate these inaccuracies.

Dr Gerald Abbott, a physician from Providence, Rhode Island, was another force in the second generation of volunteer leadership of the BIHS. Upon investigating the feasibility of completing a quality archaeological investigation, Abbott learned of the possibility of obtaining funding for such an excavation from the Rhode Island Historical Commission. Teaming with the Town of New Shoreham, which is the civic government of Block Island, the BIHS sought and obtained funding to provide the resources for a high-quality excavation.

The excavation took place on a promising spot on the island just to the north of what is today known as the Great Salt Pond, on a side of a hill with a large south-facing slope. If year-round habitation took place on the island, this would be a likely spot due to two factors. The first factor involved the nearby shell fishing in the pond, and the other, the southern slope of the land, which would have provided the most daylight and been out of the cold winds in the winter months.[14]

Towards legitimising heritage – the archaeological excavation

As the excavation commenced, evidence quickly was found that pointed to year-round habitation. The archaeologists uncovered a roughly three-acre village site with storage pits, houses, and other buildings. In addition, a sturgeon-processing area demonstrated the strong fishing heritage of these individuals. Besides footprints of buildings, a massive midden pile three-quarters of an acre in size was discovered downwind of this village (Jaworski, 1990: 32).

As in all societies, people's trash piles tell a great deal about their daily life. The midden piles found were six feet deep, hinting that this was not just a small band of individuals residing on the island for only a few months a year. However, the large amount of lime in the midden piles from the shells deposited there counteracted with the natural acidic soil of New England. This allowed not only for the preservation of shells, but also for other examples of their diet that included lobster and porpoise. This diverse food supply again pointed to year-round inhabitants. Other evidence included sturgeon bones and even the nuts from the old growth trees on the island that the Europeans later completely removed. However, what the excavation did not find caused a larger question to be asked. Of all the food sources found, corn was not one of these types, which hinted to a much older site than previously thought. The lead archaeologist, Kevin McBride, discussed the significance of this midden pile. He said, 'As far as we know, this is the oldest evidence we have for year-round villages in southern New England – and maybe for the whole Northeast' (Jaworski, 1990: 32).

Before this excavation, archaeologists theorised that the indigenous tribes of New England did not live in permanent settlements until the eleventh century, giving credence to the claims by residents discussed in the previous section. It was believed that, with the influx of corn agriculture from what is today Central America, these native bands did not have the ability to develop a food supply that could sustain a concentrated population in a given area. Thus, the theory was that no permanent villages existed within the New England region until the arrival of corn. These large piles were strong evidence of a permanent site; however, of the debris giving clues, corn was noticeably missing. This fact held the potential for reshaping not only the heritage of the Block Island Manisseans but the entire Native American narrative of the region. In fact, three radiocarbon dates placed the site at 2,400 years old (Jaworski, 1990: 33–37). Or, put another way, this site was two millennia old when the 'original' European settlers arrived in 1661.

Acknowledging Manissean heritage

Objects discovered during this excavation were incorporated into a new permanent exhibition at the BIHS (Block Island Historical Society, n.d.(b)). This exhibit demonstrated the seriousness of BIHS seeking to expand its interpretation of the history of the island to include the Manisseans. Unearthed objects, including a pointed pot for cooking and pot chards, were combined with a mockup of an archaeological excavation. An artist was commissioned in the production of paintings depicting the daily life of the Manisseans, who are shown fishing and also gathering shellfish. This exhibition not only highlighted the objects found pointing to the Manisseans' residence on the island, but also the mockup dig site illustrated the volunteer efforts of the BIHS in seeking to expand the narrative of the history of the island. For the last twenty-five years, this exhibition has introduced physical evidence and interpretation on the Manisseans to visitors of the BIHS historic house museum (Permanent Manissean Exhibition). These visitors total 2,500–3,000 visitors annually.

Seeking personal heritage through genealogy

> ...the desire to learn of their roots leads to an increased interest in travel to their ancestral homelands, which is sometimes referred to as genealy travel, roots tourism or personal heritage tourism.
>
> (Timothy, 2011: 409)

While the second generation of volunteer leadership proved inclusive in respect to pre-1661 history, they also looked to expand upon the genealogical research practised at the BIHS. This expansion, which took place in the early 1980s, sought to modernise the Society's genealogical efforts with the use of modern-era computers and the printing of easy-to-follow genealogical charts.[15] For those descended from the original sixteen families, who resided all over North American and even in the United Kingdom, this shift aided these individuals seeking their own personal heritage.

The Society from the very beginning realised the historical importance of the genealogical heritage. The original core of volunteers painstakingly researched the genealogy of the original sixteen families that extended a generation or two back to England and Scotland and continued to those born on Block Island just after World War II. The highlight of this effort was the BIHS's Helen Winslow Mansfield, who for over thirty years combed the un-mowed cemeteries of Block Island. Her efforts produced a complete listing of all the gravesites on the island, which she published in a book printed in 1956.[16] This work provided an invaluable resource not only for genealogists on Block Island, but for the increasing number of family researchers finding their Block Island heritage. Using land deeds, birth records, and the Society's growing collection of family bibles containing family information, these volunteers wrote the genealogy out by hand on sheets of paper. One volunteer used a large bed sheet and wrote out the family history of her descendants from the sixteenth century to the 1950s. This information, in the form of paper charts, was made accessible to summer visitors in the 1950s–1970s interested in their family's connection of heritage to the island (Block Island Historical Society, n.d.(c)). Genealogy allowed these visitors from all over the US to visit New England and to see their family's heritage on this small island.

The new leadership of the BIHS, realising the importance of family heritage to future visitors to Block Island, decided to focus on expanding this aspect of their heritage institution. However, in the 1980s, today's relatively inexpensive and easy-to-use genealogical software did not exist. The BIHS, wishing to display this detailed research on large printed display panels, developed their own primitive software. This software allowed for the listing of individual names, dates of birth and death, marriages, and children. After all the data was entered – which for some families totalled nearly 300 individuals – they were printed. Again, these massive charts, some over five feet in height, allowed for the display and dissemination of this complex genealogical heritage.[17] While these charts were based on all available data that could be found in the middle portion of the twentieth century, these charts, like all genealogical investigations, had limits. Family names only go so far back. In addition, information that families wished to keep secret centuries ago was very difficult to recover. The glossing over of certain issues, such as problematic heritage that could be viewed as something to be hidden not celebrated, was nearly impossible to overcome. However, the role of technology transformed the methods available to family genealogists. As a result, genealogical questions posed to the BIHS were no longer limited to just the summer months when the museum was open full time. Advanced technology in genealogical research meant the BIHS would be fielding questions year round. No longer were people limited to travelling hundreds or even thousands of miles and spending hours combing thousands of records by hand in search of heritage. With the stroke of a few keys on a computer and an internet connection, they could comb thousands of records instantly. Thousands of these inquires connected them to a place called Block Island.[18]

Coni Dubois grew up in the Midwest knowing her father was Native American. However, this exact tribal heritage was hidden from her. Her father grew up in the 1950s, and his parents, facing such prejudices as not finding employment because of their race, did not openly discuss this aspect of the family's past. Coni's father asked his adult daughter to investigate his Native American heritage.[19] He wanted to know and understand his Native American roots that had been lost to them as a result of his parent's generation purposely obscuring this heritage (Josiam and Frazier, 2008).

The challenge was significant. In the early 1990s, the experts she contacted informed her that any genealogy project would be complicated. However, for those seeking Native American genealogy, they faced an additional challenge: that of the lack of paper records. In short, the common wisdom in the early 1990s was that those seeking genealogical information on Native Americans would not identify anyone before the year 1800. The main reason for this belief was that, even if the Native Americans retained any written information that could be of use for later researchers, the majority of this material was destroyed. In addition, the other main problem was many of the Native Americans in New England who survived the diseases and wars were enslaved. As a result, if they were listed in records, they would be recorded as 'slaves' or 'mulatto', thus obscuring their Native American heritage.[20]

Undeterred, Dubois commenced seeking information of her father's Native American heritage. While findings were scattered, pieces did in fact exist. Old land deeds, wills, and lawsuits provided stepping-stones in tracing her family heritage towards the sought after Native American roots. One of the tools she utilised in completing this multi-year long genealogical research on the New England tribes was the internet. In the mid-1990s, this included starting an msn group; this allowed those seeking similar missions of heritage to communicate with each other over leads and share information. Later, as the systems of internet group communication evolved, she formed a family group, allowing researchers to share images and scanned documents related to their Native American heritage. She embraced Facebook and started a group that today boasts over 700 members and also used the genealogical software of Ancestry.com. (Dubois, 2013). Today, she has a website called 'Ever Widening Circle', on which she shares her latest findings, which includes the DNA analysis of her late father, used as a clue to their Native American past.

Dubois found her family's genealogical connection to a number of Native Americans, including one Samuel Chagum. She found evidence of him as an adult in the 1720s in the area of Charlestown, Rhode Island. Further investigation of his background provided a unique discovery for this modern-day genealogical researcher. While she found him as an adult in the colony of Rhode Island, his birth, and thus her heritage, extended to a small island off the coast – Block Island.

Chagum Pond

In Reverend Livermore's history of Block Island (1877), he uses a tour of the island to demonstrate the layers of heritage. Landmarks everywhere, such as ponds, sea-cliffs, and hills, derive their names from local culture and residents, thus these can serve those investigating heritage. His tour of the northern portion of the island describes Chagum Pond. He wrote, 'This name is commonly pronounced Shawgum, and is probably taken from an Indian' (Livermore, 1877: 160). This small description, serving as a way of describing a picturesque portion of the island, written in the late nineteenth century, provided valuable information for those seeking genealogical heritage a century later. Livermore (1877) continued:

> We have a record of one Samuel Chagum, who distinguished himself here in 1711 by stealing a canoe, running away from his master, losing the canoe, and suffering the penalty of the wardens adding six months to his former period of servitude.
>
> (Livermore, 1877: 160)

While for Livermore (1877) this small fact added colour to his narrative of the geographic aspects of the island, this provided an invaluable link to those seeking their Native American roots. This tale provided Coni Dubois with evidence to reach another layer deeper into her father's suppressed Native American heritage.

Heritage for the descendants of the Manisseans was multiform and multifaceted. The complexity was pronounced and included the issues of the Native American subjugation, enslavement, and those that fled the island. However, this was their heritage. They sought it out over years of research. They embraced this aspect of their family's heritage. While the majority of visitors to Block Island come as tourists, seeking the laid-back environs of this tucked-away corner of America's eastern seaboard, others come for more complex reasons.

Recognition of lost heritage – a stone marker

In the summer of 2011, Block Island commemorated the three-hundred-and-fiftieth anniversary of European arrival. While many of these events were celebratory in nature, the Block Island Historical Society pushed forward the remembering of a nearly forgotten people. For sixty years, the BIHS had served in the leading role of stewardship of the island's heritage with the production of exhibitions and the erection of historical markers. Continuing with these means, but expanding their scope, the BIHS voted to erect a stone marker to the very first residences of Block Island.

The BIHS sought to expand the symbolic meaning of this action by the incorporation of those connected to this Manissean heritage. The descendants of Samuel Chagum and Isaac Church were invited to the island for the event. The site selected for the stone marker retained significant heritage for those Manisseans and Africans who resided on the island, and more importantly those sired from them. The formal gathering took place to dedicate the marker to the Manisseans at what is known as Isaac's Corner. This corner is named for Isaac Church, the eighty-year-old gentleman that Livermore met in the 1870s. Isaac, who was born in 1786, died at the age of 100 in 1886. It is situated in front of the segregated cemetery. The historian Ethel Colt Ritchie, writing in the 1950s, described this site. She wrote, 'On a hill above Fresh Pond on the southeast end of the Island, is a forlorn and forgotten cemetery, its graves marked simply by small native boulders' (Ritchie, 1955: 36). This was her description of the segregated cemetery on the island; even in death the divisions between Native American/ African and European were made quite clear. Colt continued:

> This is the Indian Burying Ground dating back almost three hundred years to the earliest settlers. Here were laid to rest Island Indians, Indian bond-servants, and the negro slaves brought over by the early proprietors of the Island, together with their descendants.
>
> (Ritchie, 1955: 36)

Within this stonewalled area rest the Manisseans who were buried after the events of 1661. The majority of stones are just that, rocks marking the location of a deceased Manissean or African slave (Vascamp, 2011). While the earliest Europeans settlers and their descendants were buried in what became the main island cemetery, this segregated site marks the final resting place of the Manisseans.[21]

In front of the resting place of those Manisseans who experienced the European settlement in 1661, this ceremony finally acknowledged in stone form the Manissean heritage. At last, after 350 years since European settlement, and nearly seventy years of the Historical Society seeking to protect the heritage of the island, the Manissean story was embraced. For fifty years, stone markers laid out throughout the island have highlighted the island's heritage for visiting tourists. This marker in front of the segregated cemetery will highlight the Manissean heritage for future tourists visiting the island. While these markers in the past have informed visitors about the European descendants, this also marginalised the human heritage before 1661. Thus, this marker will serve future generations of islanders and visitors with a tangible symbol, calling attention to the original settlers of Block Island, the Manisseans.

Conclusion

Block Island presents a complex picture when considering where its 'heritage' starts and ends. What is also important to this narrative is the timeframe of whose heritage and what heritage is being recognised. It is clear that the understanding and acknowledgment of the island's heritage over the past thirty years has been re-shaped and re-framed due to a group of dedicated volunteers. This group of volunteers, local residents of the island, has been instrumental in taking the lead to uncover the island's forgotten pre-European past and as such the Manisseans are now embraced as part of the narrative of the history of the island.

The volunteers have also been instrumental in constructing family genealogy, and for the individuals descended from these forgotten peoples, Block Island has proved a powerful connection to their past, which they individually and collectively sought out. They have also embraced these descendants by formally making them part of the ceremony to the historical stone marker at Isaac's Corner, thereby creating links from the past to the future.

Furthermore, these volunteers have developed the tourism offering of Block Island. As a small New England community whose economy is primarily driven by tourism, the sharing of pre-European heritage with visitors is just one more factor in attracting potential visitors. While the island already has a strong tourist niche, with its open spaces, lovely beaches, and local charm, the inclusion of Manisseans into the heritage marker system adds one more layer of possible attraction for future visitors. This includes those researchers who are seeking specific information related to genealogy at the BIHS or just those interested in the broader history of Native Americans and the issue of slavery in New England. As a result, tourism is likely to grow as a result of the expansion of the heritage of Block Island to incorporating the Manisseans.

Notes

1 Pam Littlefield Gasner, interviewed by Benjamin Hruska on March 12, 2012, Tempe, Arizona, USA.
2 Pam Littlefield Gasner, interviewed by Benjamin Hruska on March 12, 2012, Tempe, Arizona, USA.
3 Coni Dubois, interviewed by Benjamin Hruska, March 8, 2012, Tempe, Arizona, USA.
4 Coni Dubois, interviewed by Benjamin Hruska, March 8, 2012, Tempe, Arizona, USA.
5 Dan Millea, interviewed by Benjamin Hruska, March 21, 2012, Tempe, Arizona, USA.
6 Dan Millea, interviewed by Benjamin Hruska, March 21, 2012, Tempe, Arizona, USA.
7 Pam Littlefield Gasner, interviewed by Benjamin Hruska on March 12, 2012, Tempe, Arizona, USA.
8 Coni Dubois, interviewed by Benjamin Hruska, March 8, 2012, Tempe, Arizona, USA.
9 Pam Littlefield Gasner, interviewed by Benjamin Hruska on March 12, 2012, Tempe, Arizona, USA.
10 Pam Littlefield Gasner, interviewed by Benjamin Hruska on March 12, 2012, Tempe, Arizona, USA.

11 Pam Littlefield Gasner, interviewed by Benjamin Hruska on March 12, 2012, Tempe, Arizona, USA.
12 Douglas Gasner, interviewed by Benjamin Hruska on March 13, 2012, Tempe, Arizona, USA.
13 Douglas Gasner, interviewed by Benjamin Hruska on March 13, 2012, Tempe, Arizona, USA.
14 Pam Littlefield Gasner, interviewed by Benjamin Hruska on March 12, 2012, Tempe, Arizona, USA.
15 Pam Littlefield Gasner, interviewed by Benjamin Hruska on March 12, 2012, Tempe, Arizona, USA.
16 Pam Littlefield Gasner, interviewed by Benjamin Hruska on March 12, 2012, Tempe, Arizona, USA.
17 Pam Littlefield Gasner, interviewed by Benjamin Hruska on March 12, 2012, Tempe, Arizona, USA.
18 Coni Dubois, interviewed by Benjamin Hruska, March 8, 2012, Tempe, Arizona, USA.
19 Coni Dubois, interviewed by Benjamin Hruska, March 8, 2012, Tempe, Arizona, USA.
20 Coni Dubois, interviewed by Benjamin Hruska, March 8, 2012, Tempe, Arizona, USA.
21 Dan Millea, interviewed by Benjamin Hruska, March 21, 2012, Tempe, Arizona, USA.

References

American Library Website (2012) 'Congress granted citizenship to all Native Americans born in the US, (June 2, 1924)', in *America's Story from America's Library*, accessed on March 2, 2012, www.americaslibrary.gov/jb/jazz/jb_jazz_citizens_1.html.
Block Island Historical Society (n.d.(a)) *Blaine Collection*, Block Island, Rhode Island, USA.
Block Island Historical Society (n.d.(b)) *Permanent Manissean Exhibition*, Block Island, Rhode Island, USA.
Block Island Historical Society (n.d.(c)) *Genealogical Resource Collection*, Block Island, Rhode Island, USA.
Cooley, J. C. (1898) *Rathbone Genealogy: A Complete History of the Rathbone Family Dating from 1574 to Date*, Syracuse: Courier Job Print.
Dubois, C. (2013) 'DNA Test', in *Ever Widening Circle*, accessed on March 13, 2012, http://conidubois.wordpress.com/dna test/.
Jaworski, C. (1990) 'Discovery on Block Island: 2,500-year-old village predates agriculture', *Nor'easter: Magazine of the Northeast Sea Grant Programs* 2(2): 32–37.
Josiam, B. M. and Frazier, R. (2008) 'Who am I? Where did I come from? Where do I go to find out? Genealogy, the internet, and tourism', *Tourismos* 3(2): 35–56.
Livermore, S. T. (1877) *A History of Block Island: From Its Discovery, in 1514, to the Present Time, 1876*, Hartford, CT: The Case, Lockwood & Brainard, Co.
Ritchie, E.C. (1955) *Block Island: Lore and Legends*, North Haven, CT: Van Dyck/Columbia Printing Company.
Schwartz, M (1990) 'Historical discovery on Block Island uncovered earliest settlement in southern New England', excerpted from C. Jaworski (1990), accessed on March 21, 2013, www.seagrant.gso.uri.edu/41N/Vol1No3/blockislhist.pdf.
Timothy, D. J. (2011) *Cultural Heritage and Tourism: An Introduction*, Bristol: Channel View Publications.
Vascamp, P. (2011) 'Dedication of new marker', *Block Island Times*, July 18: 8.

11 Atrocity heritage tourism at Thailand's 'Death Railway'

Apinya Baggelaar Arrunnapaporn

Introduction

The attractions of death, disaster and atrocity have long provided a reason and motivation to travel. Since it is unlikely that this particular motivation for tourism will diminish, there is a need to understand the controversies surrounding the attractions of death and disaster with regard to heritage. This is particularly important in a country like Thailand, which was neutral during the Second World War and where the so-called 'Death Railway' is located. The atrocity heritage of the 'Death Railway' is used as an example of how heritage tourism with its powerful economic drive but lack of understanding of its significance has been detrimental to the heritage environment. Furthermore, the controversy caused by poor interpretation and commodification of the site by different users (victims, perpetrators and bystanders) will be discussed. Questions also arise about certain aspects of the management, marketing and interpretation of this product of atrocity that is now the heritage.

The significance and value that lie within heritage are not only in how it is defined, but also in how it is used to create meaningful experiences for visitors, while promoting conservation values and providing benefit to most stakeholders – intellectually, socially and economically. All heritage is potentially dissonant to some extent, to some people, at some times. The origins and implications of such dissonance are an integral and unavoidable characteristic of the place of heritage within contemporary society.

Management of heritage is rarely easy, especially atrocity heritage, which is multifaceted, and has issues which may vary according to its meaning, ownership, users, the type of attraction, economic interest and benefit, and its location.

This chapter explores the multifaceted nature of the controversy generated by the use of the heritage of atrocity as tourist attractions through the case of the Death Railway. In particular, the dissonance in the interpretation of this atrocity heritage where both victims and perpetrators have become today's tourists. Furthermore, it tries to comprehend the macro-environmental factors that shape this controversy. These range from political factors (Thailand was a neutral country during the Second World War, but is now one of Japan's biggest investment countries) and economic issues (commercialisation), to social and cultural forces.

This chapter describes part of the empirical research which took place in 2009–2010 on the topic of 'Interpretation Management of Atrocity Heritage' of the 'Death Railway'. Data was gathered through interviews of the local population and tourists. Furthermore, in-depth interviews were conducted with the local authorities and the caretakers of the heritage.

The trauma of the past

By 1940, the western nations with interests in Asia (Britain, the Netherlands, France and the United States) were becoming concerned about Japanese aggression in China and, in an attempt to force the Japanese to withdraw, imposed trade sanctions on Japan. The western Allies also gave military aid to the Chinese, thus creating the situation where a greater war became very likely. For the Allies, the situation became critical after Germany launched its westward invasion of Europe in September 1939. The Netherlands and France were quickly defeated and surrendered in May and June of 1940 and Britain rapidly found itself fighting for its very survival.

As a first step towards its occupation of southern Asia, Japan easily forced the ostensibly neutral but pro-Axis French to allow it to occupy Vichy French Indo-China (what is now Laos, Cambodia and Vietnam) in September 1940. This gave Japan the security of a land base within bomber range of the British colony of Malaya and the fortress of Singapore. By the end of 1941, with Japan on the brink of economic downturn, it was not difficult for the government to take the only course it thought possible – go to war to secure the raw materials denied to it by the western trade sanctions.

Thus, the Second World War started in South East Asia on 7 December 1941, when Japan launched its attack against the western Allies with simultaneous operations against Pearl Harbour, in Hawaii, the US Navy's principal Pacific base, Thailand (Siam), the Philippines, Wake Island, Guam and the British colonies of Malaya and Hong Kong. These were quickly followed in December by full-scale invasions of Burma, Borneo and the Philippines. Furthermore, the Dutch colony of the East Indies was expected to be a buttress against the Japanese invasion of South East Asia; however, on 10 January 1942, Japanese forces invaded the Dutch Indies and by 8 March 1942 the Royal Dutch East Indies Army surrendered in Java. The vital rubber plantations and oil fields of the Dutch East Indies were in Japanese hands.

Other countries in the region were also affected, especially the European colonies, such as Indochina, Burma, Singapore and Malaya. Thailand, although not colonised, is located in the centre of South East Asia, and was forced by the Japanese Imperial Army to coordinate the construction of the strategic railway line to connect the Malay Peninsula with Burma.

There were a number of tactical reasons why the Japanese wanted to capture Burma from the British. First, they needed to cut the 'Burma Road', a highway in south-west China which extended 720 kilometres from Kunming, the capital of Yunnan province, to the railroad at Lashio in Burma. This was the only route for the western Allies to transport vital military supplies to the Chinese. Second, they needed access to raw materials vital to Japanese industry and its military, such as tungsten (wolfram) from the mines at Mawchi and oil from the Yenangyuang oil fields. Third, they could transport military supplies overland to reach India without risking allied submarine attacks on the sea-routes.

The Thailand–Burma railway, which stretched from Nong Pladuk in Thailand to Thanbyuzayat in Burma, is now widely known as the 'Death Railway' because of its wartime legacy. It was constructed between June 1942 and October 1943 by British, Dutch, Australian and American prisoners of war (POWs) and conscripted Asian labourers. These were predominantly of Indian, Tamil, Indonesian, Malay, Vietnamese and Burmese origin. During its construction, more than 13,000 (22 per cent) of the 60,000 allied POWs died; mainly of disease, sickness, malnutrition and exhaustion, coupled with brutality at the hands of their captors. They were buried along the route of the railway. While the Allied POWs suffered badly, the Asian labourers suffered horrific death rates. It is estimated that between 80,000 and 100,000 (40–50 per cent) of the more than 200,000 Asian workers perished during the construction. The Japanese kept no records of these deaths and their graves remained unmarked.

The trans-national Thailand–Burma railway line was 415 km in length with 304 km in Thailand and 111 km in Burma. It crossed mountains, rivers, streams and valleys. With such difficult terrain, harsh climatic and health conditions, logistics and the large amount of work involved, the construction of this line was extremely difficult.

After the construction of the railway, some POWs were moved to larger camps, while some remained to maintain the railway. The railway was in operation for almost two years and was used to carry troops and supplies. By the middle of 1944, the Allies had recognised the importance of this strategic rail link and began a campaign of aerial bombing. The weak spots of the railway were the bridges across rivers and streams. The bombing of bridges was ordered and one of the main targets was the Bridge over the 'River Kwai' (Bridge 277). It was bombed several times, culminating in a raid on 24 June 1945. After this, the Japanese Imperial Army gave up repairing the structure. Unfortunately, during the bombing raids, a number of the POW camps were hit and hundreds of prisoners were killed.

After the war, the Allies took control of the railway and dismantled some sections to prevent its reuse. The section of railway in Thailand was sold to the Thai government. The remains of those POWs who died (except the Americans, whose remains were repatriated to US soil) were transferred from the camp burial grounds and solitary sites along the railway to three war cemeteries. The Chongkai and Kanchanaburi War Cemeteries in Kanchanaburi province, Thailand, hold the remains of those who were recovered from the southern end of the railway. Thanbyuzayat War Cemetery in Burma holds the remains of those from the northern end. These three cemeteries are now under the care of the Commonwealth War Graves Commission.

After a technical inspection in 1947, the State Railway of Thailand (SRT) decided it was feasible to re-lay the line only as far as Namtok Station (Sai Yok waterfall, which was called 'Tarsao' during the war). During week days, there are two trains, which are mostly used by the locals for public transport, while at the weekend a tourist train service is added to the schedule.

Atrocity heritage tourism

Atrocities have occurred in many places and regions of the world. The working definition of atrocity as 'the case of deliberately inflicted extreme human suffering' used by Tunbridge and Ashworth (1996) is adopted here. Still, atrocity is recognised in two interconnected ways – first, as acts of deliberate cruelty perpetrated by people against people, and second, as occurrences, particularly shocking or horrifying to others. An important element of atrocity is the perceived culpability implicit in these occurrences, which in most cases becomes the primary source of dissonance in the interpretation.

Thus, atrocity heritage denotes all associated artefacts, buildings, sites and place associations, as well as the intangible accounts of the acts of atrocity, interpreted by the various parties involved – victims, perpetrators, bystanders and others. It needs to be considered as a separate category of heritage, first, because it is 'disproportionately significant to many users' (Tunbridge and Ashworth, 1996: 94) and, second, because 'dissonance created by the interpretation of atrocity is not only peculiarly intense and lasting but also particularly complex for victims, perpetrators and observers' (Tunbridge and Ashworth, 1996: 95). The heritage of atrocity and its interpretation is highly charged with controversy, and creates considerable heritage dissonance problems. Debates over the identity of victims, perpetrators and observers, as well as attempts to resolve such controversies, can sometimes exacerbate the problem and have serious political consequences. Usually, they mark events and places that are difficult to revisit and are memorialised mostly in physical settings. Memorial sites that recall past tragic events of a social, religious, ethnic or culture group may have varying importance in a given locale. It may be a simple plaque honouring what happened to an individual or small group in a singular event or it may carry the purposeful explanation of a string of fatal events that led to catastrophe for many.

Heritage is created wherever and whenever atrocity sites are newly designated (or redesignated) as historic sites. In the study of such sites, Tunbridge and Ashworth (1996) introduced the concepts of dissonant heritage and, subsequently, of dissonant heritage tourism. Dissonance is a tension or conflict, inherent to the nature of all heritage, which is caused by the simultaneous holding of mutually inconsistent attitudes and behaviour among heritage institutions, heritage users and other stakeholders in the process of heritage production and consumption. They argue that, in the formal recognition of large-scale atrocity sites such as memorials, dissonance will inherently evolve or prevail among the different groups involved, such as the victims, the perpetrators and bystanders (and/ or their descendants). In other words, although dissonance cannot be erased from heritage, it can be reduced and balanced. The concept of 'heritage dissonance' encompasses social, cultural, economic and political issues and has practical implications on the management level.

Dissonance in the atrocity heritage of the 'Death Railway' exists at many levels. Besides the three main parties – victims, perpetrators and bystanders – there is another group of protagonists which can be labelled the 'dual-role' countries. In Asia, the Second World War was also known as the Great Asia-Pacific War. In Thailand, it is called the Great South East Asia War. These names highlight a deeper issue. At the beginning of the war, the Japanese Imperial Army used a propaganda campaign called the 'Great Conspiracy of South East Asia' to gain support from countries under colonial rule. Its ultimate goal was to free them from the colonisers. During the war, these countries were required to cooperate with the Japanese Imperial Army and provide assistance. While these countries eventually got their independence, during the war years, numerous atrocities were instigated by the Japanese. It is therefore not surprising to see that, while some Singaporeans and Indonesians do not like how the Japanese had treated them during the war, they see the war as the event that gave them their freedom. The dissonance created by this dual-role group can be highly diverse.

So far interpretations of atrocity heritage of the 'Death Railway' at most sites (Bridge on the River Kwai, JEATH War Museum, Kanchanaburi War Cemetery, Hell Fire Pass Memorial Museum) do not include this dual-role group. So, the concept of heritage dissonance not only provides a means for taxonomic description of the issues but also directly relates to the management practices controlling it. Thus, it serves both as a tool for description and as a guide to management interventions.

The management of an atrocity site will impact not only the survivors and their families, but also the public memory of the event. The significance of these sites to the community may change over time as the healing process progresses. The passage of time has seen the sites of concentration camps and the first atomic bomb explosion in Japan take on international significance, some of which have been declared World Heritage Sites. Preservation of the sites can be important not only for maintaining the physical evidence at the site, but also for interpretation of the atrocities. One of the most evocative reminders of the atrocities of the Second World War is the Hiroshima Peace Memorial (Genbaku Dome). The first atomic bomb exploded about 600 metres above the roof of the Genbaku Dome building, which had been an important exhibition hall before the war. It was the only structure left standing in the area where the bomb exploded on the morning of 6 August 1945. It was inscribed on the list of UNESCO World Heritage Sites in 1996. It has been estimated that 140,000 Japanese died in the blast and its immediate aftermath. The Japanese government decided to leave the building as it was on the day of the explosion. The burned-out building, with only its skeletal steel construction left standing, is a remnant of that August morning that tells the story far more evocatively than any interpretative sign or display could. The memorials commemorating the dead from this atrocity were established later. They are deemed to be not only a part of the healing process, but part of the interpretation of the site itself. At the Genbaku Dome memorial garden, a peaceful area has been established in order to provide a place where survivors and families can go and reflect on the event.

The heritage production process

A selection of the past is involved in both history (scientifically based) and heritage (contemporary society) and this can potentially create discrepancies in interpretation or meaning. Tunbridge and Ashworth (1996: 7) have developed a Heritage Production Process Model, whereby a historic resource is turned into a heritage product, through a process of interpretation and packaging. The heritage production process can be said to have a consumptive foundation, as the processes of selection and targeting are also used as part of marketing process. Hewison (1987) also describes heritage as a process of commodification and trivialisation, during which history has been replaced by a heritage industry. Consequently, a false view of the past is presented. Hewison (1989) later broadens the idea and argues that heritage will reverse and influence history in the long run. This will mean that the actual understanding of history will be replaced by an image of the past as its reality. Another negative typology entails 'tabloid history' (Walsh, 1992). It can be argued that the heritage creation process is controversial in a number of respects, with one of the frequently occurring issues being commodity value above authenticity.

It is clear from a number of sources that tourist interest in recent death, disaster and atrocity is a growing phenomenon in the late twentieth and early twenty-first centuries and that theorists have both noticed and attempted to understand it. 'Dark Tourism' was first labelled by Lennon and Foley in 2000, who intended to signify a fundamental shift in the way in which death, disaster and atrocity are being handled by those who offer associated tourism products. Moreover, the politics, economics, sociologies and technologies of the contemporary world are as much important factors in the events upon which this dark tourism is focused as they are central to the selection and interpretation of sites and events which became tourism products (Lennon and Foley, 2000: 3).

Heritage tourism is intimately bound to the dichotomy of preservation/conservation and consumerism/commercialisation. It is therefore not surprising that a dialogue concerning heritage and tourism is often characterised by a series of contradictions. McKercher and du Cros (2002) in their work on the partnership between tourism and cultural heritage management discuss the problems and tensions between the two partners. They claim that cultural heritage tourism needs to include both cultural heritage management and tourism management. However, in reality, many heritage attractions fail to reach either their tourism potential or their heritage potential because ignorance leads to suspicion of other's motives (McKercher and du Cros, 2002: 3).

There are few better places to illustrate the Heritage Production Process Model, especially regarding the packaging (and sometimes re-packaging) of its historical value, than at the Bridge over the River Kwai. This is possibly the most renowned tourist location along the 'Death Railway'. After winning seven

Oscars in 1957, David Lean's Hollywood movie *Bridge on the River Kwai* (based on the 1952 novel by the French novelist Pierre Boulle) opened the 'Death Railway' to a world of mass tourism. Since then, the number of tourists arriving in the province has steadily risen, with occasional fluctuations (e.g. following the 2004 Indian Ocean tsunami). Today there are nearly 600,000 tourists with domestic visitors vastly outnumbering international tourists. For example, in 2012, Kanchanaburi province had 359,622 foreign tourists and 5,636,860 domestic (Tourism Authority of Thailand, 2013).

Few tourists are aware that during the war there never was a Bridge on the River Kwai. In fact, the bridge was built across the River Maeklong (this 145 km river continues through Ratchaburi province before it empties into the Gulf of Thailand). Unfortunately, the truth was not allowed to get in the way of what had turned into a good story. Thailand responded to the tourist interest by changing the name of the River Maeklong into the River Kwai to commodify tourists' curiosity. Moreover, during the war, the Thai government was forced by the Japanese to use the country to transit to Burma and provide some assistance. Thailand was later successful in denying its wartime cooperation with Japan. Despite the fact that the agreement to aid the Japanese Imperial Army against the Allies was signed at the most important temple (the Emerald Buddha Temple: Wat Prakeaw) in the Grand Palace, Bangkok in January 1942, the country's nationalist stance has led the citizens to believe that Thailand played no active role in the war. Thailand's political duplicity during the Second World War, by taking the side of both the Japanese invaders and the Allied Army (by supporting an underground resistance movement called 'Seri Thai'), makes for an interesting if uncomfortable case study (see Reynolds, 2010; Ngamcachonkulkid, 2010; Haseman, 2002; Wiriyawit, 1997).

Tourist commodification by using heritage to 'modify' war stories continues further at several sites. Most stories are sanitised or half truth–half fiction. Much literature about the war has been written by ex-POWs or their relatives and is often retrospective. Admittedly, interpretation of a contested heritage like this could hardly avoid controversy. It involves issues such as the war atrocities committed by Japan (presently Thailand's prime foreign investor) as well as its iconography established by the Allies, overshadowing the facts about the war victims, both the Allied prisoners of war (POWs) and the Asian impressed labourers. The whole concept of the war has become a Disney-like object for individual interpretation.

In a case like this, we are apt to confuse history and heritage, interchanging seamlessly one for another. As Lowenthal (1996) notes, heritage is not history. It uses historical fact but translates fact to sustain and support memory and values. But has the lure of heritage overtaken history as a prime way of recovering the past, as Lowenthal ventures to suggest? Heritage is then what we absorb from the past and part of the growing dependence we have on the past where we may, in fact, falsify history.

Commodification of the physical setting

One of the most successful means in heritage interpretation is to let physical fabrics and settings speak for themselves with the support of explanation. The physical fabric of the Bridge itself is almost intact. Despite bombing during the war, the Bridge was repaired and is now maintained regularly by the State Railway of Thailand. The key difference between the wartime bridge and that of today are the two square steel vaults in the middle of the Bridge which replaced the originals, which were damaged beyond repair during the last Allied raid. What is of concern is the landscape setting of the Bridge, which has been degraded, and in some cases destroyed, and commodified by mass tourism.

The collective memory of a steel bridge across the river, standing in the middle of sub-tropical rainforest scenery has long gone. The whole landscape has changed significantly. The big trees were cut down and the whole area was paved. The most radical impact is the development of tourist infrastructure. New buildings were needed to accommodate the huge volume of tourists. These include concrete shop houses; an uncontrolled number of vendors selling food, drink and souvenirs from stalls in front of the Bridge; a long-tailed boat pier almost under the Bridge built by the Municipality of Kanchanaburi; and next to it, a grand floating restaurant which can accommodate hundreds of diners extending into the river. All these developments have irrevocably altered the landscape setting, destroying the integrity of the Bridge and the train station (the River Kwai Bridge Station). It has altered the visual environment and destroyed the symbolic connections between the place and its setting completely (see Figure 11.1).

The latest development (November 2012) at the site was the completion of a huge Chinese monastery compound opposite the bridge (Figure 11.1). There are three three-storey buildings with different functions and a large garden facing the River Kwai and the Bridge. One building is a shrine for worship, one is used for visitor accommodation and the other is a vegetarian food canteen. In the garden, close to the river bank, stands an 18-metre high statue of the Chinese goddess 'Kwan Yin' overlooking the Bridge. The monastery provides tourists with a sanctuary after visiting the Bridge over the River Kwai. Since the construction of the compound started in May 2009, there has been an ongoing debate about the project, with tensions between supporters and opponents of the development. Those who opposed the development felt that the compound diminished the historical value of the bridge. Legal action was taken and a court order halted construction. The grounds used by the Court Order was that the Urban Laws had been contravened because no Environmental Impact Assessment (EIA) had been undertaken (Governing Court, 2010). Ironically, the Heritage Act was not invoked in the case because the Bridge had not been officially registered as a Thai National Monument by the government department responsible (the Fine Arts Department of the Ministry of Culture). The monastery appealed the Court's decision and referred the complaint to the Local Authority of Thamakam, who initially gave planning permission for the building. The monastery sought compensation for the cost of the building and damages (the

Figure 11.1 The Chinese Monastery has been built on the far bank while a long-tailed
boat pier and a floating restaurant sit next to the Bridge (source: author).

total budget for building the compound was $US 3.5 million). The appeal was
upheld and the monastery compound was completed in 2012. The official
opening took placed on 16 June with an official letter of congratulations from
the Governor of Kanchanaburi to mark the event.

Another contentious issue is the attempt to de-contextualise both the war narrative and heritage with the construction of modern, abstract monuments made
from non-domestic materials. These are distributed around the square where the
Bridge and the train station stand. They have little interpretive function because
few visitors (both Thai and international) read the information panels or have an
interest in the monuments. They are used instead by stall-keepers to store their
goods.

> In cultural heritage preservation, there is a habit when we de-contextualize
> our culture by building theme parks around our historic monuments and we
> treat them as garden ornaments. We also do it with intangible heritage when
> we put on dinner dance shows and treat these expressions of art and ritual as
> some kind of desert for trivial consumption. This de-contextualization of
> our culture is a very serious problem because it destroys the authenticity of
> the cultural expression.
>
> (Taylor, 2007: 8)

There is the traditional view about heritage and museums that are merely one instrument, among many in society, charged with the task of being the channel along which heritage is transmitted from past to present and from present to future. 'Museum collection is not an objective in itself but must be directed towards the transmission of the past to future generations ... cultural transmission is the central function of the museum' (Kuypers and Broekhuis, 1991: 7). This is, of course, included with the heritage.

Cultural context commodification

Following the issue of de-contextualisation, in general, there is a marked difference in the context of the way the heritage place is approached by foreigners and locals. At temples or palaces in Thailand, foreigners wonder around as tourists, but for the Thais, these heritage sites represent national treasures, symbols of national identity or active religious sites more than tourist attractions. It is a difficult issue and likely to be the opposite in case of the war heritage in Kanchanaburi. The Thai people and the locals do not have a strong sense of belonging to these places, while many visitors who are ex-POWs and families or the Allied nation citizens feel this is their heritage. For example, the Australian government and the Australian people have obviously claimed Hellfire Pass *in situ* on the railway (called Konyu Cutting during the war) as their heritage. In 1998, then Prime Minister John Howard presided over the opening ceremony of the Hellfire Pass Memorial Museum, which was built by the Australian government. This museum is under the care of the Australian government's Department of Veteran Affairs. It receives numerous local and international visitors each year – for example, around 60,000 in 2010 (Hellfire Pass Memorial Museum, 2011). Every ANZAC Day (25 April) a group of Australians who live in Thailand or come from abroad gather at Hellfire Pass for an official commemoration of the deaths in a 'Dawn Service'. It is apparent that the heritage significance of the sites along the 'Death Railway' differs according to the perspective of the three parties who share this contested heritage, the victims (the Allied countries and former Asian labourers), the perpetrators (Japan) and the bystanders (Thailand).

The Bridge over the River Kwai is popular with western tourists. The collective memory of the infamous 'Death Railway', and an extensive war-memoir literature coupled with a multi-award winning film, suffices to explain its appeal as a destination. But the marketing of the River Kwai Bridge as a tourist attraction has practically erased the horrendous past associated with the site and transformed it into a place of entertainment. The main governmental department behind the Thai tourism industry is the Tourism Authority of Thailand (TAT). Established in 1960, TAT's promotion of heritage sites for almost three decades has centred on their use as a stage setting for festivals or spectacular events, taking place in many places around the country. Undeniably, this kind of stage setting is interpretation and presentation in its own right. The Bridge over the River Kwai is also a part of these festival promotions. TAT has opted for the jocular: a week-long festival staged at the end of November and around the Bridge. The festival features 'rides on a vintage train' and whose hallmark is a sound-and-light presentation simulating an air attack of the Bridge. One can assume that, among international tourists, those interested in cultural heritage are attracted by the site, per se, and not by the attached fair, which on the other hand possesses limited appeal for recreation-seeking tourists. The situation is different for domestic tourists, who are keener than international tourists in their quest for cultural authenticity, and also are more receptive to sites, celebrations and other events that exploit the royal and religious imagery. The sound-and-light show at the Bridge is a perfect example of the commodification of heritage sites through the use of interpretation. It can be seen to display what Erik Cohen has conceptualised as '*emergent authenticity*', whereby 'a cultural product ... which is at one point generally judged as contrived or inauthentic may, in the course of time, become generally recognized as authentic, even by experts' (Cohen, 1988: 379–80).

There is common practice when culture is promoted for tourism. We tend to make the mistake of promoting simple repetition or replication of cultural forms. The same dance is performed over and over again. A similar thing happens at the Bridge on the River Kwai, the illustrated story of the show is about the origin of the railway, its construction and ending up with the bombing of the Bridge by the Allies. Between 1990–2008, an ill-fated romance between a Japanese soldier and a Thai lady was included. In doing so, there was no cultural transmission or heritage interpretation; only the atrophy of cultural forms into marketable products. The interpretation of these war heritages is seemingly designed to dispel, rather than unfold. Since 2009, the organisers have tried to interpret the heritage in more diverse ways. The show was changed into different forms. A combination of classical and contemporary dancing with a different story (a peace story) was introduced.

While the Bridge is the focus for war atrocity in Kanchanaburi, there are three other powerful mnemonic sites. These are the Commonwealth War Graves Commission (CWGC) War Cemetery of Allied Prisoners of War (Kanchanaburi War Cemetery), with 6,982 graves, the JEATH War Museum (JEATH is an acronym for Japan–England–Australia/America–Thailand–Holland) and the Thailand–Burma Railway Centre (TBRC). The JEATH War Museum was set up and is maintained by the nearby temple (Wat Chaichumphol). The museum was built in a bamboo hut as a replica of those in the prison camps during the railway's construction. POW's photographs are exhibited. However, a number of inaccurate stories are evident and the museum has a clear bias towards the Allies. This is a wider phenomenon. As Lennon and Foley have noticed in Changi prison in Singapore:

> the small chapel at Changi Gaol contains many vitriolic messages from visitors aimed at Japan in general and which indicate an absence of any healing or chronological distancing having taken place. Similar strong emotion is observable at the 'Bridge over the River Kwai' ...
>
> (Lennon and Foley, 2000: 108)

It should be noted here that the authors might be referring to the JEATH War Museum to have such an impression because there is no sign of anti-Japanese sentiment in interpretation available on site at the Bridge. A biased perspective in interpreting the war story combines with poor presentation, to make a visit to this museum an unsettling experience. Next to the main museum building, which is a bamboo structure, there is a small concrete building showing various weapons. The way it is exhibited and its setting make people believe that these artefacts are from the Second World War. In reality, these exhibits relate to other wars in the region, such as the Vietnam War or wars in Cambodia or Laos. Other poorly managed examples of tourist commodification, such as shops and stalls, have also overwhelmed the place.

At the Kanchanaburi War Cemetery, the landscape setting and visual effect have been degraded by extensive property development. As a location that is visited by foreigners, there are now numerous box-like concrete buildings built around the cemetery to serve as tourist amenity shops. There is no tranquil space between the living and the dead. The lack of tranquillity is a major problem at such a site.[1] However, there is less construction around the cemetery compared to other parts of the inner town. This may be partly because of the deeply rooted belief in Thai culture that houses should not be built close to a cemetery and as a mark of respect for the dead. Many of the western visitors were of a generation which had either fought in this war or had lost friends and relatives in it. Thus, remembrance and the visitation of death sites for this purpose are factors in the desire of the local authority and the Thai government to ensure that the Kanchanaburi War Cemetery is well tended.

The Thailand–Burma Railway Centre (TBRC) is located next to the Kanchanaburi War Cemetery. It is a private museum which is owned and run by Rod Beattie, an Australian who for two decades has dedicated his life to the survey and research of the 'Death Railway'. This museum was opened in 2003 and initially faced financial difficulty until tourist numbers increased.[2] The two-storey building provides a panoramic view from its upper floor overlooking the cemetery, and offers in-depth interpretation about the Second World War in Kanchanaburi and the surrounding region. Operated by a professional team using sophisticated presentation techniques, the museum is able to interpret the story of the war in an accessible manner.

Another site on the 'Death Railway' is the Hellfire Pass Memorial Museum, 75 kilometres north-west of Kanchanaburi in the Tenasserim Hills. Located in a remote area, Hellfire Pass was the largest cutting on the railway and was a particularly difficult section of the line to build. POWs and labourers worked around the clock in 16–18-hour shifts to excavate the 17m deep and 110m long cutting through solid rock in only 12 weeks. Forced to work at night, the combination of construction noise, the eerie illumination from fires, torches and carbide lamps, and emaciated workers created a vision of the 'Fires from Hell', from which the nickname 'Hellfire Pass' arose.

The museum is co-sponsored by the Royal Thai Armed Forces Development Command in conjunction with the Australian government. It was constructed and run by the Office of Australian War Graves (OAWG).

The museum is located on the highway to the Thailand's border to Burma, with numerous tourist attractions on the route. Tourists often stop over to have a look at the modern museum with its high standard of presentation and take a walk following the trail to see the cutting. Unfortunately, this museum has been problematic for both Thai and Australian governments. It is situated in a Thai military area where the National Security Policy is being enforced. Careful management of the museum under the military's custody is a necessity after some incidents between the Thai military on site and the museum team in 2005–2006. These revolved around a misunderstanding between the Thai military and the museum management. For instance, visitors were required to register at the military check-point at the entrance gate before entering the museum. This was not agreed by the museum at the beginning but later accepted (Australian–Thai Chamber of Commerce, 2004). More rules were introduced by the military, preventing visitors to go off the marked trail. Beside these issues, the museum has been accused of a biased interpretation of the war because it is dedicated primarily to the Australian POWs and has less of a focus on the other POWs and labourers who also died at the spot during the construction of the railway cutting. This has been an issue for debate since the museum was opened.

Lastly, a ride on a vintage train is highly recommended by most travel agencies. It is one of the best ways to understand the rail line, its construction, topography, and provides a hint at the magnitude of the task undertaken by the POWs. Contextual commodification of the war story is minimised. More tourist trains are added during the weekend or can be specially scheduled. This train service is not only for the benefit of tourists, it provides public transport for the locals. The juxtaposition between the locals using the railway to commute and the tourists experiencing the so-called 'Death Railway' makes for an interesting contrast between function and heritage.

Conclusions

Atrocity heritage that is located in a neutral country, like the 'Death Railway' in Thailand, can face some difficulties in its management. By its very nature, war heritage contains dissonance and complexity, and it is never easy to interpret such a contested heritage where there are multiple user perspectives and multiple meanings. Furthermore, this war site involves not only the three main parties, the victims (former Allied countries/former Asian labourers' countries), the perpetrators (Japan) and the bystanders (Thailand), but also another party with a dual-role. Too many parties involved, lack of knowledge in heritage management and interpretation and not enough interest and effort from the bystanders combine to prevent development of the site in a more professional way. Major economic interest has meant that Thailand has turned the heritage into a tourism product and obviously in the process has harmed its significance and values.

For preservation strategies, western standards of heritage management may or may not be relevant when confronted with different contexts. The respect due to all cultures requires that heritage properties must be considered and judged within the cultural contexts to which they belong. This applies equally to the case of the atrocity heritage of the 'Death Railway'. To be successful, a management and interpretation plan cannot depend on western technology or high-tech solutions. It must integrate the place's stakeholders, which are those four main groups of owner (the victims, the perpetrators, the bystanders and the dual-role group), to other stakeholders, such as international tourists; it must be acceptable to the local community; and it must be able to be implemented within the local political, social and technical environment.

Notes

1 Interview with Rod Beattie, Manager of Kanchanaburi War Cemetery, in May 2010.
2 Interview with Rod Beattie in May 2009.

References

Australian–Thai Chamber of Commerce (2004) *Hellfire Pass Memorial*, Bangkok: Australian-Thai Chamber of Commerce.
Cohen, E. (1988) 'Authenticity and commoditization in tourism', *Annals of Tourism Research*, 15: 371–86.
Governing Court (2010) *Governing Court Statement*, Bangkok: Governing Court.
Haseman, J. B. (2002) *The Thai resistance movement during World War II*, Bangkok: Silkworm Books.
Hellfire Pass Memorial Museum (2011) *Hellfire Pass Memorial Museum Annual Report 2010*, Kanchanaburi: Hellfire Pass Memorial Museum.
Hewison, R. (1987) *The heritage industry*, London: Methuen.
Hewison, R. (1989) 'Heritage: An interpretation', in Uzzel, D. (ed.) *Heritage interpretation*, Vol. 1, London: Belhaven Press.
Kuypers, P. and Broekhuis, C. (1991) *Treasury of the future: On museums and cultural preservation*, Amsterdam: De Balie.
Lennon, J. and Foley, M. (2000) *Dark tourism*, London: Continuum.
Lowenthal, D. (1996) *The past is a foreign country*, Cambridge: Cambridge University Press.
McKercher, B. and du Cros, H. (2002) *Cultural tourism: The partnership between tourism and cultural heritage management*, New York: The Haworth Hospitality Press.
Ngamcachonkulkid, S. (2010) *Free Thai: The new history of the Seri Thai movement*, Bangkok: Chulalongkorn University Press.
Reynolds, B. E. (2010) *Thailand's secret war: OSS, SOE and the Free Thai Underground during World War II*, London: Cambridge University Press.
Taylor, K. (2007) *Cultural landscape*, Sydney: Australia National University Press.
Tourism Authority of Thailand (2013) *Tourism statistics, Kanchanaburi Province 2007*, accessed 21 March, 2013 at http://www2.tat.or.th/stat/web/static_tst.php.
Tunbridge, J. E. and Ashworth, G. J. (1996) *Dissonant heritage: The management of the past as a resource in conflict*, New York: John Wiley and Sons.
Walsh, J. (1992) *The representation of the past*, London: Routledge.
Wiriyawit, W. (1997) *Free Thai: Personal recollection and official document*, Bangkok: White Lotus.

12 Decorated Palaeolithic cave sites as a tourism resource

The Franco-Cantabrian perspective

Jaime Kaminski

Introduction

Palaeolithic[1] cave paintings represent some of the earliest examples of human art, but presenting cave paintings and cave art to the public is becoming increasingly problematic. Escalating visitor numbers at many sites are having a detrimental effect on the cave art. This in turn is leading to some sites closing to the public or limiting visitor numbers to prevent further degradation of the art. This chapter looks at the options available that allow the public to appreciate decorated caves, and considers the role that virtual solutions can play.

The first evidence for Palaeolithic cave art in Europe was discovered in Spain in 1880 at the cave of Altamira, 30 km west of Santander. The Polychrome Ceiling in the 'Great Hall', depicting a herd of bison (*Bison priscus*), horses, a doe, and possibly a wild boar is still to this day one of the wonders of prehistoric art. But at the time, the discovery by the local landowner Don Marcelino Santiago Tomás Sanz de Sautuola (1831–1888) was not widely accepted by the antiquarian community because nothing similar had been found before and de Sautuola was not a part of academic or antiquarian circles (Bahn, 1992; Sautuola, 1880). Many simply refused to believe that early humans had the intellectual capacity for such vivid artistic expression. It would be over a decade before another decorated cave was discovered at La Mouthe in the Dordogne in 1895. It was only with subsequent discoveries of decorated caves containing Palaeolithic tools at Les Combarelles in 1901 and the Font de Gaume in 1902 that the great antiquity of cave art was finally accepted (Bahn and Vertut, 1997: 18).[2]

For the next six decades of the twentieth century, research on Palaeolithic art was driven by the abbé Henri Breuil (1877–1961), a French priest who would have a huge influence on Palaeolithic studies (Breuil, 1952). After Breuil, scholars such as André Leroi-Gourhan (Leroi-Gourhan, 1971) and Jean Clottes rose to prominence as the key drivers of Palaeolithic cave art research. During this period, numerous decorated caves were discovered across Europe, with the greatest concentrations on the Cantabrian coast of northern Spain and the southwest of France.

In the first half of the twentieth century, little thought was given to decorated caves as visitor attractions. Mass tourism was yet to develop and many caves were opened to visitors on an ad hoc basis. Prior to the work of the abbé Breuil, there was little public awareness of cave art and so consequently visitors were mainly members of the antiquarian and archaeological community, or those simply interested in the natural wonders of caves. Moreover, many caves were on private land and so were often inaccessible to the general public.

After the Second World War, travel became easier and there was greater awareness of prehistoric cave paintings as a cultural phenomenon amongst the general public, and consequently more caves opened to the public. The most famous are the richly decorated galleries at Lascaux, which opened in 1948.

Today across Europe, there are about 300 known decorated caves, although not all are open to the public and some have only one or two painted figures (e.g. Bouvier, 1993, records 291 sites). Moreover, cave art is continually being discovered, although in the twenty-first century far fewer new discoveries are opened to the public as a matter of course.

European cave art has an important role to play as a heritage tourism resource because of a number of factors, including:

- **Geography**: Although Palaeolithic cave art is found globally, the most famous corpus of sites is found in Western Europe in the Iberian Peninsula and France. These sites are easily accessible to tourists. In contrast, there are many more palaeoart sites across Australia and India (mostly rock art rather than cave art) but these are generally widely distributed and less accessible to mass tourism.
- **Interpretation**: The long period of study of Pleistocene art in Europe has created a huge corpus of interpretative material. This both adds value to the visitor experience and has generated awareness of cave art amongst the general public.
- **World Heritage status**: Numerous decorated cave sites have achieved World Heritage status, such as the 'Prehistoric Sites and Decorated Caves of the Vézère Valley', which has 25 decorated caves, including Lascaux, and the 'Cave of Altamira and Palaeolithic Cave Art of Northern Spain', which includes 17 decorated caves.
- **Antiquity**: Recent research has highlighted the great antiquity of cave art. An Aurignacian date[3] of around 32,000 BP has been recorded for ceiling imagery from the collapsed rock shelter at Abri Castanet, in the Dordogne, France (White *et al.*, 2012), while U-series dates from 11 Palaeolithic caves in Spain also demonstrate that cave decoration extends back to at least the Early Aurignacian period. A red disk from the walls of El Castillo Cave was dated to a minimum of 40,800 BP. This led the researchers to note that cave art was certainly a part of the cultural repertoire of the first anatomically modern humans in Europe, but potentially Neanderthals could have engaged in cave painting (Pike *et al.*, 2012). Cave sites are one of the few cultural heritage sites open to the public that are of this great antiquity.

The dilemma of access and preservation

The cave art (sometimes referred to as parietal decoration) has frequently been preserved because of its location. Often deep inside cave systems, the environment is relatively constant. There is no possibility of weathering from wind or rain, there is little variation in temperature (usually cave temperatures stay around 11–13 degrees centigrade), humidity is constant and it is unlikely that abrasion caused by the movement of people or animals will be an issue.[4] Naturally there are issues specific to cave systems, such as flooding, water seepage, rock falls and calcite formation, that can degrade or destroy cave art. But more recently the opening of some cave sites to visitors has disturbed their fragile ecological balance.

Increased opportunities for tourism in the last half century has seen interest in, and visitor numbers to, decorated caves increase markedly. It is precisely this increase in visitor numbers in some decorated caves that has led to the deterioration of some cave art. The most famous example is of the caves at Lascaux, located near the village of Montignac, in the Dordogne, France. The cave decoration was only discovered in September 1940 by four teenagers (Marcel Ravidat, Jacques Marsal, Georges Agnel and Simon Coencas) and their dog, Robot (Bahn, 2007: 81–5). Lascaux was opened to the public in 1948 and immediately attracted huge numbers of visitors, who came to see the spectacular cave paintings. These included nearly 2,000 individual figures, which comprised animals, human figures and abstract signs. On some days, visitor numbers could exceed 1,200 and this rapidly began to affect the environment of the cave. The simple act of breathing by large numbers of visitors increased levels of carbon dioxide and water vapour. The introduction of lighting raised temperatures and so modified the micro-climate, while changes in air circulation patterns caused further problems.

As early as the late 1950s, lichens and crystals were beginning to appear on the cave walls. This became serious enough that, in 1963, just 15 years after they were opened to the public, the caves were closed. Visitor numbers were limited while a replica of the decorated caves was constructed. In 2001, the air conditioning system was changed, which rapidly caused an infestation of a white mould (*Fusarium solani*), which may have been exposed by the tradesmen who installed the air conditioning (Dupont *et al.*, 2007). This particular mould was treated with quicklime, but in 2007 a new, more damaging fungus caused grey and black blemishes to degrade the decorations. This has proved far more difficult to eradicate. An International Scientific Committee for Lascaux has been established to assess how to deal with the infestations and is studying how much access should be permitted in caves containing prehistoric art (Coye, 2011).

Clearly the vulnerability of decorated caves to these phenomena is dependent on the specific attributes of each individual cave. Some caves are less susceptible to the degradation of their art than others. For example, Rouffignac, a privately owned cave 25 km west of Lascaux, is less liable to micro-climate modifications because of its huge size (there are 8 km of tunnels). Moreover, visitor management policy and infrastructure at the site further reduce risks; an electric train transports visitors through the tunnel so visitors do not walk in the cave, reducing the potential for abrasion and other damage, and there is no fixed illumination to increase the temperature. Visits are limited to 550 people per day.

Presenting decorated caves to the public

It is evident that management of the caves is crucial to their sustainability (Ashworth, 2009). Currently there are a number of options available for presenting decorated cave sites to the public. These are:

- **Open access**: Access to some cave sites is unrestricted to visitors. Some caves have only one or two examples of cave art or may be difficult to access (e.g. to cavers only). These sites would not provide an economic return as visitor attractions (e.g. La Chaire à Calvin, France).
- **Controlled access**: Public access is only limited by opening hours, entrance fees, and/or physical capacity but within those boundaries there is no restriction on the number of people who can visit. This is currently the most common type of access (e.g. the Font de Gaume, France).
- **Controlled and restricted access**: Another possibility is that the number of visitors is restricted to a specific number of individuals per day in order to lessen the potential environmental impact (e.g. the iconic decorated cave at Pech-Merle, France restricts visitor numbers to 700 per day, El Castillo, Spain limits numbers to 380 per day, while Gargas limits numbers to 250 per day).
- **Partial closure**: In some cases, sensitive galleries within cave systems may be closed off to the general public, while the remainder of the cave remains open or accessible.
- **Closure**: The cave is closed to visitors entirely and access is limited to scientists and those monitoring the cave. This closure can take place after problems are observed or in some cases caves have never be open to tourists (e.g. privately owned caves like Tuc d'Audoubert and Trois Freres).
- **Reconstruction**: In other cases, a physical (e.g. Lascaux and Altamira) or virtual replica (e.g. Santamamiñe and Lascaux) of the cave art has been created for tourists to experience instead of the actual cave.

Physical replicas

Today when prehistoric caves are discovered, they themselves are unlikely to become tourist attractions. For example, the Chauvet Cave was discovered in December 1994 in the Ardèche valley of south-east France by the cavers Jean-Marie Chauvet (after whom the cave is named), Christian Hillaire and Eliette Brunel Deschamps (Chauvet *et al.*, 1996). At the time it was the oldest securely dated Palaeolithic cave art site dating from about 32,000 years BP (Clottes *et al.*,

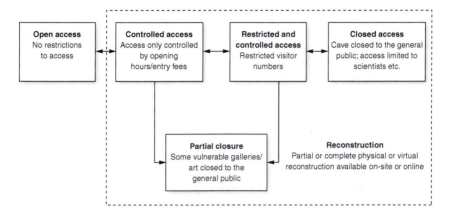

Figure 12.1 Options available to access decorated cave sites.

1995). It was also one of the most densely decorated caves known, with over 400 painted or engraved animals, including mammoth, rhinoceros, bison, lion, bear, and horse (Clottes, 2003). Soon after the discovery, the cave was closed to the general public to protect the paintings. An exact replica of the Chauvet Cave is currently being constructed 2 km away from the original site and is due to open in 2014. It is estimated that it will attract about 350,000 visitors each year.

Chauvet Cave is not alone. The most famous decorated Palaeolithic cave sites in Spain (Altamira) and France (Lascaux) have been closed to visitors and physical replicas constructed in their place. Physical replicas have a number of advantages. They can create a highly realistic representation of the cave environment that is well lit, with none of the negative issues associated with poor accessibility or degradation of the art.

For example, Bahn (2007: 141–2) notes that the facsimile of Altamira is 'in many ways better than the original'. The replica of the decorated chamber has been placed in a position relative to the cave's entrance and daylight that is no longer possible to see in the original cave. It is also possible to see the whole ceiling, unlike the original where the floor has only been lowered in some areas. The facsimile does not have the unattractive concrete pillars that were installed in the original cave to prevent the roof from collapsing, and the engravings on the original ceiling are not as visible as those on the facsimile because of enhanced lighting and less degraded paint. Overall the facsimile provides a better visual experience; 'the only things missing are the odour of the cave and the emotion of knowing that one is seeing an original' (Bahn, 2007: 141). However, despite their benefits, physical replicas have certain disadvantages. These include:

• **Cost**: Creating a physical replica can be expensive. Clearly it is possible to limit physical reproductions to certain panels of cave art which can then be displayed in museums (e.g. examples in the Parc de la Prehistoire, near Toulouse, or the Musée National de Prehistoire, near Les Eyzies). However, major replicas of entire chambers like those at Lascaux II, Altamira II or the Chauvet Cave are hugely expensive. The facsimile at Lascaux II, which opened in 1983, required 11 years of work by 20 sculptors and artists, who used the same materials and methods as the original cave painters. The museum and the reconstruction of the cave cost over 500 million francs.

- **Context**: Some cave systems are quite substantial. Cave art can be limited to specific chambers or areas of the cave. Physical reconstructions are usually limited to the areas of cave art (such as the polychrome ceiling at Altamira) and cannot realistically be expected to recreate anything more than a small part of the cave system and so consequently the context is lost.
- **Fixed location**: Although small-scale facsimiles of panels are potentially movable, the large-scale facsimiles are static.

Virtual representations

Caves and the associated cave art can also be represented virtually. Virtual representations do not need to be highly sophisticated. At the Ekain Cave in the Basque Country, Spain, a 'virtual reconstruction' has been made using simple 360 degree panoramas. Clearly this is a cost-effective mechanism for cave sites to increase accessibility and generate awareness of the site. As a way of facilitating access while the replica of the Chauvet Cave was being built, the filmmaker Werner Herzog made a 3D documentary about the caves called the 'Cave of Forgotten Dreams'. However, virtual reconstruction has the potential to go much further. 3D scanning allows either decorated chambers or the entire cave to be visualized.

Potential benefits of virtual reconstructions

Virtual reconstructions have the potential to mitigate some of the issues associated with the interpretation and presentation of decorated cave sites, thereby adding value to the presentation. Such issues include the following.

Better interpretation

Many examples of cave art are in poor condition. Colours have degraded or calcite formations obscure the details. Digitization can potentially add information (enhance colours) that allows for better interpretation of the art.

Moreover, digital interpretation methods can simulate the cave environment in a way that is far closer to that experienced to early humans. Today, visitors to decorated caves view cave paintings under electric light or by battery operated torchlight. This may provide the optimal lighting conditions but it is not how early humans would have seen the art. Their light would have been fires, burning torches or lamps. This flickering light that illuminated small portions of the cave wall would provide a completely different experience to electric light. In fact, the flickering light in conjunction with the 3D rock surface could have appeared to animate the painted figures on the cave walls (Chalmers *et al.*, 2000).

Presenting multi-period art

Dating cave art has proved extremely difficult. Until recently, most cave art was dated on stylistic grounds, although the assumptions behind this have been questioned in recent years. It is now understood that in many cases what appears to be the most sophisticated art is often some of the earliest (Bednarik, 1995).

Modern scientific techniques have been brought to bear on the subject, although such dating is itself not without its controversies. For example, radiocarbon dating using accelerator mass spectroscopy has allowed minute traces of charcoal used for pigments on the art to be dated. However, this dates the charcoal only. Charcoal was often left by prehistoric artists in caves and so could have been used by generation after generation of artists. Moreover, only small samples can be dated to minimize damage to the art, and this then amplifies the potential effects of contamination and can lead to less accurate results (Bednarik, 2002).

Today the most widely used technique is uranium-series disequilibrium dating, which measures the uranium isotopes in the thin calcite flowstone growths that form on the surfaces of some paintings and engravings (Pike *et al.*, 2012). This technique avoids the problems related to radiocarbon dating.

These more advanced dating techniques have begun to reveal that some parietal art is a palimpsest. Rather than being created in one session, figures in some scenes have been painted over a far longer period than previously thought. Some examples of cave art appear to have been produced over thousands of years, with scenes modified and repainted over many generations. The polychrome ceiling at Altamira was updated over a period of 20,000 years (Pettitt and Pike, 2007). Scenes are difficult to identify because, until more scientific dating takes place, it is not possible to prove that figures are associated rather than just being in proximity to each other.

This clearly has implications for how cave painting and rock art are presented to the public. What appears to be a single scene may often be a palimpsest that has been produced over thousands of years. Digital visualizations are one mechanism that could allow the development of such scenes to be presented. Such visualizations would be better able to convey the uncertainty of interpretation compared to physical means.

2D and 3D presentation

While photography is an important mechanism for capturing and presenting cave art, it creates a 2D representation (Ruspoli, 1987). Cave walls are anything but a flat canvas. Moreover, in some cases, the physical shape of the cave wall appears to be an integral component of cave art. It is becoming apparent that the decoration found in caves is often far from randomly placed. For example, research by Gonzalez Garcia at the Cantabrian caves of Castillo, La Pasiega, Las Chimeneas, and Las Mondeas found a relationship between the types of figures represented and the 3D shape of the cave wall beneath. The analysis found that 88.8 per cent of horses, 93.1 per cent of hinds, 87.7 per cent of caprines, 100 per cent of stags and hand stencils occurred on concave surfaces. Conversely 78.7 per cent of bison and 82.8 per cent of cattle occurred on convex surfaces (Gonzalez Garcia, 1987). Other relationships between space and art have also been found in caves. While extrapolating these findings to the entirety of the Palaeolithic would be problematic, there do appear to be other instances of the concave and convex surfaces being used selectively.

Moreover, some cave surfaces have been deliberately modified to receive the art. For example, in the French Pyrenees, a specific style of cave art involved using clay to modify surfaces or create sculpture on the cave floor, such as the two bison made of clay in the cave of Le Tuc d'Audoubert and the headless bear in the cave of Montespan.

It is evident that Palaeolithic cave art was part of a three-dimensional realm. The location within the cave, shape of the cave wall, the stalactites and acoustics of the cave may have had significance for various cultural groups over time. Recording and presenting it in 3D is far more appropriate than in 2D. Moreover, many examples of cave painting and especially rock art (e.g. the Coa Valley, Portugal) are created by scratching the rock surface (sgraffiti). 3D is one mechanism for recording these art forms and the 3D structure of the rock.

Accessibility

Accessibility is another issue where both physical and virtual replicas can aid visitors. Caves are very difficult environments to make accessible. Many are unsurprisingly located in mountainous terrain. Car parks and visitor centres are often located some distance from the caves themselves. In many cases, this distance is over difficult terrain, often uphill. Even if the cave can be easily reached, it is unlikely that the interior would be accessible to wheelchairs. Narrow passages, stairs, and inclines are just some of the difficulties encountered. Moreover, some cave art is located deep in cave systems. Therefore, caves are generally inaccessible to the disabled and those with mobility issues.

Two sites where disabilities are accommodated, at least in a limited manner, are the Font de Gaume and Les Combarelles, which provide special tours for the blind. During these, the visitors are given texts, plans, and reproductions of the main figures in Braille and statuettes of the principal animal species to feel. They can touch the rock surface outside the caves and are taken inside the entrances to feel the temperature and humidity. The sounds of echoes are used to estimate the volume of the caves (Bahn, 2007: 10).

From an accessibility perspective, the virtual reconstructions can be made available online (e.g. Lascaux) or as part of the on-site experience (e.g. Santamamiñe).

Economics

Clearly, decorated caves are a cultural entity but they can also be important economically. The dilemma between access and preservation also has economic implications. Closing a decorated cave can have an economic impact on a local area. The cave could be the principal reason for visitors to come or it could be part of the wider touristic offering of the area.

In many cases, it is simply not cost effective to create a physical replica of a decorated cave, but an on-site or online virtual experience may be feasible. The cave of Santimamiñe is located 150 m above sea level at the foot of Mount Ereñozar, overlooking the Urdaibai estuary, 4 km north-east of Guernica in Spain's Basque Country. It is close to the Hermitage of San Mamés, from which the cave gets its name. It was discovered by chance in 1916, when local children searching for stalactites in the cave discovered a chamber with cave paintings. The cave includes a nearly complete archaeological sequence from the Aurignacian to the Iron Age. However, it is best known for its charcoal mural paintings of the Magdalenian period, over 13,000 years ago, depicting bison, horse, goat and deer. Unfortunately, the deterioration of the art caused by 90 years of visitation led to the closure of the cave in 2007. A 3D laser scan of the entire cave was used as the foundation for a virtual presentation of the site. The 3D experience was housed in an unused chapel. Within two years of the virtual experience being opened, 11,500 visitors were coming to the site per annum, which was as many as when the original cave was open.

The content from virtual replicas can be created anywhere and is not just limited to the physical environment of the cave. This has advantages in their use as an educational resource, or even as part of a mobile tour. This then has the potential to act as a mechanism for revenue generation.

Conclusions

Over a century of access to decorated caves has left a legacy of damaged and degraded art, as well as a greater understanding of the need to protect these fragile and finite resources. While closing cave sites to visitors or restricting visitor numbers is a commonly adopted mechanism to mitigate these issues, it does reduce accessibility. This conflicts with the widely accepted goal of increasing access to culture and heritage as a 'public good'.

There is no substitute for seeing some of the earliest artistic achievements of humankind in their original settings, which are often in regions of outstanding natural beauty. Moreover, the context of the cave, including its sounds, smells, humidity, and temperature, contribute to the authenticity of the experience and provide a direct and tangible link to the environment of the early humans who produced the cave art. But allowing unrestricted public access to decorated cave sites is becoming increasingly problematic because it can lead to degradation of the art. Caves are highly sensitive environments and it can only be expected that over time potential tourist numbers are likely to increase because of better transport links and increased awareness. Decorated Ice Age caves are a finite resource. They have a huge role in understanding not only how art developed, but also what it is to be human.

Physical replicas are used with great success but they are a high-cost solution, in reality limited to those sites with the highest footfall. Virtual surrogates are one way forward that allows a flexible approach to public presentation. Palaeolithic art is more than simple two-dimensional art; 3D shape is clearly important. The rock face is the canvas. In some cases, the 3D form of the rock face is used to provide a structure for the images. Many painted scenes are palimpsests that are visually complex to interpret.

Recording caves by 3D scanning is an important way of capturing the 3D context, which can have additional implications for conservation. A scenario could be envisaged where a 3D visualization of a prehistoric cave is played in an auditorium, the temperature in the auditorium could be air conditioned to the average temperature of the caves being represented, a simulated flickering light could be used to illuminate the art, while the appropriate smell of the damp cave environment could be released (complemented by the smell of smoke to emphasize how the art would have been illuminated), and a background soundtrack to simulate the echo of the cave sounds could be played if appropriate. Such a multisensory experience could bring visitors closer to the cave environment of our earliest ancestors.

Virtual or physical reconstructions will never replace the experience of viewing images produced by prehistoric peoples tens of thousands of years ago, but this has to be balanced with protection of the art itself. Virtual decorated caves can be enjoyed in a sustainable and responsible way.

Acknowledgements

This research has been made possible by V-MUST (the Virtual Museum Transnational Network). V-MUST is funded by the European Commission under the Community's Seventh Framework Programme, contract no. GA 270404.

Notes

1 The Palaeolithic extends from the earliest known use of stone tools by hominins, to the end of the last glaciation around 10,000 BP. Cave art was produced in the Upper Palaeolithic along with other artistic expressions, such as Venus figurines, animal carvings, and rock paintings.
2 These discoveries led to the publication of one of archaeology's most famous retractions when Emile Cartailhac penned the article 'Mea culpa d'un sceptique', which was published in *L'Anthropologie* in 1902. Sadly, Sautuola had died 14 years earlier and so never benefited from the restoration of his character.
3 The Aurignacian Culture existed between ca. 45,000 to 35,000 years ago, and derives its name from the type site of Aurignac in France's Haute-Garonne area. The imagery at Abri Castanet was dated to 32,400 BP.
4 This differs from 'rock art' sites, which are exposed to the elements and so vulnerable to degradation (Giesen *et al.*, 2013).

References

Ashworth, G. J. (2009) 'Do tourists destroy the heritage they have come to experience?', *Tourism Recreation Research*, 34(1): 79–83.

Bahn, P. G. (1992) 'Expecting the Spanish Inquisition: Altamira's rejection in its 19th century context', in A. S. Goldsmith, S. Garvie, D. Selin, and J. Smith. (eds.) *Ancient images, ancient thought: The archaeology of ideology*, Calgary: Archaeological Association, University of Calgary: 339–46.

Bahn, P. G. (2007) *Cave art: A guide to the decorated Ice Age caves of Europe*, London: Frances Lincoln.

Bahn, P. G. and Vertut, J. (1997) *Journey through the Ice Age*, London: Weidenfeld & Nicolson.

Bednarik, R. G. (1995) 'Refutation of stylistic constructs in Palaeolithic rock art', *Comptes Rendus de L'Académie de Sciences Paris*, 321(série IIa, No. 9): 817–21.

Bednarik, R. G. (2002) 'The dating of rock art: A critique', *Journal of Archaeological Science*, 29: 1213–33.

Bouvier, J.-M. (1993) 'Généralités', in GRAPP (ed.) *L'Art pariétal paléolithique: techniques et méthodes d'étude*, Paris: Ministère de L'Enseignement Supérieur et de la Recherche: 7–19.

Breuil, H. (1952) *Four hundred centuries of cave art*, Montignac: Centre d'Études et de Documentation Préhistoriques.

Chalmers A., Green C., and Hall M. (2000) 'Firelight: Graphics and archaeology', Electronic Theatre, SIGGRAPH 2000, New Orleans, July 2000. *Electronic Art and Animation Catalogue*: 115, New York: ACM.

Chauvet, J-M., Deschamps, E. B., and Hillaire, C. (1996) *Dawn of art: The Chauvet Cave*, New York: Harry N. Abrams.

Clottes, J. (2003) *Return to Chauvet Cave, excavating the birthplace of art: The first full report*, London: Thames & Hudson.

Clottes, J., Chauvet, J.-M., Brunel-Deschamps, E., Hillaire, C., Daugas, J.-P., Arnold, M., Cachier, H., Evin, J., Fortin, P., Oberlin, C., Tisnerat, N., and Valladas, H. (1995) 'Les peintures paléolithiques de la Grotte Chauvet-Pont d'Arc, à Vallon-Pont-d'Arc (Ardèche, France): Datations directes et indirectes par la méthode du radiocarbone', *Comptes Rendus de l'Académie des Sciences Paris*, 320: 1133–40.

Coye, N. (ed.) (2011) *Lascaux and preservation issues in subterranean environments: Proceedings of the international symposium (Paris, February 26 and 27)*, Paris: Éditions de la Maison des sciences de l'homme.

Dupont, J., Jacquet, C., Dennetière, B., and Lacoste, S. (2007) 'Invasion of the French Paleolithic painted cave of Lascaux by members of the Fusarium solani species complex', *Mycologia*, 99(4): 526–33.

Giesen, M. J., Ung, A., Warke, P. A., Christgen, B., Mazel, A. D., and Graham, D. W. (2013) 'Condition assessment and preservation of open-air rock art panels during environmental change', *Journal of Cultural Heritage*. Available online: doi: 10.1016/j.culher.2013.01.013 (accessed March 17, 2013).

Gonzalez Garcia, R. (1987) 'Organisation, distribution and typology of the cave art of Monte del Catillo, Spain', *Rock Art Research*, 4: 127–36.

Leroi-Gourhan, A. (1971) *Prehistoire de l'art occidental*, Paris: Mazenod.

Pettitt, P. B. and Pike, A. W. G. (2007) 'Dating European Palaeolithic rock art: Progress, prospects, problems', *Journal of Archaeological Method and Theory*, 14(1): 27–47.

Pike, A. W. G., Hoffmann, D. L., García-Diez, M., Pettitt, P. B., Alcolea, J., De Balbín,

R., González-Sainz, C., de las Heras, C., Lasheras, J. A., Montes, R., and Zilhão, J. (2012) 'U-Series dating of Paleolithic art in 11 caves in Spain', *Science*, 336, June 15: 1409–13.

Ruspoli, M. (1987) *The cave of Lascaux: The final photographic record*, London: Thames and Hudson.

Sautuola, M. S. de (1880) *Breves apuntes sobre algunos objetos prehistóricos de la* provincia de Santander, Santander: Telesforo Martinez.

White, R., Mensan, R., Bourrillon, R., Cretin, C., Higham, T. F. G., Clark, A. E., Sisk, M. L., Tartar, E., Gardère, P., Goldberg, P., Pelegrin, J., Valladas, H., Tisnérat-Laborde, N., de Sanoit, J., Chambellan, D., and Chiotti, L. (2012) 'Context and dating of Aurignacian vulvar representations from Abri Castanet, France', *Proceedings of the National Academy of Sciences*, May 29, 109(22): 8450–5.

Part 3
Economics and impact

13 Seasonal tourism flows in UNESCO sites

The case of Sicily

Tiziana Cuccia and Ilde Rizzo

Introduction

It is commonly acknowledged that tourism can play a strategic role in fostering local development and, from this perspective, increasing attention is being paid by policy-makers to the specific sector of cultural tourism. Even if the definition of cultural tourism is rather elusive – and, therefore, the related data are not always reliable – it is widely stressed that this segment of tourism, based on the tangible and intangible cultural endowment of a destination, shows an overall positive trend, almost everywhere. Among the claimed beneficial effects of cultural tourism, it is common opinion that it can contribute to reduce one of the main problems of tourism, i.e. its seasonality, with the related effects on sustainability. In this chapter, we investigate how seasonality is affected by the different features of cultural tourism supply and demand, using Sicily as a case study. First, we review the main issues related to cultural tourism definition and measurement, focusing attention on the relationship between cultural heritage tourism and cultural destinations listed in the World Heritage List. Second, using Sicily as a case study, we try to assess whether an outstanding cultural endowment, officially recognized and preserved by UNESCO, affects cultural tourism and makes a difference as far as seasonality is concerned. We also investigate different segments of cultural tourism demand, distinguishing between domestic and foreign tourists, to see whether they exhibit different behaviours as far as seasonality is concerned. Finally, we explore how the decision-making process, involving different public and private actors and different layers of government, can be designed to enhance the positive role of cultural tourism and to reduce seasonality.

The chapter is organized as follows: in the second section, a brief review of some economic issues of cultural tourism is offered. The third section presents the main features of the case study. In the fourth section, the empirical analysis is carried out and the major results are presented. Some policy implications are investigated in the fifth section and concluding remarks are offered in the final section.

Cultural tourism: definition and measurement issues

Cultural tourism definition

Cultural tourism is increasingly recognized as an important economic phenomenon. Different approaches to define cultural tourism have been developed by international organizations as well as in the literature. Nowadays the prevalent idea is that cultural tourism 'should not be regarded as a definable niche within the broad range of tourism activities, but encompasses all experiences absorbed by the visitor to a place that is beyond their own living environment' (ICOMOS, 2002).[1]

At the same time, in parallel to the enlargement of the concept of culture which has been witnessed in industrialized countries in recent decades (Towse, 2011), it is widely agreed that cultural heritage tourism demand is not confined to 'sites and monuments' but has a wider scope, ranging from cultural events, architecture and design to creative activities and intangible heritage, just to mention some of the most significant items (Bonet, 2011; Richards, 2003; OECD, 2009). Recently, Richards (2011) outlined the growing integration of tourism and creativity leading to 'creative' tourism, as an extension of cultural tourism. A side effect, with relevant policy implications (see below), of the continuous enlargement of the scope of cultural tourism is that the attractiveness of a region relies on its cultural assets but its competitiveness with other destinations strongly depends on 'its ability to transform the basic inherited factors into created assets with a higher symbolic or sign value' (OECD, 2009).

This expanding notion of the cultural consumption of tourists makes the definition of cultural tourism increasingly difficult. Among the attempts made in the literature to overcome such a problem and to identify different typologies of cultural tourists (Richards, 2003), the two-dimensional approach developed by McKercher (2002) is interesting, aimed at classifying cultural tourists according to their motivations for the trip and on the level of engagement with the cultural attractions.[2]

Cultural tourism measurement

Further problems arise when we come to the measurement of cultural tourism. Indeed, international statistics do not distinguish between 'leisure' and culturally motivated tourists. As the OECD (2009) outlines, relatively few countries or regions collect specific data; however, based on UNWTO's data it is estimated that cultural tourism increased from 37 per cent of global tourism in 1995 to 40 per cent in 2007. These figures include all visitors to cultural attractions without taking into account their motivation. Notwithstanding these difficulties, the OECD (2009) offers some evidence from the US and Canada suggesting that cultural motivations account for an important share of tourism. According to the Eurobarometer (Gallup Organisation, 2009a, 2009b), cultural motivations appear to be relevant also for Europeans when making their travel decisions.[3]

At a smaller scale, a survey run by ATLAS (Richards, 2007) for a few selected countries revealed the motivations and behaviour of tourists in respect to culture. Almost 20 per cent of those surveyed could be identified as cultural tourists since visiting a cultural attraction was the main reason for travelling; for those taking a holiday, almost 35 per cent declared a cultural motivation, showing an increasing trend with respect to previous surveys. Overall, more than 60 per cent visited a museum during their trip, almost 50 per cent a monument, more than 20 per cent an art gallery and more than 10 per cent a theatre. The survey results confirm that visits to cultural attractions should not be assimilated into cultural tourism and that, over time, there is a tendency for the growth of cultural consumption.

UNESCO sites and tourism

Notwithstanding the above-mentioned measurement problems, there are many quantitative estimations of cultural tourism economic impact but comparability is difficult because of the differences in cultural tourism definitions (Del Corpo *et al.*, 2008). According to Bellini *et al.* (2007), tourism specialization has a positive impact on the *level* of both income and prices, this effect being stronger in World Heritage Cities, suggesting that cultural tourism has a stronger impact on local economies than other types of tourism.

The link between cultural tourism and inclusion in the World Heritage List has received great attention in recent years. It is worth noting that the World Heritage List is highly heterogeneous and has been growing and expanding over time.[4] The effectiveness of this type of heritage in fostering tourism is somehow taken for granted. Apart from official statements ('It is an inevitable destiny: the very reasons why a property is chosen for inscription on the World Heritage List are also the reasons why millions of tourists flock to those sites year after year', Pedersen, 2002: 1), in the theoretical literature such a perception is widespread (Frey and Steiner, 2011). Heritage sites included in the UNESCO World Heritage List are used as indicators of attractiveness of travel destinations as measured by the Competitive Monitor (Mazanec *et al.*, 2007) and are also identified as powerful factors to foster sustainable tourism competitiveness clusters at regional level (Hawkins, 2004).

However, the overall effects of inscription on tourism are to be considered in a wide perspective: Tisdell and Wilson (2002) outline that inclusion in the World Heritage List may bring about complementary as well as substitution effects; the latter are stressed by Gamboni (2001), arguing that by focusing attention on designated buildings or areas, inscription is likely to generate a 'displacement effect' to the disadvantage of other heritage.

Empirical evidence is ambiguous. Arezki *et al.* (2009) consider the World Heritage List as an example of tourism specialization and find positive and significant effects on economic growth through specialization in tourism; a recent debate in the latest issues of the journal *Tourism Management* (Yang *et al.*, 2009, 2011; Cellini, 2011) shows that the effectiveness of the World Heritage

List in promoting tourism and, therefore, economic local development is an open and controversial question.

In what follows, we indirectly enter such a debate, investigating the effects of World Heritage List inscription on the domestic and foreign tourism flows in the Sicilian UNESCO sites.

The case study: Sicilian UNESCO sites

Sicily has five sites included in the World Heritage List: four of them are cultural and one is natural.[5] Moreover, since 2008 Sicily also has an inscription in the UNESCO Representative List of the Intangible Cultural Heritage of Humanity: the puppet theatre (Opera dei Pupi). Given the scope of this study, attention will focus on cultural sites, though the connection between tangible and intangible heritage is worth mentioning and will be explored in the fifth section.

The four cultural sites were included in the World Heritage List in different years and for different reasons. In 1997, Agrigento and Piazza Armerina were included for the universal relevance of the archaeological sites located in their area: the Greek acropolis (Valle dei Templi) in Agrigento and the Roman Villa (Villa Romana del Casale) in Piazza Armerina. In 2002, the Baroque churches and private and public buildings of the historical centres of the towns in Val di Noto ('Le città barocche del Val di Noto') have been included in the World Heritage List as a serial site spread in urban centres and rural agglomerations.[6] In 2005, another site ('Siracusa and the rural necropolis of Pantalica'), which comprises the historical centre of Siracusa and the archaeological site of Pantalica, was inscribed.

The different characteristics of Sicilian UNESCO sites as well as their geographical locations (shown in Figure 13.1) can be relevant for the following analysis of seasonality. Except for Piazza Armerina, which is located in the Sicilian interior, the other three UNESCO sites are located close to the Sicilian coast[7] and tourists can be attracted both by the cultural heritage and by the landscape and the seaside.

The characteristics of the Sicilian sites protected by UNESCO and their geographical locations make the study of the effectiveness of the UNESCO recognition more difficult in terms of tourism attractiveness. The characteristics of the sites do not allow cultural tourism to be easily distinguished and measured: we could identify and measure cultural tourists by the number of visitors of the archaeological sites of Agrigento and Piazza Armerina but the same measure cannot be adopted in the case of Val di Noto and Siracusa. In fact, even if in Val di Noto and Siracusa there are some noteworthy museums that can be attractive for cultural tourists, the inscription in the World Heritage List refers to historical centres and rural agglomerations: the architectural style of these two destinations testifies to the uniqueness of the Baroque style adopted after the earthquake of 1693 in Val di Noto and the accumulation of three millennia of architectural styles in Siracusa. Moreover, for the reasons outlined before, cultural tourism cannot be simply identified with the number of visitors of museums and heritage

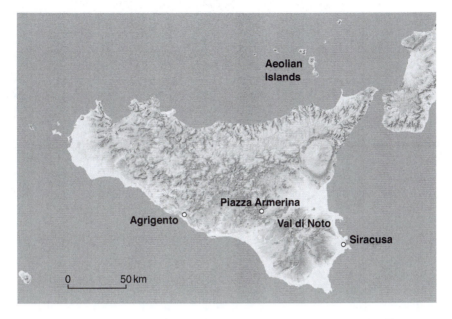

Figure 13.1 UNESCO World Heritage Sites in Sicily. © OpenStreetMap contributors.

sites and such an indicator, referring to a very narrow definition of cultural tourism, would be in any case unsatisfactory. For these reasons, an alternative indicator is called for.

Since this study is focused on tourism destinations with a very important cultural endowment, it can be assumed that the main component of the tourism flows to these UNESCO sites is cultural tourism. It can also be easily assumed that cultural tourism is less seasonal than other types of tourism, such as 'sun and sea' tourism. Therefore, from the analysis of the pattern and the seasonality of a traditional tourism indicator – the monthly overnight stays – we think it might be possible to estimate directly the relevance of the cultural segment of tourism demand in the Sicilian UNESCO sites and, indirectly, the effectiveness of the UNESCO certification in terms of attractiveness of tourist visits.

The analysis of seasonality

The methodology

Seasonality in tourism can be measured in different ways (for a review of the literature, see Lundtorp, 2001). A first method consists of considering simple descriptive statistics, among which we have selected the Gini index. The Gini index is a concentration index that we report in this study to measure the concentration of tourist stays across months: the higher the concentration, the higher the

Gini index. A second way consists of considering time-series properties and regression analysis. To model and measure seasonality, deterministic and stochastic models are available. The deterministic model may employ seasonal dummy variables to capture the seasonality. Alternatively, the components (i.e. trend, cycle, seasonal and residual) of the series can be disentangled through different procedures; among these procedures, in this study, we have used the X12 program, provided by the Census Bureau. The Census-X12 program automatically provides some tests on the significance of seasonality and the stability across years of seasonal factors. This approach to seasonality with reference to tourism has been used, for example, by Hui and Yuen (2002) and is strongly advocated by Candela *et al.* (2007). In this study, we focus more on this approach because it allows certain characteristics of tourism flows to be observed, such as the seasonal peaks during the year and the dynamics of seasonality in the time series, that the descriptive indicators of seasonality do not capture.

The data set refers to domestic and foreign tourist visits to Sicily and in the UNESCO destinations, as measured by the monthly overnight stays, registered over the period January 1998–December 2009.

Before examining the pattern and the seasonal characteristics of the flows of tourist stays (i.e. the demand side), it is useful to point out that the Sicilian UNESCO destinations have different accommodation capacity (i.e. the supply side) and, even if the supply of different accommodations – hotels and extra-hotels – has increased in Sicily in these years, the difference still persists. On average, the rate of growth of establishments and beds has been slightly larger in the UNESCO cultural destinations (Cuccia and Rizzo, 2011a), compared to the regional average; a sharper increase has been registered in the municipalities of Val di Noto (Cuccia, 2012). The increasing quantity of accommodation is one of the measures that the regional government adopted to support the tourism industry; no specific measures have been devoted to the regional UNESCO destinations.

The pattern of tourism flows

Figures 13.2 to 13.6 show the patterns of overnight stays of domestic and foreign tourists in Sicily and in the Sicilian UNESCO destinations.

At a first glance, the pattern of tourist visits to Sicily increased until 2006–2007 and then declined, probably because of the international negative business cycle, with a positive recovery in 2009. The foreign component of the tourist demand shows a more stable trend and the decline has a slower pace.

UNESCO destinations have tourism flows of very different sizes, depending on the capacity of their establishments. The pattern of tourism visits varies across UNESCO sites:

- Piazza Armerina (see Figure 13.5) registers a negative pattern since 2001;
- Agrigento (see Figure 13.6) has a very unstable pattern;

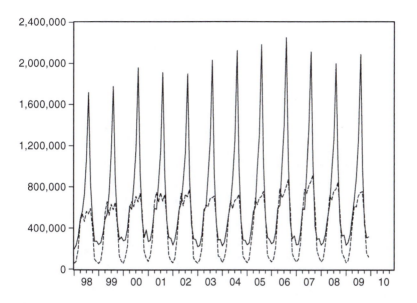

Figure 13.2 Pattern of overnight stays of Italian (solid) and foreign (dotted) tourists in Sicily.

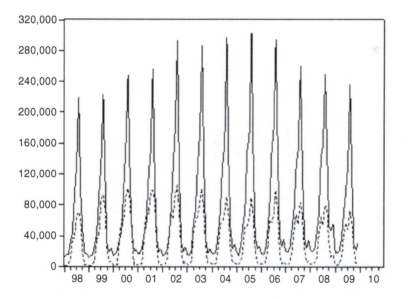

Figure 13.3 Pattern of overnight stays of Italian (solid) and foreign (dotted) tourists in Val di Noto.

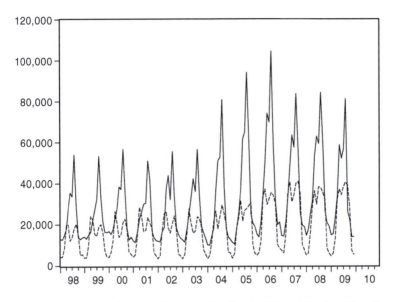

Figure 13.4 Pattern of overnight stays of Italian (solid) and foreign (dotted) tourists in Siracusa.

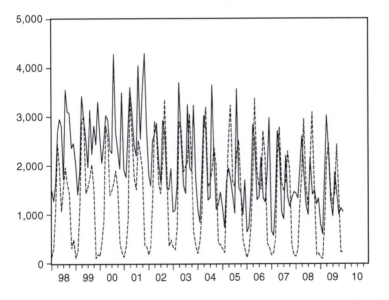

Figure 13.5 Pattern of overnight stays of Italian (solid) and foreign (dotted) tourists in Piazza Armerina.

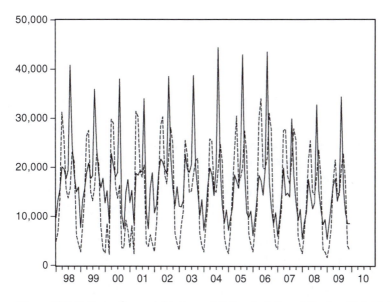

Figure 13.6 Pattern of overnight stays of Italian (solid) and foreign (dotted) tourists in Agrigento.

- Val di Noto (see Figure 13.3) shows a positive trend in 2002 (the year of World Heritage inscription);
- Siracusa (and Pantalica) (see Figure 13.4) shows a positive trend in 2004 (the year before inscription);
- all the UNESCO destinations except Siracusa (and Pantalica) show a recovery in 2009.

Does the above evidence suggest the existence of the effects of UNESCO recognition on tourism? Cuccia (2012) stresses that the recognition generates only very short-term effects. The causes of this weak effect can depend on both regional and international factors: they can be due to the inefficiencies in the organization of the tourism supply in Sicily and/or to the international negative business cycle. Further hints can be derived by a closer analysis of seasonality.

Looking at the seasonality of the overnight stays, we observe that seasonality characterizes Sicily as well as all the destinations under scrutiny. It seems that tourists are more interested in the geographical attractiveness of the destinations and in their proximity to the coast and the seaside than in their cultural endowments. Piazza Armerina has a lower level of seasonality, probably because of its interior geographical location.

Seasonality characterizes both domestic and foreign tourist stays; however, these two segments of the tourism demand have different individual preferences or are subject to different institutional constraints that influence the choice of the peak period. Italian tourist stays are mainly concentrated in the summer season, with a peak in August, while foreign tourist stays extend over a longer period, from spring to early autumn (September) and have their peaks in September, with differences across the different destinations.

Statistical analysis on the seasonality

In this section, we develop the analysis further, providing a description of the seasonal component of the monthly data. We base our analysis on some descriptive statistics and on the regression supporting the X-12 Census Bureau procedure to disentangle seasonality (X-12 Census Bureau, n.d.).

As observed in the graphs and documented in Table 13.1, the Sicilian UNESCO destinations are of very different sizes. Average, minimum and maximum monthly overnights are reported for each destination, and for Sicily as a whole, in columns 1–3 of Table 13.1. Columns 4 and 5 report the month with the minimum and maximum average value. All the columns report separately the Italian and foreign monthly overnight stays. In percentage terms, the foreign average monthly presence is higher in the Sicilian UNESCO sites that were inscribed first – the single sites of Agrigento (47 per cent) and Piazza Armerina (41 per cent) – than in Sicily (38.6 per cent). Siracusa and Val di Noto, the UNESCO serial sites that have more recently received World Heritage status, have a lower percentage of foreign average monthly stays than in Sicily, respectively 37 per cent and 31 per cent. The data can have a twofold interpretation: on the one hand, the UNESCO recognition can take time to be appreciated by foreigners and to promote arrivals and visits; on the other hand, the increasing number of sites inscribed in the UNESCO World Heritage List could reduce the impact in terms of foreign recognition of the importance of the sites.

It is worth noting that for Italian tourists the maximum data occur in August, while for foreign tourists they occur in shoulder months (April, May or September according to the different destinations under consideration), with the exception of Val di Noto, where the foreign maximum is also registered in August. It is likely that the characteristics of this serial site allow enjoyment of both the cultural and the natural attributes of the destination simultaneously; this kind of site does not help to reduce seasonality as it is generally assumed in the case of cultural sites but, on the contrary, it increases seasonality in domestic and foreign tourism.

Table 13.2 (columns 1 to 5) reports statistics on seasonality, computed on the basis of the X-12-Arima procedure (F test and K test). In Sicily and in all the selected destinations, there is seasonality in tourism; the Gini index (column 5) shows that Val di Noto has the highest value of concentration: its Gini index is higher than the index for the whole of Sicily; the other cultural destinations have lower values of the monthly overnight concentration index. Tests on moving seasonality (F test, column 3), on the basis of X-12 Arima procedure, leads to the conclusion that in Val di Noto and in Agrigento seasonality is not moving, while it is moving in Sicily and in the other destinations selected. The analysis of the seasonal factors, reported in column 4 only for the destinations where the

Table 13.1 Descriptive statistics on monthly overnights

		(1) Average	(2) Minimum*	(3) Maximum*	(4) Month with minimum average	(5) Month with maximum average
Agrigento	Total	31,435	7,003	65,455	Jan 12,659	Aug 58,608
	Italian	16,602	5,338	44,390	Jan 9,582	Aug 39,624
	Foreigners	14,833	1,665	33,969	Jan 3,076	May 28,423
Piazza	Total	3,413	686	7,001	Jan 1,717	Apr 5,701
Armerina	Italian	2,024	569	4,292	Feb 1,277	Aug 3,396
	Foreigners	1,389	90	3,397	Jan 183	May 2,826
Siracusa	Total	49,051	13,566	139,988	Jan 16,994	Aug 91,666
	Italian	30,923	9,992	104,485	Jan 12,223	Aug 67,365
	Foreigners	18,128	3,460	40,772	Jan 3,999	Apr 25,571
Val di Noto	Total	110,914	12,702	397,597	Jan 17,694	Aug 363,961
	Italian	76,366	11,646	303,318	Jan 15,542	Aug 269,488
	Foreigners	34,549	1,056	105,065	Jan 2,152	Aug 94,473
Sicily	Total	1,107,230	253,068	3,050,152	Jan 300,236	Aug 2,653,004
	Italian	679,413	194,767	2,251,563	Jan 237,583	Aug 1,984,012
	Foreigners	427,816	55,783	916,817	Jan 62,652	Sep 726,145

Note
The minimum and maximum values for Italian and Foreign tourists may occur in different months, so their sum does not necessarily coincide with the minimum and maximum value of total.

Table 13.2 Statistics on seasonality: whole sample

	(1) F test on seasonality $(F_{11,132})$	(2) K test on seasonality $K(11)$	(3) F test on moving seasonality $F_{(11,121)}$	(4) Seasonal factors (min–max 1998, min–max 2009)	(5) G
Agrigento	F = 72.6*	K = 118.7#	F = 1.27		0.269
Piazza Armerina	F = 90.3*	K = 128.4#	F = 2.41§	0.51–1.45 0.29–1.81	0.256
Siracusa	F = 341.1*	K = 132.9#	F = 3.28§	0.49–1.96 0.31–1.99	0.332
Val di Noto	F = 959.6*	K = 138.3#	F = 1.75		0.500
Sicily	F = 2371.1*	K = 141.0#	F = 5.67§	0.29–2.36 0.26.2.47	0.366

Notes
In column 1, * denotes that seasonality is present at 0.1 per cent; in column 2, # denotes that p-value is lower than 0.01; in column 3, § denotes that moving seasonality is present at 1 per cent; in column 4, minimum–maximum seasonal factors are not reported in cases where moving seasonality is not present; in column 5, G denotes the Gini index.

F test rejects the null of absence of moving seasonality, shows that seasonality has been increasing.

If we consider separately the domestic and foreign monthly overnight stays (see Table 13.3), we can observe that both Italian and foreign monthly over-nights are seasonal but the seasonality of Italian overnights has increased in some destinations (Sicily and Siracusa), while the seasonality of foreign over-nights is stable. Therefore, it is the Italian quota of tourism visits that determines the increasing seasonal variation.

The presence of seasonality in the foreign quota deserves a better explanation. The foreign monthly overnights cover a longer season than the Italian monthly overnights, which extends from April to September and its peak is generally not in August but in shoulder months, in spring or early autumn; this could be due to the milder climate, which allows foreigners to enjoy the cultural as well as the natural attractions and/or to the cultural priority they attribute to the visit. Seasonality is still present in foreign overnights because of the large difference between the monthly overnights in the long high season and the very low monthly overnights registered in the rest of the year, particularly in the winter months. The difference in monthly overnights in high and low season is larger among foreigners than among Italians. Probably, Italians that live closer to the selected destinations can come more often and enjoy the cultural and natural attractions of the destinations in different periods of time.

In conclusion, we can say that the common assumption that cultural tourism is less seasonal is not verified in the case of the Sicilian UNESCO cultural sites. This can be explained by both demand and supply side motivations. As far as the demand side is concerned, the common institutional constraints, leading Italians more than foreigners to concentrate their holidays in the summer period, are stronger than any other determinants of the tourism demand.

As far as the supply side is concerned, the geographical location of most of these UNESCO sites near the sea makes it problematic to estimate seasonality, since they can attract both 'sun and sea' and cultural tourists. However, the presence of outstanding cultural heritage can lower the concentration index registered in the single sites – as documented by Piazza Armerina and Agrigento – and can make the seasonality more stable, as documented by the serial site of Val di Noto.

It is an open question if the different effectiveness of UNESCO recognition on seasonality depends on the geographical location, on the characteristics of the cultural site or on the number of years of recognition. The increasing number of sites under the protection of UNESCO could lower the marginal productivity of this international recognition in terms of tourism attractiveness. In the short term, the international recognition can affect the level of tourism visits but not its rate of growth (Cuccia, 2012); over the long term, the UNESCO sites that first received protection and that consist of single monuments show a lower degree of seasonality.

Even if both Italian and foreign tourism flows show seasonality, the peak season is different: spring for foreigners and summer for Italians. Therefore,

Table 13.3 Statistics on seasonality: Italians and foreigners

	(1) F test on seasonality $(F_{11,132})$	(2) K test on seasonality $K(11)$	(3) F test on moving seasonality $F_{(11,121)}$	(4) Seasonal factors (min–max 1998, min–max 2009)	(5) G
Agrigento:					
Italians	F = 96.6*	K = 114.4#	F = 2.16		0.240
Foreigners	F = 63.7*	K = 118.5#	F = 1.63		0.351
Piazza Armerina:					
Italians	F = 23.0*	K = 103.3#	F = 2.11		0.238
Foreigners	F = 173.6*	K = 133.1#	F = 0.42		0.395
Siracusa:					
Italians	F = 251.1*	K = 132.1#	F = 4.52§	0.57–2.24	0.343
Foreigners	F = 211.9*	K = 128.3#	F = 1.27	0.36–2.25	0.351
Val di Noto:					
Italians	F = 1056.5*	K = 138.1#	F = 2.36		0.496
Foreigners	F = 339.9*	K = 133.3#	F = 0.81		0.522
Sicily:					
Italians	F = 2503.1*	K = 139.7#	F = 9.06§	0.38–2.86	0.380
Foreigners	F = 1054.2*	K = 137.9#	F = 0.26	0.33.2.98	0.360

Note
See notes in Table 13.2.

foreigners show a clear priority for the cultural attractions of the sites but we cannot deny that also Italians, who should have more opportunities to visit the sites during the year, are able to enjoy the different attractiveness of the destination in the more suitable period of the year: sun and sea in summer and cultural sites in the rest of the year.

However, in the case of Sicily, we observe that the first UNESCO single sites to be inscribed – Piazza Armerina and Agrigento – clearly attract cultural tourism, as their lower degree of seasonality shows, but still suffer from too low a level of tourism visits. The most recent serial sites of Val di Noto and Siracusa attract a larger number of tourists who want to enjoy a more complex cultural experience that is not only aimed at visiting a single monument but the whole landscape. Therefore, if it is difficult for policy-makers to build an attractive cultural tourism supply on a single outstanding monument, it could be much more difficult to plan a cultural tourism supply on a serial cultural site that can attract a highly diversified demand. Statistics on seasonality do not help to understand univocally the preferences of the visitors of serial sites.

Some policy implications

Broadly speaking, our results, coherently with Cuccia and Rizzo (2011a) show that UNESCO inscription does not seem effective in reducing seasonality and, therefore, in fostering cultural tourism, at least under the reasonable assumption that cultural tourism is less seasonal than other forms of tourism. The above-mentioned differences in the seasonality experienced by Sicilian World Heritage Sites depend on the type of tourists, whether Italian or foreigners, and on the type of site, whether serial or single sites, and have to be taken into account in public decision-making when intervening to reduce the seasonality.

Moreover, when addressing this segment of demand, it should be taken into account that the increasing number of sites in the World Heritage List enhances competition among them, in terms of tourism attractiveness and, therefore, stresses the importance of transforming destinations into 'distinctive places' and of promoting the destination adequately, coherently with the policy goals and objectives (see below). The UNESCO recognition needs time to be appreciated by foreigners and to promote arrivals and visits and, therefore, long-term strategies are needed. Indeed, a network strategy could be developed, using the established reputation of the 'older' sites as a resource; reciprocal benefits would occur, since it might contribute to increase the number of visitors, enlarging their attractiveness to meet a demand which looks for more complex cultural experiences.

Looking at the type of tourist, the empirical results presented in the preceding section would suggest different lines of action. Foreign tourists seem to recall the model of 'purposeful cultural tourist' (McKercher, 2002): in this case, seasonality mainly explains the large gap between the long high season (April–October) and the short low season. For this group, a policy objective might be to reduce the gap, lengthening the high season, offering specialized holidays, 'cultural experiences' tailored to the various segments of the demand, in line with their specific interests. Domestic tourists do not show cultural motivation as a priority since it is overshadowed by the motivation of 'sun and sea'. For this group, a pragmatic policy objective might be to lengthen their stay, using the cultural endowment of the destination as a further attraction.

To pursue the above-mentioned objectives, different strategies are required, involving different actors. A first point to be considered is that the existence of cultural heritage, even if outstanding, is a necessary but not a sufficient condition for reducing seasonality through cultural tourism. As was outlined in the section on definition and measurement issues above, cultural heritage is not the only element affecting cultural tourism demand: cultural tourism has evolved towards the notion of 'cultural experience' and of 'creative tourism'.[8] To meet such a changing demand, cultural supply has to be dynamic, ready to evolve, being the result of several inputs variously combined.

As Richards (2011: 1238) points out, 'every location has the potential to provide a unique combination of knowledge, skills, physical assets, social capital and "atmosphere" which make certain places particularly suited to specific creative activities'. Without offering an exhaustive overview, in our case study, some specific creative traditions can be given as examples, such as: the artistic ceramic production of Caltagirone; the chocolate production in Modica; the particular cultural 'scene' developed by the 'Scicli group'[9]; the puppet theatre in Catania (all in Val di Noto); the Classical Tragedies Festival (in Siracusa); the Pirandello literary park (in Agrigento); or the widespread quality-certified eno-gastronomic productions (olive oil, wine, cheese, etc.). These offer just a few examples of such characteristics.

Combining creative approaches with tourism may lead to the emergence of 'distinctive places', not only in urban environments but also in rural areas and, therefore, to exploit the potentialities of heritage. Elsewhere (Cuccia and Rizzo, 2011b), it has been stressed that cultural heritage can be a powerful input of cultural tourism only if cultural heritage as output of a public policy is sustainable, i.e. if policy-makers plan cultural initiatives that create a 'cultural atmosphere' in the destination.

In this direction, policy-making requires the involvement of many public and private (for profit and no profit) actors: regional and local governments, heritage authorities, museums, cultural heritage owners (e.g. the Church), cultural institutions, 'creative' producers, tourism operators, associations. Coordination is needed to favour the creation of cultural networks and itineraries since isolated heritage is unlikely to stand out in the tourism market (Bonet, 2011).

Vertical fragmentation

As has been pointed out elsewhere (Cuccia and Rizzo, 2011b), coordination would allow *vertical fragmentation* (between regional and local government)[10] (Rizzo and Towse, 2002), derived from the coexistence of different layers of government, to be overcome, as well as overcoming *horizontal fragmentation* derived from the coexistence of public and private actors at each of the wide range of levels mentioned above.

Vertical fragmentation can be minimized with a clear definition of objectives and allocation of functions to reduce overlap and to enhance the accountability of each level of government. For instance, the coordination of regional and local competences is needed since regional regulation aimed at heritage conservation impinges upon local choices about the revitalization of historical centres as well as the use of public spaces (for instance, ancient theatres): too conservationist an approach may prevent private investments in the heritage sector and reduce the scope of local policies to foster cultural tourism (Rizzo, 2011). Alternatively, the same applies when regional industrial policies are not coherent with local cultural tourism policies.

Moreover, vertical coordination is needed whenever local governments rely on grants from the regional government: in fact, local cultural policies to effectively meet the international tourism demand require long-term strategic planning that, in turn, has to be based on a clear long-term financial framework. In Sicily, the public decision-making process does not fulfil such a requirement because financing decisions referring to the above-mentioned cultural resources are adopted by different regional departments – depending whether they refer to heritage, theatres, crafts or eno-gastronomic products – and, therefore, fragmentation is likely to occur.

In the case of World Heritage Sites, the need for vertical coordination is enhanced by the fact that a supra-national institution, such as UNESCO, is involved and, therefore, it is advisable that regional/local decision-makers develop a unitary approach. Actually, when it is not the case and contrasting policies are pursued, the monitoring function of UNESCO can be helpful to reach an agreement.[11]

Horizontal fragmentation

Looking at horizontal fragmentation, policy-making has to face other challenges. The promotion of UNESCO tourism destinations, especially with the objective of reducing seasonality, requires a strong coordination of several (public as well as private) actors operating at local level.

A clear map of *who does what and why* is the starting point for developing policies aimed at enhancing the tourism potentialities of cultural endowment and fostering specific objectives, such as the reduction of seasonality. Public and private actors play different roles and face different challenges. Each publicly funded institution (e.g. museums, archaeological sites, galleries, theatres, etc.) has to be accountable: autonomy, responsibility and an adequate set of incentives are necessary to stimulate *demand-orientated* (Peacock and Rizzo, 2008) strategies[12] and activities to attract more visitors, to offer high-quality services and to cooperate with the other actors. At the same time, all the other heritage owners, namely the Church and the private owners, have to coordinate their activities so that the fruition of heritage can be promoted effectively (for instance, different closing days, jointly organized guided tours on itineraries, etc.). Moreover, to meet the demand of cultural tourism for 'cultural experiences', creative producers need to be involved in the promotion of the destination to contribute to its 'distinctive identity', not to mention the producers of tourism services (tour operators, hotels, restaurants, etc.).

Clear strategies and well-defined priorities and objectives have to be set by local policy-makers and shared by all the other partners, having in mind the different segments of demand, whether from foreign or domestic tourists. For instance, if reducing seasonality through the extension of the shoulder season is a policy objective, coordinated actions are needed to organize off-season events (exhibitions, festivals) and activities (laboratories, courses) in connection with local creative productions and relying on a complementary offer of tourism services. In such a process, representation of local communities is called for to enhance the long-term sustainability of cultural policy, to favour voluntary action and to strengthen local identity. The involvement of local communities enhances 'cultural experience' and may prevent the above-mentioned risk that UNESCO sites might generate 'displacement' or 'substitution' effects with respect to other sites. In other words, a comprehensive and coordinated cultural supply has to be planned as a condition for the competitiveness of the destination. Carefully planned promotion is also needed to provide information to reach different target groups: several tools can be used, ranging from well-designed websites to the provision of information through travel magazines or through consulates (see also Pederson, 2002).

What type of governance is needed to generate the above-mentioned comprehensive cultural supply? As Cuccia and Rizzo (2011b) point out, different solutions can be envisaged and, regardless of the solution adopted, what matters is the identification of clear objectives and incentives to enhance the accountability towards stakeholders. What is the role of UNESCO sites in such a framework? The answer to such a question crucially also depends on the type of site. Single sites, such as Agrigento and Piazza Armerina, are the 'core' of the corresponding archaeological parks, administrative structures recently created[13] within a wide organizational reform of the heritage administration undertaken by regional government in 2010 and still ongoing. One of the claimed objectives of these new organizations seems to be the coordinated management and valorization of archaeological sites in the same area but with incomplete autonomy and responsibility and, therefore, limited accountability. This institutional feature somehow endangers the role that archaeological parks might play to promote cultural tourism following the lines described above.

Governance issues are even more complicated in serial sites such as Val di Noto where the site does not even have a single identity: eight municipalities coexist across three provinces and so far have experienced competitive rather than cooperative behaviours. In such a case, the need for coordination is especially relevant: Val di Noto as unitary institutional actor does not exist yet and until the governance issue *within* the site is solved, it will be difficult for the UNESCO site to play any strategic role to promote cultural tourism through interaction with the other actors.

Concluding remarks

In this chapter, we have analysed the role that sites included in the World Heritage List could play in reducing tourism seasonality through cultural tourism, using Sicily as a case study. As the empirical analysis shows, generally, UNESCO inscription does not seem effective in fostering cultural tourism and, as a consequence, in overcoming seasonality. However, some differences arise depending on the type of site – whether serial or single – as well as on the type of visitors – whether foreigner or domestic.

The potential of the Sicilian UNESCO sites still needs to be fully exploited to make them competitive destinations – for example, able to meet the demand for 'cultural experiences', which nowadays characterizes cultural tourism. In this perspective, clear strategies and well-defined priorities and objectives have to be set by local policy-makers and shared by all the other partners, and vertical as well as horizontal fragmentation needs to be overcome to generate a well-coordinated cultural supply.

Notes

1 A similar approach is adopted by the UNWTO.
2 Five typologies are obtained, ranging from the purposeful cultural tourist (high motivation/deep experience) to the incidental cultural tourist (low motivation/cultural experience).
3 In 2008, 17 per cent of Europeans decided their destinations focusing primarily on cross-cultural experiences; in 2009, cultural attractiveness was considered important by 31 per cent of respondents.
4 In 2011–2012, it included 936 properties (725 cultural, 183 natural and 28 mixed, i.e. combining cultural and natural) in 153 countries.
5 The natural site is the Aeolian Islands, under the protection of UNESCO since 2000.
6 The World Heritage inscription includes eight towns in the Val di Noto region of south-eastern Sicily. These are Caltagirone, Militello Val di Catania, Catania, Modica, Noto, Palazzolo, Ragusa and Scicli, which were all rebuilt after 1693 on or beside towns existing at the time of the earthquake of that year.
7 For serial sites such as Val di Noto and Siracusa and Pantalica, this is true only for some of the cities included.
8 According to UNESCO (2006: 3):

> Creative tourism is travel directed toward an engaged and authentic experience, with participative learning in the arts, heritage, or special character of a place, and it provides a connection with those who reside in this place and create this living culture.

9 An artists' group created in Scicli named after a well-known artist, Piero Guccione.
10 Unlike other regions in Italy, in Sicily, the regional government is fully responsible for cultural policies within the general principles set by central government (the various dimension of such an autonomy are investigated by Rizzo and Towse, 2002).
11 For instance, this happened in Sicily: in 2007 the regional government tried to allow oil drilling in the south-east (where Val di Noto is located) and the interested municipalities, claiming that it would have endangered local sustainable development and cultural tourism, protested and succeeded in stopping it.
12 The potential shortcomings of public decision-making in the heritage field, leading to supply-oriented policies, are explored by Peacock and Rizzo (2008).

13 Actually, the archaeological park of Agrigento already existed, though with different features.

References

Arezki, R., Cherif, R. and Piotrowski, J. (2009) 'Tourism specialization and economic development: Evidence from the UNESCO World Heritage List', *IMF Working Paper*, No. 176.

Bellini, E., Gasparino, U., Del Corpo, B. and Malizia, W. (2007) *Impact of cultural tourism upon urban economies: An econometric exercise*, Fondazione Eni – Enrico Mattei, Working Paper No.85.

Bonet, L. (2011) 'Cultural tourism', in R. Towse (ed.) *A handbook of cultural economics*, Cheltenham: Edward Elgar, 166–171.

Candela, G., Giannerini, S. and Scorcu, A. E. (2007) 'Flussi e caratteristiche delle destinazioni e dei turismi. Una nota introduttiva', *Economia dei Servizi*, 2: 47–58.

Cellini, R. (2011) 'Is UNESCO recognition effective in fostering tourism? A comment on Yang, Lin and Han', *Tourism Management*, 32(2): 452–454.

Cuccia, T. (2012) 'It is worth being inscribed in the World Heritage List? A case study of "The Baroque cities in Val di Noto" (Sicily)', *SSSRN Working Paper*, No. 2027892.

Cuccia, T. and Rizzo, I. (2011a) 'Tourism seasonality in cultural destinations: Empirical evidence from Sicily', *Tourism Management*, 32(3): 589–595.

Cuccia, T. and Rizzo, I. (2011b) 'Heritage and tourism: Theoretical and empirical issues', *Tourismos*, 6(3): 37–56.

Del Corpo, B., Gasparino, U., Bellini, E. and Malizia, W. (2008) 'Effects of tourism upon the economy of small and medium-sized European cities. Cultural tourists and "the others"', *FEEM Working Paper*, No. 44, http://papers.ssrn.com/sol3/papers.cfm?abstract_id=1140611.

Frey, B. and Steiner, L. (2011) 'World Heritage List: Does it make sense?' *International Journal of Cultural Policy*, 17(5): 555–573.

Gallup Organisation, Hungary (2009a) 'Survey on the attitudes of Europeans towards tourism', Analytical Report conducted on behalf of the Directorate General Enterprise and Industry, Flash EB Series #258, http://ec.europa.eu/public_opinion/flash/fl_258_en.pdf (accessed March 23, 2013).

Gallup Organisation, Hungary (2009b) 'Europeans and tourism', Analytical Report Autumn 2009, conducted upon the request of Directorate General Enterprise and Industry, Flash EB Series #281, http://ec.europa.eu/public_opinion/flash/fl_281_en.pdf (accessed March 23, 2013).

Gamboni, D. L. (2001) 'World Heritage: Shield or target', *Conservation: The Getty Conservation Institute Newsletter*, XVI/2: 5–11.

Hawkins, D. E. (2004) 'Sustainable tourism competitiveness clusters: Application to World Heritage Sites network development in Indonesia', *Asia Pacific Journal of Tourism Research*, 9(3): 293–307.

Hui, T. K., and Yuen, C. C. (2002) 'A study in the seasonal variation of Japanese tourist arrivals in Singapore', *Tourism Management*, 23(2): 127–131.

ICOMOS (2002) *International cultural tourism charter. Principles and guidelines for managing tourism at places of cultural and heritage significance*, ICOMOS International Cultural Tourism Committee.

Lundtorp, S. (2001) 'Measuring tourism seasonality', in T. Baum and S. Lundtorp (eds.) *Seasonality in tourism*, Oxford: Pergamon, 23–50.

Mazanec, A., Wober, K. and Zins, A. H. (2007) 'Tourism destination competitiveness: From definition to explanation?', *Journal of Travel Research*, 46(1): 86–95.

McKercher, B. (2002) 'Towards a classification of cultural tourists', *International Journal of Tourism Research*, 4: 29–38.

OECD (2009) *The impact of culture on tourism*, OECD: Paris.

OpenStreetMap. Available at www.openstreetmap.org/ (accessed June 28, 2013).

Peacock, A. T. and Rizzo, I. (2008) *The heritage game: Economics, policy and practice*, Oxford: Oxford University Press.

Pedersen, A. (2002) *Managing tourism at World Heritage Sites: A practical manual for World Heritage Site managers*, UNESCO, whc.unesco.org/uploads/activities/documents/activity-113-2.pdf.

Richards, G. (2003) 'What is cultural tourism?', in A. van Maaren (ed.) *Erfgoed voor Toerisme*, Nationaal Contact Monumenten (www.docstoc.com/docs/2554594/).

Richards, G. (2007) 'ATLAS Cultural tourism survey: Summary report', www.tram-research.com/atlas/ATLAS%20Cultural%20Tourism%20Survey%202007.PDF (accessed March 23, 2013).

Richards, G. (2011) 'Creativity and tourism: the state of the art', *Annals of Tourism Research*, 38(4), 1225–1253.

Rizzo, I. (2011) 'Regulation', in R. Towse (ed.) *Handbook of cultural economics*, Cheltenham: Edward Elgar: 386–393.

Rizzo, I. and Towse, R. (2002) *The economics of the heritage: A study in the political economy of culture in Sicily*, Cheltenham: Edward Elgar.

Tisdell, C. and Wilson, C. (2002) 'World Heritage listing of Australian natural sites: Tourism stimulus and its economic value', *Economic Analysis and Policy*, 32(2): 27–49.

Towse, R. (ed.) (2011) *A handbook of cultural economics, II*, Cheltenham: Edward Elgar.

UNESCO (2006) 'Towards sustainable strategies for creative tourism', Creative Cities Network, *Discussion Report of the Planning Meeting for 2008 International Conference on Creative Tourism, Santa Fe, New Mexico, USA, October 25–27, 2006* (Ref CLT/CEI/CID/2008/RP/66) (http://unesdoc.unesco.org/images/0015/001598/159811e.pdf, accessed March 23, 2013).

X-12 Census Bureau (n.d.) 'The X-12-Arima Seasonal Adjustment Program', www.census.gov/srd/www/x12a/ (accessed September 7, 2013).

Yang, C. and Lin, H. (2011) 'Is UNESCO recognition effective in fostering tourism? A comment on Yang, Lin and Han: Reply', *Tourism Management*, 32(2): 455–456.

Yang, C., Lin, H. and Han, C. (2009) 'Analysis of international tourist arrivals in China: The role of World Heritage Sites', *Tourism Management*, 31(6): 827–837.

14 Tracing the relevance of Borobudur for socio-economic development through tourism

Devi Roza Kausar

Introduction

This chapter explores the role of the Borobudur Temple Compounds World Heritage Site in Central Java, Indonesia for socio-economic development through tourism. Built in the eighth century AD, the Borobudur temple complex is one of the principal tourism attractions in Indonesia. The Buddhist temples are located in Magelang Regency, Central Java Province and incorporate multiple sites, including the Borobudur Temple (the main temple) and the smaller Mendut and Pawon Temples. Between 1973 and 1983, the temple compounds were restored under the coordination of UNESCO in conjunction with a national executive agency and an international supervisory committee. The complex became a UNESCO World Heritage Site in 1991. Although the Buddhist temple is situated in a predominantly Muslim community, it is still used by Buddhists, especially for the Vesak ceremony on the day of the full moon in May, which celebrates the birth, enlightenment and death of Buddha.

The stone temple is in the form of a stepped pyramid consisting of nine superimposed terraces and crowned by a huge bell-shaped stupa. On the walls and balustrades of the temple are bas-reliefs describing the life of the Buddha and other Buddhist stories. On each of the four sides of the pyramid, running up through its centre to the circular terraces, are stairs and gateways framed by ornaments. Devotees and visitors are encouraged to circumambulate the monument level by level, proceeding to the higher terraces on these staircases to the summit.

The relevance of heritage sites can assume different forms for different stakeholders. For instance, the sites may have cultural relevance as places to perform religious practices; heritage relevance as a reminder of historic pasts; or as a symbol of identity; or political relevance as an instrument for the exercise of power; and economic relevance as a source of income for government (Ashworth, 2008).

Borobudur is widely used to construct the image of Indonesia in its tourism promotion activities (see Figure 14.1). However, Hampton (2005) has argued that it is actually an image that could appear to be dissonant with the present local community. Borobudur, for instance, has little relevance as a place to worship for the majority of the Muslim community living in its shadow.

Figure 14.1 Borobudur Temple (© Borobudur Heritage Conservation Office).

This chapter evaluates the relevance of Borobudur to the livelihoods of rural people living in the surrounding area by assessing the socio-economic impacts of tourism generated by the site. Visits to cultural and heritage resources have become one of the largest and fastest growing sectors of the tourism industry (Timothy and Nyaupane, 2009). Tourism's economic potential means that World Heritage Sites are often seen as resources to promote social and economic development (cf. Rizzo and Mignosa, 2006). At Borobudur, which is situated in a rural region, there are high expectations for the site to bring benefits, such as rural development to nearby communities (JICA, 1979; Black, 1997). Since 1985, the focus for tourism has been the Borobudur Temple Recreation Park, which was developed around the main Borobudur temple. Around two million visitors visit the park every year, 80 per cent of whom are domestic tourists.

However, the length of stay for the majority of visitors is generally rather short (3–4 hours) because many of them use Yogyakarta as a base to visit Borobudur in Magelang Regency. Yogyakarta, the second most important tourism destination in Indonesia, is about 43 km by road from the temple compounds. Nevertheless, there are also international and domestic visitors who stay for a few days in the accommodation which is available in the vicinity of Borobudur.

A study by Hampton (2005) indicated that only limited economic benefits filtered to the surrounding rural area from tourism. The informal sector in Borobudur has the greatest local significance in providing employment. The number of people working in this sector, especially the street vendors, can reach 2–3,000 people in the peak seasons (Taylor, 2003; Soeroso, 2006, 2007). This sometimes chaotic environment is only exacerbated by the sometimes-aggressive selling tactics of the vendors. There have also been concerns that there are few locally made products, most of which are of low quality (Nagaoka, 2011). Soeroso

(2007) noted that, out of about 170 souvenirs offered in the recreation park, only seven were made locally. This contrasts with Greffe's (1994) proposition that tourism requires goods and services from the rural area and promotes the demand for craftwork and labour-intensive products.

The issue of the limited economic benefit from heritage tourism rose to prominence in 2003 when Borobudur was celebrating the twentieth anniversary of its restoration (Adishakti, 2006). On this occasion, a number of local community members made a vocal declaration that questioned the role of management bodies, especially that of the state-owned company (mandated to manage the recreation park), both in managing the site and in ensuring tourism benefits for local communities. In 2006, a monitoring mission carried out by UNESCO's World Heritage Committee recommended that more benefits from the heritage site should be brought to the wider rural area (Boccardi *et al.*, 2006). Poverty has also remained an issue in the vicinity of Borobudur (Nagaoka, 2011).

Clearly there should be a balance between the need to preserve heritage for future generations and the economic and social aspirations of local communities. This perspective is in line with developments in World Heritage Site discourse, which have moved beyond conservation issues, which were the original focus of the 1972 World Heritage Convention. Now World Heritage Sites are seen to have a role in development and even poverty alleviation.

This chapter is divided into seven sections. The following section will discuss the shifting paradigm in World Heritage Site management. The third section will present the methodology of the research, followed by a section presenting findings on the socio-economic impact of tourism in Borobudur based on the author's research in the area. The fifth section will discuss the findings on socio-economic impacts in light of the management of the World Heritage Site and its vicinity. Before the conclusion and policy recommendations, the sixth section will present current progress in Borobudur, especially the rehabilitation works and tourism after the Mount Merapi volcanic eruption in 2010.

The shifting paradigm: World Heritage in development

The aim of inscription to the World Heritage List is to encourage conservation of heritage resources and to foster a sense of collective global responsibility through international cooperation, exchange and support (Leask, 2006). Engelhardt (2005) suggested that to ensure the sites have positive social impact and relevance both to humanity and to local communities, the paradigm of World Heritage Site management needs to be changed. The old paradigm of World Heritage Site management which implied that the sites were monuments of 'princes, priests, and politicians' needs to be shifted to: 'monuments of princes, priests, politicians, and people' (Table 14.1).

Engelhardt's (2005) proposal for a paradigm shift in World Heritage management is in line with developments in World Heritage discourse over the last few years, which has extended beyond conservation issues. Matsuura (2008) indicated that, despite the primary aim of World Heritage Convention to conserve

Table 14.1 Paradigm shifts in World Heritage management

Old versus new	Remaining gaps between old and new paradigms
Monuments of princes, priests and politicians versus Places and spaces of ordinary people	Who are the ordinary people? Giving access to visitors is one of the ways of accommodating ordinary people in heritage sites. However, some communities feel alienated from their own heritage when outsiders take charge of heritage management for the sake of conservation and tourism (Ndoro and Pwiti, 2005; Keitumetse, 2009).
Abandoned, relic sites versus Continuing communities	Some heritage sites are dissonant. They represent ideologies, religions and values that are different to those of the current communities or the ones endorsed by the current authority (Ashworth, 2006). As such, contemporary communities can face challenges in sustaining such dissonant heritage. Moreover, when heritage is located where communities live, there needs to be a commitment from all stakeholders to minimize the negative impact on residents (Engelhardt, 2005, uses the example of Lijiang in China).
Physical components versus Living traditions and practices	Conservation efforts often concentrate on the physical aspects, but neglect the living traditions and practices that used to be an integral part of the heritage site (Keitumetse, 2009). Heritage is often part of a wider cultural and natural landscape, but conservation only deals with heritage as a structure. In communities, this can reduce the sense of ownership; while in terms of tourism, the potential of heritage and its landscape as a tourist attraction may not be developed optimally.
Management by central administration versus Decentralized community management	National governments are ultimately responsible for World Heritage Sites. Consequently, management by central administration is common practice. However, such centralized management can be more effective if there is a mechanism that facilitates coordination between the central government, other organizations and stakeholders for the benefit of heritage conservation and socio-economic development.
Elite use (for recreation) versus Popular use (for development)	For heritage to have benefit in the wider development context, it should encourage the development of other sectors in the local economy and linkages with other attractions in the locality (Boccardi *et al.*, 2006; Timothy and Nyaupane, 2009). However, this is often not the case, because tourism can be seen as a driver for revenue generation while the development of other sectors in the local economy is neglected.

Source: Engelhardt (2005), modified by author based on Ashworth (2006), Boccardi *et al.* (2006), Keitumetse (2009), Timothy and Nyaupane (2009) and Ndoro and Pwiti (2005).

cultural and natural heritage, the designation of World Heritage Sites has to look also at efforts to reduce poverty.

However, complementing Matsuura's (2008) statement, Araoz (2008) argued that the social and economic conditions of the population in and around World Heritage Sites had not actually been a priority in the content of nomination dossiers, nor in the monitoring process that followed inscription to the World Heritage List. Hence, he asserts that there is the need for World Heritage Convention's Operational Guidelines to offer guidance for nomination dossiers to present or analyse demographic information about the population in and around sites proposed for inscription and to address the potential impact of the inscription on the local, regional or national economy.

In addition to the growing notion of the role of World Heritage Sites in development and poverty alleviation, another evolution in the World Heritage discourse involves the adoption of participatory process in nomination and management of World Heritage Sites. The fourth version of UNESCO's Operational Guidelines issued in 1996 included for the first time an article concerning the necessity for local people's participation in the nomination process in order for them to have a shared responsibility with the national government in maintaining the site. Since 2005, the Operational Guidelines have provided a more detailed elaboration on participation in article III.A.123:

> Participation of local people in the nomination process is essential to enable them to have a shared responsibility with the State Party in the maintenance of the property. States Parties are encouraged to prepare nominations with the participation of a wide variety of stakeholders, including site managers, local and regional governments, local communities, NGOs and other interested parties.
>
> (UNESCO, 1996: Article III.A.123)

There are numerous challenges in involving multiple stakeholders in World Heritage Site management and, in many cases, local people, community groups and local businesses are left out of the consultation and management processes despite the need to have a link between the universal and local values. World Heritage Site management often emphasizes the global and national interests at the expense of local people's interests (Millar, 2006). In the case of Borobudur, the development of a recreation park as the access point to the heritage site and as a place to provide for visitors' needs seems to fulfil global and national interests for conservation and access to the site, and for tourism as an income generator. On the other hand, local people's desire for a wider distribution of tourists to the other attractions in the local area has not been accommodated.

Methodology

The socio-economic impact analysis that is presented here is based on three field research campaigns conducted in the Borobudur District between 2007 and

2009. Survey research targeting local people, focus group interviews and key informant interviews, has been used to investigate the socio-economic impacts of cultural heritage tourism from the perspective of the local community.

Surveys are one of the methods that can be used in social impact assessment, such as changes in employment and improvement in living standards (Crandall, 1994). This survey also assessed perceived impacts because these may be different from actual impacts (Pizam, 1978). Therefore, this research also used other data sources to better understand the socio-economic impacts of tourism.

There were 119 respondents in the survey. They were over 20 years old, literate and spoke the national language (Indonesian). The majority were involved in tourism-related jobs. The survey was developed using the livelihoods framework approach (Ashley, 2000; Novelli and Gebhardt, 2007), which not only included direct costs and benefits, such as profits and jobs generated, but also included a range of indirect, positive and negative impacts. This study adopted and developed the framework into a set of questionnaires, with the working variables shown in Table 14.2.

Socio-economic impacts of tourism in Borobudur

The survey results indicate that respondents' opinions towards tourism impacts were generally positive in the following areas: improvement of households' income; improvement of skills; conservation of local culture; sense of pride towards Borobudur; sense of ownership towards Borobudur; positive impact in rural infrastructure; positive impacts on improvement of public facilities; and improvement of well-being.

Despite these generally positive perceptions, the majority of respondents agreed that tourism has had negative impacts on the social and natural environment. According to the respondents, the negative impacts include: the inappropriate way tourists dress; the increasing amount of garbage in the area; competition over raw materials such as bamboos because they are often used for making handicrafts; competition over freshwater resources with the recreation park; persistent poverty despite tourism; local people are rarely invited to participate in tourism; the centralization of tourism within the park; and higher land and building taxes in some areas near to the recreation park but little commensurate change in income.

Moreover, although the survey indicates that there are positive perceptions of tourism impacts, this is not supported by data, such as the actual level of household income and the magnitude of tourism impacts on employment. The tourism impact has been most significant in providing employment in the informal sector, such as street vendors. The monthly household income for the majority of sample households (43 per cent) is less than 500,000 Indonesian Rupiahs (this is below the regional minimum wage of 650,000 Indonesian Rupiahs per month set by the government of Magelang Regency). The focus group interviews highlighted that many participants felt that working as street vendors was attractive because of the potential to earn cash every day rather than waiting until the

Table 14.2 Working variables developed to assess socio-economic impacts

Livelihoods framework approach	Working variables/indicators	
	Economic impacts	*Social impacts*
Impacts of household assets • Financial assets • Physical assets • Human resources • Natural resources • Social capital	Increased income* Increased land value*	Opportunity for skills improvement* Tourism impacts on the social and natural environment* Sense of pride towards the heritage site* Sense of ownership towards the heritage site* Preservation of local culture* Changes in social relationships induced by tourism*
Impacts on household activities and strategies	Opportunity for starting small business (entrepreneurship opportunity)* Tourism promotes assistance for local product development** Opportunity to engage in economic activities in heritage site (recreation park)* Position of tourism jobs (if any) relative to other jobs (e.g. agriculture work), as a substitute or complementary job**	Access to the heritage site (recreation park) for recreational purposes*
Contribution to household goals	Improved well-being* The type of income received from tourism-related jobs	Tourism impact on rural infrastructure development* Impact of tourism on improvement of public facilities*
Participation		Opportunity to participate in forums or meetings on tourism development in the area**

Source: Kausar (2010), based on Ashley (2000), Crandall (1994) and Novelli and Gebhardt (2007).

Notes

* Presented in the questionnaire as a five-point Likert scale.

** Yes or no question.

harvest season, such as with farming. Cukier-Snow and Wall (1993), in their study of the street vendors in Bali, revealed that tourism jobs might be highly prized by local residents when compared to farming small plots of land.

In the Borobudur District, agriculture is still the main sector in the local economy. It is the biggest contributor to the district's gross regional domestic product (GRDP) and it employs 40 per cent of the workforce. However, the importance of this sector has gradually diminished since tourism has prompted a shift from agricultural occupations to ones related to tourism. Urry (1996) has noted that such a shift is often one of the effects of tourism upon pre-existing agricultural activities.

Analysis of different sectors' contribution to GRDP reveals that the service and tourism-related sectors have been growing at a higher rate compared to the agriculture sector. Between 2003 and 2007, the trade, restaurant and hotel sector witnessed an average growth of 4.26 per cent per annum, while the service sector has achieved an average growth of 10.64 per cent per annum (Regional Planning Agency of Malang Regency, 2007). In contrast, during the same time frame, the agriculture sector in the district grew only at 0.2 per cent compared to 2.02 per cent growth in the Magelang Regency as a whole (see Table 14.3). The harvested area for rice has also decreased at an average rate of 7.8 per cent per annum from 1999 to 2006 and rice production has decreased at an average rate of 8.7 per cent per annum during the same period (BPS, 2006). A longitudinal study by Winarni (2006) on the changes in land use in the area revealed that the conversion of land from rice fields to other purposes accelerated after Borobudur was inscribed in the World Heritage List in 1991.

Agriculture is growing at a much slower rate than sectors related to tourism in Borobudur, which could be an indication that tourism development does not

Table 14.3 Comparison of average growth rate in sectors' value added between the Borobudur District and Magelang Regency (2003–2007)

Economic sector	Average growth rate (%)	
	Borobudur District	Magelang Regency
Industrial origin		
Agriculture	0.20	2.02
Mining and quarrying	7.78	4.57
Manufacturing	4.63	7.46
Electricity, gas and water supply	6.43	6.32
Construction	9.24	7.65
Trade, restaurant and hotel	4.26	4.27
Transportation and communication	5.32	5.02
Financial, ownership and business services	3.21	3.14
Services	10.64	8.99
Total GRDP	4.64	4.69

Sources: Regional Planning Agency of Magelang Regency (2007) and BPS (2006), calculated by author.

encourage development in agriculture. This means that tourism has a limited impact for the majority of the local people who still rely heavily on the agricultural sector. In addition, it indicates that the impact of tourism is not evenly distributed across different economic activities. Liew (1980) has previously argued that tourism in developing countries does not always stimulate local agricultural production because of weak inter-sectoral linkages.

These weak inter-sectoral linkages are emphasized in the responses of the survey participants, who felt that tourism had done little to promote assistance for local product development. While participants agreed that tourism had provided business opportunities over the years, its impact on other sectors was limited to those activities that were closely related to tourism, such as the development of the tourist village and handicrafts. However, agriculture and food production have largely been neglected.

In contrast to the shortcomings in the beneficial impacts for local communities, the study found that heritage tourism in Borobudur had contributed significantly to the local government's tax revenue and the development of infrastructure in the area.

Managing the Borobudur World Heritage Site and its environs

If heritage tourism is to raise the standard of living of the majority of local people in Borobudur, it faces numerous challenges. These include how to create better linkages between tourism and the agriculture sector, which involves over 40 per cent of the workforce; how to develop other rural opportunities, such as local home-based industries; and how to create more employment opportunities (Kausar, 2011).

How tourism is planned and managed can affect its impact (Mason, 2003). At Borobudur, there has been a lack of clarity about which organization would lead the efforts to overcome the challenges mentioned above (Kausar, 2011). The Presidential Decree No. 1/1992, which is the highest law stipulating management of the site, specifies that the Borobudur Heritage Conservation Institute (BHCI) manages the core conservation area (Zone 1 or the main temple); a state-owned enterprise (PT Taman or Taman Limited) manages the Borobudur Temple Recreation Park (Zone 2); and the Magelang Regency Government manages the surrounding rural environment and residential areas (Zone 3).

The zoning system stipulated in the decree was adopted from the area Master Plan that was developed by the Japan International Cooperation Agency (JICA) in 1979 for Borobudur. The Master Plan comprises five zones instead of three. Zone 1 is the innermost zone, which includes the Borobudur temple; surrounding this is Zone 2, which comprises the archaeological park; beyond this is Zone 3, the regulated land-use zone, which includes the temples at Mendut and Pawon; further still is Zone 4, the historical scenery preservation zone; and finally Zone 5 is the national archaeological park zone. The Presidential Decree No. 1/1992, however, only recognizes Zones 1–3.

The local government of the Magelang District, which is responsible for the management of the residential areas, has carried out some assistance programmes to promote rural industries. However, the communities where the programmes took place often complained of a lack of continuity and long-term vision in the assistance programmes (Kausar, 2010). For instance, training on product development in several villages has not been followed up with guidance and assistance on capital provision and marketing strategies.

The Presidential Decree does not specify the obligations of the three organizations towards community development. It has also been criticized because it only emphasizes the commercial value of the Borobudur Temple as part of the recreation park. Furthermore, as a legal instrument that was created specifically for the World Heritage Site, it fails to acknowledge the sites as heritage with international significance, and not merely another tourism attraction. Moreover, this legal framework also complicates the power relations between the three organizations because it gives more emphasis to the rights of the state-owned enterprise PT Taman. This led to a situation in which the company dominated the management and decision-making processes of the site.

The national tourism policy of Indonesia, which places much emphasis on economic growth, may have contributed to the enactment of this decree. The Indonesian government sees tourism as a vital tool for economic growth, regional development and employment creation (Dahles, 2001). Consequently, planning in Borobudur was undertaken with an economic/industry-based perspective (Hampton, 2005); however, prioritizing economic goals over social and cultural aspects may lose sight of who actually benefits or loses (Hall, 2000).

Another important issue in the planning and management of Borobudur is the absence of a formal management plan. Management plans typically consist of some shared purpose, the presence of a leading body, steering committee, annual action plan, monitoring measures, performance indicators and consultation arrangement. In 1997, a management plan became a prerequisite for inscription to the World Heritage List. Furthermore, all sites listed before 1997 were actually required to prepare and submit a management plan by 2005 (Wilson and Boyle, 2006). However, no sanction has been imposed for sites that have no management plan. The World Heritage Convention is a 'soft law', which is not legally binding, thus the degree of compliance depends on each government (Hall, 2006).

The absence of the management plan in Borobudur has led to a lack of shared purpose between the organizations, especially one concerning community development. Instead, each organization in the management system has its own organizational purpose with differing interests (i.e. PT Taman is more business oriented, BHCI's main function is conservation and the local government's main interest is the contribution of tourism to regional income; see Figure 14.2).

The lack of shared organizational purpose between the organizations in the management system has had several impacts. First, no unified direction permeates the management system as a whole. Unity of direction, which is one of the principles of effective management identified by Henry Fayol (Weihrich and

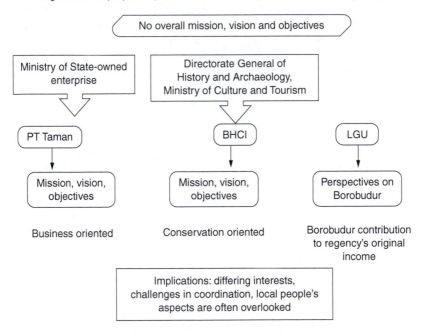

Figure 14.2 An illustration of the current organizational structure of the Borobudur
heritage site (source: Kausar, 2010).

Note
LGU is local government unit.

Koontz, 1993), is difficult to achieve when there is no shared or agreed purpose
between the three organizations. Defining purpose and problems together is par-
amount if autonomous organizations wish to resolve problems (Gray, 1989;
Jamal and Getz, 1995).

Second, local people's perspectives are largely overlooked in both PT
Taman's and BHCI's objectives. For instance, PT Taman does not specify any
measurable objective related to community development or the promotion of
more tourism benefit for the communities in its company objectives. The BHCI
does not specify community strategy in its objectives. The survey revealed that
the respondents saw Borobudur as a tourism attraction, an economic driver and a
Buddhist monument. Such views limit the potential of the heritage site to play a
greater role in community life, such as being the setting for community activities. Such multiple uses of cultural heritage could lead to an improved sense of
ownership and respect towards the heritage site, and such attitudes would
provide community support for conservation.

Developing a management plan requires skills and commitment from organizations to work together (Wilson and Boyle, 2006). However, Nuryanti (1996)

has noted that inadequate institutional capabilities have plagued many World Heritage Sites in developing countries. Issues such as lack of budget, lack of priority given to the culture and tourism sector, and potential political issues, such as a partial loss of decision-making autonomy in each organization, may be the reason for the absence of Borobudur (and Prambanan) management plans.

Existing problems in the local rural area, such as poor farming conditions in parts of the district, small land holdings, low educational attainment, which limits job opportunities, poverty and scarce employment opportunities, have contributed towards a high dependency on tourism. On the other hand, Hall *et al.* (2003) suggested tourism in rural areas should complement an existing thriving and diverse rural economy; otherwise it can create income and employment inequalities. Hall *et al.* (2003) also underscored that rural tourism planning must be a part of a wider integrated planning of all sectors in the rural economy.

The lack of a management plan in Borobudur has led to the absence of a continuous heritage tourism planning mechanism between the three organizations, not to mention a lack of integrated planning between tourism and other sectors. The lack of integrated planning is a constraint for tourism development (Gunn, 1994). Table 14.4 summarizes the institutional problems that relate to the absence of both a management plan and an integrated plan between tourism and other sectors.

The shifting paradigm in World Heritage management is also significant. Today, World Heritage Site nomination dossiers are required to address the potential impact of inscription on the local, regional or national economy (Araoz, 2008). The nomination dossiers of the Borobudur Temple Compound World Heritage Site make no mention of local communities or how they would benefit from the presence of a World Heritage Site (UNESCO, 1990) because at the time of inscription this was not required in the nomination process. Therefore, the original nomination process, which emphasized conservation but disregarded community development, has influenced the limited view of the World Heritage Site for conservation and tourism.

Current progress in Borobudur: post-disaster rehabilitation works and efforts to achieve sustainable development

In October 2010, one of the most active volcanoes on earth, Mount Merapi in Central Java, erupted. In a series of prolonged eruptions more than 380 people were killed, 776 injured and 136,585 displaced. This natural disaster also had an impact on Borobudur and the communities living in the vicinity of the temple because the volcano is only 30km away. Corrosive ash covered the temple, blocked the drainage system and penetrated the cracks and gaps in the stone (Nagaoka, 2011).

Emergency action was immediately taken to limit the disaster's effect on the temple itself and the livelihoods of the surrounding communities. Borobudur Temple was closed to the public. Volcanic ash was cleaned from the surface of the monument to prevent the deterioration of its stonework. Staff from the

Table 14.4 Institutional problems found at Borobudur and their implications

Functions carried out in the management process	Problems	Implications
Planning: developing a rational approach to achieving preselected objectives (Weihrich and Koontz, 1993).	No overall organizational purpose (mission and objectives) of the heritage site. Each organization in the management system has its own organizational purpose with differing interests based on the underlying function of each organization. The 1979 Master Plan encompassing the core conservation zone, recreation park and surrounding villages lacks implementation and has not been institutionalized. Lack of integration between tourism planning and planning from other sectors.	No unified direction, needed for effective management, between organizations. Local people's perspectives are largely overlooked because there are no specific and measurable objectives related to community development. Other rural potential and intangible heritage, such as local knowledge in performing arts, rituals, crafts and food from traditional villages, is poorly developed alongside the core heritage site.
Organization: identification and classification of required activities to accomplish goals and the grouping of activities (Weihrich and Koontz, 1993).	Issue of power relations. Issue of clarity in identification of required activities needed to help the local communities who are responsible for carrying out these activities.	No coordinated effort on achieving sustainable development in the area.
Coordination: achieving harmony among different efforts towards accomplishment of mutual goals (Weihrich and Koontz, 1993).	Coordination is very much affected by other managerial functions. Thus, problems in planning and organizing are indeed impacted on coordination.	Planning does not involve a shared mission and objectives, and a common perception of problems that exist in the locality, thus coordination between the organizations becomes a real challenge. Coordination with other sectors is difficult when there is no integrated planning mechanism. Tasks for increasing the benefits of heritage tourism for the local people have not been identified and divided between organizations; hence, coordinated effort to tackle local problems is hard to achieve.

Source: Kausar (2010).

Borobudur Heritage Conservation Office and the state-owned enterprise PT Taman, as well as local volunteers, began the colossal task of clearing the ash using simple equipment such as brooms, dustpans and vacuum cleaners. The quantity of ash was relatively small and the work was nearly completed within a week. Unfortunately, a larger eruption occurred on November 5, 2010 and once again Borobudur was covered in a thick layer of ash, this time up to 45 mm deep.

The disaster led to the closure of Yogyakarta Airport for three weeks, which caused serious problems for local and regional tourism. However, it also brought new hope through a recovery programme that was designed to contribute to the sustainable development of the Borobudur region (Nagaoka, 2011). A group of individuals with a keen interest in the long-term protection of Borobudur, called the 'Friends of Borobudur', raised funds to assist the authorities in carrying out emergency joint operations for the mitigation and restoration of the site.

The joint operation was divided into three phases. The first was the emergency response, the second was a recovery phase, while the final phase was aimed at the improvement of the livelihood of the local community through tourism and the cultural industries (Nagaoka, 2011). Two main activities were carried out in the emergency response phase: a community-driven emergency cleaning operation and tree planting activities within the temple compounds to replace the many trees and plants that had been destroyed during the volcanic eruption. The community-driven cleaning operation began in January 2011 and involved 60 local workers, who were guided by the Borobudur Heritage Conservation Office. By the end of the preservation work in November 2011, 600 community members were involved in the cleaning operation, which included the entire surface of the monument as well as inside the stone cracks and fissures, the drainage systems, the reliefs, Buddha statues, façades and balustrades (Nagaoka, 2011). This operation was crucial because the corrosive ash could trigger damage to the architectural structure of the monument. In the recovery phase, a scientific damage assessment was made of the ash erosion to the stone temple.

Practical involvement with the monument had also revived the community's awareness of the importance of taking care of the structure (Nagaoka, 2011). One of the local workers involved in the cleaning operation said that being involved in the operation reminded him of his childhood, when his house was located at the foot of Borobudur Temple before it was relocated during the establishment of the park (Nagaoka, 2011). He felt that Borobudur was not a monument for him then, instead it was part of his environment.

In 1982, approximately 250 families were moved from the vicinity of the monument into four new settlements (Black, 1997). Many were naturally opposed to being moved because they felt a strong attachment to the land they were living on and they were worried that they would be deprived of their livelihood if they could no longer access the tourist market from their homes (Black, 1997; Winarni, 2006).

The final phase of the joint operations was aimed at improving the livelihood for the local community and mainly took the form of training sessions to improve the local tourism and cultural industries. Previously there were relatively few locally made products available to tourists and many of these were of poor quality (Nagaoka, 2011). The shortage of appealing local products makes income generation difficult for the local community.

One of the training sessions in the final phase aimed to revive the local handicrafts industry. The handicraft training therefore promoted the production of high-quality craft products using traditional skills and local materials. One innovation was to use the lava stones abundant after the eruption as the material for producing a wide range of home accessories and high-quality souvenirs. There were also training sessions to improve hygiene and sanitation at community-based tourism venues, such as traditional food and snacks factories and guest houses. This training brought new hope of integrating the local food industry into the tourism market (Kausar, 2010).

Conclusions

This chapter has explored the relevance of one of the largest Buddhist monuments in the world, the Borobudur World Heritage Site, to the predominantly Muslim communities living in its vicinity. Although the temple does not have much relevance as a place to perform religious activities for the majority of local people, it influences the socio-economic development of the area, particularly through tourism. Tourism at the site has triggered infrastructure development and increased the area's accessibility and connectivity to other areas and communities. It opens business opportunities and contributes significantly to local government tax revenue. Tourism-related industries have also contributed to the growth of the service sector's share of the GRDP.

Tourism impacts on the livelihoods of the local communities, however, have been limited in scope. The most evident impact of tourism has been the provision of employment in the informal sector, which is characterized by low and unstable income. Although the survey results indicate that the community perceives many tourism impacts positively, these perceptions are not supported by other evidence, such as the level of income of the majority of the sample, which is still below the minimum regional wage. Tourism in Borobudur has seen only limited success in stimulating the development of other sectors, especially agriculture.

Alongside these problems, the study found a lack of coordination between organizations involved in the management of the World Heritage Site and its environment because of the inadequate legal framework and the absence of coordination mechanisms and a World Heritage Site management plan. Clearly, Borobudur is in need of a management plan to improve coordination between organizations. Moreover, Borobudur's function as the centre of community cultural activities should be revived in order to increase local people's sense of ownership, which has declined since the site's inscription.

One positive aspect of the 2010 volcanic eruptions is that the post-disaster activities have helped to unify the local communities under the coordination of organizations involved in the management, improved sense of ownership and triggered innovations in ways to enhance the community's livelihoods through the development of sustainable tourism activities.

Since the inscription of Borobudur on the World Heritage List in 1991, heritage tourism has become an increasingly important phenomenon. Managing the effects of this for the benefit of the local community will be one of the challenges for the coming decades.

References

Adishakti, L. T. (2006) *Borobudur heritage site and area management: From temple to saujana heritage and for a better conservation and management of the World Heritage Site*, presentation paper. Yogyakarta: ICOMOS Indonesia, Indonesian Trust, Centre for Heritage Conservation – Department of Architecture and Planning, Gadjah Mada University.

Araoz, G. (2008) 'World heritage and public works: Development cooperation and poverty reduction', in *World Heritage and Public Works: Development Cooperation for Poverty Alleviation Seminar*, Tokyo, Japan, August 29. Tokyo: United Nations University.

Ashley, C. (2000) *The impacts of tourism on rural livelihoods: Namibia's experience. Working paper 128*. London: Overseas Development Institute.

Ashworth, G. J. (2006) 'The commodification of the past as an instrument for local development: Don't count on it', in McLoughlin, J., Kaminski, J. and Sodagar, B. (eds.) *Heritage Impact 2005: Proceedings of the first international symposium on the socio-economic impact of cultural heritage*. Budapest: Archaeolingua, 81–88.

Ashworth, G. J. (2008) 'Paradigms and paradoxes in planning the past', in Smith, M. and Onderwater, L. (eds.) *ATLAS Reflections 2008: Selling or telling? Paradoxes in tourism, culture and heritage*. Arnhem: ATLAS, 23–24.

Black, H. (1997) *Monumental problems: Cultural heritage and communities in Indonesia and Thailand*. Unpublished MA Thesis, School of Planning, University of Waterloo, Canada.

Boccardi, G., Brooks, G. and Gurung, H. (2006) *Mission report. Reactive monitoring mission to Borobudur temple compounds*. Indonesia: World Heritage Property (February): 18–25.

BPS (2006) *Kabupaten Magelang Dalam Angka*. Indonesia: Central Bureau of Statistics

Crandall, L. (1994) 'The social impact of tourism on developing regions and its measurement', in Ritchie, J. R. B. and Goeldner, C. R. (eds.) *Travel, tourism and hospitality research: A handbook for managers and researchers* (2nd edition). Toronto: John Wiley, 413–423.

Cukier-Snow, J. and Wall, G. (1993) 'Tourism employment: Perspectives from Bali', *Tourism Management*, 14(3): 195–201.

Dahles, H. (2001) *Tourism, heritage and national culture in Java: Dilemmas of a local community*. Richmond: Curzon.

Engelhardt, R. A. (2005) 'World Heritage: Its implication and relevance for humanity', presentation paper, *Training workshop on the conservation and management of World Heritage Sites*, April 18. Hiroshima: UNITAR Hiroshima Office for Asia and the Pacific.

Gray, B. (1989) *Collaborating: Finding common ground for multiparty problems*. San Francisco: Jossey-Bass.

Greffe, X. (1994) 'Is tourism a lever for economic and social development?', in Bramwell, B. and Lane, B. (eds.) *Rural tourism and sustainable rural development.* Clevedon: Channel View Publications, 22–40.

Gunn, C. A. (1994) *Tourism planning: Basics, concepts and cases* (3rd edition). Philadelphia: Taylor & Francis.

Hall, C. M. (2000) *Tourism planning: Policies, planning and relationships.* Harlow: Prentice-Hall.

Hall, C. M. (2006) 'Implementing the World Heritage Convention: What happens after listing?', in Leask, A. and Fyall, A. (eds.) *Managing World Heritage Sites.* Oxford: Elsevier Butterworth-Heinemann, 18–32.

Hall, D., Mitchell, M. and Roberts, L. (2003) 'Tourism and the countryside: Dynamic relationships', in Hall, D., Mitchell, M. and Roberts, L. (eds.) *New directions in rural tourism.* Aldershot: Ashgate, 3–15.

Hampton, M. P. (2005) 'Heritage, local communities and economic development', *Annals of Tourism Research*, 32(3): 735–759.

Jamal, T. and Getz, D. (1995) 'Collaboration theory and community tourism planning', *Annals of Tourism Research*, 22(1): 186–204.

JICA (1979) *Borobudur Prambanan national archaeological parks final report.* Tokyo: Japan International Cooperation Agency.

Kausar, D. R. (2010) 'Socio-economic impacts of tourism on a World Heritage Site: Case study of rural Borobudur, Indonesia', unpublished PhD dissertation. Nagoya: Nagoya University.

Kausar, D. R. (2011) 'Socio-economic impacts of heritage tourism on its locality: A case study of Borobudur temple compounds World Heritage Site, Central Java', *Forum of International Development Studies*, 40: 131–150.

Keitumetse, S. O. (2009) 'Sustainable development and cultural heritage management in Botswana: Towards sustainable communities', *Sustainable Development*, 19(1): 49–59.

Leask, A. (2006) 'World Heritage designation', in Leask, A. and Fyall, A. (eds.) *Managing World Heritage Sites.* Oxford: Elsevier Butterworth-Heinemann, 5–19.

Liew, J. (1980) 'Tourism and development: A re-examination', in Pearce, D. (ed.) *Tourism in the South Pacific. The contribution of research to development and planning.* Christchurch: University of Christchurch, 13–17.

Mason, P. (2003) *Tourism impacts, planning and management.* Oxford: Butterworth-Heinemann.

Matsuura, K. (2008) Keynote speech, in *World Heritage and public works: Development cooperation for poverty alleviation seminar*, Tokyo, Japan, August 29. Tokyo: United Nations University.

Millar, S. (2006) 'Stakeholders and community participation', in Leask, A. and Fyall, A. (eds.) *Managing World Heritage Sites.* Oxford: Elsevier Butterworth-Heinemann, 37–54.

Nagaoka, M. (2011) *Borobudur the road to recovery: Community-based rehabilitation work and sustainable tourism development.* Jakarta: UNESCO.

Ndoro, W. and Pwiti, G. (2005) 'Heritage management in Southern Africa', in Corsane, G. (ed.) *Heritage, museums and galleries: An introduction.* Abingdon: Routledge, 154–168.

Novelli, M. and Gebhardt, K. (2007) 'Community based tourism in Namibia: "Reality show" or "window dressing"?', *Current Issues in Tourism*, 10(5): 443–479.

Nuryanti, W. (1996) 'Heritage and postmodern tourism', *Annals of Tourism Research*, 23(2): 249–260.

Pizam, A. (1978) 'Tourism impacts: The social costs to the destination community as perceived by its residents', *Journal of Travel Research*, 16(3): 8–12.

Regional Planning Agency of Magelang Regency (2007) *Regional income report*. Magelang, Central Java Province: Regional Planning Agency of Magelang Regency.

Rizzo, I. and Mignosa, A. (2006) 'Policy decisions and cultural heritage impact', in McLoughlin, J., Kaminski, J. and Sodagar, B. (eds.) *Heritage Impact 2005.* Budapest: Archaeolingua, 58–68.

Soeroso, A. (2006) 'Valuing Borobudur heritage area in a multi-attribute framework environmental economic perspective and its ecotourism management policy implications', unpublished PhD dissertation (in Indonesian). Yogyakarta: Gadjah Mada University.

Soeroso, A. (2007) 'Nilai Ekonomi Konservasi Saujana Budaya Kawasan Borobudur: Sebuah Eksperimen Pilihan' ('Economic value of the Saujana Borobudur cultural conservation area: A choice experiment'), *Journal Of Indonesian Economy and Business*, 22(3), 343–61.

Taylor, K. (2003) 'Cultural landscape as open air museum: Borobudur World Heritage Site and its setting', *Humanities Research*, 10(2): 51–62.

Timothy, D. J. and Nyaupane, G. P. (2009) *Cultural heritage and tourism in the developing world: A regional perspective*. London: Routledge.

UNESCO (1990) *Nomination Dossier of Borobudur and Prambanan Temple compounds Indonesia for inclusion in the World Heritage List*. Paris: UNESCO.

UNESCO (1996) *Operational guidelines for the implementation of the World Heritage Convention*. Paris: UNESCO World Heritage Centre.

Urry, J. (1996) 'The changing economics of the tourist industry', in Apostolopoulos, Y., Leivadi, S. and Yiannakis, A. (eds.) *The sociology of tourism: Theoretical and empirical investigations*. London: Routledge, 193–218.

Weihrich, H. and Koontz, H. (1993) *Management: A global perspective.* New York: McGraw-Hill.

Wilson, L. and Boyle, E. (2006) 'Interorganisational collaboration at UK World Heritage Sites', *Leadership and Organization Development Journal*, 27(6): 501–523.

Winarni, G. (2006) 'Kajian Perubahan Ruang Kawasan World Heritage Candi Borobudur' ('Changes in space studies at the Borobudur World Heritage Area'), unpublished Master's thesis, University of Gajah Mada.

15 'Mobile heritage'

Motor vehicle heritage tourism in the United Kingdom

Jaime Kaminski and Geoffrey Smith

Introduction

Heritage tourism takes many forms. Despite the growing awareness that heritage can include almost anything from the past that has a meaning for individuals or groups in the present (cf. Ashworth, 1991), the academic literature still places much emphasis on tourism associated with sites and monuments. There are, however, other forms of heritage that have not been as widely studied. One such area is 'historic motor vehicle event tourism', in which individuals and groups travel to take part as participants, competitors or spectators in events focused on heritage vehicles.[1] This gives rise to the interesting phenomenon of both the heritage and the tourists being mobile.

Recent research on the economic and social benefits of the historic vehicle movement on the UK indicates that between 2010 and 2011 heritage vehicle enthusiasts spent 855,000 nights away from home in the UK whilst attending historic vehicle events. Enthusiasts spent a further 300,000 nights abroad attending historic vehicle events (Frost *et al.*, 2011: 15). Clearly the historic vehicle movement is a significant driver for tourism.

Despite this, little academic consideration has been given to the actual economic impact of historic vehicle events on communities. Such events can be important tourist attractions but appear to exist on the margins of tourism research. Moreover, the situation is doubly complicated because the study of motor vehicle history is not widely studied as part of traditional academic historical research. Academically, heritage vehicle research is marginalized and publically only a minority considers vehicles to be 'heritage'. This combination of factors goes some way to explaining the dearth of research on heritage vehicle tourism.

In order to understand how historic vehicle events can impact local communities, research was initiated to assess and understand the economic impact of three separate events: the 2010 London to Brighton Veteran Car Run on the city of Brighton and Hove (Smith *et al.*, 2011), the 2012 Beaulieu Autojumble on the New Forest region (Kaminski *et al.*, 2013a) and the 2012 Goodwood Revival Festival (Kaminski *et al.*, 2013b). These events were chosen because they represent a cross-section of different event types (a run, an autojumble and a festival) and have heritage tourism characteristics. This research was assessed in conjunction with previous studies on the value of the historic vehicle movement to the UK.

Methodology

An economic impact assessment of each of the chosen events was conducted by the University of Brighton and the Federation of British Historic Vehicle Clubs (FBHVC). Three principal avenues of enquiry were pursued:

- Spectators were selected at random during the events and were questioned in order to ascertain their financial expenditure within the respective study areas (the city of Brighton and Hove; a radius of 24 km [15 miles] around Beaulieu; and 20 km [12 miles] around Goodwood).
- The participants were questioned in order to establish their expenditure within the study areas during the events.
- Additionally, the organizers were questioned in order to ascertain their expenditure on the events in the study areas.

The London to Brighton Veteran Car Run 2010

Organized by the Royal Automobile Club (RAC), the annual London to Brighton Veteran Car Run is the longest-running motoring event in the world. The first Run took place on Saturday 14 November 1896 and was organized by the Motor Car Club to celebrate the passing of the Locomotives on the Highway Act 1896. But the beginning of the 'London to Brighton Veteran Car Run' as it is known today can be traced to 1927 when a re-enactment of the Emancipation Run, called the 'Run to Brighton', was sponsored by the *Daily Sketch* and the *Sunday Graphic* newspapers. This arrangement continued until 1930 when Britain's oldest motoring club, the Royal Automobile Club, took over the organization of the Run. The event has taken place annually since 1927, with the exception of the war years and 1947, when fuel rationing was in force (Montagu, 1990).

The 'Brighton', as the Run is widely known in historic vehicle circles, has taken place on the first Sunday in November since 1956 and starts at sunrise from Hyde Park, London. To qualify for entry, the motor vehicles must have been manufactured prior to 1 January 1905 and be of four-wheel, tri-car or motor tricycle design. There are two official stops along the way: Crawley (for coffee) and Preston Park (a suburb of Brighton, in East Sussex, UK), which is currently the official finishing point; the cars then proceed to Madeira Drive on the seafront where the majority of the spectators gather. Participants are not permitted to exceed an average speed of 20 mph (32 km/h) and those who finish before 16.30 are awarded a bronze 'finisher's medal'. The medal is based on the medals awarded by the Motor Car Club to the first eight finishers of the original Emancipation Run.[2] Today the London to Brighton Veteran Car Run is one of the largest meetings of veteran cars in the world.

The year 2010 saw the seventy-seventh Run, which took place 114 years after the Emancipation Run. Five-hundred and seventy cars registered, including 150 makes of vehicles ranging in age between 105 and 116 years old. The demand for places on the 2010 London to Brighton Veteran Car Run was such that all the allotted places were filled six months before the event. The 2010 event included a record 137 overseas entries (24 per cent of all registrations). These included cars from China, Australia, USA, Canada, Mexico, Argentina, South Africa and Europe. Of the 505 starters, 434 reached the finish at Brighton (see Figure 15.1).

The spectators

The 2010 London to Brighton Veteran Car Run took place on Sunday 7 November; a sunny day with temperatures in the low teens and only a light breeze. These fine conditions encouraged spectators to come out in considerable numbers on the seafront. With any impact study, the number of spectators and participants is the foundation for all other subsequent calculations (Davies *et al.*, 2010). Therefore, considerable effort was devoted to ensuring the greatest possible accuracy. However, the Veteran Car Run is an entirely unrestricted free-to-view event. With no tickets, and spectators free to move about the route and city, and mix freely with non-spectators, assessing spectator numbers was particularly problematic. A variety of mechanisms was therefore used, including video recording of the spectators along the seafront area and along the route in Brighton, manual counting and estimation of turnover of spectators during the event. These observations revealed that an estimated 20,300 spectators watched the Run in Brighton.

A questionnaire was administered to spectators across the entire route through Brighton during the event. This generated 595 usable responses, or 3 per cent of

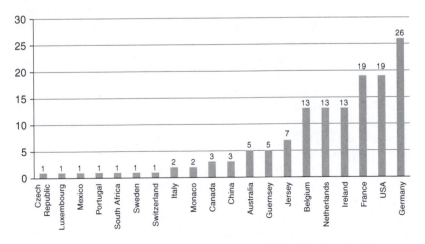

Figure 15.1 Non-UK entries in the 2010 London to Brighton Veteran Car Run.

the estimated population.[3] The survey revealed that, of the 20,300 spectators who watched the Run in 2010, 37 per cent were residents of Brighton and Hove (7,600), while 63 per cent were from outside of the city (12,700). Of these spectators who had come from outside of the city, 72 per cent had come specifically to see the Run (14,700). Therefore, 48 per cent of all spectators were from outside of the city and had come specifically to watch the Run (see Table 15.1).

The majority of the spectators were day visitors (52 per cent) and residents (34 per cent), the remaining 14 per cent staying overnight in the city. This is primarily because the event is highly accessible to day visitors. Although the Run begins at Hyde Park in London at sunrise and the first vehicles can potentially arrive at Madeira Drive on the Brighton seafront from 10.00, the majority of vehicles arrive between noon and 15.00. This timing means that spectators can travel to Brighton and return home on the day of the event.

The spectator's average spend within the city was quantified. It was found that non-Brighton residents visiting Brighton specifically to attend the event spent on average £43.87 per person in the city (see Table 15.2). Naturally Brighton residents attending the event spent less, averaging £8.97 per person.

The large disparity in expenditures between tourists who came to Brighton specifically to watch the Run and those for whom the Run was a secondary activity can be explained by motivation and opportunity to spend. The majority of the spectators were day visitors, so their time in the city was limited. These visitors were sufficiently motivated to travel to Brighton for the express purpose of viewing the final stages of the Run. It is therefore natural that much of the time they spent in the city was devoted to watching the Run and so these spectators had less opportunity and time to spend money in the city.

If these figures are extrapolated to the total population of spectators at the London to Brighton Veteran Car Run then the 5,000 Brighton residents who came specifically to view the Run would have spent £44,800 in their city. The

Table 15.1 Estimated size of different spectator groups at the London to Brighton Veteran Car Run

	In Brighton specifically for the Run	*In Brighton but **not** specifically for the Run*
Residents	5,000 (24%)	2,600 (13%)
Visitors	9,700 (48%)	3,000 (15%)

Table 15.2 Estimated expenditure per person of different spectator groups at the London to Brighton Veteran Car Run

	In Brighton specifically for the Run	*In Brighton but **not** specifically for the Run*
Residents	£8.97	£8.74
Visitors	£43.87	£98.27

total expenditure in Brighton by the 9,700 London to Brighton Veteran Car Run visitors from outside the city who came specifically to view the Run was £425,800 (see Table 15.3).

The economic benefits of the Run accruing to Brighton and Hove include the immediate additional inward expenditure on accommodation, food, entertainment and, to a lesser extent, travel. The Run organizers do not provide catering for the public, so almost all of the non-participant spectators' food requirements are met by the city.[4] Some minor event-related souvenirs, such as programmes, are provided by the organizers but aside from this all other retail expenditure is in the local community.

The participants

A postal survey was sent to participants of the 2010 Run in mid-December of that year from which 138 responses were obtained (27 per cent). Aside from the drivers, there are often numerous other associated participants, such as friends, family and mechanics, hence the average party size for participants was 5.2. The expenditure of these 721 participants in Brighton and Hove totalled £102,400. This yielded an average spend per person of £142.00. During the 2010 Veteran Car Run, 434 cars finished, giving an expenditure of £320,500 based on 2,257 participants and their associates (see Table 15.4).

Table 15.3 Total expenditure by different spectator groups at the London to Brighton Veteran Car Run

	In Brighton specifically f or the Run	In Brighton but **not** specifically for the Run
Residents	£44,800	£22,700
Visitors	£425,800	£294,800

Table 15.4 Participant expenditure in Brighton relating to the Veteran Car Run

Expenditure type	Amount
Accommodation	£137,100
Food/drink	£76,000
Private car expenses	£43,200
Other transport	£13,200
Entertainment	£9,000
Retail shopping	£42,000
Total	£320,500

The economic impact on the city

The London to Brighton Veteran Car Run results in a number of injections of capital from outside the city (see Table 15.5). These are:

- *Spectator expenditure*: The expenditure of visitors from outside of the city who came specifically to see the Run was £425,800. The expenditure of the 3,000 (15 per cent) spectators (£294,800) who were from outside of the town and did not come specifically to see the Run was excluded from the impact assessment even though they may have been partially motivated to come to the city on that weekend because of the Run.[5] Residents' expenditure totalling £67,500 was excluded because that money may have been spent in the city anyway.
- *Participant expenditure*: The total expenditure of the participants was £320,500. Interestingly, it was the participants in the Run who made the largest relative contribution to the local economy (38 per cent of Run-related expenditure). This group had an average spend per person of £142.00 compared to £43.90 for Run-specific spectators. Much of this expenditure is associated with accommodation (43 per cent) and food (24 per cent). The reason for this disparity is because the participants predominantly stayed in the city overnight. This is because after the Run finishes in the afternoon, there are formal dinners for the participants, which provides an incentive to stay. This figure seems unlikely to decline because year on year since 2003 registrations have increased.
- *Organizers' expenditure*: The total expenditure incurred by the organizers in Brighton and Hove was £84,500. This included the license fee, infrastructure costs, services, catering and other general event costs.

The direct financial impact of the event on the town is only part of the benefit. A multiplier is used to capture the secondary effects of spending on the city's economy. This provides an indication of the number of times these external injections of capital from visitors and the organizers are circulated in the Brighton and Hove economy. In the case of the London to Brighton Veteran Car Run, the £830,800 expenditure on the event by those specifically visiting the Run and on the Run itself translated to £1,124,000 worth of income for the city through indirect and induced effects. Clearly this impact relates to one small part of the route; the total economic impact of the entire event will be considerable.[6]

Table 15.5 Expenditure sources used to calculate the impact of the Veteran Car Run

Expenditure in Brighton and Hove	Amount
Spectator spend (non-residents who came specifically for the Run)	£425,800
Participant spend	£320,500
Organizer spend	£84,500
Total spend	£830,800

Intangible benefits

It is evident that the financial impact of the London to Brighton Veteran Car Run on the city is considerable. However, simply using the financial expenditure associated with the Run to provide an estimate of the economic value on the city of Brighton and Hove will underestimate the event's overall impact and benefit. Financial expenditure associated with the Run does not come close to capturing the brand value of the event to the city. The event is world famous, as attested by the vast geographical distances participants are willing to travel with their cars to take part. Moreover, it is not only the participants; some spectators are willing to travel huge distances as well.

Perhaps more significantly, the London to Brighton formula is the foundation for a plethora of other motoring events. These include runs for Minis, Land Rovers, Citroën 2CVs, Jaguars, MGs, Smart Cars, Volkswagen vans and campers, Triumph TRs, Pioneer motorcycles, vintage motorcycles and vintage commercial vehicles. Many of these motoring events start in London and finish at Madeira Drive on Brighton's seafront, highlighting the symbolic familial relationship with the Veteran Car Run.

The cumulative benefit of all these events and the publicity they generate for the city is huge and can in part be attributed to the original London to Brighton Veteran Car Run.

The Beaulieu International Autojumble

The first Beaulieu 'Autojumble' took place on Sunday 17 September 1967, in a field within the grounds of the Beaulieu Estate, in Hampshire, UK. It was open from 11.00 to 17.00 and was billed as 'a grand event for the buying, selling and swapping of spare parts, accessories and other desiderata for motorcars and motorcycles of all ages'. The aim was to 'provide a market-place in which both private enthusiasts and the trade will be able both to dispose of surplus items useful to other restorers, and to buy what they themselves require'. The only restriction on items for sale was that they were to be 'clearly connected with motoring or motorcycling, and that there must be no complete vehicles offered for sale'.

Sellers were able to hire a pitch with a table and two chairs, while visitors paid half a crown to enter. Unfortunately for both, it rained heavily some of the time but this did not affect things unduly. That first event attracted 76 stalls and 4,933 visitors. Unlike today's huge Beaulieu Autojumbles, only three of the stalls belonged to full-time professional traders; most were motoring enthusiasts who were clearing out their garages. The event quickly gained in popularity. By 1969, it could boast its first American stallholder along with 200 other traders. By 1976, the first automart of complete cars was held and the event attracted 14,000 visitors. By 1980, it was so large that it was no longer practical to hold the event on one day and the Autojumble became a weekend event with 1,286 stalls. Since this time, it has generally been held on a weekend early in September.

The forty-sixth Beaulieu International Autojumble took place between 7 and 9 September 2012. The event is the largest of many special events that take place at the Beaulieu Visitor Attraction during the course of year and had over 2,400 stalls and automart/dealermart pitches with headline visitor numbers exceeding 38,000. The rules on what may, or may not, be sold in the Autojumble area remain much as in the early days – items must have a transport connection, and complete vehicles may only be sold from an automart or dealermart pitch.

Such events generate income to support the on-going costs of maintaining Beaulieu and its associated enterprises. These are important and significant employers in a largely rural region that relies heavily on tourism.

The focus of most historic vehicle events is the vehicles: the public attend in order to see the vehicles on display. The Beaulieu International Autojumble is different: the focus of the event is trade, with the vehicles themselves almost incidental. The trade in question, though, is the sale of items that relate to transport: it can range in scale from the sale of a motor-related post-card at a few pence to original works of art at several thousand pounds; from an obsolete nut and bolt at under a pound to complete cars costing tens, or even hundreds, of thousands of pounds.

While this trade may take place at Beaulieu, most of it is between parties based a significant distance away. Consequently, the core business undertaken at the Beaulieu International Autojumble has no more direct effect on the local economy than any other event taking place over a similar duration and attracting a similar number of people.

The research indicated that the Beaulieu International Autojumble generates overall economic activity of over £13 million, of which nearly £3 million is of direct benefit to the local area (i.e. within a 15 mile/24 km radius). Despite the fact that the main sales activity relates to the non-taxable disposal of secondhand items, £570,000 VAT is generated. The figures are summarized in the Table 15.6.

The majority of the money received by the Beaulieu Visitor Attraction is used within the study area. A significant proportion of it contributes to the general estate income, which provides employment for over 200 people, including the staff who organize this and other major events taking place through the year. Approximately 25 per cent of this income is spent on direct additional costs associated with the event, such as hire of infrastructure, printing and promotion, temporary additional staff and security (where feasible, local firms were used for these items).

The Beaulieu Visitor Attraction spent £16,000 on temporary staff for the Autojumble, comprising an extra 32 temporary staff for 'front of house' duties and 42 members of the 'Friends of Events' group. This group is a team of local people who are available to be called upon to help at events taking place at Beaulieu and who help behind the scenes. Additionally, the catering concessions and security contractors between them take on over 150 temporary staff drawn from the locality.

The Autojumble comprised over 2,000 stall pitches for the sale of vehicle parts and other automobilia and some 300 'dealermart' or 'automart' pitches where complete vehicles could be offered for sale. The survey revealed gross

Table 15.6 Economic impacts of the Beaulieu International Autojumble (all figures rounded down to nearest £5,000)

Description	Gross	Destination		
		Local economy	General economy	VAT
Autojumble and Dealermart activity, including receipts by the Beaulieu Visitor Attraction from exhibitors, sponsors, dealers and the public	£7,745,000	£1,170,000	£6,520,000	£55,000
Deduction for amounts going overseas			£1,000,000	
Bonhams auction	£2,865,000		£2,750,000	£115,000
Stallholder and public spending	£2,400,000	£1,685,000	£310,000	£400,000
Total	£13,010,000	£2,855,000	£8,580,000	£570,000

spending of over £7 million within this market, of which £1.4 million was between stallholders. Most of this trade is in secondhand items being sold by private individuals or small traders who are not registered for VAT. Eight per cent of stall holders are based in the study area, so it has been assumed that 8 per cent of this element of spending remains within the study area. The average turn-over per pitch was just under £3,000. More than 10 per cent of stallholders are from outside the UK, and it is likely that much of the value of their sales (estimated at £1 million) will not come into the UK economy.

The Bonhams auction, which was part of the event, took £2,757,383 net, including both buyers' and sellers' premiums. These premiums are subject to VAT and the value of VAT shown is an estimate based on Bonhams' standard premium rates. The facility fee paid by Bonhams to Beaulieu is included in the overall revenue received by Beaulieu.

Spending within the study area and beyond by those attending the Beaulieu International Autojumble is substantial and breaks down as indicated in Table 15.6. The local economy benefited to the tune of £2,855,000. A proportion of spending by visitors to any community is subsequently re-circulated within the local economy, thus enhancing the financial benefit such visitors bring to the area being studied. The application of a multiplier to the direct economic expenditure in the study area would generate an overall economic benefit of over £3.3 million.

Spectators and participants of the Beaulieu Autojumble spent 43,000 nights away from home, with over 27,000 of these in the study area, in accommodation ranging from tents to hotels. As a direct result of the event, 11,000 person nights were spent in hotels and guest houses in the study area. The minimum estimated value of spending on accommodation by those attending the Autojumble but staying outside the study area, in centres such as Bournemouth, in Dorset, and Southampton, in Hampshire, was £377,000.

The Goodwood Revival Festival

The Goodwood Revival, so-named because it revives motor racing at the Goodwood Motor Circuit, in West Sussex, UK is an annual extravaganza of nostalgia built around a three-day motor race meeting for historic cars and motorcycles that celebrates the history of motor sport at Goodwood.

The Goodwood Motor Circuit and its immediate environs have hardly changed since the circuit was opened in 1948. The area is steeped in history and provides a setting that helps create a sense of theatre and occasion. Many aficionados consider the 1950s to have been the most exciting era for motor sport, when it was possible to see the drivers at the wheel of open-wheeled single-seater racing cars while the sports racing cars bore close resemblance to the cars the public could buy. Goodwood was at the heart of that golden period of British motor sport, hosting many international events in the 18 years it was open.

The Revival has been running annually since 1998. It is as much a celebration of the garden-party atmosphere of the circuit's heyday as it is a celebration of the racing. No modern vehicles (except for emergency vehicles) are allowed within the perimeter of the circuit. Track marshals are taken to their positions by a fleet of 1950s coaches. Everyone is encouraged to come in appropriate attire for the 1940s, 1950s or 1960s and, where possible, in period vehicles. There is a period fashion show, period themed motor-show and exhibitions arranged in period style. There is a race for children in 1950s style pedal cars and a period fun-fair. Hence the Revival has been marketed as 'a magical step back in time, a unique chance to revel in the glamour and allure of motor racing in the romantic time capsule of the world's most authentic motor circuit'.

In 2012, 145,398 people attended the Revival between 14 and 16 September. This represents the total number of day passes issued and includes everyone involved, from catering staff to VIP guests; from race officials to celebrity drivers. No tickets were sold on the gate, so the event was open only to those who had planned to attend and purchased their tickets in advance.

The Revival is one of three particularly high-profile events that take place on the Goodwood Estate annually – the others are the Goodwood Festival of Speed, which takes place in July, and the five-day 'Glorious Goodwood' horse race meeting at the end of July/beginning of August. These special events generate income to support the on-going costs of maintaining the Goodwood Estate and make the many lesser events that take place viable. This activity is an important source of local employment in this largely rural area.

The 2012 Revival brought over £12 million revenue for the local community (i.e. a 20 km radius area around Goodwood) while generating £36 million gross turnover for the wider national economy over three days. The UK's Exchequer benefited from over £4 million VAT. It generated over 23,000 person nights' accommodation for local hotels and guest houses and 25,000 person nights outside of the local area.

Just over half the local financial activity is channelled through the Goodwood Estate in the form of extra services hired in from local suppliers, employment of temporary staff and so on, with the remainder being spent by those attending the Revival on goods and services. The figures are summarized in Table 15.7.

Spending within the study area on non-automotive items by those attending the Revival was substantial, and breaks down as indicated on the pie-chart in Figure 15.2. This does not include the spending by those who said they were based in the study area, in order to ensure that the figures quoted represent money coming newly in to the area from elsewhere.

The figures on the chart (which have been rounded down to the nearest £1,000) are gross and add up to £7,129,000. The value quoted in the gross column of Table 15.7 includes a further £2,156,000, which represents the £1,137,000 minimum estimated value of spending on accommodation by those attending the Revival but who stayed outside the study area, in centres such as Portsmouth and Worthing, and the £1,019,000 spent by those attending the Revival on automobilia purchased from the exhibition stands. There were 262 exhibition stands, selling items from under £5 to complete cars at over £50,000. Four per cent of exhibitors were based in the study area.

Table 15.7 Economic impacts of the Goodwood Revival Festival (all figures rounded down to nearest £5,000)

Description	Gross	Local economy	Wider economy	VAT (estimate)
Revenue from ticket sales, grandstands, hospitality deals, sponsorship, etc.	£13,600,000	£6,340,000	£4,995,000	£2,265,000
Bonhams auction	£13,095,000		£12,590,000	£505,000
Spectator and competitor spending	£9,285,000	£6,050,000	£1,715,000	£1,520,000
Total	£35,980,000	£12,390,000	£19,300,000	£4,290,000

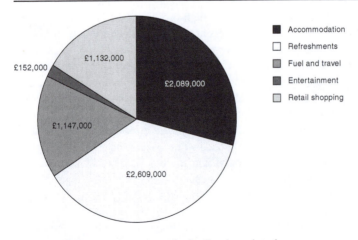

£1,132,000
£152,000
£2,089,000
£1,147,000
£2,609,000

- ■ Accommodation
- □ Refreshments
- ▨ Fuel and travel
- ■ Entertainment
- ▨ Retail shopping

Figure 15.2 Gross amounts spent in the Goodwood study area.

A portion of spending by visitors to any community is subsequently re-circulated within the local economy, thus enhancing the financial benefit such visitors bring to the area concerned. Accounting for this induced and indirect activity would give a total economic benefit to the local area of £13,920,000.

Included in Goodwood's overheads for the Revival is over £100,000 that was spent on employing over 350 temporary extra staff to cope with the volume of work generated by a meeting of this magnitude. This is in addition to any additional staff that may have been employed by the many contractors that provide services before, during and/or after the event.

The Goodwood Revival Festival generated 23,000 person nights of accommodation for local hotels and guest houses, and a further 25,000 person nights in hotels and guest houses outside of the study area. The event benefited the local economy to the tune of £12,390,000, while the national economy saw a turnover of £35,980,000.

Aggregate visitor and spectator demographics

Analysis of the visitor demographics and attendee composition of the three events yielded useful comparative data about the age, male/female ratio and loyalty of the attendees.

As might be expected, the London to Brighton Run received most visitors from the south-east region. Of those spectators who came to Brighton specifically to watch the Run, 39 per cent came from Sussex, 13 per cent from London, 9 per cent from Surrey, 7 per cent from Kent and 5 per cent from Essex. International visitors who came specifically to watch the Run comprised 4 per cent of the spectators, with those from Australia and Burma travelling the furthest.

The Beaulieu International Autojumble lives up to the 'international' element in its name, with 37 per cent of public attendees and more than 10 per cent of traders coming from outside the UK. Countries represented include New Zealand, Australia, South Africa, Brazil, Mexico, USA and Canada as well as most European countries. Within the UK, the distribution was concentrated on southern counties, with 50 per cent of spectators coming from the south-east, 10 per cent from the south-west, 7 per cent from Greater London and 7 per cent from eastern England. Eight per cent of both the public and the stallholders live within the study area.

At the Goodwood Revival, 21 per cent of competitors and crew came from outside the UK, which is almost double the proportion of overseas spectators. This probably reflects that the opportunities to take part in top-flight historic racing are relatively few and far between, so those wishing to race have a greater incentive to make the journey. Within the UK, the population distribution is heavily biased towards southern counties, with the south-east, south-west and Greater London regions accounting for more than 65 per cent of all spectators, and nearly half of all competitors and crew. This proportion barely changed amongst the spectators attending for only one day. The study area itself falls entirely within the south-east region. Eighteen per cent of spectators and 4 per cent of competitors and crew live within the study area.

This provides a parallel to the research undertaken by the FBHVC and the Heritage Vehicle Research Institute (HVRI) on the activities attended by historic vehicle enthusiasts. In a 2009 survey of the UK historic vehicle movement, 68 per cent of respondents indicated the distance from home was an important consideration when choosing which events to attend (see Table 15.8). Research in 2011 indicated that 40 per cent of events attended were within 50 miles of the home base (Frost *et al.*, 2011: 4). This is clearly reflected in the visitor origins seen in the three case studies.

Heritage interests

There was no surprise in finding that a majority of those attending the Beaulieu International Autojumble and the Goodwood Revival had a strong interest in historic vehicles, as demonstrated by the number who own such vehicles or belong to clubs catering for historic vehicle interests. However, the extent of wider interest in heritage matters as indicated by membership of organizations such as the National Trust and English Heritage was double what would be expected from the general population at Beaulieu and four times at Goodwood. Twenty-one per cent of visitors at Beaulieu (29 per cent of traders) and 39 per cent (57 per cent of the Goodwood Road Racing Club) at Goodwood were members of heritage-related organizations such as the National Trust and to a lesser extent English Heritage. It is apparent that heritage vehicle enthusiasts have a broader interest in heritage than just automotive heritage.

Spectator loyalty

It is also apparent that the heritage vehicle events studied attract a loyal following of spectators and attendees. At the London to Brighton Veteran Car Run, 65 per cent of the respondents had seen the event previously, while 92 per cent expressed an intention to see the event again. Clearly the Run has a huge potential to convert spectators into return visitors to the city. Moreover, 27 per cent stayed longer in Brighton because of the event.

At the Beaulieu Autojumble (80 per cent) of visitors had attended the event previously (64 per cent more than three times) and 92 per cent intended to come to the Autojumble again. These figures are reinforced by the statistics from the traders at the event, of whom 91 per cent had been more than three times

Table 15.8 Factors that influenced visits to historic vehicle events (Frost *et al.*, 2009: 4)

Importance	Very (%)	Important (%)	Neutral (%)	Least (%)
Distance from home	21	47	26	6
Single marque	15	32	35	18
Value for money	13	43	33	11
Family friendly	15	32	35	18
Multi-marque	8	26	51	15

previously, while 99 per cent intended to return. Some of the stallholders have attended Beaulieu every year since its opening in 1967. Over the years, a strong social scene has developed in parallel with the Autojumble.

At the Goodwood Revival, 37 per cent of the general public (and members) had attended the event previously, while 92 per cent intended to see the event again. The figures rose considerably with the members of the Goodwood Road Racing Club, 97 per cent of whom had attended previously, while 98 per cent intended to see the event again.

The extent to which those attending annual events return is a clear measure of the success and health of those events – if people enjoy themselves and perceive value for money, they are likely to return whenever they are able: if they do not enjoy themselves, or sense the cost of attending outweighs the pleasure, they tend not to come again. Clearly these events have the capacity to engender strong loyalty and repeat visits (see Table 15.9).

The bigger picture

The three studies give an indication of the economic impact of prestigious historic vehicle events on communities and regions. How this relates to the wider consumption of historic vehicle events in the UK is only just beginning to emerge. Research by the Federation of British Historic Vehicle Clubs (FBHVC) and the Heritage Vehicle Research Institute (HVRI) indicates that the historic vehicle movement was worth £4.3 billion to the UK economy in 2010–2011. Part of that figure is made up of historic motor vehicle tourist activities. Segmentation analyses revealed that there are three principal groups of consumers of heritage motoring events: heritage vehicle owners, enthusiasts who do not own heritage vehicles and the general public. The research established that non-owner enthusiasts spent an average of £920 per annum on their hobby. These costs include the costs of attending events (fuel, meals, accommodation, etc.) and buying historic vehicle media etc. (Frost *et al.*, 2011).

The types of historic vehicle event attended by respondents were predominantly non-competitive, but a significant minority participates in competitive motor sport. Owners use historic vehicles when attending events on 86 per cent of occasions. They are active participants at 67 per cent of the events they attend. It is also apparent from this research and the three case studies that large numbers of the general public attend historic vehicle events (Frost *et al.*, 2011: 18).

Table 15.9 Spectator visitation statistics for the three case study events

	London to Brighton (2010)	*Beaulieu Autojumble (2012)*	*Goodwood Revival (2012)*	*Average (%)*
Attended previously (%)	65	80	37	61
Intend to come again (%)	92	92	96	93

In the UK in 2012, there were over 900 events (see Figure 15.3), in which over 25 heritage motor vehicles participated.[7] These range from similarly high-profile events, such as the Classic Motor Show at the National Exhibition Centre, Birmingham, to local historic vehicle shows that can be no larger than a village fête. The range of event types is hugely diverse with club meets, fairs, rallies, hill climbs, concours d'elegance and autojumbles to name but a few.

In the UK, the (heritage) motoring event season picks up in April, peaking in the summer months (June–August) and declining once more in October. A small peak is evident in January with a number of events held on New Year's Day, such as the 'Brooklands New Year's Day Event' at the Brooklands Museum, Surrey, which is the largest New Year classic gathering of classic cars and motorcycles in the south-east. Over 1,000 vehicles usually attend.

Some heritage motor car and bike events include other heritage vehicles as an added attraction. Conversely, some heritage 'vehicle' events include a heritage car component as part of a wider offering of other vehicles, such as trains, traction engines, boats or planes. For example, the Pickering Traction Engine Rally in Yorkshire is one of the largest steam fairs in the north of England and has over 700 cars and commercial vehicles attending in early August; similarly the Great Dorset Steam Fair in early October is one of the south's biggest steam traction events but still has a significant classic car presence, while Cornwall's Morval vintage steam rally hosts over 200 classic cars. But the possible range of combinations is immense. The 'Pembroke Horticultural and Classic Show' held in August combines the Welsh national vegetable championships and a flower show, with a classic and vintage car and vintage tractor display. Clearly from an impact perspective, attributing the effect of the vehicle component of such events is complicated.

Moreover, new events are being created every year. For example, 2012 saw the first 'Destination Manchester' event, which brought together over 1,000 classic cars in the city in April.

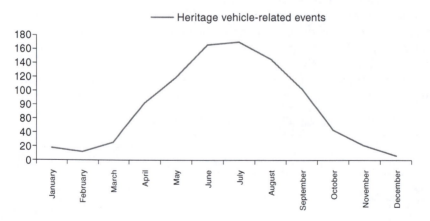

Figure 15.3 Heritage vehicle-related events with more than 25 participating heritage motor vehicles in the UK in 2012.

Discussion

It is evident that heritage motor vehicle events have certain characteristics that differentiate them from many heritage events.

- *Mobility*: The objects of interest (motor vehicles) are mobile.[8] This means that the events associated with these vehicles do not have to be bound to a specific place. This gives heritage motor vehicle events an immense degree of flexibility in that they can, if necessary, change location according to public demand. The vehicles can go to the people. The benefits (and any negative externalities) are transferable. Related to these points, heritage vehicle events are unique every time they take place, because different motor vehicles tend to take part. Heritage vehicle events are anything but static.
- *Public ownership*: Although some heritage vehicles can be found in museums, these are not the vehicles that tend to be found at heritage vehicle events. In contrast, other transport heritage, such as trains, planes and boats, tend to be expensive to purchase and maintain. This leads to a much more restricted ownership. In contrast, most of the vehicles which attend motor vehicle events are owned by individual members of the general public. Individual choice has a significant bearing when heritage vehicle owners decide which events to attend as participants or spectators.
- *Funding*: Many events are funded by the heritage vehicle enthusiasts themselves, either through club fees or through their attendance fees for having their cars at specific events.
- *Negative externalities*: Despite the obvious economic benefits of heritage motor vehicle events to local communities, there can be negative issues. The two most widely quoted negative externalities are traffic congestion and noise. Clearly a large event of any description has the potential to overwhelm the local infrastructure of a small community. The issue is that the 'zone of inconvenience' is far smaller than the 'zone of benefit'. While problematic noise can travel 2–3 miles and traffic congestion can affect a similar radius in large events, the positive benefits can be felt across entire regions. At some events studied, spectators stayed over 25 miles from the venue. Moreover, the traffic congestion is limited to peak times at the beginning and end of each day's activities.

Conclusions

It is widely acknowledged in academic circles that the definition of heritage is expanding. Motor vehicle heritage is one area where academic thought is catching up with this new all-encompassing definition of heritage. Of course for the heritage car movement this is not news. There have been heritage car clubs for almost as long as there have been cars in the UK (the Veteran Car Club of Great Britain was formed in 1930). But there is an underlying feeling that motor vehicle heritage does not have the gravitas of a stately home, monument or castle. Yet ironically, for good or for bad, motor vehicles have had a greater global impact than any of these forms of traditional heritage. Motor vehicles as we know them today have been around since the 1880s when Karl Benz developed his automobile in Mannheim, Germany. Yet with the global population of motor vehicles topping one billion in 2010, the motor car and motor vehicles have had a fundamental effect on society, the economy and the environment. In the developed world, almost every aspect of life has been influenced by motor vehicles, allowing people greater mobility than ever before. Although this freedom has not been without its costs, the heritage of the motor vehicle is now an important area of public interest.

The three events studied in this chapter attracted over 203,000 visitors. These visitors spent over 143,000 person nights away from home in order to attend, of which over 35,000 were in local hotels and guest houses. The benefit of all this activity was almost £15.3 million for their local economies without the addition of a multiplier. Moreover, research indicates that motor heritage vehicle events are thriving in the UK, with over 900 events with more than 25 cars attending in 2012. Clearly the UK's heritage motoring events are an important driver for both domestic tourism and inbound foreign tourism.

Acknowledgements

The research team is indebted to the Royal Automobile Club, who organize the London to Brighton Veteran Car Run, and Motion Works, who have been of exceptional help in this research. Peter Foubister of the Royal Automobile Club and Roger Etcell of MotionWorks gave considerable support for the London to Brighton Veteran Car Run research. Lord Montagu of Beaulieu and Stephen Munn of the National Motor Museum were instrumental in the study of the Beaulieu International Autojumble, while Lord March and Lloyd McNeill provided unfailing support for the Goodwood Revival case study. Without the input of Jim Whyman, this would have been a lesser chapter.

Finally, we would like to express our sincere thanks to the many participants and spectators of the 2010 London to Brighton Veteran Car Run, the 2012 Beaulieu Autojumble and the 2012 Goodwood Revival Festival who responded to the questionnaires. About 3,000 people gave up their time to answer our questions; without which this research would simply not have been possible. Thank you.

Notes

1 In this context, 'historic' and 'heritage' vehicles are defined as those made more than 30 years ago. Such vehicles have usually been retired from the purpose for which they were built and are now being preserved for posterity. Subdivisions in the broader definition of historic vehicles in the UK include veteran (built before 1918), vintage (1919–1930) and classic (post 1930); there are many variations on the definitions in different countries.
2 The medal has the logo of the Motor Car Club (Munro, 1964).

3 With a 98 per cent confidence level and a 5 per cent margin of error.
4 A few brought food with them from outside of the city.
5 It is essential to count only expenditure that would not have occurred in the absence of the Run. This is why expenditure by tourists who would have visited regardless is excluded.
6 The research does not compute the social cost of the Run. For example, issues to do with parking difficulties and traffic congestion relating to the event may result in a social cost for some; however, in this case the short duration of the event reduces these potential costs.
7 This is by no means a complete picture. In the absence of a central authority for such events in the UK, it is also conceivable that some have been omitted. Clearly there are a significant number of events with fewer than 25 motor vehicles attending that have not been included.
8 At any point in time, some heritage vehicles will be 'off the road' because of breakdowns, repairs or restoration.

References

Ashworth, G. J. (1991) *Heritage planning*, Groningen: Geo Press.

Davies, L., Ramchandani, G. and Coleman, R. (2010) 'Measuring attendance: Issues and implications for estimating the impact of free-to-view sports events', *International Journal of Sports Marketing and Sponsorship*, 12(1): 11–23.

Frost, P., Hart, C., Kaminski, J., Smith, G. A. and Whyman, J. (2011) *The British historic vehicle movement – A £4 billion hobby*, Stonewold: Federation of British Historic Vehicle Clubs.

Frost, P., Hart, C., Smith, G. A. and Edmunds, I. (2009) *Maintaining our transport heritage*, Stonewold: Federation of British Historic Vehicle Clubs.

Kaminski, J., Smith, G. A., Frost, P. and Whyman, J. (2013a) *Economic impact of the Beaulieu International Autojumble on the New Forest area*, Stonewold: Federation of British Historic Vehicle Clubs.

Kaminski, J., Smith, G. A., Frost, P. and Whyman, J. (2013b) *Economic impact of the Goodwood Revival meeting on the immediate area*, Stonewold: Federation of British Historic Vehicle Clubs.

Montagu, E. D. (1990) *The Brighton Run*, Princes Risborough: Shire Publications.

Munro, I. C. (1964) 'A "Brighton" puzzle solved', *Veteran Car*, October, 77–8.

Smith, G. A., Kaminski, J. and Frost, P. (2011) *Economic impact of the London to Brighton Veteran Car Run on Brighton and Hove*, Stonewold: Federation of British Historic Vehicle Clubs.

16 The value of intangible cultural heritage

The case of the Fallas Festival in Valencia, Spain

Begoña Sánchez Royo

Introduction

Europe's cultural heritage is both rich and diverse. This huge wealth of heritage can engender a range of community benefits and act as an economic driver, so much so that the cultural heritage of Europe has been estimated to generate an annual revenue of 335 billion euros for the tourism industry, and many of the nine million jobs in the tourism sector are directly or indirectly linked to it. This heritage is both tangible (e.g. buildings, monuments, objects) and intangible (e.g. song, music, drama, skills, crafts). The study of the impact, value and benefits of tangible heritage has a long history, but intangible cultural heritage (ICH) is less-well studied. ICH is far more nebulous and difficult to pin down compared to assessing economic impact, for example. Moreover, it was only in 2003 that UNESCO launched the 'Convention for the Safeguarding of Intangible Cultural Heritage' for its protection and promotion (UNESCO, 2003).[1] The UNESCO Convention lists the following examples of ICH: oral traditions and expressions; performing arts; social practices, rituals and festive events; knowledge and practices concerning nature and the universe; and traditional craftsmanship, and defines intangible heritage as:

> the practices, representations, expressions, knowledge, skills – as well as the instruments, objects, artefacts and cultural spaces associated therewith – that communities, groups and, in some cases, individuals recognize as part of their cultural heritage. This ICH, transmitted from generation to generation, is constantly recreated by communities and groups in response to their environment, their interaction with nature and their history, and provides them with a sense of identity and continuity.
>
> (UNESCO, 2003)

The importance of ICH lies in its intrinsic values which, when shared among and between communities, can encourage mutual respect and in so doing promote social cohesion, intercultural dialogue and sustainable development. There are, however, many different expressions of ICH, of which community heritage festivals are one form.

Decisions to safeguard ICH are based on the articulation of heritage values as a reference point, whether they are concerned with deciding on a specific sample of ICH status to be inscribed on the 'Representative List of the Intangible Cultural Heritage of Humanity', on the 'List of Intangible Cultural Heritage in Need of Urgent Safeguarding' or even inscribed in any other national or local safeguarding list. Assessment of the values attributed to ICH is therefore an important activity in any safeguarding initiative, since values strongly shape the justification of funding decisions.

Specific research into the relationship between ICH and heritage festivals is under-researched by the academic community. Creating a model of that relationship, which can be used as a foundation for examining the value of ICH and cultural heritage festivals, is an entirely novel area of research.

This research was part of a larger study which aimed to:

- explore value and impact assessment of ICH as a particular aspect of fundraising, management and safeguarding decision-making;
- be an example of building a cohesive value and impact assessment of ICH and cultural festivals for towns and regions in Europe;
- build a methodology for strategies to involve partners from different fundraising authorities in order to;
- support more stable long-term protection of ICH; and
- encourage increased economic and cultural benefits from ICH.

The case study of the Fallas Festival is used as an example to pursue these aims and illustrate how the approach could establish the basis for planning, monitoring and evaluating heritage festivals.

This chapter presents an overview of a subset of this research. The following section discusses the relationship between ICH and the identity of its creators and bearers. A literature review follows this. The next section has an overview of the methodology used to assess the value and impact of ICH, while the following section considers the case of the Valencian Fallas Festival using a subset of the assessment methodology. The chapter concludes with an assessment of the values of the Fallas Festival to those who take part.

The relationship between ICH and the identity of its creators and bearers

In recent decades, there has been an important shift in the safeguarding of intangible heritage by the international community, from the focus on legal concepts, such as intellectual property, copyright, trademark and patent, or the basis for protecting what was then called folklore[2] to the culmination of the UNESCO Convention on the Safeguarding of the Intangible Cultural Heritage in 2003. This Convention defines, in article 2, the notion of ICH and highlights implicitly or explicitly the main elements of meaning and worth for the international safeguarding. Despite all these elements being interrelated to each other, the aspect of self-identification of ICH as an essential element of the cultural identity by its creators and bearers stands out for inferring the differences in the rationale underlying the protection/safeguarding of tangible and intangible cultural heritage for the international community. The World Heritage Convention (UNESCO, 1972) states that tangible heritage deserves international protection in the light of its outstanding *universal* value.[3] In other words, the criteria for selecting heritage are based on an 'objective' evaluation of its outstanding worth from a general and worldwide appreciation of value. In the case of ICH, the criteria to be considered as a value for international safeguarding are undertaken by the subjective appreciation of the creators and bearers of a given heritage who recognise ICH as an essential part of their idiosyncratic cultural inheritance, even though it may appear worthless to external observers.

The notion that the value of ICH is bounded to the subjective perspective of its creators and bearers is also highlighted in the international context of culture and development. In 1996, the Report of the World Commission on Culture and Development emphasised that 'It is essential to understand the values and aspirations that drove its makers, without which an object is torn from its context and cannot be given its proper meaning. The tangible can only be interpreted through the intangible' (World Commission on Culture and Development, 1996). In relation to the safeguarding of intangible cultural heritage at a European level, there is a strong and clear position in EU policy that:

> The Community shall contribute to the flowering of the cultures of the Member States and Associated Countries, while respecting their national and regional diversity and at the same time bringing the common cultural heritage to the fore. Action by the Community shall be aimed at ... supporting and supplementing action in the following areas ... conservation and safeguarding of cultural heritage of European significance.
>
> (European Union, 1992)

This provision in the Treaty on European Union is further clarified by the Council Conclusions of 17 June 1994, in which the Council points out that Article 128 of the Treaty establishing the European Community selected cultural heritage as a priority field of action for the Community in both movable and immovable heritage. Cultural heritage research has been present in European Framework Programmes since 1986, with a particular emphasis on research into preservation.

Within the Sixth Framework Programme (2002–2008), the 'Citizens and Governance in a Knowledge-based Society' Programme looked at cultural heritage in the context of perceptions of history and identity. In November 2011, the European Commission proposed the 'Creative Europe Programme'[4] with the general objectives of fostering the protection and promotion of European cultural and linguistic diversity and strengthening the competitiveness of the cultural and creative sectors with a view to promoting smart, sustainable and inclusive growth. Although the proposal is under discussion in the Council of

EU Ministers and the European Parliament and some adjustments and reviews have been proposed, it recognises,[5] on the one hand, culture's intrinsic and artistic value and, on the other, the cultural sector's economic value, including its broader societal contribution to creativity, innovation and social inclusion.[6] In the Seventh Framework Programme (FP7: 2008–current), one of the research activities prioritised was: 'Social Sciences and Humanities theme exploring European identity, diversities and commonalities'. The European Union has been collaborating with UNESCO through its regional programmes in the Mediterranean, and more specifically the Euromed Heritage programme. UNESCO is the leader of the Mediterranean Living Heritage Project (MedLiHer) to support the implementation of the Convention for the Safeguarding of the Intangible Cultural Heritage in Egypt, Jordan, Lebanon and the Syrian Arab Republic, with the participation of the Maison des Cultures du Monde (France).

There is a currently a gap in the available research at the European level regarding the methodologies that can be used to provide clear evidence of the multiple benefits which ICH can have for European society. This is clearly relevant to the EU's overall 2020 vision and Sustainability Agendas. In this regard, the European Heritage Alliance 3.3 called for a comprehensive and comparative study to be undertaken at the European level in their document 'Towards an EU Strategy for Cultural Heritage – a Case for Research', published on 25 April 2012 by Europa Nostra.[7] There have been, of course, examples of European projects covering particular aspects of ICH in specific parts of Europe, such as the Euro-Festival,[8] ICH (Intangible Cultural Heritage) Europe (www.patrimoineimmateriel.net)[9] and the Mediterranean Voices Project,[10] but they do not consider the measurement of its value or indeed its impact.

Literature review of ICH and heritage festivals

Community festivals have been depicted as 'themed public occasions designed to occur for a limited duration that celebrate valued aspects of a community's way of life' (Dimmock and Tiyce, 2001: 358). Community festivals are of limited duration and have a clear 'community and celebratory focus' (Arcodia and Robb, 2000: 157), often celebrating a theme which has developed from within the community itself, where a 'community' refers to a group of people who have a geographic or locational commonality (Butcher, 1993). In this regard, community festivals often reflect what is distinctive about a particular community, providing insights into the 'values, interests, and aspirations' of the host community (Derrett, 2000: 120). Likewise, community festivals are typically organised by the host community using local volunteers and organising committees (Getz, 1991), further reinforcing the links that these festivals have to their host community.

While there is an extensive literature on the impact of festivals, much of this is related specifically to their economic impact. Moreover, far less emphasis is devoted to heritage festivals compared to the plethora of other festival types. Indeed, festivals as one manifestation of intangible cultural heritage are what

Formica (1998) describes as a 'young and developing academic field'. Formica (1998) conducted a meta-analysis of the festival and special event research field based on festival- and special event-related articles found in four leading tourism journals in the period between 1970 and 1996. Some of the results elicited by his analysis are nevertheless still relevant today. Among other things, he pointed to the overwhelming majority of quantitative studies. Of the reported studies, 63 per cent were quantitative, whilst 7 per cent were qualitative and 30 per cent were what the author termed conceptual (meaning they were descriptions of, or reports from, special events or festivals). These investigations were mainly limited to economic/financial impact of festivals, marketing, profiles of festival/ event, sponsorship, management, trends and forecasts. All the studies had a general lack of a 'robust theoretical background' in common (Formica, 1998: 135). Moreover, the majority of papers explored festivals held in North America and were written by authors working for North American institutions. This bias was so clear that the author feared it could lead to ethnocentrism within the research field.

Quantitative studies still constitute much of the research into festivals, whilst conceptually orientated articles occur, surprisingly, in journals mainly dedicated to empirical research. In addition, there is a range of articles treating the festival phenomenon from a more theoretical or even philosophical angle. However, economic and related matters dominate such investigations. The North American bias is not so overwhelming as it was ten years ago, at least not when looking at the field from a wider perspective, but it nonetheless still seems to suffer from a Western orientation dominated by North American, European and Australian researchers.

When reviewing the literature available, the lack of theory is noticeable in many of these studies. For instance, authors write about festivals and their significance for the development of community identity without taking into consideration any aspects of identity theory, either at the level of the individual or that of the municipality. Further, several authors complain about the lack of empirical research into festivals (see, for instance, Formica, 1998; Quinn, 2005; Waterman, 1998).

Methodology for value and impact assessment of ICH

The value that a community places in ICH is key for its survival. No community will make an effort to safeguard and sustain something that is not perceived to have value. Methodologically, the assessment of ICH values is fraught with difficulties. These problems stem from different factors, including: the diverse nature of ICH values (bearers and carers of ICH can have many kinds of values, such as: cultural, economic, political or aesthetic, and some of them may even overlap others or compete); the fact that ICH evolves as society does (values change over time and are shaped by contextual factors, such as economic and environmental changes); and the wide variety of methodologies and tools for assessing the values in cultural heritage.

For purposes of ICH safeguarding planning and sustainability (funding the protection of ICH), value assessment presents a threefold challenge: identifying the values that bearers and carers have of a particular form of ICH; describing them; and connecting them with those willing to fund sustainability. Underpinning these challenges is the question of how assessment of ICH values can be used by the stakeholders involved in safeguard planning so a wider participation in the planning process can be achieved.

Consequently, the original case study research used a holistic socio-economic impact methodology (McLoughlin *et al.*, 2007) for addressing the subjectivity and contingency of ICH values. As values of ICH are embedded by the social, historical and spatial context of its bearers and creators, the holistic framework provides the necessary systematic identification of those values that are held universally (or nearly) in order to facilitate the value and impact assessment of ICH for safeguarding planning and fundraising purposes.

The methodology for the full study focused on values associated with notions of governance, environmental sustainability and the cultural values of bearers and creators of this festival. By suggesting these values, it is not claimed that this (or any) selection will be appropriate for all situations or stakeholders involved – it is simply an attempt to create a common starting point from which assessment of ICH value can be constructed and evidence provided to support debate on safeguarding planning and fundraising initiatives.

When considering the task of constructing different scenarios for long-term safeguarding and fundraising for ICH, the constraints on time and resources to undertake a rigorous specification for the scenarios was recognised. The aim for the scenarios was to take a 'snapshot' of how the actor who gives value to ICH reacts against three main trends of impact on safeguarding and fundraising ICH. The actors considered for framing the scenarios were: the bearers of this particular festival, the communities in which the ICH was embedded (through neighbourhood associations) and local stakeholders: the municipality and local businesses of cultural tourism. Methodologically, these scenarios were integrated into questionnaires where the neighbourhood associations displayed their reactions against three trends for protection and fundraising.

A questionnaire was developed to use as a data-generating tool for the analysis and the quality of the final results is, to a large part, determined by the quality of the questionnaire applied (Louviere *et al.*, 2000; Bateman *et al.*, 2002). The questionnaire underwent revisions following a focus group of six members of neighbourhood associations and a pilot study on a sample of 30 respondents.[11] Several interviews with survey participants and the festival's key stakeholders were also undertaken.

The technique of Choice Experiment (CE) was selected for addressing the scenario for local public/private partnerships (governance) for long-term protection and fundraising ICH. The survey instrument presented hypothetical combinations of interests in managing and funding the cultural heritage festival, with different levels of participation intensity for the local authority, private sponsorship and the communities, as shown in Table 16.1.

Table 16.1 Attributes and attribute levels

Attributes and attribute levels	Description	Attribute level
Political funding	Financial support to the Fallas Festival made by the local council (Ayuntamiento de Valencia)	60% (High) 30% (Medium) 10% (Low)
Market funding	Financial support to the Fallas Festival made by the private companies and individuals in the search for profit	60% (High) 30% (Medium) 10% (Low)
NGOs' funding	Financial support to the Fallas Festival made by the members of the different neighbourhood associations in the city of Valencia	60% (High) 10% (Low)

Every alternative for funding consists of three attributes: 'political funding', 'market funding' and 'NGOs' funding' (community association funding), which had a proposed payment attached which the respondent must also consider. The payment is described in the questionnaire as 'an annual fee paid by the funding agent', with two alternative funding levels and the option for the responder to choose neither. Each such triple choice set (local authority, private sponsors and communities) is known as a choice occasion (Hanley *et al.*, 1998) with 18 possible choice sets. Figure 16.1 shows an example of a choice set used in the questionnaire.

The technique of Contingent Valuation (CV) was selected for addressing the scenario of planning long-term ICH protection and environmental sustainability of the cultural heritage festival. Members of the communities were presented with two hypothetical scenarios and asked about their willingness to pay in order to address the consequences and allow the festival to continue. One scenario related to environmental damage generally perceived as a remote possibility and the other to reducing environmental damage by agreeing to use more expensive materials (i.e. investigating personal concerns about the environment and environmentally friendly behaviour).

The results of the questionnaires were analysed both by individual question and by looking at patterns of correlations between answers to different questions using techniques drawn from data-mining, in particular decision trees. This technique was used to find attributes across the different questions in the questionnaire related to three categories: level of governance and payment; preference to negotiate about management and fundraising; and level of cultural value and the socio-demographic variables. This chapter concentrates on presenting the results from the third of these sections, drawing on descriptive statistics associated with the values of ICH. These and the results of the choice experiments, contingent valuation and decision tree analysis are described in more detail in Sánchez Royo (2011).

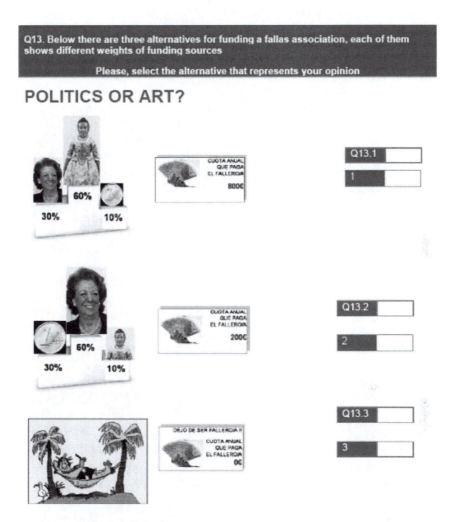

Figure 16.1 Choice set example.

The case study of the Fallas heritage festival in the city of Valencia

The Fallas Festival, which takes place in the city of Valencia every March, is an example of intangible cultural heritage funded by local neighbourhood associations called 'comisiones falleras'.[12] Today the Fallas Festival celebrates the festival of Saint Joseph but its origins are lost in history. The most common origin myth of the festival dates back to the Middle Ages. It is said that, in order to provide light to work by during the winter, Valencian carpenters hung their candles on planks of wood called parots. When spring arrived, they were no longer necessary, and so were burned to celebrate the spring equinox. Over time, the date of the burning of the parots was aligned with the festival of Saint Joseph, the patron saint of carpenters.

The Fallas Festival is a social festival run by the local community as a tradition. There are 382 neighbourhood associations called 'comisión fallera', who drive the festival (see Figure 16.2). These associations are a network of voluntary organisations with more than 200,000 members in the Valencian region. This figure is quite significant considering that the city of Valencia itself has only 815,440 residents. The members of these associations are called falleros and falleras. Each civil association is rooted in a neighbourhood community (barrio) or even in a smaller area, such as a street. The headquarters of each 'comisión fallera' is called the 'Casal'. This is where a wide range of social activities take place during the course of the year. The network of these neighbourhood associations is coordinated by a central committee, which has links with the council of the city of Valencia (Ayuntamiento).

Each neighbourhood association erects two temporary monuments, one called Infantil (Chidren's Falla) and another one called Falla Mayor (Big Falla). Most of the neighbourhood associations hire the services of specialist artists to make the 'Falla' monument. These monuments are made of wood, cardboard, polystyrene and glass fibre. They comprise free-standing satirical figures (ninots) of mythical and fictional characters and popular celebrities drawn from Spanish life and global culture (see Figure 16.3).

Figure 16.2 An example of a neighbourhood association (comisión fallera) in a parade (source: author).

Figure 16.3 An example of a 'Big Falla' monument in Valencia.

The themes and characters of Fallas monuments are essentially of two types. One type is related to current social and political life. Consequently, politicians are usually the object of criticism and satire, so that Fallas monuments produce a critique of established power. The other type is related to Valencian traditions and popular myths. Monuments often present the human body in a grotesque way, displaying exaggerations, distortions and metamorphoses of certain parts of it.

These monuments constitute a sort of static theatre depicting popular or topical themes. They are exhibited in the streets during the climax of the festival (between 15 and 19 March). At midnight on the last day, they are set on fire. This burning can either symbolise a gesture for washing away winter worries in a tribute to spring or is a way to purge the satirical and critical meaning that these monuments represent.

The 'Children's Falla' is small (1.5–3 metres), and it usually has fairies, cartoons or other characters for children. The 'Big Falla' Mayor is bigger, and the topic depends on what the people (or the artist) have selected. Mostly it is based on a satire about something that happened during the year, something traditional, something the people have been talking about, etc.

Both 'Children's Falla' and 'Big Falla' monuments are divided into categories according to their price. For 'Children's Falla' monuments, there are 16 categories, and a special category. The latter category consists of more expensive monuments costing over €20,000 each. In 2012, there were 13 monuments in this category. The cheapest category is the sixteenth, and in 2012 there were 27 monuments in this category, costing more than €350 each. In 2011, the 382 'Children's Fallas' monuments erected cost a total of €1,925,995. For 'Big Falla' monuments, there are seven categories, from first to seventh, and a special category. The latter category consists of more expensive monuments costing over €100,000 each. In 2012, there were 13 monuments in this category. The cheapest category is the seventh, and in 2012 there were 20 monuments in this category, costing more than €1,250 each. In 2011, the 382 'Big Fallas' monuments erected cost a total of €6,856,349 (Junta Central Fallera, 2012). All these Falla monuments are paid for by contributions made by the neighbourhood associations in the city of Valencia, together with donations from residents and businesses.

Symbols and cultural expressions of the Fallas heritage festival

The term 'cultural expressions' refers to the various ways in which the creativity of individuals and social groups takes shape and manifests itself. These manifestations include expressions transmitted by words (literature, tales...), sound (music...), images (photos, films...) – in any format (printed, audiovisual, digital etc.) – or by activities (dance, theatre...) or objects (sculptures, paintings...) (UNESCO, 2005).

The idea of focusing on the symbols and cultural expressions transmitted in this festival may help to understand the way in which the local community expresses its identity and values, and frame the socio-economic impacts of this festival. The core symbols and cultural expressions of the Fallas Festival are: the Falla monument, the 'Mascletà' fireworks, the traditional costumes, the Valencian flag and hymn and the Offering of the Flowers to our Lady.

The Falla monument

The Fallas monuments satisfy the human feeling of satirical criticism and effective change. The instrument for achieving that is humour. The message and content of this critique is social, economic and political. It is exposed to the public and burnt, to be reborn again afterwards. The logic behind this process is to criticise something controversial and the next year to criticise something else. Future monuments grow again from the ashes, like the Phoenix.

Fallas monuments are burnt on 19 March. Once the figures and statues are burnt, the conception of a new Falla monument starts. It is surprising to notice how a *static* monument has the power to '*move*' people even after disappearing; it is as if the feeling of emptiness left by the monument gives light to the consciousness that it was indeed occupying a place. This renewal is expressed in satire. Fallas monuments symbolise this satirical perspective which links catharsis and cyclical renovation.

The 'Mascletà' fireworks

Mascletà is a coordinated firecracker and firework display lasting around five minutes. It takes place in each neighbourhood at 2.00 pm every day during the climax of the festival; however, the main Mascletà is the municipal Mascletà in the *Plaça de l'Ajuntament*. The Mascletà is a collective ritual where people enjoy the beauty of the ephemeral with the emphasis on marvellous sights and sounds in the context of social enjoyment.

The traditional costumes

The men and women of the different neighbourhood associations wear the traditional Valencian costume, at every official act and during the climax of the festival. The traditional dress for the women is more sophisticated than the one for men. Most of these costumes are individually tailor-made, in natural silk with gold or silver garments and embroidery. There is an entire industry manufacturing the intricate fabrics and accessories for the falleras, apart from the specialist hairdressers who are tasked with arranging the women's hair in traditional style.

The Valencian flag and hymn

The streets are decorated with Valencian flags and coloured lights, while a varied repertoire of music animates the events of the festival. The essence of this festival concerns the role of the civic symbols in the main formal celebrations, such as the nomination and proclamation of the Queens of the Fallas for the year, the Exaltation, the Crida, the parade of the Ninots, the Offering of Flowers, the Planta and the Cremà. In addition, the gala costume of falleros includes the Valencian flag, which gives the Fallas Festival a closer link to the 'civic' institutional symbols than to religious ones.

The Offering of the Flowers to our Lady

As Costa and Hernández (1998) note, members of the different neighbourhood associations do not regard the Fallas Festival as being as religious as other local traditional festivities of 'saints' and 'virgins'. The Offering of Flowers to Our Lady of the Unprotected is the principal religious symbol of the Fallas Festival. However, it is not as 'officially religious' as it would appear to an outside observer. During the climax of the festival, the gigantic Virgin's body is constructed with the flowers offered by the falleros along their festive parade. This event combines these two perspectives: the devotion of the participants and the emotion of social union and enjoyment of parading in the centre of the city. It was created by the Fallas Central Committee in 1944. This event became established some years later as its success increased. During the 1960s and 1970s, the Offering took the form of a spectacular mass offering held in the open Square of the Virgin, where her Basilica is located. By contrast, a plan to develop an Offering of Flowers to Saint Joseph failed when the Franco authorities proposed it in the 1950s.

The City Council of Valencia organises the Offering and has representatives during the two days of the huge ritual, but the Catholic Church is not continuously represented. The presence of the Church is reduced to the reception of the Festival Queen by the Archbishop in the Basilica. The participants in the Offering, organised by the different Falleros Commissions and the neighbourhood's territorial sections, parade towards the centre of the Virgin's Square. Women and men, dressed up in gala costumes, carry flowers to the central figure of the Virgin.

The figure of the Virgin is a gigantic lattice-work of wood and her body and clothing are made of the flowers that the participants offer in accordance with a specific timetable and colour scheme (see Figure 16.4). A group of skilled people climb up through the wooden structure to arrange the flowers in an artistic display. Each bunch of flowers contributes to the floral composition of the Virgin's mantle and robe. Each year the design on the robe is different. This flowered design is an ephemeral construction. Therefore, the understanding of this so-called 'officially' religious symbol turns up also from the perspective of the ephemeral. Her dress and figure is 'destroyed' (i.e. the flowers perish after a few days) and renewed next year, like the Fallas monuments.

Applying the methodology to the Fallas Festival

A questionnaire was designed, tailored to evaluate the specific aspects of the Fallas Festival, and deployed during March 2010 across the different community districts in the city of Valencia where the neighbourhood associations were located (see Figure 16.5).

Following a pilot of the questionnaire as described above, the full-scale study was conducted by interviewing 382 random members of neighbourhood associations (falleros from comisiones falleras) throughout the city of Valencia.[13] Because there are no official statistics about the number of members in each

Figure 16.4 The Offering of Flowers to Our Lady during Fallas Festival (source: author).

neighbourhood association in the city of Valencia, the base criterion for the sample was the number of associations by municipal districts (see Table 16.2).

Of the 382 questionnaire respondents of the neighbourhood associations, 49 per cent were women and 51 per cent men. The profile of the respondents indicates that 28 per cent were under 25, 47 per cent were 25–40, 21 per cent were

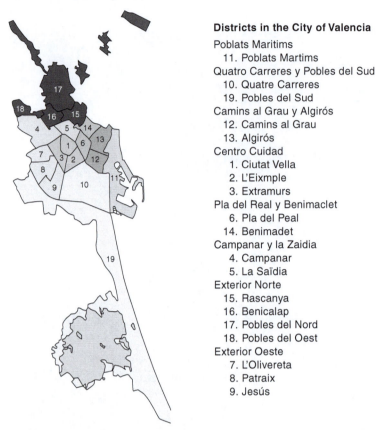

Districts in the City of Valencia

Poblats Maritims
  11. Poblats Martims
Quatro Carreres y Pobles del Sud
  10. Quatre Carreres
  19. Pobles del Sud
Camins al Grau y Algirós
  12. Camins al Grau
  13. Algirós
Centro Cuidad
  1. Ciutat Vella
  2. L'Eixmple
  3. Extramurs
Pla del Real y Benimaclet
  6. Pla del Peal
  14. Benimadet
Campanar y la Zaidia
  4. Campanar
  5. La Saïdia
Exterior Norte
  15. Rascanya
  16. Benicalap
  17. Pobles del Nord
  18. Pobles del Oest
Exterior Oeste
  7. L'Olivereta
  8. Patraix
  9. Jesús

Figure 16.5 Districts in the city of Valencia.

41–55 and 3 per cent were over 55. The respondents were fairly equally split between those who were single (47 per cent) and those who were married or cohabiting (48 per cent), with divorcees and widowers making up the remainder.

The values associated with the Fallas cultural festival

In the questionnaire, respondents were asked which components of the Fallas Festival were of most importance to them and to rank these using a seven-point Likert scale. The results are shown in Figure 16.6. They clearly show that the Falleros fraternity was the lowest ranked component (13 per cent). This may be because the fraternity is part of the community year round. Therefore, the respondents favoured things that were a specific part of the festival itself.

The monuments (24 per cent), the music (35 per cent), the customs (37 per cent) and the fireworks (44 per cent) are moderately ranked. Interestingly, the two highest ranked components were the Offering of the Flowers to the Virgin and the gastronomy associated with the festival. The Offering of the Flowers is

Table 16.2 The distribution of questionnaires according to municipal district

No. district	District subnumber	District name	Valencian municipal districts	No. comisiones falleras associations within each municipal district	No. questionnaires for municipal district
13		ALGIROS	ALGIROS	15	15
16	16.1.	BENICALAP	BANICALAP	14	14
18		POBLES DE L'OEST	BENIMAMET-BURJASOT-BENIFERRI	18	18
3	3.1., 3.3.	EXTRAMURS	BOTANIC-LA PECHINA	15	15
12		CAMINS DEL GRAU	CAMINS AL GRAU	18	18
4, 5	4.1.	CAMPANAR Y SAÏDIA	CAMPANAR	17	17
11	11.2., 11.1., 11.5.	POBLATS MARITIMS	CANYAMELAR-EL GRAU-NAZARET	14	14
1	1.3.	CIUTAT VELLA	EL CARME	14	14
1	1.4., 1.2., 1.5.	CIUTAT VELLA	EL PILAR-SANT FRANCESC	13	13
9		JESUS	JESUS	13	13
9		JESUS	LA CREU COBERTA	13	13
3	3.2., 3.4.	EXTRAMURS	LA ROQUETA-ARRANCAPINS	15	15
1	1.1., 1.2., 1.5.	CIUTAT VELLA	LA SEU-LA XEREA-EL MERÇAT	13	13
11	11.3., 11.2., 11.4.	POBLATS MARITIMS	MALVARROSA-CABANYAL-BETERO	17	17
			MISLATA	11	11
7		OLIVERETA	OLIVERETA	18	18
8	8.1.	PATRAIX	PATRAIX	12	12
6, 14		PLA DEL REIAL Y BENIMACLET	PLA DEL REIAL-BENIMACLET	19	19
2	2.2., 2.3.	L'EXAMPLE	PLA DEL REMEI-GRAN VIA	13	13
19		POBLES DEL SUD	POBLATS AL SUD	11	11
			QUART DE POBLET-XIRIVELLA	13	13
10		QUATRE CARRERES	QUATRE CARRERES	18	18
15		RASCANYA	RASCANYA	18	18
2	2.1.	L'EXAMPLE	RUZAFA "A"	12	12
2	2.1.	L'EXAMPLE	RUZAFA "B"	11	11
4, 5		SAÏDIA	ZAIDIA	17	17
				382	382

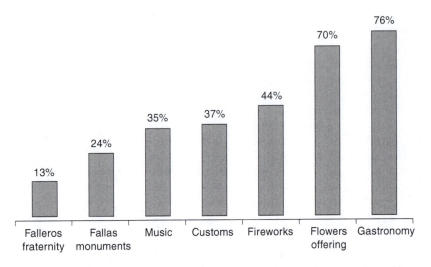

Figure 16.6 Aspects of the Fallas Festival of most importance for respondents (% most popular).

clearly an important component of the festival. Entirely televised, it takes two days for the tens of thousands of Falleras to give their offerings of flowers to the Virgin. But it was the gastronomic elements of the festival that were most important to the respondents. There are foods that are associated with the festival such as the doughnut-like buñuelos, churros (a fried-dough pastry) and hot chocolate. During the festival, mobile stalls selling these delicacies can be found on many streets. However, feasting has a more fundamental role in the community activity of the festival. The community associations gather during the festival for feasts, in which large paellas are often cooked outside on the streets. Such feasts are a highlight of the festival when the Falleros and Falleras can gather with friends and family.

In the questionnaire, respondents were also asked which elements of the Fallas Festival kept the festival alive and to rank these using a seven-point Likert scale (Figure 16.7). These results are instructive from a number of perspectives. Tourism is the lowest ranked option (15 per cent). Clearly, with nearly a million visitors coming to see the festival, tourism has an important role, but it is not of immediate concern to the participants. The influx of visitors will have an economic benefit to the city, some of which will be invested in the festival organisation and infrastructure (everything from funding additional police and fire fighters to road cleaners) but this is of marginal relevance to the neighbourhood associations who directly fund the festival (the monuments, fireworks and parades).

According to the respondents, the artistic and religious elements of the festival have a moderate importance in keeping the festival alive (25 and 26 per cent, respectively). While the heritage value of the festival (33 per cent) is clearly

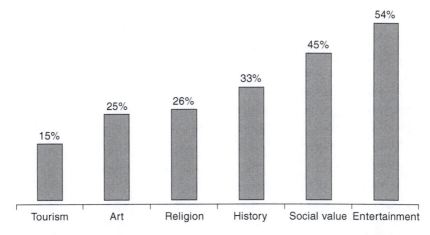

Figure 16.7 The elements that keep the Fallas Festival alive according to respondents (% most popular).

important to the respondents, the social and entertainment aspects of the festival are clearly the most significant. It is these 'current' values that keep the festival alive.

It is evident that the festival evokes a range of values to the respondents, ranging from social and religious to historic. The respondents whose reactions were sought were those from the local communities, which places a particular emphasis on these stakeholders. It is difficult to be certain whether the importance placed on the social elements results from an underlying assumption that the festival is based inextricably on the cultural heritage and therefore inevitably preserved by continuing the festival. Were the festival continued in a different guise (with different content) a new debate would arise as to whether its cultural heritage, as a re-formulated event, would in fact nevertheless be heritage in terms of representing the significance current society placed on the original cultural values.

The date on which Christmas falls reputedly aligns with dates on which pre-Christian pagan festivals were held. At some level, it could be argued that the celebration of Christmas in midwinter to replace the pagan festivals was a conscious act of planning continuity with society's prior expectation of celebration at that time. However, it seems unlikely that Christmas could ever be construed as the cultural heritage of pagan festivals.

As heritage is defined as elements from the past that have meaning in the present so the festival is re-imaged to the needs of the present. Given that the historic elements (art, religion and history) do not seem to figure as highly as the sense of occasion in social value and entertainment terms, the degree to which the cultural heritage elements are integral to the success of the occasion is not obvious. The data gathered so far does not investigate the degree to which tourism is an essential component of the economics of the occasion. Stakeholders such as the local authority and potential private company sponsors are very likely to regard the economic return from tourists as integral to their continued support and hence to place importance on the tourists' perception of the cultural heritage value of the occasion, but these reactions were not sampled in the data surveyed.

When asked who should be responsible for funding the festival, 52 per cent felt it was the duty of the Falleros, highlighting the importance the community attaches to this festival. Twenty-one per cent felt that it should be supported by sponsorship and donations, 15 per cent felt the private sector should have a major role in funding, while only 12 per cent felt the government should fund the festival. The question of the protection and sustainability of the ICH represented by the Fallas Festival is highly relevant, especially in a context of the financial crisis, which is affecting Spain and numerous other countries in the developed world.

Despite the increasing awareness of the UNESCO Convention for safeguarding ICH and encouragement for its implementation within both public and private sectors, there remains a significant challenge in sustaining and protecting ICH. This study explores new forms of funding ICH beyond the conventional one of public funding. To be specific, it analyses the relationship between the values of the bearers and carers of the Fallas cultural festival and their contribution for funding the safeguarding of this festival. Consequently, it raises the question of what kind of benefits would encourage these agents to support such a festival and how impacts on their cultural values, ways of governance for the festival and climate change can influence their decisions to support the festival. The preceding assessment opens a wide range of issues for consideration by policymakers and institutions concerned with safeguarding ICH.

Values for safeguarding ICH are dynamic as society evolves. Considering that these values cannot be planned or mapped but lived and chosen by its bearers and carers, they can reflect the dominant values that shed light about why they are engaged and how long-term safeguarding and sustainability of ICH can be assured. In the case study of the Fallas cultural festival, the multivariate and descriptive statistics underscored the historic and community value as the dominant ones, that respondents with such dominant values pay a high membership fee for the safeguarding of the Fallas cultural festival. When expressing opinions about which social agents they would wish to negotiate with about the management and fundraising of this festival, stakeholders expressed a preference to negotiate with politicians rather than profit-seeking companies.[14]

Interestingly, these community-level historic and identity values are by no means incompatible with the environmental sustainability agenda or even with the conservation of biodiversity (see, for example, Pathak and Kothari, 2003). To this regard, the case study of the Fallas Festival sheds some light about how the bearers and carers of this festival respond to ecological concerns under two scenarios: environmental damage generally perceived as unlikely and remote and that perceived as a personal concern about an environmentally friendly behaviour (i.e. a moral sense of duty to protect the environment).

The analysis of these questions was undertaken using a contingent valuation methodology where members indicate their willingness to pay for avoiding a potential environmental damage associated with the Fallas Festival and the funding formulas that members of these associations were willing to pay for safeguarding the Fallas Festival. The results indicate a positive attitude. Interestingly, in both scenarios, 12 euros was the marginal price. Therefore, members' of 'comisiones falleras' for safeguarding their cultural festival did not differentiate in terms of willingness to pay if an environmental damage is unlikely and remote or derived from an environmentally unfriendly behaviour. They elicited the same importance to avoiding damage in terms of their willingness to pay.

Conclusion

It is widely understood that cultural heritage has a huge social and economic benefit for Europe. This is manifested both in revenue from tourism and in its role in strengthening European identity, encouraging intercultural dialogue and enhancing well-being. At a time when increasing globalisation is insidiously eroding cultural identities, the more evidence that can be produced from assessments of the values associated with ICH and heritage festivals, the more likely policy makers are to consider ICH when planning legislation and allocating public funding.

Cultural heritage is both dynamic and reactive to economic and political conditions, and is influenced by them. In times of economic uncertainty, such tangible and intangible assets are important drivers for the economy and society.

In the case of the Fallas Festival, the participants hold strong community and historic values for the event. It might be inferred that members of the neighbourhood associations perceive benefits from supporting the festival. The fact that, despite the economic difficulties in Spain in 2011–2012, the total spent for celebrating this cultural festival[15] has remained constant gives an indication of the value that the community places on this festival.

Notes

1 It was only in 1950 that Japan introduced the 'Law for the Protection of Cultural Properties', which was the first to introduce legislation to preserve and promote intangible as well as tangible culture.

2 The Recommendation on the Safeguarding of Traditional Culture and Folklore on the General Conference of the United Nations Educational, Scientific and Cultural Organisation in 1989.

3 The definition of 'outstanding universal value' is not offered by the Convention in 1972, but only by its successive reforms, to its 'Operational Guidelines for the Implementation of the World Heritage Convention' (2005 version), and still in rather vague terms:

> Outstanding universal value means cultural and/or natural significance which is so exceptional as to transcend national boundaries and to be of common importance for present and future generations of all humanity. As such, the permanent protection of this heritage is of the highest importance to the international community as whole.

4 The Creative Europe Programme, providing support to the European cultural and creative sectors, will run between 1 January 2014 and 31 December 2020.

5 The version presented to the Council. Footnote 6), Article 5a (1) on European added value (former Article 3) has been modified to include the intrinsic and economic value of culture, in addition to the shared cultural arena (footnote 9). Proposal for a Regulation of the European Parliament and of the Council on establishing the Creative Europe Programme (Brussels, 30 April 2012). Inter-institutional File: 2011/0370 (COD). No. doc. 9097/12 AUDIO 42 CULT 68 CADREFIN 210 RELEX 359 CODEC 1063.

6 Although there is not an explicit reference in this proposal so far about intangible cultural heritage, its role is implicitly included in European cultural and linguistic diversity.

7 www.europanostra.org/news/238/. The European sectoral platform of the European Heritage Alliance 3.3 was launched in June 2011 in Amsterdam by 27 European or international networks active in the wider field of cultural heritage. On 25 April 2012, 11 member organisations, who attended the second plenary meeting, adopted the first document jointly produced by the Alliance with the title: 'Towards an EU Strategy for Cultural Heritage – a Case for Research'.

8 The Euro-Festival project was set up in 2008 to evaluate the impact of arts festivals on society, and their relevance to Europe and to the aims of the EU. The project looked at 13 arts festivals across a range of genres.

9 This three-year project set up in 2010 investigates the current establishment of this heritage domain at the European level and compares how these concepts are interpreted in the implementation of the 2003 UNESCO Convention for the safeguarding of intangible cultural heritage in southern, central and eastern European countries (Italy, France and Hungary).

10 This three-year project was carried out within the framework of the project Mediterranean Voices, which is a EuroMed heritage II project, supported by the European Union. It aimed to analyse the living history of the historic centres of the participant cities from the perspective of cultural anthropology.

11 The pilot survey took place at the beginning of the festival (called La Crida). In the evening, crowds gather beneath the Serranos Towers. After a display of fireworks, the 'Fallera Mayor' of Valencia invites everyone to enjoy the fiesta, extolling its qualities.

12 This festival is in the process of being included in the UNESCO World Heritage List as an example of intangible cultural heritage, in accordance with the 'Convention for the Safeguarding of the Intangible Cultural Heritage'. In addition, it is nominated for declaration as an Asset of Cultural Interest by the Dirección General de Patrimonio Cultural Valenciano de la Consellería de Cultura y Deporte.

13 These kinds of neighbourhood associations can be found in other locations around the province of Valencia, but those are beyond the scope in the present study.

14 The decision tree algorithm does not find any pattern for association rules with the socio-demographic variables.

15 In 2011, this amount was €6,704,461 and in 2012 was €6,858,349. The expected budget for 2013 is not confirmed yet but the prospects are in line with these figures. Data supplied by the official website of Junta Central Fallera, www.fallas.com (last accessed on 15 January 2013).

References

Arcodia, C. and Robb, A. (2000) 'A future for event management: A taxonomy of event management terms', in J. Allen, R. Harris, L. Jago and A. J. Veal (eds.) *Events beyond 2000: Setting the agenda, Proceedings of Conference on Event Evaluation, Research and Education*: 154–160, Sydney: Australian Centre for Event Management.

Bateman, I., Carson, R., Day, B., Hanemann, M., Hanley, N., Hett, T., Jones-Lee, M., Loomes, G., Mourato, S., Ózdemiroglu, D. and Pearce, D. (2002) *Economic valuation with stated preference techniques*, Cheltenham: Edward Elgar.

Butcher, H. (1993) 'Introduction: some examples and definitions', in H. Butcher, A. Glen, P. Henderson and J. Smith (eds.) *Community and public policy*: 3–21, London: Pluto Press.

Costa, X. and Hernández, G.M. (1998) 'The Offering of Flowers to the Virgin in the Festival of the Fallas of Valencia', *Social Knowledge: Heritage, Challenges, Perspectives*, XIV International Sociology Association World Congress of Sociology, Montréal: ISA.

Derrett, R. (2000) 'Can festivals brand community cultural development and cultural tourism simultaneously?', in J. Allen, R. Harris, L. Jago and A. J. Veal (eds.) *Events beyond 2000: Setting the agenda, Proceedings of Conference on Event Evaluation, Research and Education*: 120–129, Sydney: Australian Centre for Event Management, School of Leisure, Sport and Tourism, University of Technology, Sydney.

Dimmock, K. and Tiyce, M. (2001) 'Festivals and events: celebrating special interest tourism', in N. Douglas and R. Derrett (eds.) *Special interest tourism*: 355–383, Milton, Queensland: John Wiley and Sons, Australia.

European Union (1992) 'Treaty on European Union', article 128, signed on 7 February 1992, *Official Journal of the European Union*, C 191/01, 35, 29 July 1992.

Formica, S. (1998) 'The development of festivals and special events studies', *Festival Management and Event Tourism*, 5(3): 131–137.

Getz, D. (1991) *Festivals, special events and tourism*, New York: Van Nostrand Reinhold.

Hanley, N., Wright, R. E. and Adamowicz, W. (1998) 'Using choice experiments to value the environment: Design issues, current experience and future prospects', *Environmental and Resource Economics*, 11(3–4): 413–428.

Junta Central Fallera (2012) Available online at www.fallas.com (last accessed 15 January 2013).

Louviere, J. J., Hensher, D.A., Swait, J. D. and Adamowicz, W. L. (2000) *Stated choice methods: Analysis and applications*, Cambridge: Cambridge University Press.

McLoughlin, J., Kaminski, J. and Sodagar, B. (2007) 'Assessing the socio-economic impact of heritage: From theory to practice', in J. McLoughlin, J. Kaminski and B. Sodagar (eds.) *Technology strategy, management and socio-economic impact: Heritage Management Series Volume II*, Budapest: Archaeolingua, 17–42.

Pathak, N. and Kothari, A. (2003) 'Community-conserved biodiverse areas: Lessons from South Asia', in D. Harmon and A. D. Putney (eds.) *The full value of parks: From economics to the intangible*: 211–226, Lanham, MD: Rowman & Littlefield.

Quinn, B. (2005) 'Arts festivals and the city', *Urban Studies*, 42(5/6): 927–943.

Sánchez Royo, B. (2011) *An approach towards holistic assessment of socio-economic impacts*, unpublished PhD thesis, Valencia: University of Valencia.

UNESCO (1972) *Convention concerning the protection of the world cultural and natural heritage*, adopted by the General Conference of UNESCO on 16 November 1972, Paris: UNESCO. Entry into force: 17 December 1975, in accordance with Article 33. Accessed online in April 2013 at http://whc.unesco.org/archive/convention-en.pdf.

UNESCO (2003) *Convention for the safeguarding of the intangible cultural heritage*, MISC/2003/CLT/CMISC/2003/CLT/CH/14, Paris, 17 October 2003. Available online at http://unesdoc.unesco.org/images/0013/001325/132540e.pdf.

UNESCO (2005) *30 frequently asked questions concerning the convention on the protection and promotion of the diversity of cultural expressions*. Available online at http://unesdoc.unesco.org/images/0014/001495/149502e.pdf (last accessed June 2013).

Waterman, S. (1998) 'Carnivals for elites? The cultural politics of arts festivals', *Progress in Human Geography*, 22(1): 54–75.

World Commission on Culture and Development (1996) *Our Creative Diversity*, Paris: UNESCO, Office for Culture and Development. Available at http://unesdoc.unesco.org/images/0010/001055/105586Eb.pdf (last accessed 15 January 2013).

Part 4

Future directions

17 Cultural heritage tourism and the digital future

David Arnold and Jaime Kaminski

Introduction

In this chapter, we consider how information and communication technologies (ICTs) are currently used in ways that are specific to cultural heritage tourism attractions and their assets. We will assess how tourism based on cultural heritage differs from other forms of tourism, and how this influences the ICT applications that add value in this domain. However, in addition to reviewing the range of digital applications, we will also consider the digital future and some of its many paradoxes.

The ubiquity and pervasiveness of technology has become so much part of our everyday lives that we expect to be surprised as novel applications that we had not thought about emerge routinely. The unexpected developments make it hard to predict winning developments and it is easy to allow ourselves to cease to evaluate in any systematic way the areas where we might gain most from targeted applications. In many cases, technologies open up possibilities that challenge our underlying assumptions of the 'right way'. Things we thought were impossible become commonplace, whilst known 'truths' about the best way of meeting an enterprise's business objectives are suddenly thrown into irrelevance or obsolescence by disruptive technologies that simply bypass the 'unavoidable constraints' of previous working methods.

These influences throw up many paradoxes, which we will explore in this chapter through examining the evidence of what has become possible through developments in technologies and what the implications may be for the way that the cultural heritage tourism sector will use ICTs in the future. There are however some apparent empirical truths with technologies – most obviously the well-known and remarkably robust 'Moore's Law'. This has many variants, but at its simplest states that computing power doubles every 18 months to two years. Actually the same exponential development has applied to many aspects of technologies over a long period of time, including: memory capacity; processing speed; network speeds; information stored; and pixels per digital image. The law, which is actually rather more of an observation, has in some ways become self-fulfilling in that technology R&D companies set targets based on the expectation that the law will continue to apply (Intel, n.d.). Hence successful

ICT developers will benchmark that success against this rate of performance improvement.

The implications of this are that innovative applications need to be conceived against a backdrop of technological possibilities that can be anticipated when the application is first conceived. If it takes several years to digitize a collection in a museum and develop an interactive application, then the application's specification needs to anticipate future comparators not current ones. Thus for the image quality to appear up-to-date, any digital images that are included will need to be impressive when compared to the camera technologies at the time the application goes live rather than at the time of embarking on the project.

In this chapter, the material is structured so as to progress from generic technologies and applications through to specialist and more experimental technologies that are specific to cultural heritage contexts and where their innovative nature inevitably means that their adoption as standard techniques in the market will be further in the future. Nevertheless with the pace of change in technology adoption, we can predict confidently that amongst today's speculative applications there will be some that get adopted widely in the sector. The trick of course is to be able to predict which!

An essential part of the process of gaining market penetration is the education of the visiting public about the mechanisms by which the digital content is expected and designed to be used. The public has an expectation that in visiting a museum, for example, they are not allowed to touch the exhibits and it is not unusual to see visitors who refuse to touch interactive screens despite large signs exhorting them to do so.

The next section touches on the more mundane, general uses of ICTs within tourism and is followed by a section in which we consider the specifics of cultural heritage tourism and the opportunities, challenges and paradoxes that are inherent and unavoidable. This section is followed by one considering the need for an integrated view of the uses of technology with cultural assets and argues that the real benefits of ICT applications will lie in the reuse of digital cultural assets. The fourth section examines a number of different ways in which ICTs can enhance the on-site experience. We consider the on-site experience to be at the core of cultural heritage tourism – adopting the definition that tourism involves travelling rather than merely being a form of leisure where 'visitors' could, in theory, never leave home. Four subsections examine first the improved access that ICTs can allow to cultural heritage; second, the opportunities to use technologies to improve visitor management; third, the use of online resources to complement and enrich in-person visits; and finally using ICTs to augment the tangible evidence of the past through digital reconstructions, augmentation and narrative.

The final section examines the uses of technologies to create links beyond the freestanding tourist attraction, through collaborations between sites and the role of digital surrogates for purposes that may be disconnected with the physical visit, but maintain the emotional connection with the venue through digitally created souvenirs and gifts.

The chapter then concludes with some final thoughts on the likely future of ICTs in cultural heritage tourism.

Cultural heritage information systems

Information and communication technologies (ICTs) have the potential to influence almost every aspect of the cultural heritage tourism experience. Some applications of ICTs are immediately evident to potential visitors, such as the presence of heritage-related materials on the internet which can inform the pre-visit planning or provide additional material for post-visit experience. For example, cultural heritage tourism statistics for the USA (Office of Travel and Tourism Industries, 2010) reveal that around 50 per cent of international cultural heritage tourists use personal computers in planning their journeys, while TripAdvisor™ (Market Metrix, 2009, in World Tourism News) reports that 88 per cent of their 30 million monthly visitors are influenced by the hotel reports filed by other hotel guests. Such statistics, while demonstrating the increasing use of technologies in travel and tourism in general, are not influenced by underlying characteristics that are specific to the cultural heritage offering. However, they do illustrate that technologies are being used in planning and hence that a site with rich digital assets may have a market advantage.

At their simplest, these more obvious forms of ICT application with cultural heritage tourism are little more than the information systems that would accompany any tourism offering, providing information about what is on offer at a venue and perhaps the opportunity to plan the journey and book entrance tickets. They become more interesting for cultural heritage tourism as they extend to more dynamic systems that could provide information on how busy the attraction is and whether there is any temporary news – for example, temporary closures for restoration, or on a more positive note, temporary exhibitions of additional material that may enhance the visit. Of interest to the operators of heritage sites may be the potential to use online booking as a way of controlling overall visitor numbers and hence limiting wear and tear on the heritage and on its supporting infrastructure – for example, by issuing a maximum number of tickets online and avoiding visitors travelling to the site only to be refused access.

Potentially more interesting cultural heritage innovations arise when digital cultural heritage content is available and suitable for use in different contexts and with different audiences. This spreads the investment in creating the digital assets of a historic site beyond reasons of attracting visitors on the internet and the assets may subsequently be repurposed for use with internet advertising to potential tourists.

The cultural heritage tourist attraction

For current purposes, we consider that the core elements of a cultural heritage tourist attraction revolve around the physical artefacts – tangible heritage that can be viewed and accessed at venues varying in scale from a complete historic city to an archaeological site, individual building or monument, and down in scale to a collection of physical artefacts in a museum. In contrast, natural heritage sites may be accompanied by associated heritage narratives describing their signifi-cance to previous inhabitants, but such sites present different challenges to ICTs and the cultural heritage value lies in the associated intangible heritage rather than necessarily in the physical properties of the site. We therefore concentrate here on sites that involve at least elements of man-made tangible heritage.

There are many examples of digital models of cultural sites and artefacts, but the quality varies widely and many are prototypes created as part of getting familiar with the technological potential. The whole sector is gradually becom-ing aware of the possibilities and slowly becoming trained to understand the strengths and weaknesses of the available technologies. As with any technolo-gical innovation, there is a long assimilation period of experiment, education and refinement for any individual cultural heritage site and its staff. This is not a mature market where attractions can go and buy their technology solutions off the shelf with guaranteed success. In addition, designing tourist experiences is a creative process and success relies as much on the quality of the creative talent as on the underpinning digital assets.

As viable digital content becomes available, additional applications and chal-lenges arise. At one end of the spectrum, high-quality content may be considered as digital surrogates, providing very detailed and accurate documentation. This can enhance the visitors' experience by providing access at a level of detail that cannot be achieved either through the real object or site, or through a physical replica.

The paradox here could be that a tourist is in the presence of the original arte-fact, but places more attention and value on the digital surrogate. The equivalent might be to attend a rock concert where the artist performs live and in full view of the audience but the 20 m high projected image of the artist is more the centre of attention than the person performing in the flesh in front of the projection. In such cases, insurers and venue managers might ask 'What is the value added from having the original available alongside the digital?'. A partial answer is 'the atmosphere' that visitors report as the second highest motivation for their visit (Richards, 2007; Palmer and Richards, 2007), which might equate to a sense of place or history.

Beyond the simplest forms of ICT applications (for example, audio guides), technologies are increasingly being used for applications that are specific to cul-tural heritage, with digital heritage content and various forms of ICTs used on-site to enhance and inform the visitor experience. 2D multi-media technologies are in common use but are more difficult to repurpose for new applications. 3D recording offers more flexibility and presentational technologies are being used with 3D assets allowing the digital object to be relit and visualized accurately in synthetic environments (see below).

In theory, archaeological sites and historic urban environments present very similar challenges, but might be distinguished by the degree to which they are integrated in the fabric of current human activity. For example, recent work in documenting the Naples Roman theatre faced the challenge that the original structure is now integrated into the fabric of the city of Naples with current housing being constructed on the Roman amphitheatre, which is in essence acting as the foundations for modern building. In practice, the heritage of large-scale structures lies on a continuum between abandoned ruins and modern urban environments with historic but functional buildings, in which the balance of challenges may vary between documenting what is there, to modelling what is thought to have been there in the past.

This range of venues and scales also introduces additional distinctions between movable and immobile heritage – a historic city typically remains in one place, though there are examples of museums of individual buildings that have been moved to a site as a collection (Central Museum of Textiles, n.d.; Norsk Folkemuseum, n.d.; Odense City Museums, n.d.) These are all classed as museums rather than sites, since museums bring together collections, normally around a theme and containing objects that have been physically moved from their original context to a museum venue. The difference in this case is that open-air museums of buildings are collections of items that might under other circumstances be considered immovable, whereas a typical museum contains collections of thousands or even millions of objects that can be, and are, moved quite frequently.

In some definitions, any collection of items that has been deemed worthy of collection probably constitutes 'cultural heritage' – for example, under the UK Heritage Lottery Fund's somewhat tautological definition of heritage that might be characterized as 'that which is valued by the people' (HLF, 2013).[1]

This definition does of itself give rise to some paradoxes due to the relatively common practice of using surrogate objects even within physical collections. Surrogates may be used in museums for reasons of restricted access to originals by reason of value, fragility or availability. Thus security concerns may make it challenging to place particularly valuable objects in public locations; or concerns over potential risks of damage may make it hard to take fragile objects as part of a touring exhibition. There are examples however of surrogates being the subject of a museum collection in their own right – a notable example being the Cast Court of the Victoria and Albert Museum in London (V&A, n.d.), in which casts of works of art or architectural details mainly from the nineteenth century are on permanent exhibition. Other well-known plaster casts include some taken from the remains found at Pompeii, including casts of people and animals caught in the poses in which they died, which formed part of an exhibition about the site which toured in the USA for a period of two years from October 2011. Such plaster casts are frequently lent or toured to add to the visibility of the materials (British Museum, 2013). There is even an International Association for the Conservation and the Promotion of Plaster Cast Collections, and the Association's database (AICPM, n.d.) lists almost 250 cast collections in 33 countries across six continents.

The other dimension to a site or museum collection is that the significance and compelling tourism engagement that they can present relies less on the objects themselves than the narrative they represent. Thus places come alive when the narrative of the events they have witnessed is revealed and objects' significance beyond intrinsic artistic value is usually revealed in the context of their significance to figures from the past. Son-et-lumière offerings show a range of early examples of the use of technologies to augment the physical site with narrative content.

Repurposing digital heritage assets – the workflow pipeline

For the purposes of cultural heritage tourism, one paradox is that the production of digital content is often focused on satisfying an audience, whereas to derive the most benefit from creating digital records of cultural material other uses in documentation, preservation and curatorial research need to be factored in. Designers of websites of cultural content and interactive experiences for museum visitors will typically start by considering what potential demand the digital content is seeking to serve. Historically the materials required to support such end use applications might well have been produced explicitly for these applications without much consideration of the re-use of assets. Multi-media CDs of cultural content would be built from scratch using specially scripted text, photos, videos, accompanying soundtracks and occasionally 3D virtual objects or environments. A great deal of the material would be commissioned for individual projects in part because there was no supply of pre-existing materials. It is in general impossible to reverse engineer from touristic materials to derive materials for professional quality documentation of the cultural assets, whereas extracting cultural heritage tourism materials from professional documentation is just one of many uses to which the data may be put.

By the late 1990s, the rate at which there was demand for designing new websites, and extending or updating existing sites, coupled with the associated costs of producing material. There was a realization that content needed to be re-used. At about the same time, digital imagery reached the stage where images could be mapped to a screen one to one and fill a screen so that the quality of visual materials was as good as the screen was able to display, so re-use of existing materials would not seem as dated. The stage was set for the development of content management systems.

As soon as the design of websites ceased to be a completely bespoke solution in every case, the development of content, from scripting a page of text to film production, was separated from the production of the style of a page and treated as the maintenance of a library of resources. Assets from this library would then be assembled into the online presence that was the new website and similarly library assets could be used within a scripted framework to provide gallery tour guides or other interactive systems (e.g. see Boast, 2009; Morgan, 2009); in parallel to this process libraries and museums were also migrating their inventories of information about their holdings into digital archives – initially at the level of information about the collection, and then quickly to the level of information about the individual catalogue entries. A natural step was therefore to link the information in the catalogue as an online resource for cultural professionals and members of the public alike, to allow them to browse information about museum holdings, for example, and identify artefacts of interest to them. These sources were largely text based – catalogues might not even have photographs of the individual artefacts – and the entertainment and touristic value of these resources was limited. However, as photographic documentation moved from analogue film to digital cameras during the 2000s, so the catalogue became enhanced with digital imagery.

Projects at a European level sought to amalgamate the information about museum holdings at these levels too (MICHAEL, 2004–08, MICHAEL+, 2006–09, MINERVA, 2006, and Athena, 2008–11) and the concept of a European Digital Library of cultural assets has evolved rapidly (Kaulins, 2009). In commercial circles, including the tourism sector, enterprises that aggregate information from multiple sources have also sprung up. These organizations may draw information from restaurant guides, tourist venues, travel services and hotels, for example, into a single one-stop website and information service. Increasingly these services will include information on the best routes for tourists travelling through a region and viewing several visitor attractions, including cultural sites on route (for example, the Parador world heritage city routes in Spain [Paradores, 2013]).

In this section, we have seen the way in which a desire to satisfy the tourism demand for content related to tangible cultural heritage leads naturally and logically to the need to make resources available by documenting the underpinning tangible heritage with accurate, visually compelling imagery and well-researched and curated factual information. Thus cultural heritage institutions are increasingly interested in their digital documentation not only in its own right as a means to support the curation, preservation, analysis and integrity of the source material but as a basis for repurposing digital assets to allow the development of digital systems to communicate with the public.

The economics of cultural heritage and the degree to which a return on investment can be demonstrated are both factors that will continue to influence the availability of cultural heritage assets for touristic applications as well as the degree to which cultural heritage institutions will use digital technologies to enhance their visitors' experience. Variations in accuracy required for different applications, and in levels of detail that are recorded, are apparent and any digital object may well be suited for one set of applications but unsuited for many other purposes. Recording at the highest achievable accuracy will, in general, improve the shelf life of a digital model and the degree to which content can be repurposed but also will incur greater initial costs. Balancing cost and future potential remains a complex business decision.

In the following sections, we consider the types of application that digital assets will support. Most of these can be considered under the umbrella of improving access to heritage assets, whilst some will improve the sustainability of the assets to which access is provided.

Enhancing the on-site experience

Technology has much to offer in enhancing the on-site experience, but equally the on-site experience requires careful design and, as noted elsewhere, a visiting public that is comfortable with the technologies offered. Digital models of cultural objects and environments are used increasingly to:

- provide access by making it easier to view details and by allowing items that are physically inaccessible for whatever reason to be professionally documented and viewed at a separate location and time;
- provide insights and interpretations of the previous condition or states of a site or object, for example, by using digital models to give an impression of the artefact in its former pristine state, repairing damage or even just showing documented condition which predates more recent damage;
- place content in other location-based augmented reality, including both so-called 'digital repatriation' (see below) and to contextualize artefacts, for example, showing the way a tool might have been used (See Figures 10–12, Hamer *et al.*, 2011);
- present representations of tangible heritage as part of the narrative of intangible heritage with digital story-telling.

Accessing the inaccessible

At its most obvious, technology can provide virtual access to aspects that are not available physically. The most common situation where this occurs is because a very high percentage of museum collections is normally kept in storage that is much less accessible to the public, but even items that are on display are usually inaccessible at some level. For example, curators are unlikely to be willing to allow visitors to handle unique museum artefacts, to get a closer view of the objects, or when the size and detail of an object makes it hard for the tourist to see, then an accurate digital model can be scaled and manipulated to show detail that is not visible to the naked eye.

A classic example of this type of application occurs with the intricacy that craftsmen in the Far East have achieved with carved objects in wood, ivory and stone. For example, a small number of objects from the National Palace Museum in Taiwan were digitized in 3D to a high standard in around 2000, including a carved boat, which is described on the museum's website as follows:

> Ch'en Tsu-chang, originally from Kwangtung, had already entered the Imperial Bureau of Manufacture in the Yung-cheng reign (1723–1735). In 1737, he followed the natural shape of an olive pit to carve a small boat. On the boat are eight figures, each of which is animated and expressive in an individual manner. What is most fascinating is that the entire text of Su Shih's 'Latter Ode on the Red Cliff', including more than

300 characters and upon which this work is based, is engraved with exquisite detail on the bottom of the boat, testifying to the heavenly craftsmanship of the artist.

(Taiwan National Palace Museum, 2013)

In the museum, this artefact is in a glass cabinet and so can only be viewed from a distance. Even with a magnifying glass in front of the object, it is impossible to appreciate the full complexity of the piece and the magnification is only available from one point of view. In the 3D model, however, the individual carvings can be viewed in detail and the interior carving appreciated by removing the roof of the boat. Other examples from the National Palace Museum include a carved ivory ball containing 22 concentric layers that can be peeled away to reveal elements that could not otherwise be appreciated without handling and manipulating the original, fragile piece. From the same museum, the *Turning Vase* is decorated with fishes on an inner sleeve that are revealed through the openings in an outer shell as the sleeve is turned inside. Again this manipulation would never be available to the public with the original artefact.

Other classes of cultural heritage where access may be an issue include the following:

- physical access, where the object is in storage or physically inaccessible for other reasons – for example, the detail of the roof of a building or where the archaeology is submerged (Gallo *et al.*, 2012);
- no longer exists or, in some cases, has never existed in reality.

By way of illustration of these cases, Figure 17.1 shows the digital representation of an ivory Jacob's Ladder wallet from China, dating from about 1920 and measuring 9 cm by 5 cm. Having a digital model, the object can be rendered in many ways, including as a reproduction of the object with the original visual properties, as in the left-hand image, or as a simulated line drawing, as in the right-hand image. It is clear that more detail can be seen even in these images than would be readily observable from handling the original.

Scale is one limiting factor on capacity to appreciate what we are looking at. Artefacts may also be inaccessible because they are in storage, as a very high proportion of museum collections are. Estimates vary about the fraction of museum artefacts that are in storage. On 31 March 2012, for example, the Victoria and Albert Museum in London had 60,039 collection items on display, out of a total of 221,829 items in the so-called 'Display Collections' – museum objects and works of art suitable for long-term gallery display. In addition, 2,011,464 items were included in the reference collections (V&A, 2012). In this case, less than 3 per cent of the overall collections are on view and the remainder may only be brought out for public viewing very occasionally – for example, as part of a special exhibition or on request for scholarly study.

There can be other reasons why the remains of tangible cultural heritage are not easily accessible to cultural heritage tourists. For cultural sites, this may vary

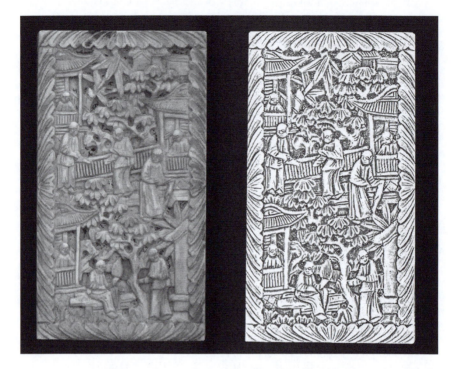

Figure 17.1 Digital model of an ivory wallet, China (~1920), scanned in 3D and displayed (a) as a reproduction of the object with the original visual properties, left, and (b) as a simulated line drawing, right.

from the intended characteristics of the original (for example, a deliberately inaccessible fortified structure, which is still in good condition), to unsafe state of repair in a ruined building, or through change of circumstances through volcanic activity, leading to a site becoming buried or submerged.

Digital documentation records the state of a cultural site or artefact at a particular time. Digital restoration, reconstruction and visualization are all terms that describe means to augment the current evidence to give an impression or hypothesis of what might have been there in the past (for example, see Adami *et al.*, 2012). Figure 17.2 shows an example which goes a stage further, a hypothetical reconstruction of a building that was designed but never built. This example is based on Le Vau's 1663 design for extending the Louvre Palace in Paris (Berger, 1993). No one can view the 'original' building and this is one of a number of competing designs, only one of which was completed. Where a building was never completed, even the remaining drawings provide only partial evidence of the architect's intentions.

Figure 17.3 shows a model of the entrance porch to Brighton Royal Pavilion, from an angle that it is impossible to see as a cultural heritage tourist. This model was constructed to show the building's structure and makes no pretence

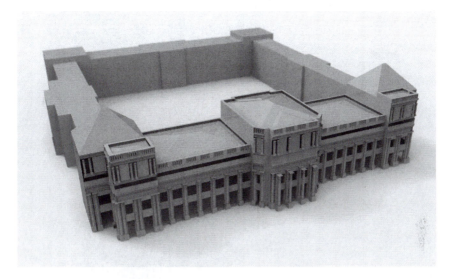

Figure 17.2 Digital reconstruction of a proposed extension of the Louvre Palace, designed by le Pau in 1663.

of giving a photographic representation of the visual quality of the original. However, with suitable professional recording of the structure, the visitor would be able to see details that were impractical to view from the original. If 3D documentation of historic buildings and monuments were routine, then such models could be used for tourist purposes as well as providing records for condition monitoring and other conservation applications.

Clearly these three instances, and the project decisions that led to their creation, represent very different purposes and challenges. Whilst all involve the use of ICTs with cultural artefacts, the approach taken to their creation, and the costs involved, varies to match the narrative they support as well as their potential use in documenting heritage for other purposes. ICTs can assist in any of these circumstances through the production of digital representations of the inaccessible heritage.

Despite advances in disability legislation in recent years, some heritage sites remain inaccessible to disabled visitors, clearly ICT has a role in potentially allowing these groups to at least experience these sites (Buhalis and Darcy, 2011), but while this may increase access on one hand, the digital divide may exclude others.

Managing visitor numbers: less favoured, spreading load

Heritage tourism is characterized by an imbalance of visitors, with 90 per cent of visitors going to 10 per cent of the sites, whilst the remaining 90 per cent of usually smaller sites receive the remaining visitors. ICT has the potential to

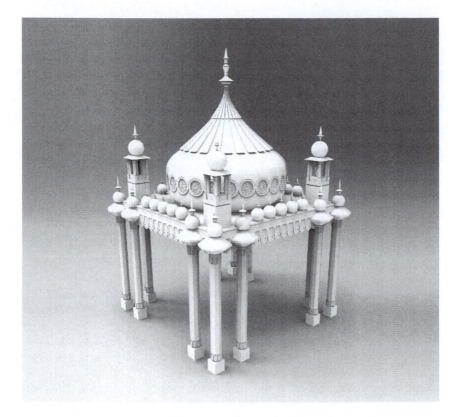

Figure 17.3 Procedural model of the west porch of the Royal Pavilion in Brighton, UK.

address this rapid decay in visitor numbers and spread the load, but with the larger sites having the skills and financial resources to invest in ICT to a greater extent than smaller sites, will this merely reaffirm the status quo?

For example, there is the possibility that virtual reality may allow some users to experience heritage sites from their own homes. For some, this may become the visit. But communicating the essence of the experience without travelling to the site is a tourism paradox; does this reduce physical visits or increase them? Does the online presence become a replacement for physical visits or a trailer to encourage visits?

Online resources, physical presence and the virtual museum

The virtual museum is the result of the conjunction of the traditional concept of a museum with the multimedia computer and communication technology of the Internet.... It dematerializes the museum itself by making possible a remote visit.

(Moscati, 2007)

At one level, this is the ultimate paradox for use of digital technologies in cultural heritage tourism, challenging as it does the very definition of tourism as an activity involving travelling. The concept of a virtual exhibition drawing together material from several sites or presenting material that may not exist in any physical form has been growing in parallel to the general growth of the internet (see, for example, Chittaro *et al.*, 2010). However, the idea of the virtual museum is still relatively recent and extrapolates the pre- and post-support for a tourist's visit to a site, conceptually reaching the situation where the physical visit itself is now superfluous. Two arguments would counter that assertion.

First, it was widely reported (but little evidenced) in the initial developments of electronic books that, at least initially, placing the entire text of a book online led to more copies of the physical book being sold. If this were ever true, then the absence of suitable e-readers at the time was probably a major factor. More recently, however, press reports are clearly indicating that e-books are taking over. For example, James Hall, consumer affairs editor of the *Telegraph* newspaper, reported that, 'Sales of printed books have fallen by a quarter in the first two months of this year due to the increased popularity of e-readers such as the Kindle' (Hall, 2012).

Hall's (2012) hypothesis was that the availability and acceptance of the e-reader has led to the downturn in sales of printed books, evidenced by a dramatic rise in sales of e-books and e-readers over the same period. Except in extreme circumstances, it seems unlikely that the same would be true for e-tourists, since the e-experience would in no way be seen as sufficiently close to the real visit as to satisfy the appetite of those who were able to undertake the real visit. Where people have the wherewithal (such as finance and accessibility), it seems likely that they will continue to want to incorporate their cultural heritage visits into the overall experience of travel, holidays or add-ons to business trips, etc.

Of course, factors beyond the control of the visitor may reduce the accessibility to sites over time – for example, the rationing of visits for the protection of sites from wear and tear, such as the ticketing limitations imposed on visits to the burial chamber in the Great Pyramid at Giza, the Hypogeum of Hal-Saflieni in Malta or many of the decorated caves of France and Spain. Additionally, travel may become limited by the imposition of controls on the use of fossil fuels, although it seems unlikely that the political will would be there to implement such radical measures anytime soon.

The second argument is that the virtual museum serves a different purpose and market. With some iconic exemptions, it seems unlikely that a museum will have so many visits as to lead museum authorities to seek a virtual presence that would materially reduce the number of physical visits. The Sistine Chapel, Mona Lisa or Michelangelo's David may attract so many visitors as to impact on the quality of the experience, but few museums or cultural heritage sites, if any, are in a situation that would not be controlled by rationing of access. What the virtual museum concept could do is provide a mechanism for different, but related experiences and hence augment any physical visit. So museum curators might, for example, use the virtual museum to display artefacts that are currently in storage, or to mount different narratives as special exhibitions. Cooperation between several museums could allow a virtual museum in a space that is entirely fictitious. Such experiences can be expected to encourage interest in heritage and hence it could be argued will actually continue to promote additional physical visits to museums and culture heritage sites.

Augmentation of the physical visit with a virtual presence is a slightly different use of the technologies from the virtual museum. The virtual museum sets out to be a complete experience in its own right, whereas those museums that are engaged in providing pre- and post-visit augmentation are setting these offerings in the context of the physical visit.

Interpretation: previous states, story-telling and augmentation

The representation of history and its use in augmenting our appreciation of the remaining tangible evidence of historic places, events and artefacts offers some of the most striking challenges to cultural heritage tourism. These challenges are amplified with the use of ICTs and the internet, through the persistence of the visibility of information that is presented. A factual inaccuracy may become magnified and take on the status of accepted wisdom through propagation over the internet.

The statement that 'History is written by the winners' (often attributed to Winston Churchill, but origin unknown) describes one of the challenges and paradoxes. Much of the most evocative surviving tangible heritage relates to the commemoration of religion or conflict, but in both of these spheres there are by definition multiple perspectives. However, although the remembrance of war inevitably provides stark illustrations of opposing views, conflicting narratives and extreme perspectives, these narratives typically represent a nuanced range of perspectives that surround tangible heritage and serve to highlight both its embedded significance and the degree to which it is interpreted. A civilian account of war may differ substantially from a military account, even from the same side. The official version is unlikely to align with any individual's perspective of the 'truth' and individuals' versions can easily become distorted over time and with the frailties of memory.

Experts disagree at some level on many small details of historic buildings, so a virtual reconstruction of a historic building is always an interpretation. The intangible narratives of its significance and use are likely to be even more uncertain, yet tourists have a thirst for 'knowledge' and certainty that may not be achievable.

To complicate matters, if the vested interests are served by hijacking this uncertainty to reinforce political agendas, then technology allows unofficial versions of 'the truth' to be presented with apparent authority. The paradox is that the more nuanced and inclusive the interpretation is, the less satisfying and entertaining the result appears to be to a broader, mass audience.

Personalization of narratives could in principle make matters worse. Profiling systems are built around positive reinforcement. Goods are marketed to people by reinforcing their expressed preferences – so having bought a watch online the likelihood is that the consumer continues to be bombarded with advertising for watches. If personalized narratives are tailored to the receivers' expectations, then all the worst elements of fallacies, misrepresentation and prejudice are merely reinforced.

Personalization relies on visitor profiles being kept and further developed though monitoring visitor behaviour, which has ethical and practical implications, both for the visitor and for the organization holding the data. For some visitors, the benefits of a tailored experience will outweigh both the risks of inappropriate use of personal data and the irritations that can arise from unwanted suggestions. The organization must balance their responsibilities for data protection against the desire to provide tailored narratives.

As data about the collections on a route improve and as user profiling becomes more sophisticated, personalization should also improve. Visitors will become more familiar with the paradigms of consumption and some approaches will emerge as winners, with people typically able to operate a basic system without training, as they do with a mobile phone or TV remote without instruction. Of course, advanced functionality continues to either remain unused or be learnt only by early adopters – frequently the young!

A different form of augmentation can be expected to emerge, where the experience at a venue is increasingly linked to online resources. So, for example, the visitor to a war cemetery might photograph an individual headstone and be linked through optical character recognition of the inscriptions to information about military records of individual soldiers, connected to information about the battlegrounds on which they fought and to content about the routes of military campaigns. They might also link to census data and information about their prior lives, origins and family. It is clear that the decisions to make such data available need to be made with thorough consideration of privacy and ethical issues, and this in itself presents one paradox to cultural heritage tourism – the balance between an enriched and enriching experience for the tourist and respect for personal privacy and cultural sensitivity.

Another paradox for cultural heritage tourism is that the information is being viewed out of context – the experience for the cultural heritage tourist is itself consumed within the experience of their own background and culture, so the exploits of a national hero may be the unacceptable face of terrorism. This is not a situation that is created by the use of ICTs, but ICTs exaggerate the potential because of the difference between a controlled, locally presented in-person experience and de-contextualization of content over the internet. However, matching the narratives to the cultural background of the visitor would be to deny the pluracy of perspectives.

This draws attention to the final paradox in this section, namely that the personalization of the experience may be seen to close down the visitors' opportunity to broaden their interests and the joy of serendipitously discovering unexpected treasures for themselves.

Displaced heritage, digital repatriation and digital cooperation

The cultural heritage associated with the colonial past of European countries is a specific example of displaced heritage and occurs in both directions – heritage brought back from colonies to cultural institutions in the colonizing country and the remains of the colonizing culture left behind in the colonies. These are examples of 'displaced cultural heritage', a term which could also be used to describe cultural artefacts plundered in times of war or displaced for other reasons. The original Elgin marbles might be used within a virtual environment of the Parthenon, or even used as templates to manufacture physical copies for restoration work. Of course, the curatorial challenges and politics of such proposals would be complex.

As with the Elgin marbles, depending upon the circumstances in which heritage becomes displaced can provoke strong nationalistic or emotional reactions and the resolution is in practice a political and inter-cultural matter. In some circumstances, the displacement may be accepted, but ICTs could present physically separated elements of tangible cultural heritage within a single user experience. So, for example, many of the tombs of the Valley of the Kings have been emptied by archaeologists and others, either plundered for valuables or removing them for safety. In such circumstances, it may be possible to create experiences integrating elements that are no longer co-located into a single experience that can be offered to augment the elements either in their current locations or as a stand-alone presentation available in another location or online.

The cultural significance of publicly accessible tangible heritage (historic places and public artworks) changes over time as new generations experience them and absorb them into their own heritage. For example, over time a public statue may cease to embody the memorial narrative that led to its erection and become a meeting place for a younger generation.

Similarly, the motivation that led to the introduction of cultural artefacts from the colonizing power is highly unlikely to be appreciated in the same way in a post-colonial independent nation, but may acquire different cultural significance, or equally be allowed to decay through lack of interest or purposeful neglect. Over time, however, the remaining tangible cultural heritage may become an attractant to tourists from the former colonizing power and an important economic factor for the host country.

ICTs can be used to collect different cultural perspectives and, if this process is repeated over time, then the evolution of the significance and the accompanying narratives can be used within tourism offerings. However, the paradox is that we seek to use ICTs so as to retain information that fallible humans might forget, but selective forgetting is at one level a useful healing process and heritage, as described elsewhere in this book, is about the current significance of history, rather than a fixed historical perspective.

The digital surrogate: restoration, digital gifts and souvenirs

In the introduction to this chapter, we saw how surrogates have been used historically to allow risk-free access to fragile, valuable or remote objects. Using digital copies of artefacts will become increasingly sophisticated and provide a potential basis for replicating physical objects through 3D printing and/or manufacturing duplicates using numerically controlled cutting tools. Thus the digitization of a statue could be used as input to a numerically controlled machine tool that is used to cut a replica in marble or other material at any scale.

The paradox is that the digitization that could secure a site by reducing the need for physical visits could at the same time reduce security by informing criminals of the placing and layout of valuable heritage. Equally, raising awareness of the existence of an artefact and, through that, producing additional revenue streams to the owners through souvenir production could also undermine those revenue streams by empowering the unscrupulous production of bootleg copies.

Physical copies could in principle be used in restoration and reconstruction and hence in maintaining at least a representation of the original environment. The paradox here is that, although the technology would support the approach, every time the decision is taken to replace a piece, the physical environment becomes less authentic. Such decisions are of course curatorial rather than technical and there are many examples of manual processes being used to produce replacement pieces to 'restore' a historic site (Figure 17.4 shows an obvious case).

Physical copies have a long tradition of being used as souvenirs – one need think no further than the plaster models of the Leaning Tower of Pisa or metal copies of the Eiffel Tower. The concern with digitally derived copies is the opportunity for unauthorized reuse coupled with simple technologies for mass production. One imagines that there must have been similar concerns to protect Jacquard weaving patterns in the nineteenth century.

These paradoxes are management challenges to those embarking on a digital strategy. Careful planning for the use of ICTs can of course also help address the paradox – for example, through the use of digital watermarking technologies to allow identification of unauthorized digital copies and clear identification of physical reproductions.

Conclusions

This chapter has explored the impact of ICTs on cultural heritage tourism and considered where it is going and what paradoxes it faces. In many cases, these predicted 'future' applications are technically possible now – limited more by the available data and the creative narratives. These factors also dictate the viability of the applications – whether individual museums and tourist sites will find it is economic to become engaged in the technologies. The analysis of return on investment is complicated. Having a maintained cultural fabric may be considered a public service, but the organizations that benefit most economically rarely contribute to the investment in maintaining the assets. Thus hotels and

Figure 17.4 Replacement stones in Ankor Wat in Cambodia. Whilst at least three of the stones are clearly recent replacements, the variability of the condition of the carvings suggests that this process of replacement has been going on for a long time.

tour operators may benefit from a tourism industry based on cultural assets, but most of the turnover accrued may be in the services that bring tourists to the sites, fed and accommodated, rather than at the turnstiles of the heritage venues.

Politicians require better appreciation and justification for investment of public finance in our cultural fabric, since much is publicly owned. Political and societal appreciation of the value of heritage and the importance it holds in defining citizenship, cultural identity, the sense of belonging to the community in which we live and the place of heritage in educating the next generation may also be factors that impact the growth rate of cultural heritage tourism.

We have examined what the digital future holds not just for cultural heritage tourism but also for the custodianship of human heritage, because of the broader technological potential in repurposing digital materials.

All of the applications we have outlined involve using digital content and, whether that content is used on or off site, it amounts to a cultural asset that exists separately from the physical material. These digital assets can be repurposed and re-presented to suit a whole range of new business propositions, many as yet unimagined, although these are somewhat distinct areas where the use of ICTs is increasingly adding value to the visitor experience.

The potential of digital assets challenges the imagination of the developers of touristic experiences, the owners of cultural assets, regional economic development officers and curators alike. Continued innovation in the range of these applications can be confidently predicted and each of these stakeholder groups will bring their own perspectives to the desirability of innovations and potential new cultural heritage 'products'.

At the same time, the visiting public will learn to understand the expected paradigms of consumption in the same way as most of us have learnt to use games controllers, mobile phones and computers – albeit at a range of proficiencies. Audiences need to be able to learn how to consume within the new technological paradigms or the products will fail as business propositions.

As noted above, the concept of 'culture trails' is fairly well established (see, for example, Sussex Sculptures Recording Project, 2013). An obvious development would be to create tailored culture trails in which personalized online commentary would not only provide a succession of downloadable audio guides to your mobile phone at each site you visited, but create a profile of your interests. This could draw on analysis of your pattern of movement at each site, knowledge of the collection and what is on show, and the dwell times at each exhibit. As the systems become more capable and voice-based question and answer interfaces are used to improve the visitor's experience, so the system would potentially be able to tailor what you are told about exhibits depending upon the level of interest and expertise that was detected in your profile. The system would remember your questions and the answers and build a model of the knowledge you have to help construct an appropriate reply to the next question. Will tourists ever become comfortable with talking to machines and having their profiles recorded and analysed, for example?

Digital copies allow mass production of accurate reproductions, raising issues of the underlying enterprise models in which owners of cultural assets will have to take a view of the overall good and balance protection of their ownership, with demand for access to the original in terms of on-site visits and online shopping for copies. These decisions are not new and are judgements that are in part political. There is no doubt that ICTs make such applications possible and hence active decisions are needed. The fact that systems that create digital models from tourist photos are improving all the time means that in many cases the decisions are overdue. However, accurate documentation, which supports the making of copies, also supports the identification of those copies and the protection of the assets, as well as the other innovations. The possibility of misuse of a digital photograph does not preclude high-quality photography for insurance purposes.

3D digital documentation would allow more accuracy and even permit entire cultural sites to be reproduced, even allowing overall dimensions to be adjusted. For example, this would allow accurate scale models if required, but only politicians, historians and curators, and perhaps planners, can take the more difficult decisions on their desirability. The effort of achieving this or the comparable challenges of digitizing all the collections of a museum (including those in store) would be considerable and challenging for three reasons. First, since digitization only records some elements of an object which are required to support the applications envisaged, the purpose of recording needs to have been understood in order to design the digitization campaign. Second, current technologies are limited in what material types can be faithfully recorded and in what combinations. Third, the sheer operational logistics of recording collections of (say) two million items in 3D imply a very long and difficult digitization campaign. Fourth, and last, a long and complex campaign would require major financing and the economics of the benefits are not yet well understood. Even applying Moore's Law to the number of 3D digitized cultural artefacts, it will be many decades until the world's museums are truly online.

Nevertheless, we would argue that the future is constrained not so much by technological considerations, but by human considerations, ranging from political to curatorial. The danger is that, in many instances, the opportunity for considered decisions may be sidelined by the pace at which technology empowers new scenarios that are enacted by technologically savvy entrepreneurs, before the custodians of our heritage feel equipped to address legitimate concerns.

We must conclude that ICTs are already exerting a profound influence on tourism and cultural heritage tourism, which can only continue to grow. Technological developments continue at a frantic pace. Mobile devices allow heritage tourists to carry a huge amount of (networked) computing capacity around with them. When seen in conjunction with developments in visualization, cloud computing and big data they have the potential to enhance every aspect of the value chain. The capacity to achieve 'wonderful things' with ICTs in cultural heritage is very much here. But of course not everyone can engage in the digital world (the digital divide), and not all heritage organizations have the resources or capacity to support its development. The application of ICTs to cultural heritage tourism will continue to provide more than its fair share of paradoxes.

Note

1   Our view of heritage is broad, progressive and inclusive.... We take a distinctive, integrated approach – grounded in what people value...

(HLF, 2013)

References

Adami, A., Carlani, R., van Kampen, I., Pietroni, E. and Sannibale M. (2012) 'Digital techniques for Etruscan Graves: the Etruscanning Project', in Arnold, D., Kaminski, J., Niccolucci, F. and Stork, A. (eds.) *VAST (2012) 13th International Symposium on Virtual Reality, Archaeology and Cultural Heritage*: 129–136, Goslar, Germany: The Eurographics Association.

AICPM (n.d.) *Database of cast collections*, International Association for the Conservation and the Promotion of Plaster Cast Collections, accessed online (April 2013) at www.plastercastcollection.org/en/database.php.

ATHENA (2008–11) *Access to Cultural Heritage Networks across Europe*, accessed online (April 2013) at www.athenaeurope.org.

Berger, R. (1993) *The Palace of the Sun: The Louvre of Louis XIV*, University Park, PA: Pennsylvania State University Press.

Boast, R. (2009) *Open Source Collections Management System*, Museum3, accessed online (April 2013) at http://museum3.org/group/engaginginsocialmediainmuseums/forum/topics/open-source-collections.

British Museum (2013) *Life and Death: Pompeii and Herculaneum*, accessed online (April 2013) at www.britishmuseum.org/whats_on/exhibitions/pompeii_and_herculaneum.aspx.

Buhalis, D. and Darcy, S. (eds.) (2011) *Accessible tourism: Concepts and issues*, Bristol: Channel View Publications.

Central Museum of Textiles (n.d.) *Open-air Museum of the Łódź Wooden Architecture*, Lodz, Poland, accessed online (April 2013) at www.muzeumwlokiennictwa.pl/o-skansenie/.

Chittaro, L., Ieronutti, L., Ranon, R., Siotto, E. and Visintini, D. (2010) 'A high-level tool for curators of 3D virtual visits and its application to a virtual exhibition of Renaissance frescoes', in Artusi, A., Joly-Parvex, M., Lucet, G., Ribes, A. and Pitzalis, D. (eds.) *The 11th International Symposium on Virtual Reality, Archaeology and Cultural Heritage VAST (2010)*: 147–154, Goslar, Germany: The Eurographics Association.

Gallo, A., Angilica, A., Bianco, G., De Filippo, F., Muzzupappa, M., Davidde, B. and Bruno, F. (2012) '3D reconstruction and virtual exploration of submerged structures: A case study in the underwater archaeological site of Baia (Italy)', in Arnold, D., Kaminski, J., Niccolucci, F. and Stork, A. (eds.) *VAST (2012) 13th International Symposium on Virtual Reality, Archaeology and Cultural Heritage*: 121–128, Goslar, Germany: The Eurographics Association.

Greg Richards, (2007) *ATLAS Cultural Tourism Survey, Summary Report 2007*, retrieved 9 December 2012 from www.tram-research.com/atlas/ATLAS%20Cultural%20Tourism%20Survey%202007.PDF?3e3ea140.

Hall, J. (2012) 'Printed book sales slump', Consumer Affairs, *Telegraph online*, 8 March, accessed online (February 2013) at www.telegraph.co.uk/news/uknews/9131135/Printed-book-sales-slump.html.

Hamer, H., Gall, J., Urtasun, R. and Van Gool, L. (2011) 'Data-driven animation of hand-object interactions', *IEEE Conference on Automatic Face and Gesture Recognition*: 360–7, accessed online (April 2013) at www.vision.ee.ethz.ch/publications/papers/proceedings/eth_biwi_00793.pdf.

Heritage Lottery Fund, HLF (2013) *Strategy and planning*, accessed online (April 2013) at www.hlf.org.uk/aboutus/howwework/strategy.

Intel (n.d.) *Moore's Law inspires Intel innovation: Bold forecast drives groundbreaking new technologies and more power-efficient processors*, accessed online (April 2013) at www.intel.com/content/www/us/en/silicon-innovations/moores-law-technology.html.

Kaulins, A. (2009) *Relaunch of Europeana: The European Union digital cultural resource project appears in improved form with over 4 million digital items*, accessed online (April 2013) at eupundit.blogspot.com/2009/03/relaunch-of-europeana-european-union.html.

Market Metrix (2009) 'The expanding role of user-generated hotel reviews' 2 March, reported in *World Tourism News*, accessed online (April 2013) at www.world-tourism-news.eu/news/the-expanding-role-of-user-generated-hotel-reviews/.

MICHAEL (2004–08) and MICHAEL plus (2006–09) *Multilingual Inventory of Cultural Heritage in Europe*, accessed online (April 2013) at www.michael-culture.org/about/project.html.

MINERVA-EC (2006) *MINERVA EC Thematic Network in cultural, scientific information and scholarly content*, accessed online (April 2013) at www.minervaeurope.org.

Morgan, R. (2009) *Moving a major cultural institution onto an Open Source WCM environment, presentation of experiences from the V&A*, accessed online (April 2013) at www.slideshare.net/OpenSourceCMS/va-museum-migrating-content-management-systems-open-source-cms.

Moscati, P, (ed.) (2007) 'Virtual museums and archaeology: The contribution of the Italian National Research Council', *Archeologia e Calcolatori*, Supplemento 1: 9–14. Available online at soi.cnr.it/archcalc/images/VM.pdf.

Norsk Folkemuseum (The Norwegian Museum of Cultural History) (n.d.) *The Open Air Museum*, accessed online (April 2013) at www.norskfolkemuseum.no/en/exhibits/The-Open-Air-Museum/.

Odense City Museums (n.d.) *Funen village open-air museum*, accessed online (April 2013) at museum.odense.dk/en/museums/funen-village.

Office of Travel and Tourism Industries (2010) *Cultural Heritage Traveler US*. Department of Commerce International Trade Administration, accessed online (April 2013) at www.tinet.ita.doc.gov/outreachpages/download_data_table/2010-cultural-heritage-profile.pdf.

Palmer, R. and Richards, G. (2007) *European Cultural Capital Report*, Arnhem: ATLAS.

Paradores (2013) *World Heritage City Route*, Paradores of Spain Routes 2013, accessed online (April 2013) at www.paradores-spain.com/offers/routes.html.

Sussex Sculptures Recording Project (2013) *Sculpture Trails*, PMSA Regional Archive Centre for Sussex, accessed online (April 2013) at www.publicsculpturesofsussex.co.uk/sculpture-trails.

Taiwan National Palace Museum (2013) *Carved olive-stone boat, Ch'en Tsu-chang, Ch'ing Dynasty (1644–1911)*, accessed online (April 2013) at www.npm.gov.tw/en/Article.aspx?sNo=04001107.

V&A (n.d.) *The Cast Court Collection*, Victoria and Albert Museum, accessed online (April 2013) at www.vam.ac.uk/users/node/15151.

V&A (2012) *How many items are there in the V&A collections?*, accessed online (April 2013) at www.vam.ac.uk/content/articles/s/size-of-the-v-and-a-collections/.

18 Strategic planning for sustainability and the effect of the recession at the Roman Baths, Bath, UK

Stephen Bird

Introduction

This chapter is a case study which discusses the process by which Bath and North East Somerset Council's Heritage Services division has devised and implemented a framework for strategic business planning that will ensure the sustainability of the Roman Baths, the audiences they attract and the income streams those audiences bring. It looks at the philosophy underpinning the investment made in the Roman Baths, and it considers the effect of the worldwide economic downturn on the visitor attractions sector through the experience of the Roman Baths at Bath. It outlines the long years of successive crises which have affected visitor behaviour and decision-making, and it discusses the ways in which managers at the Roman Baths have monitored their effects and implemented service delivery and marketing measures to mitigate them. The chapter concludes with an assessment of the problems of planning for sustainability in the longer term.

The city of Bath

The spa city of Bath lies in the valley of the River Avon 20 km east of the port city of Bristol in the west of England. Although it has a population of only 85,000 residents, it receives around four million visitors each year, attracted by its Georgian architecture and the substantial *in situ* remains of a Roman thermal complex built around Britain's only hot springs. The complex was constructed over the largest of the city's three hot springs, the King's Spring, which disgorges over one million litres of geothermal water per day at a constant temperature of 46°C. The springs are the outflow from a regional thermal aquifer buried at depths >2.7 km beneath the city and surrounding area. The aquifer is recharged via rainfall on limestone outcrops to the south and west. The time required from rain falling on these outcrops to its subsequent emergence in the city's hot springs is thought to be between 6,000 and 10,000 years. Hydrological research suggests that this flow has continued unbroken for thousands of years (Atkinson and Davison, 2002; Stanton, 1991).

Tourism is the principal industry in Bath. It supported 8,652 jobs – one in ten of the local employment market – and contributed £373 million in 2008 to the local economy (South West Tourism Research, 2008). The engine of the city's tourism industry is the Roman Baths and Pump Room complex: the economic impact of this site alone is estimated to be £92 million per annum (Bath and North East Somerset Council Heritage Services, 2010; Dawson, n.d.).[1] It is the only local authority-run member of the Association of Leading Visitor Attractions (ALVA) and ranks amongst the UK's most important and most popular heritage sites with over one million visitors to the Roman Baths and Pump Room complex per annum since 2009 (ALVA, 2012).

Although a resort for much of its 2,000-year history, Bath's treatment facilities fell into decline in the second half of the twentieth century. This was rectified by the opening in 2006 of the Thermae Bath Spa complex, using the city's unique thermal waters, which heralded a new era of spa culture in the city. This gave a major new impetus to the tourism economy; Bath, in common with other heritage cities in the UK, has however witnessed a decline in visitor numbers in the face of tough competition from low-cost flights to short breaks in European cities and from big-spending former industrial UK cities marketing themselves as exciting destinations.

The Roman Baths

The Roman Baths is one of the UK's foremost heritage attractions. The Roman Baths received circa 978,000 visitors in 2011/12 (Bath and North East Somerset Council Heritage Services, 2010), a figure which has risen from a previous ten-year constant of circa 840,000 following a major development programme of conservation, access and interpretation measures. Care of the hot springs of Bath is vested in Bath and North East Somerset Council, whose Heritage Services division manages the Roman Baths and Pump Room complex. In addition to the Roman Baths and Pump Room, Heritage Services manages the Fashion Museum and Assembly Rooms, the Victoria Art Gallery and Bath Record Office. Within these buildings, the division is responsible for all displays and exhibitions, collections care, study facilities, front-of-house services, museum shops, education programmes, community events, corporate hospitality and catering services. Because of the commercial nature of many of its activities, Heritage Services functions as an internal business unit and returned a surplus of circa £4.3 million in 2011/12 to the Council (Bath and North East Somerset Council Heritage Services, 2012a,b). The primary income stream, about 70 per cent of the total, comes from admission charges, supported by secondary income sources from museum shops, corporate hospitality and commission on the catering franchise.

The Roman Baths has always charged for admission, providing the authority with one of its three principal income streams, the others being rents from its commercial property portfolio and charges from public car parks. All three sources of income reflect the city's long-standing role as a destination for visitors, a tradition stretching back as far as the first century AD and the construction by the Romans of a huge religious spa complex of baths and temple around the natural phenomenon of the hot springs. The historic city, much of which takes the form of a planned eighteenth century urban landscape, contains over 6,000 listed buildings and, in December 1987, the 'City of Bath' in its entirety was inscribed on the UNESCO World Heritage List as 'a place of outstanding universal value whose protection must be the concern of all' (HBMCE 1987). 'Roman Archaeology' was identified as one of its outstanding universal values (OUVs).

The ancient monument takes the form of the almost complete footprint of the Roman bath house with remains standing up to three metres high in places, (Cunliffe, 1969) as well as substantial *in situ* elements of the Temple of Sulis Minerva beneath the eighteenth-century Pump Room excavated between 1981 and 1983 (Cunliffe and Davenport, 1985; Cunliffe, 1988; Bird and Cunliffe, 2006; Erfurt-Cooper and Cooper, 2009: 72–73). The archaeological collections in the Roman Baths Museum have been 'Designated' by the UK government as collections of national importance in a non-national museum.

The Heritage Services business plan: investing in sustainability

The concept of sustainable tourism is well documented in the academic literature (Benson, 2012). Further, Benson (2012) outlines that the Centre International de Recherches et d'Etudes Touristiques (CIRET) in 2012 showed that there were 5,712 published documents on the theme of sustainable tourism; Bramwell and Lane (2012: 1) examined approximately 500 papers from the *Journal of Sustainable Tourism*; Buckley (2012) examined 250 papers using five themes: population, peace, prosperity, pollution and protection. These themes overlap with the UNWTO (2005) challenges (managing dynamic growth, climate change, poverty alleviation, support for conservation, and health, safety and security) associated with sustainable tourism.

This chapter, therefore, adds to the literature on 'sustainable management' by offering an in-depth examination of the commercial environment within which Heritage Services operates. Unusually for a local authority service, the division has political endorsement for a business plan to reinvest a proportion of earned income in measures that will protect or extend existing income streams and develop new ones. The rolling five-year business plan, underpinned by detailed financial models and informed by market research and visitor feedback, is revised and updated annually and sets out strategies on pricing policy, marketing, investment and future development.

The Heritage Services business plan is sub-titled 'A Plan for Sustainability and Continuity' and herein lies its fundamental rationale. The business plan does not seek to maximise income to the exclusion of all other considerations; rather, it seeks to ensure the ongoing and long-term sustainability of three key areas of activity – conservation, customer care and commercial activity ('the three Cs'). This is represented as the 'tripod of sustainability' (see Figure 18.1).

This business philosophy argues that, in order to ensure the long-term sustainability of the Roman Baths, the three key areas of activity need to be kept in

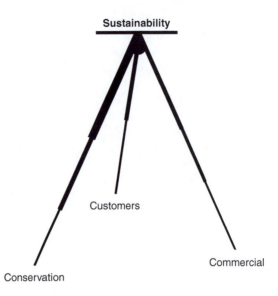

Figure 18.1 The 'tripod of sustainability' – the business philosophy behind the Heritage Services business plan.

balance and afforded equal consideration in forward planning. The model suggests that, the more one disturbs this balance by unduly extending or contracting any one of the tripod legs, the less sustainable the service becomes. For example, if investment were directed solely to commercial activities leaving conservation and customer care neglected, the monument would deteriorate at an unacceptable rate, jeopardising its long-term sustainability and visitor expectations would not be met. A crumbling monument and dissatisfied visitors would quickly lead to a downturn in reputation and income and, consequently, a lower proportion of earned income available to re-invest.

Furthermore, the 'tripod of sustainability' indicates that the three legs of the tripod are inter-dependent. Investment in conservation gives a better quality of experience and creates higher customer satisfaction ratings; this generates more visitors, which in turn creates more commercial activity; and more commercial activity leads to a greater sum available for re-investment in all three areas – conservation of the historic fabric, customer services such as interpretation, public toilets and visitor seating, and commercial imperatives such as marketing, retail product development and shop refurbishment. When arguing for political endorsement of the division's investment strategy, this rationale was summed up as:

- investment in conservation – preserving our heritage for future generations;
- investment in customer services – meeting the needs of all our audiences;
- investment in commercial activities – sustaining and developing our business.

Working within the framework of a local authority, investment takes a variety of forms. Revenue expenditure is used to invest in routine cleaning, interpretation, replacement of equipment, marketing, branding, websites, market research and staff development. Property maintenance budgets are invested in planned and responsive building maintenance and monument conservation; and capital funds are sourced for major investment projects and new developments.

Staff structure: walking the talk

The 'tripod of sustainability' business model was devised during the early 2000s during the early years of business planning activities by Heritage Services. As it was developed and its principles applied to the management of and investment in Heritage Services' activities, it became clear that the staff structure inherited from earlier years did not reflect the principles underpinning the new way of working as a business unit. Traditionally, most senior museum managers are curators; marketing people are viewed with deep suspicion and customer care staff are thought to lack the gravitas essential for an academically credible institution. However in Bath, with the introduction of the new Heritage Services business model represented by the 'tripod of sustainability', it became clear that if equal status were to be afforded to conservation, customers and commercial activity, this should be reflected in the staff structure. A restructuring of Heritage Services was therefore undertaken in 2004/05, creating three core teams of equal status. These are the:

- **Public Services Team** (conservation): Staff caring for collections and monuments and delivering services based upon them; i.e. curators, archivists and education staff.
- **Visitor Services Team** (customers): Front-of-house staff, including reception, guides, interpretation and retail sales staff.
- **Commercial Team** (commercial): Marketing, sales, room hire, PR and media management, catering and retail trading and merchandising strategy.

In addition to the existing Finance support team, a new Facilities support team was created under a new senior post of Facilities Manager sitting alongside the managers of the three core teams in the structure. The purpose of this new post was twofold:

- to relieve curators of the premises-related tasks they had hitherto undertaken and free them up to devote their time to Public Services Team duties; and
- to provide the project management skills that would be needed for the Roman Baths Development Plan investment projects which started in 2006/07.

The new basic arrangement of teams in Heritage Services is shown in Figure 18.2 below.

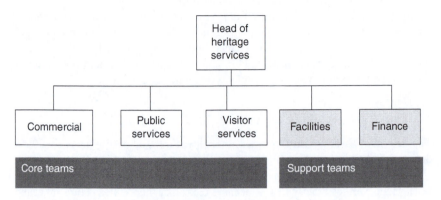

Figure 18.2 The basic staff structure of Heritage Services showing the equal status afforded to the three core areas of activity.

Market research: informing the decision-making

To inform the business planning process, Heritage Services undertakes extensive data-gathering exercises to discern:

a) how visitors to the Roman Baths and Pump Room respond;
b) how the site performs in relation to other leading visitor attractions; and
c) the ongoing trends and market forces that influence visitors in their preferences.

In addition to the usual vehicles of visitor feedback forms and comments books, Heritage Services participates in reciprocal mystery visit schemes with other ALVA members, buys into industry market research and undertakes detailed peer group benchmarking through ALVA. Valuable information about visitor behaviour on site is also derived from data downloaded from the audio guides, which, being included in the admission charge, have a very high take-up rate that makes the information gathered statistically very reliable.

Benchmarking with ALVA takes place in two areas: financial performance and quality of visit. Detailed 'quality of visit' exit surveys are conducted three times a year using a professional market research company, which analyses and presents the data in a way that each participating attraction can see how it performs in relation to the others but can only identify itself and no other attraction. Comparison of these results over a period of time reveals whether investment made at the Roman Baths to address a weakness has had an effect.

A particular indicator, the 'enjoyment/value for money' graph, had started to cause particular concern at the Roman Baths. A series of results in the years following 2000 indicated a worsening trend in the enjoyment/value for money perceptions of visitors to the Roman Baths. When the full sequence of graphs from 2001 to 2006 was examined, it became evident that over the previous few years there had been a marked decline in visitors' 'enjoyment' and 'value' ratings of the Roman Baths, when compared with the scores achieved by its ALVA peer group. The Roman Baths' performance can be summarised separately to demonstrate this downward trend, as shown in Figure 18.3.

This decline in the enjoyment and value of the Roman Baths in comparison with the ALVA mean illustrates the need for investment. The reversal of the downward trend in 2006/07 may reflect only modest price increases and early improvements made in the visitor experience.

It was this evidence, more than any other, which helped Heritage Services to persuade the council to give it additional financial freedom to borrow funds on the open market to invest in a major capital development of the Roman Baths aimed at reversing this trend. Using the UK government's recently introduced 'Prudential Code of Borrowing' for local authorities (CIPFA, 2003, 2011), borrowed funds would have to be funded through the business plan and amortised over twenty-five years. An advisory board of external experts was established to challenge the investment assumptions and give the council comfort that its officers were committing it to long-term investment on grounds that were sound.

The Roman Baths Development Plan

The council approved the 'freedom to borrow' in 2004/05 after which detailed plans were drawn up for a major development at the Roman Baths to take place in a series of manageable 'mini-projects' implemented between 2007 and 2011. After careful consideration, it was decided that it would not be commercially viable to close for a few months and implement the Development Plan as one major project and so the Plan was implemented through a series of 'mini-projects', which saw only small areas of the visit closed off at any one time.

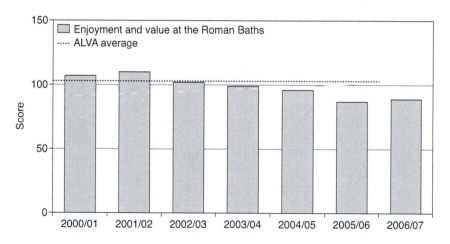

Figure 18.3 Roman Baths enjoyment and value against ALVA average.

The Development Plan had two principal aims:

- to maintain the Roman Baths' position as a leading UK visitor attraction;
- to transform the accessibility of the Roman Baths.

It followed the business philosophy established by the 'tripod of sustainability' in that the investment planned aims to sustain the 'product' (conservation), sustain the audiences that visit it (customers) and sustain the income streams they bring (commercial). The work undertaken between 2007 and 2012 fell into all three categories and, while there were many facets to it, the main elements may be summarised as follows.

Conservation

- The installation of environmental monitoring and control in the Temple Precinct area of the site to minimise damage caused to Roman remains by rising salts; it was also to improve visitor comfort following feedback that many found it hot in that area during summer months. The new system is powered using energy derived from the hot spring water rising immediately adjacent to this area.
- Cleaning of all Roman stonework and consolidation of Roman plasterwork and *opus signinum* surfaces around the Great Bath.
- Cleaning of all nineteenth-century stonework around and overlooking the Great Bath, including columns, balustrades and statues.

The conservation programme in the Great Bath had the added benefits of giving visitors a cleaner monument to enjoy and, in commercial terms, allowing better quality marketing and holiday photographs to be taken. With sustainability in mind, laser cleaning techniques were used in places to minimise intervention in the fabric of the monument.

Customers

- Two lifts were installed to enable visitors with mobility impairments to gain access first to the museum and then to the Baths at the ancient ground level, six metres below present street level.
- A British Sign Language tour using the existing audio guide equipment (in large screen format) was introduced for visitors with little or no hearing.
- Tactile interpretation in the form of models and relief plans was introduced for visually impaired visitors, and a straight 'audio description' option was added to the audio guides.
- Innovative new interpretation was installed using high-tech and low-tech interactives throughout the museum and Baths; interpretation became more people-led, reflecting visitors' current preference for human stories that can bring a monument to life; as part of this new approach the following have already been introduced:

- costumed interpretation beside the Great Bath every day, delivered by actors in the roles of people known from inscriptions to have been present at the Baths in Roman times;
- film of life-sized male bathers projected onto the walls of the Roman Circular Bath with speech and sound effects.

In terms of sustainability, the two new measures immediately above are an alternative to conventional interpretation in the form of graphic panels and labels attached to the fabric of the building. They complement the existing non-intrusive interpretative medium, which is the portable audio guide carried around by visitors; being a digital self-contained device, no wiring is required in the building.

Commercial

- Both shops on site were refurbished; the main Roman Baths shop was extended into a back-of-house area to create more front-of-house retailing space.
- Investment was made in the existing Roman Baths website to enable the electronic pre-purchasing of tickets and the electronic purchase of retail merchandise.
- A new till system was installed in the Roman Baths reception hall.
- Investment was made in researching and developing new site-related retail merchandise.

In addition and in response to visitor feedback requesting an accessible family-friendly café at the Roman Baths, Heritage Services took possession of a council-owned commercial property opposite the Roman Baths main entrance to complement the period splendour of the Pump Room restaurant with a contemporary, good-quality cafeteria strongly themed to the Baths. The 'Roman Baths Kitchen' was opened in May 2012.

The transformation of the Roman Baths visitor experience undertaken between 2007 and 2011 resulted in a string of awards regionally, nationally and internationally, the most influential being short-listed in the last four of The Art Fund Museum Prize 2011 (it was pipped as winner by the British Museum). The national publicity this generated, supported by additional investment in marketing, and consequent word-of-mouth recommendations, saw visitor numbers rise in 2011 to a twenty-five-year high of 980,000.

Challenges

Bath and North East Somerset Council has robust risk management arrangements in place and these, along with market intelligence-gathering activities, are used by Heritage Services to anticipate and plan strategies for dealing with local, national and international issues likely to affect the financial performance of the

Roman Baths and Pump Room. The year 2000 is still taken as the baseline for current forecasting, being the last year untroubled by events likely to influence people's decisions as to where – and whether – to travel.

The Roman Baths has traditionally strong markets in North America and Western Europe, with new emerging markets in Eastern Europe and China, which are growing significantly. For many years, its visitor profile was split roughly down the middle, with 50 per cent being UK residents and 50 per cent coming from overseas. This split varied at the margins according to the relative strengths of the pound, euro and dollar, but fluctuated by only a few per cent over many years. However, in today's competitive visitor attractions sector, the Roman Baths faces a number of challenges. From 2009 onwards, the 'stay-cation' phenomenon of UK residents taking holidays at home rather than over-seas was reflected in a shift of balance which, at the time of writing, stands at 55 per cent UK residents and 45 per cent overseas visitors. To test the perceived affordability of the Roman Baths to visitors and gauge likely customer resistance to prices, Heritage Services benchmarks its headline (i.e. adult single) admission charge against the euro, the dollar and the yen.

Around 33 per cent of all visitors come in groups, some on pre-paid package holidays that take in the most popular 'must-see' destinations, others on day excursions from London. Although these are markets that attract group discounts and therefore bring a lower spend-per-head per visitor, their volume makes them an important source of income and, for some visitors, they are the inspiration for longer-stay holidays in future years. Consequently, the Roman Baths is com-peting against the big London attractions on unequal terms; London-based tour-ists must decide whether to pay to travel 100 miles for a day visit to Bath and then pay to enter the Roman Baths, or to succumb to the lure of several world-class national museums which offer free admission and are on their doorstep.

The turn of the millennium saw new investment in many attractions through Millennium and National Lottery funding, while government-sponsored free admission to national museums was introduced in 2001. Recent figures indicate that 73 per cent of inbound tourists are very likely to visit castles/stately homes and sightsee famous monuments/buildings while in Britain, with 65 per cent claiming it was very likely they would go to museums, 63 per cent to churches/cathedrals and 60 per cent to locations associated with the monarchy and Royal Family.[2] During the 2000s, security threats, environmental scares and economic fluctuations all affected numbers visiting the nation's attractions. The terrorist attacks of September 2001 in America (9/11) were the biggest factor, causing a lasting change to the worldwide tourism industry. In 2001, UK visitor attractions were also affected by foot-and-mouth disease (FMD), which, as it occurred in the spring of that year, had a greater influence on people's decision-making than did 9/11, which occurred after the high season was over. Unlike 9/11, however, the effect of the FMD outbreak was confined to one year only.

The most serious incident to occur in the UK was the London bombings in July 2005, which caused a short-term drop of 30 per cent in the number of people visiting London. Despite this, the early years of the twenty-first century in the UK were a period of relative stability in which visitor attractions jostled for attention in a cluttered leisure-time market place. Cinema, shopping, eating out, home entertainment and cheap flights to European cities or short breaks in Britain's rejuvenated industrial city and port destinations were just some of the activities competing with visitor attractions for the disposable income and spare time of the nation. Perhaps the most influential factor was the health of the UK economy and the level of public confidence engendered by it. There can be no doubt that the weak pound and concerns over disposable income were significant contributors to the 'stay-cation' phenomenon. Market research conducted for Visit Britain late in 2008 revealed widespread pessimism, with 90 per cent of the population claiming to be cutting back on spending as a result of the economic downturn, with 45 per cent cutting back on holidays and breaks.[3] However, for many, holidays and short breaks were still considered essential rather than a luxury, with the 'quality of experience' being as important as ever. The research indicated that, while short breaks abroad and to London were likely to be sacrificed, there remained the potential for holidays to be taken in the rest of the UK. At the Roman Baths, the result was a 6 per cent increase in visitors to around 880,000, the highest annual total for ten years. Many other major visitor attractions experienced results that were similar or better, particularly those offering free admission.

These uncertainties reflected what managers at many attractions were thinking – that forward planning and forecasting were difficult at the best of times but, against the backdrop of a world recession, would be even harder. Nevertheless it is worth noting that experience of adversity caused by factors beyond their control has taught visitor attractions many lessons in coping with the unexpected. Economic downturn is but one factor capable of influencing performance; other general trends over the past ten years are shown in Table 18.1.

Every year of the twenty-first century to date has seen one or more dramas take place which have affected the holiday plans and travel decisions our

Table 18.1 General trends affecting site performance

Factors	Specific events
Geo-political/'world events'	Wars, terrorist attacks and the consequent fear of flying.
Health scares	Bovine spongiform encephalitis/Creutzfeldt-Jakob disease (BSE/CJD), foot-and-mouth disease (FMD), severe acute respiratory syndrome (SARS), 'flu pandemics.
Environmental events	Climate change, extremes of weather, volcanic eruptions, etc.
Competition	Shopping, leisure, home entertainment, cinema, major sporting events, national museums going free, cheap flights overseas.
Economic	Relative strength or weakness of the pound, concerns over pensions and job security, visa costs in emerging markets.

potential customers have made. The sequence has been unrelenting, as shown in Table 18.2.

It was not just national and international events that influenced visitor performance. The delayed opening of the new spa in Bath from 2003 to 2006 led to widespread confusion that the Roman Baths were closed and, even after the spa eventually opened, the residual confusion was deeply embedded in the UK psyche and is still encountered today. Dramatic events, such as widespread flooding in the West Country in the summer of 2007, had a severe impact on a limited geographical area.

Other pressures are more predictable and can be factored into our business planning, as the sequence in Table 18.3 demonstrates. Global sporting events during the peak tourist season affect the behaviour of significant numbers of people, while every four years significant numbers of well-to-do politically active Americans stay at home to campaign in advance of the autumn presidential election. Analysis of exit surveys has even revealed a slight 'bulge' in American visitor numbers in the weeks after presidential elections as those same visitors sought a post-election vacation.

Table 18.2 Specific events or influencing factors which have affected site performance between 2000 and 2012

Year	Event or influencing factor
2000	Bovine spongiform encephalitis (BSE)/Creutzfeldt-Jakob disease (CJD)
2001	Foot-and-mouth disease (FMD); terrorist outrages in America (9/11)
2002	War in Afghanistan; Bali bomb
2003	Wars in Afghanistan and Iraq; SARS scare
2004	Wars in Afghanistan and Iraq; Madrid bombs
2005	Wars in Afghanistan and Iraq; London bombs
2006	Wars in Afghanistan and Iraq
2007	Wars in Afghanistan and Iraq; FMD; Glasgow Airport attack
2008	Wars in Afghanistan and Iraq; credit crunch
2009	Wars in Afghanistan and Iraq; recession; swine 'flu
2010	War in Afghanistan; recession; volcanic ash cloud
2011	War in Afghanistan; recession
2012	War in Afghanistan; recession; London Olympics and Paralympics; record rainfall

Table 18.3 Recurring events which affect site performance

Event	Time of year	Year
Olympic Games	Summer	2000, 2004, 2008, 2012
Football World Cup	Summer	2002, 2006, 2010
USA Presidential Election	November	2000, 2004, 2008, 2012

The effect of the 2012 London Olympic Games

The announcement in July 2005 that London would be the host city for the 2012 Olympic and Paralympic Games was overshadowed by the London bombings the very next day. Following the 2008 Beijing Games, attention turned to the effect that the 2012 Games would have on tourism in general and on visitor attractions in particular. Many were sceptical that the Games would be unremittingly good for tourism, as the government confidently expected them to be. Research undertaken by the European Tour Operators Association (ETOA) and published in a series of reports between 2006 and 2010 (ETOA, 2006, 2008, 2009, 2010) analysed the detrimental short-term effect on tourism of the Olympic Games in Sydney (2000), Athens (2004) and Beijing (2010) and cautioned against over-optimism for London 2012. Many leading visitor attractions that receive large numbers of groups brought by tour operators allowed for a downturn in their visitor numbers in 2012 and, in the case of the Roman Baths, where circa 33 per cent of visitors each year come in groups, a downturn of 8 per cent in overall visitor numbers in July and August 2012 was factored into the Heritage Services business plan.

Under normal circumstances, 66 per cent of overseas visitors to Britain cite 'heritage' as the main purpose of their visit, but it was recognised that many of these visitors would be displaced out of London in the summer of 2012 by Olympic-related visitors, who would be there purely for the sport and who would not visit attractions. This forecast was based on ETOA's research into visitor behaviour at Sydney, Athens and Beijing. At the Roman Baths, there was some evidence of in-year displacement in 2012, with some visitors, child groups being the most noticeable, coming between January and March rather than between April and July. This had the effect of taking visitors out of financial year 2012/13 into financial year 2011/12.

When comparing performance in 2012 with that in 2011, it was recognised that 2011 saw a twenty-five-year high in visitor numbers which would not be repeated in 2012 and this was recognised in the annual update of the Heritage Services business plan for 2012–17. This planned for a downturn of 5 per cent in Roman Baths' visitors in the financial year 2012/13, with a greater shortfall of visitors, including a reduction of circa 25 per cent in group sales business, during the months of July and August. Actual sales in July and August did indeed reduce significantly; during the seventeen days of the Olympics themselves, total sales were 27 per cent lower than in the same period in 2011. Fortunately, the Roman Baths escaped the worst effects which were felt by many London attractions, which during the first week of the Games were between 48 per cent and 61 per cent down on the previous year's visitor numbers.

Long-term trends

Figure 18.4 shows the pattern of visitation at the Roman Baths over the last forty years. The steep rise in visitor numbers during the early 1980s was due in part at

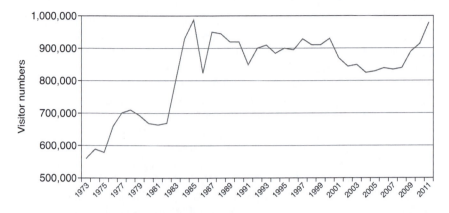

Figure 18.4 The fluctuations in visitor numbers at the Roman Baths between 1973 and 2011 (note that the scale begins at 500,000).

least to national media coverage of the Temple Precinct excavations beneath the Pump Room. The big discernible dips in performance were in 1986, when the USA bombed Tripoli from bases in southern England, and the nuclear explosion and subsequent fall-out at Chernobyl, and in 1991 and 2001 when Britain and the USA intervened in the Middle East.

The other lesson from this graph is that, despite expectations of governing bodies for a smooth and constant incremental performance in financial return, no two consecutive years have been the same. This not only reflects the influence that the significant drivers described above can have, it suggests that other more local and/or less obvious determinants can affect performance from year to year.

While the Roman Baths benefited from the 'stay-cation' effect, it also had new stories to tell. Access was improved to enable visitors with mobility difficulties to descend the six metres to Roman level, and new 'people-led' interpretation was introduced to tell the story of the Baths and Temple through the lives of people who were known to have visited or worked at the site in the Roman period – priests, pilgrims, soldiers and local stonemasons, for example. This new approach to interpretation included the introduction of first-person costumed interpreters using a local theatre company, which now gives the site a very human dimension and enables visitors to meet a 'real Roman'. These family-friendly improvements broadened the target audience and presented marketing opportunities to exploit. Existing marketing activities in the form of leaflet distribution, website development, on-street signage and media coverage were augmented by local and sub-regional out-of-home promotions and, for the first time, TV advertising in regions with greatest potential for new visitors.

While some of these measures were born of necessity – conservation of the ancient monument is not only a legal duty of the landowner but is now increasingly expected and appreciated by visitors – others were driven by visitor feedback. At the Roman Baths, the utmost importance is given to understanding what visitors expect of the attraction when they arrive and how the experience lives up to that expectation. The results of 'quality of visit' exit surveys and feedback from mystery visits, comments forms and visitors' books are analysed monthly and action plans drawn up to tackle issues that arise from them. Information about visitor preferences and patterns of behaviour can be downloaded from the audio guide system and is also analysed (Bird, 2007). Since the audio guide is available at no extra charge in eight languages and has a take-up rate of well over 90 per cent, these data are particularly comprehensive. The result is that over many years managers have built up an understanding of visitors and how their needs and expectations change over time, and this has been a significant factor in helping to survive the recession.

Every visitor attraction will have evolved strategies for dealing with the recession, many of them learned from the experience of responding to successive crises over the years, such as those listed above. Numerous lessons have been learned and applied at the Roman Baths and these strategies include the following.

Know your audiences

The Roman Baths joined the Association of Leading Visitor Attractions (ALVA) in 1998. The market intelligence gained through the detailed 'quality of visit' benchmarking and mystery visits undertaken with other attractions has proved invaluable and, without it, the management team would have been flying blind when unforeseen crises required quick decisions to be made.

Benchmark your performance

The Roman Baths has also benchmarked its financial performance against other ALVA attractions for many years, which, as the only local authority-run attraction in ALVA, has been an interesting experience. The encouraging news is that the private sector does not necessarily do things better or perform more commercially successfully than the public sector.

Discount where necessary, but add value where possible

Managers resisted cutting prices to attract new visitors and looked instead to add value to the visit – for example, by introducing new family-friendly activities. Discussion with other ALVA attractions revealed that many had taken a similar approach. However, it is still important to be flexible: the price of the three-year season ticket was reduced and this resulted in significantly increased take-up.

Forge partnerships to add value

Find partners to work with to share the marketing burden and add value to your shared customers. In 2008 and 2009, the Roman Baths fronted a major 2-for-1 off-season promotion with Great Western Trains. A popular 'Spas Ancient and Modern' package was developed with Thermae Bath Spa, which includes a visit to the Roman Baths, two hours in the spa and lunch in the Pump Room.

Do not compromise on quality – visitor expectations have not dropped

Do not assume that in a recession visitors will be pathetically grateful that they can afford to visit you at all. Visitors value their holidays and excursions as much as ever and, if anything, their expectations of both value-for-money and value-for-time have risen.

Do not cut the marketing budget

At times of financial restraint, it is natural to look down your budget list for the meatier figures to slice. Do not! If anything, increase the marketing budget so that you can raise your profile, contribute to partnership campaigns and try new things.

Do things you have not done before

As a matter of principle, managers should be prepared to try new things, whether in the 'visitor offer', pricing policy or marketing initiatives. The mantra that 'if you always do what you always did, you'll always get what you always got'[4] is pertinent here. But perhaps now more than ever, as attractions find themselves in new territory and the deepest recession for many decades, it is time to find new ways of working. For some, these might include benchmarking with a peer group, a partnership with a neighbouring attraction or new added-value measures for their visitors. For the Roman Baths, it was TV advertising in the Meridian region and a 'romantic couples' summer evening campaign to build on the Roman Baths' status of 'Britain's Most Romantic Building'[5] and promote its late night opening to 22.00 in July and August.

Keep investing – the competition will be

Do not stop moving your attraction forward. As mentioned above, visitor expectations have not dropped. Refresh your offer, find new stories to tell and keep your visitor facilities fresh and user-friendly. To stand still while other attractions continue to invest – and some are, even in the current financial climate – is actually to regress.

Longer term strategic planning

Heritage Services is also turning its attention to the longer term future, in two particular respects.

The long-term sustainability of affordable long-haul flights

Currently around 28 per cent of visitors to the Roman Baths are from non-European countries of origin, the vast majority of them from the United States of America. While Visit Britain advises that the Japanese market is in long-term decline, it also reports growing markets arriving from the Indian sub-continent and from China. So what is the problem? All those concerned with the airline industry in the UK remain bullish about the long-term prospects of affordable international flights; airport expansion programmes show no sign of faltering and the fear of flying appears to have receded as a deterrent to international travel.

The problem is that, when the issue is assessed in terms of risk, there remain two great uncertainties. One is whether airlines can be sure of access to affordable and reliable fuel supplies in the long term. Might we now be living in the golden age of cheap flight? Could it end more quickly than we might imagine?

The second uncertainty is to do with climate change. At present, there seems to be little sign that significant numbers of people refrain from flying because of their concerns about the damage it causes to the ozone layer and other potential climatic implications, although many of us must know at least one individual that does. Yet as the consequences of climate change become ever more apparent, the proportion of the world's population unwilling or unable to fly is likely to increase. Again, could this happen more quickly than we anticipate, and might it be accelerated by belated inter-governmental action to curb those activities known to be fuelling climate change?

The easy course of action is to do nothing. After all, time and energy are already sapped just keeping on top of our current business planning activities. Nevertheless Heritage Services is already turning its thoughts to the question of how to replace those long-haul markets, should they start to contract for any of the reasons mentioned above. The answer must lie in developing new markets much closer to home and as a strategic planning objective relevant to the financial sustainability of the Roman Baths, it is now very much on the agenda. Significant work has already been undertaken to better understand the full spectrum of audiences (Clews, 2001), and this has led to the preparation of a detailed audience development plan and, most recently, proposals for a new Learning Centre adjacent to the Roman Baths, which will serve not only existing formal education markets but also a wide range of community and lifelong learning audiences. Looking at the bigger picture, the plans also include a World Heritage Interpretation Centre for the city that will benefit local people and overseas visitors alike (Bath and North East Somerset Council Heritage Services, 2011).

Conservation of the Roman Baths

After spending many centuries buried beneath the city of Bath, the Great Bath, the centrepiece of the bathing establishment, was discovered in 1880 and stripped of its overburden of collapsed building material and layers of mud.

Since that time, although the bath itself has been kept full of spa water to protect its *in situ* sheets of Roman lead lining, the surrounding pavements, walls and column bases have been exposed to the seasonal extremes of the weather. Periodic programmes of conservation have removed the detritus of industrial pollution and the corrosive excrement of pigeons and seagulls, although nothing can be done to prevent the ongoing erosion of nineteenth-century stonework in the form of architectural ornamentation and the features of the statues overlooking the Great Bath. A conservation statement (Clews, 2000) has been a key document in identifying areas under greatest threat and planning programmes of interventive and preventative conservation accordingly.

In the years after the discovery of the Great Bath, schemes were prepared for building a vaulted roof over the bath to replicate the Roman brick and tile roof whose fallen fragments were found when the bath was cleared. In the end, the favoured scheme left the Great Bath open to the sky, allowing the splendid view up out of the bath to Bath Abbey enjoyed by so many today. But with the weather taking its inexorable toll on both the Roman and the nineteenth-century monument, is it now time to consider action more radical than simply repeating the once-in-a-generation conservation programme? One answer might be to find a twenty-first century engineering solution to placing a lightweight glass roof over the bath that would allow the environment around the monument to be controlled while still permitting the view from the side of the bath to the tower of the Abbey.

Such a project would be fraught with difficulties. An appropriate design acceptable to the planning and regulatory authorities would be needed; structural surveys would need to ensure that the additional load could be borne by the Roman foundations; and capital funds running into many millions of pounds would need to be found. But the benefits could be many. Not only could it solve the long-term problem of erosion, it could improve interpretation by demonstrating where the high Roman vault once stood. It could also provide Bath with its own iconic glass structure, assuming that this medium is still in favour by the time the project is realised.

Conclusions

It would be easy to dismiss these notions as too fanciful to consider. Nevertheless it is incumbent on the present generation to consider the long-term sustainability of one of the UK's most important ancient monuments, even if the solutions identified are only realised by a future generation. Today's five-year business planning, although very important, is doing little more than keeping the show on the road. It is necessary to think much further into the future to ensure that there is a road there at all.

Notes

1   In addition to the exit surveys on quality of visit conducted each year, we participated in an independent economic impact survey organised by Dr Peter Dawson
of the University of Bath. His estimate of the economic value of the Roman Baths
to the Bath area in 2009 was £92 million. It was already known that the Roman
Baths is the biggest driver for the tourism industry in Bath, but the impact is even
greater than realised.

(Bath and North East Somerset Council Heritage Services, 2010)

2 Culture and Heritage Profile, Visit Britain, February 2010.
3 Sharon Orrell of Visit Britain, Visit London/Visit Britain seminar presentation, January
2009.
4 Attributed to Henry Ford (1863–1947).
5 RIBA Poll, 2009.

References

ALVA (2012) *Visitor statistics. Visits made to visitor attractions in membership with
ALVA*, London: Association of Leading Visitor Attractions. Online at www.alva.org.
uk/details.cfm?p=423 (accessed April 2013).

Atkinson, T. C. and Davison R. M. (2002) 'Is the water still hot? Sustainability and the
thermal springs at Bath, England', *Geological Society, London, Special Publications*,
193: 15–40.

Bath and North East Somerset Council Heritage Services (2010) *Heritage Services
annual review 2009/10*, accessed online (April 2013) at www.victoriagal.org.uk/pdf/
HerSer%20AnnRev%2009-10%20FINAL.pdf.

Bath and North East Somerset Council Heritage Services (2011) *The Archway Project: A
learning centre for the Roman Baths*, Bath: Bath and North East Somerset Council.

Bath and North East Somerset Council Heritage Services (2012a) *Financial and business
review 2012/13*, Bath: Bath and North East Somerset Council.

Bath and North East Somerset Council Heritage Services, (2012b) *Heritage Services
annual review 2011/12*, accessed online (April 2013) at www.romanbaths.co.uk/pdf/
HerSer%20AnnRev%2011-12%20FINAL.pdf.

Benson, A. M. (2012) 'Editorial: Special issue: Sustainable tourism management and
marketing', *Journal of Hospitality Marketing and Management*, 21(7–8): 703–709.

Bird, S. E. (2007) 'Deploying and assessing the impact of audio guides at the
Roman Baths, Bath, UK', in McLoughin, J., Kaminski, J. and Sodagar, B. (eds.) *Technology strategy, management and socio-economic impact*, Budapest: Archaeolingua,
65–82.

Bird, S. E. and Cunliffe, B. W. (2006) *The essential Roman Baths*, London: Scala Publications.

Bramwell, B. and Lane, B. (2012) 'Editorial: Towards innovation in sustainable tourism
research?', *Journal of Sustainable Tourism*, 20(1): 1–7.

Buckley, R. (2012) 'Sustainable tourism: Research and reality', *Annals of Tourism
Research*, 39(2): 528–546.

CIPFA (2003; 2nd edn 2011) *The prudential code for capital finance in local authorities*,
London: Chartered Institute of Public Finance and Accountancy.

Clews, S. (ed.) (2000) *Roman Baths and Pump Room conservation statement*, Bath: Bath
and North East Somerset Council.

Clews, S. (2001) 'Engaging with the individual – A strategy for development and survival at the Roman Baths Museum, Bath', in *Archäologische Museen und Stätten der Römischen Antike*, Cologne: In Kommission bei Habelt, 114–117.

Cunliffe, B. W. (1969) *Roman Bath*, Oxford: Society of Antiquaries Research Report No 24.

Cunliffe, B. W. (1988) *The Temple of Sulis Minerva at Bath, volume II: The finds from the sacred spring*, Oxford: Oxford University Committee for Archaeology Monograph No 16.

Cunliffe, B. W. and Davenport, P. A. (1985) *The Temple of Sulis Minerva at Bath, volume I: The site*, Oxford: Oxford University Committee for Archaeology Monograph No 7.

Dawson, P. (n.d.) 'Economic impact of cultural activities in Bath and North East Somerset', unpublished Report for Bath Cultural Forum and Bath Festivals, University of Bath. Accessed online at https://wikis.bris.ac.uk/download/attachments/55972470/Economic+Impact+Report+-+Bath.pdf?version=1&modificationDate=1363248296458.

Erfurt-Cooper, P. and Cooper, M. (2009) *Health and wellness tourism: Spas and hot springs*, Bristol: Channel View Publications.

ETOA (2006) *Olympic report*, London: European Tour Operators Association.

ETOA (2008) *Olympics and tourism: Update on Olympic report 2006*, London: European Tour Operators Association.

ETOA (2009) *Beijing Olympic update*, London: European Tour Operators Association.

ETOA (2010) *Olympic hotel demand*, London: European Tour Operators Association.

HBMCE (1987) *World Heritage convention cultural properties: UK nomination The City of Bath*, London: Historic Buildings and Monuments Commission for England.

South West Tourism Research (2008) *Value of tourism 2008*, accessed online (April 2013) at www.swtourismalliance.org.uk/files/download.php?m=documents&f=100419150927-5FormerAvonUAs08FINAL.pdf.

Stanton, W. I. (1991) 'Hydrogeology of the hot springs of Bath', in Kellaway, G. A. (ed.) *Hot springs of Bath: Investigations of the thermal waters of the Avon Valley*, Bath: Bath City Council, 127–142.

UNWTO (2005) *Tourism, microfinance and poverty alleviation*, Madrid: UNWTO.

19 Volunteering and cultural heritage tourism

Home and away

Angela M. Benson and Jaime Kaminski

Introduction

The concept of volunteering is influenced by economics, culture, religion, society and politics. Despite these influencing factors volunteering, in various forms (aiding others), is a phenomenon that is found across the globe and an integral part of the majority of societies. It is also evident that the discourses around volunteering are influenced by western concepts and perspectives. Events like the International Year of Volunteering 2001, the International Year of Volunteers + 10 (IYV+10), European Year of Volunteering (EYV, 2011) and International Volunteering Day (which is an annual event held on 5 December since 1985) are testament to this.

Despite this all-encompassing view of volunteering, there is no comprehensive, comparative study of worldwide volunteerism (UNV, 2011). Even at the European level, the EYV Alliance (EYV, 2011: 28) note that there are 'difficulties in providing accurate data on the size, scope, dynamics, and the impact of volunteering at national and European level'. This is also evident when examining volunteering and cultural heritage tourism. Whilst examples of volunteering from around the globe, both domestically and internationally, indicate significant contributions, there is little empirical evidence that gives a clear picture as to its magnitude. This is compounded by the lack of a consistent definition of what constitutes 'cultural heritage' (see chapter 1 in this volume) or 'cultural heritage volunteering' and the lack of a central authority to monitor such activities.

This is further exacerbated when examining the role of visas in this process as currently there is no systematic evidence to indicate which countries include volunteering as part of their visa procedures. In 2011, the EU Alliance suggested the development of a special visa category for volunteers that enables a fast-track procedure, allowing volunteers from developing countries easy access to operate within the EU. Another example of where volunteering is acknowledged is that, when applying as a UK citizen for a visa to enter Ghana, the application form includes a box for volunteers to tick. Further, Tanzania also introduced a system for volunteers and since 2009 a volunteer visa fee has been in existence. However, rather than acting as a systematic data collection and/or monitoring tool, the raising and lowering of the visa fee tends to suggest an attempt to capitalise on the volunteering market. The fee in 2012 stabilised at between $200 and $550, the exact fee being dependent on single or multiple entries and length of the volunteer programme. Anecdotal evidence suggests that volunteering in Tanzania has not attracted as many volunteers as in previous years, as volunteers seek value-for-money alternative projects. Another consideration here is that of diaspora volunteering (discussed later in the 'Away' section) in that many diaspora volunteers may hold two passports and, therefore, even if volunteering visa mechanisms were in place, they could 'fall through the net' and not be recorded as 'volunteering' since they had no requirement to apply for a visa.

This being said, there are some measurements that give an insight into the wider volunteering phenomenon. Terrazas (2010: 2) suggests that 'about 1 million Americans volunteer overseas each year'. In Australia, 38 per cent of the 6.4 million adult population volunteer; this has been estimated to have doubled in the period between 1995 and 2010 (Volunteering Australia, 2011). In a recent report by the European Commission (2007: 34), it was suggested that over 100 million people in Europe are volunteers, of which 8 per cent are involved in 'education, arts, music or cultural activities'. In the UK, it has been estimated that each year over 20 million people volunteer. In total, they donate over 100 million hours to their communities every week, which is estimated to have an economic value of over £40 billion (Davis Smith, 2012: n.p.).

In the decade between 2001and 2011, the level of UK formal and informal volunteering by the general public stayed fairly static at around 23–25 per cent (DCLG, 2010, 2011). Table 19.1 outlines detailed data available from 2005–2011 on areas related to volunteering and cultural heritage. As can be seen, these figures have also remained fairly static; the activity that shows the greatest change is arts volunteering in 2010/2011.

Table 19.1 UK volunteering in areas of cultural heritage, 2005–2011 (%)

	2005/2006	2006/2007	2008/2009	2009/2010	2010/2011
Volunteered in the last 12 months	23.8	24	25	N/A*	24.2
Connected to the following areas:					
Arts	6.3	7.0	6.4	N/A	8.1
Museums/galleries	1.4	1.2	1.1	N/A	1.4
Heritage	4.9	4.0	4.7	N/A	4.2
Libraries	0.8	0.5	0.7	N/A	0.8
Archives	0.7	0.5	0.6	N/A	0.6
Sport	19.2	19.6	21.3	N/A	20.7
Any other sector	75.0	74.9	74.4	N/A	74.2

Source: https://www.gov.uk/government/publications/taking-part-2011-12-quarter-1-statistical-release and https://www.gov.uk/government/uploads/system/uploads/attachment_data/file/78414/Y7Q1_Volunteering.xls.

Note
* Data unavailable for 2009–2010.

In a context of reduced funding caused by economic difficulties in some parts of the world, a rise in unemployment in many countries and increasing numbers of visitors at attractions, the need for volunteering in cultural heritage tourism has probably never been greater. Consequently, this chapter gives a broad overview by examining volunteers in the cultural heritage sector from the perspective of both volunteers who engage in volunteering at 'home' in the more traditional tourism settings (e.g. museums and heritage sites) and the volunteers that travel 'away' (i.e. internationally) in order to engage in volunteering activities associated with cultural heritage tourism.

After this introduction, section one, the chapter is divided into four key sections. The second section examines the concept of 'home', while the third section examines the concept of 'away'. The fourth section outlines the blurring of the boundaries between artificially constructed barriers of home and away. The fifth and final section draws some conclusions.

Home

Whilst volunteering at a national level takes place across many sectors (including, for example, social care, health, hospitals and libraries), this section examines volunteers who undertake volunteering activities within their own country (domestic/local/home volunteering) where the volunteering takes place in sites, venues or attractions where tourism, and more specifically cultural heritage tourism, takes place, but regardless of the activities undertaken. Much of the volunteering that takes place in this context enhances the visitation of other visitors, both domestic and international.

Research within the framework is often contextualised within the leisure-related literature. Stebbins (2004) suggests that, in respect of leisure, volunteering can be viewed in three forms: serious, casual and project-based. Volunteers engaging in cultural heritage can be found in all three categories. However, they are often framed within serious leisure (Stebbins, 1992, 1996, 2007; Stebbins and Graham, 2004; Orr, 2006). From both within and outside the framework of serious leisure, volunteering in museums has been examined by a number of authors.

The main themes of research are management, organisations and professionalisation of volunteers (McIvor and Goodland, 1998; Holmes, 1999; Graham, 2000; Edwards, 2004; Edwards and Graham, 2006) and motivations of volunteers (Henderson, 1981; Holmes, 2001; Graham, 2001; Edwards, 2005). Other perspectives include that of Holmes and Edwards (2008), who have examined the relationship between museum visiting and volunteering and suggest that volunteering is an extension of visiting.

Between 2005 and 2008, the Institute for Volunteering Research (IVR) evaluated the role and development of volunteers in the museums, libraries and archive sector in Britain (Howlett *et al.*, 2005). The research involved a survey to a random sample of 1,892 organisations (464 to museums, 952 to libraries and 476 to archives) across England. The response rate was 31 per cent (585 organisations). The results indicated that 95 per cent of museums, 79 per cent of archives and 67 per cent of libraries involved volunteers (Howlett *et al.*, 2005: 3). Recruiting volunteers allowed the organisations 'to do things they would not normally be able to do' (74 per cent). The majority of organisations had 1–20 volunteers (54 per cent), while only 6 per cent had over 100 volunteers. The profile of the volunteers was predominantly white, female and older. Interestingly, 63 per cent of organisations involved disabled volunteers and 54 per cent of organisations indicated they did not have sufficient volunteers and could easily absorb more. Of the organisations surveyed, only 16 per cent did not use volunteers.

Whilst it is clear that volunteering is extensively part of the literature associated with museums, they are also evident in the wider context of cultural heritage. For example, the raison d'être of the UK's Heritage Lottery Fund (HLF), which commenced operation in 1994, is to distribute money raised by the National Lottery to UK heritage projects. Between 1994 and 2012, over £5 billion was invested in: historic buildings and monuments (£1,883 million); museums, libraries, archives and collections (£1,432 million); land and biodiversity (£1,049 million); industrial, maritime and transport (£400 million) and cultures and memories (£248 million). What is pertinent here is the extent to which volunteering is an integral part of HLF funding mechanisms; over 90 per cent of HLF-funded projects engage volunteers – 'Volunteering is the cornerstone of HLF funding. Almost all projects work with volunteers in some capacity, and many have volunteers that play critical roles in the management, design and leadership of projects' (HLF, 2010: 2).

In 2008, HLF engaged a team of consultants to undertake a three-year investigation of the experience and impact of volunteers within HLF-funded projects. The profile of volunteers was similar to the findings by Howlett *et al.* (2005) in that they were predominantly older, white, well-educated with slightly more women than men, who lived in affluent areas. In respect of gender, some differences were evident in terms of the type of heritage for which men and women volunteered. For example, proportionally more male volunteers (62 per cent) were attracted to industrial and maritime heritage projects compared to female volunteers (HLF, 2011: 30). Across the three years of the study, 10 per cent of volunteers considered themselves as having a disability; however, the report suggests this is largely as a result of the older age profile. The main motivation for volunteering is 'having an existing interest and passion in the subject area of the projects' (HLF, 2011: 1). The level of volunteering has remained constant over the three years; however, in the third year of the project, greater numbers of unemployed volunteers were evident. They appeared to view volunteering in part as an opportunity to get back into the labour market. The report could not attribute positive social outcomes to a distinct HLF project or even a heritage-based experience and concluded that the positive outcomes and experiences of the HLF volunteers were a result of volunteering per se.

English Heritage (2012) also identifies volunteers as playing an increasingly important role in supporting the work they do. They, like many other organisations, realised they needed to gain greater understanding of their volunteers.

In 2012, they conducted their first national evaluation of volunteering. The results suggested that 'of the 830 registered volunteers, 98% said they were happy with their volunteering role and 97% said they would recommend volunteering with English Heritage in the future' (English Heritage, 2012). Whilst these results might suggest a 'self-fulfilling prophecy', what is important here is that English Heritage has engaged in a dialogue with volunteers.

In 2008–2009, the National Trust (NT) had engaged 55,000 volunteers; by 2011–2012, this had risen to 67,000, with volunteer donated time totalling four million hours (National Trust, 2012). The volunteers are considered to be the face of the Trust and as such welcomed 19 million visitors in 2011–2012 (National Trust, 2012: 29). The National Trust also surveys their volunteers annually. One of the key measurements is the extent to which volunteers would recommend the National Trust to others; the performance target is for 62 per cent of volunteers strongly recommending the Trust. In 2011–2012, the target was 3 per cent below this requirement. However, 92 per cent of the properties met the required level and best practice is now being shared. The Trust recognises the importance of volunteers in their organisation and has included them as a priority in the forthcoming years: 'We still have work to do to get the basics of volunteering right everywhere. We need to make sure we organize and manage our volunteers well, that we listen more and improve communications' (National Trust, 2012:13). One of the initiatives launched (2012) to assist in this endeavour was the MyVolunteering website for volunteers. Whilst the NT annual report (2012) does not distinguish between volunteer staff and other volunteers, there is evidence to suggest that volunteers are used in positions of leadership. Jackson (2011) outlines the case of volunteer leaders for the UK's National Trust's (NT) 'Working Holiday' programme, which has remit for the preservation and conservation of natural and built heritage.[1] Jackson (2011) purports that the volunteer leaders play a pivotal role between volunteer participants and the NT paid staff.

Both English Heritage and the National Trust are organisations that support large numbers of cultural heritage tourism venues. Without the support of volunteers, they would struggle to maintain a viable level of service. What is interesting here is the extent to which organisations are actively seeking a greater understanding of volunteer dynamics (through activities such as consultancy and internal surveys, and including them in annual conferences) and also the extent to which this understanding is changing operational, management and strategic practices.

The above examples highlight areas where domestic volunteers undertake heritage activities that may support cultural heritage tourism. However, volunteers can engage in domestic volunteer heritage tourism activities in their own right. For example, in the UK, the National Trust's Working Holidays programme utilises volunteers both to run the activities and to take part in the activities as volunteer tourists. In the USA, the Forest Service runs the 'Passport in Time' volunteer archaeology and historic preservation programme, where volunteers can work with professional archaeologists on projects that, in addition to archaeological excavation, include rock art restoration, survey, oral history

gathering and analysis, artefact curation, archival research and restoration of historic structures (Osborn and Peters, 1991; Osborn, 1994; Jameson, 2003: 156).
For example, the Gifford Pinchot National Forest is one of 137 National Forests
in the US that participates in the Passport in Time programme. Between 1992
and 2004, 339 volunteers at the National Forest contributed 15,389 hours of volunteer labour to heritage projects. Of these, 10,262 hours were for purely archaeological projects (Kaminski *et al.*, 2010). Although international volunteers do
participate in the programmes, they predominantly tend to be oriented towards
domestic volunteers; however, because of the size of the USA, this can involve
considerable mobility and domestic tourism.

The long-term, incremental impact of volunteers can be considerable. At
George Washington's Mount Vernon mansion near Alexandria, Virginia, USA,[2]
predominantly domestic volunteers and interns have helped the site's archaeologists since 1987. The Mount Vernon estate also provides a range of volunteer
opportunities in the museum, site administration, archives and elsewhere. By
2010, the volunteer programme had contributed more than 50,000 hours towards
researching and restoring the estate.

Away

The literature associated with volunteering in an 'away' context falls predominantly into two domains; one is associated with international tourism, the other
with international development. There are overlaps between these two discourses, particularly when considering the concept of volunteering. This section
will predominantly focus on cultural heritage tourism and international (volunteer) tourism; however, it would be remiss not to engage in a discussion of international development and diaspora volunteering because of its potential to have
a significant impact on both tangible and intangible cultural heritage tourism.

The concepts of volunteering and tourism both have long histories. However,
the combining of these phenomena into 'volunteer tourism' (also known as vol-
untourism) is more recent. Despite the growing popularity of volunteer tourism,
systematic academic research in this area is still in its infancy but growing
(Benson, 2011). Whilst there were a small number of papers on the subject prior
to 2000, the book by Wearing (2001) was the catalyst for the articles that have
followed. According to the Centre International de Recherches et d'Etudes Touristiques (CIRET), there are 444 documents on volunteerism (CIRET, 2012).
Within this literature, there is some recognition of the leisure and serious leisure
related contexts, particularly in terms of the 'project-based' form (Stebbins,
2004), although this is often marginalised in respect of a wider tourism framework. There are varying definitions of volunteer tourism (Wearing, 2001; Brown
and Lehto, 2005; McGehee and Santos, 2005), and in addition the passive
acceptance of volunteer tourism as a 'saving-the-world' (Benson, 2011: 2)
concept in the early part of the decade was substantially criticised in the latter
part. There are now a number of discussions around key issues, such as:
volunteer tourism and mass tourism; sustainability; commodification; the

altruistic–egoistic debate; host community benefits and engagement; neo-colonialism; the north–south flow and the quality of the projects (see Benson and Wearing, 2012). At present, there is minimal literature that discusses these critical debates on international volunteer tourism in the context of cultural heritage.

In 2008, Tourism Research and Marketing (TRAM) estimated that there were 1.6 million volunteer tourists each year (2008: 5) and suggested that volunteer tourism generated a total expenditure of between £832 million ($1.66 billion) and £1.3 billion ($2.6 billion) (2008: 42).Volunteer tourism and travel volunteering has become an international phenomenon with future market predictions indicating growth, both in size and in value (Mintel, 2008; TRAM, 2008). These figures, however, do not outline the extent to which volunteering impacts upon cultural heritage tourism in an overseas context, nor do they reflect the economic downturn after 2008.

The ever-growing number of organisations and the myriad of projects that make up the global volunteer tourism market make examining it holistically challenging. The most comprehensive study of the global market is the study by TRAM (2008); however, even this document does have its limitations. There have been several attempts at grouping activities, in an effort to better understand the volunteer 'offer' (TRAM, 2008; Callanan and Thomas, 2005). However, the grouping of culture and heritage are generally absent. This is also made more complex because the organisations themselves group their projects under different headings and this lack of consistency makes searching for cultural heritage projects specifically challenging. This said, cultural heritage tourism volunteering projects can be broadly grouped into two areas: archaeological tourism, and historic and heritage tourism opportunities.

Volunteering on archaeological sites abroad is one of the most visible manifestations of volunteer tourism in cultural heritage (Timothy, 2011). Archaeology has had a long association with (initially domestic) volunteers because it is such a labour-intensive process. One of the principal mechanisms for data acquisition in archaeology is excavation. Although scientific techniques such as geophysical survey can refine where and how much to excavate, mechanical means cannot replace human labour.[3] Despite the widespread use of volunteers at archaeological sites, it was only in the 1960s that volunteer archaeological tourism in the modern sense was instigated (Kaminski *et al.*, 2010). One of the earliest examples of volunteer tourism was the excavation at the fortress and palace at Masada in Israel's Southern District.[4] The excavation's director, Yigael Yadin (1917–1984), advertised for volunteers in the UK and Israel. Crucially, no background in archaeology was required from the volunteers. For the Masada excavation, the volunteers were required to pay their travel expenses to the site and to stay at the dig for a minimum of two weeks. The sheer number of volunteers who signed up for the expedition allowed Yadin to run 23 two-week shifts with an average of 300 participants each (Yadin, 1966: 13–14; Bacon, 1971: 181; Atkinson, 2006: 14). Yadin achieved far more than he ever could if he had been reliant on a purely professional excavation team. The Masada excavations would become the blueprint for future archaeological excavations wishing to make use of volunteers. Importantly, these developments came at a time when (air) travel was becoming a mass-market phenomenon.[5]

By the 1980s, the use of volunteers in archaeology was unmatched in any other field (Rosen, 2006: 20). Since then archaeology has been eclipsed numerically by many other forms of volunteer opportunity. This is principally because there is a limit to the number of archaeological excavations that take place each year, and of these not all can, or are willing to, accept volunteer placements. The limitation on the number of excavations accepting volunteers globally is determined by a number of factors (Kaminski *et al.*, 2010):

- *There has to be archaeology*: Archaeology is the evidence of past human activity. That evidence is not evenly distributed across the globe. Some societies, such as hunter gatherers, have left far less evidence of their passing, compared to more sedentary societies. Therefore, there is a disparity in the density of archaeological sites per unit area in different parts of the world.
- *Some countries are difficult to work in*: Some countries with interesting archaeology are plagued by political instability, unrest and other safety concerns. Others may have complex visa requirements for entry, reducing the potential of short-term volunteer-orientated visitors (cf. Kenoyer, 2008).
- *There has to be the capacity and resources to conduct excavation*: Archaeology is a specialist technique; there are only so many university departments and archaeological organisations that can run excavations. Some countries simply do not have a well-established archaeological infrastructure and so are reliant on outside organisations conducting the majority of excavations.
- *Willingness to accept volunteers*: Not all excavations have the ability or willingness to accept tourist placement volunteers. Such an undertaking may require marketing efforts in different channels. Tourist placements require administration and training, and they can carry a greater administrative overhead compared to local volunteers. For example, tourist volunteers may require higher standards of safety and hygiene than is normally available in some countries (McCloskey, 2003: 11).
- *Language support*: Currently most consumers of volunteer archaeological tourism experiences come from the developed world (especially the USA and UK) but seek experiences in both the developed and the developing world. These volunteers are more likely to have the disposable income and free time to take part in such activities. The majority of volunteer archaeological opportunities outside of the English-speaking world need to offer support for English language in order to attract these volunteers. This can act as a limiting factor for the number of excavations which can accept volunteers.

To many volunteers, 'archaeology' is synonymous with excavation. Naturally, excavation is a crucial part of archaeology because it is the means of acquiring data, and is the most publically visible component of archaeology. However, even on an archaeological dig, there is a greater range of activities than just excavation. These could include: recording (drawing plans and elevations), finds processing, photography, environmental sampling and surveying. Furthermore, archaeological work related to excavation carries on throughout the year. Organising the excavation, conducting post-excavation, analysing the results and publishing are activities that most volunteers are blissfully unaware of. Some volunteer archaeology programmes emphasise these alternative components of archaeology or have a wider historic or heritage component.

Of course, while archaeology is a highly visible element of volunteer cultural heritage tourism, there are many other opportunities in the historic and heritage arenas. For example, organisations such as 'Adventures in Preservation', 'Preservation Volunteers' and 'Restoration Works International' focus specifically on historic restoration projects. All provide services whereby volunteers can take part in the restoration of historic structures, ranging from a 1930s gas station in Virginia, USA to a Buddhist Temple, in Mongolia. These projects can include a mix of local volunteers and those from different countries.

Yaxunah, in the state of Yucatán, Mexico, is the location of a pre-Columbian site and has numerous ruins of colonial era haciendas. The Maya Research Program runs a programme whereby volunteers can live with the local community and work at the Cultural and Historical Interpretive Centre, which explains the history and culture of the Yaxunah community and local region.[6] These kinds of activities naturally feed into the narrative of international development.

Diaspora volunteering

Whilst the concept of diaspora tourism (Coles and Timothy, 2004; Basu, 2007; Kelner, 2010; Newland, 2011) is established as part of the discourse of tourism per se, some view diaspora tourism as a sub-category of domestic tourism rather than international tourism (Barkin, 2001; Erb, 2003; Scheyvens, 2007). Furthermore, the diaspora niche has been explored as a potential aid for development and, therefore, is often viewed within the context of the development landscape (Newland and Taylor, 2010; Scheyvens, 2007). The discussions around diasporas and volunteering are more recent; Terrazas (2010: 2) notes that often diaspora volunteers have sufficient contacts to work outside of formal programmes. He further suggests that, at both national and community levels, diaspora volunteers make value contributions but there is no systematic analysis at a country level of this phenomenon. Whilst the work of Terrazas is predominantly from an American standpoint, there are similar findings from the UK. The Diaspora Volunteer Alliance is a UK-based organisation that managed the Diaspora Volunteering Programme (DVP) on behalf of the Department of International Development (DFID). This was a £3 million, three-year project with: Diaspora Organisations; Voluntary Services Overseas (VSO); DFID; and the Big Lottery Fund. This project was in recognition of the many diaspora communities in the UK that offer financial and professional support to their countries 'back home' or 'continents of heritage' (Diaspora Volunteer Alliance, 2013: n.p.).

There are similar initiatives in the USA – for example, Volunteers for Economic Growth Alliance (VEGA) and International Diaspora Engagement Alliance (IdEA). It comes as no surprise that the majority of this work, under the banner of international development, is focused on transformation, capacity building and poverty alleviation and as such the majority of the projects are orientated towards areas like entrepreneurship and business; agriculture; public health; education, etc. However, there are also a small number of projects directly related to cultural heritage; for example, the project through VEGA on protection, preservation and conservation of the archaeological, natural and cultural heritage of Petra and the Petra region in Jordan. What perhaps is more interesting though is the extent to which diaspora volunteering has the potential to engage and influence, or be influenced by, the intangible aspects of cultural heritage in the country that volunteers are returning to.

Of course, diaspora can be an important driver for volunteering in cultural heritage tourism. In 1963, Yigael Yadin advertised for volunteers to take part in the excavations at Masada, Israel in both the *Observer* newspaper in the UK and Israeli newspapers. The advertisements were forthright about the potential conditions that volunteers could expect at the site but this did not deter thousands from signing up. The opportunity to excavate on such an iconic archaeological site, with deep meaning for Jewish national identity, brought (predominantly Jewish) volunteers from across the globe to Masada (Kaminski *et al.*, 2010).

Moreover, diaspora volunteering, regardless of the type of project, is being contextualised within the heritage of the country. For example, the Ethiopian Diaspora Volunteer Programme (EDVP) recruits volunteers in healthcare to help with the treatment of HIV/AIDS and other diseases. Between 2006 and 2010, the EDVP programme placed 45 volunteers in more than 30 sites. The volunteers' motivations were a desire to help to tackle HIV/AIDS in the country, a need to give something back to Ethiopia and 'pride in Ethiopian heritage' (United Nations Volunteers, 2011: 32).

Home and away: blurring boundaries

The complexities of volunteering make discussing it in terms of domestic and international increasingly difficult. As such, this section offers three cases in which volunteering does not neatly fit into to these categories – hence, blurring boundaries.

Online volunteering

Volunteering is often viewed as a face-to-face activity; however, technological advances now allow people at home to volunteer online in order to assist others. Online volunteering is also known as virtual volunteering, cyber volunteering, or cyber service. Online volunteering began in the 1990s when the internet began to gain critical mass and, as with other forms of volunteering, there is no real sense of the numbers involved; however, anecdotally it does appear to be growing. Online volunteering can be undertaken in a 'home' to 'home' context in that the online volunteering is within the boundaries of a country, or 'home' to 'away' where online volunteers do not travel but nevertheless help others in another country.

Numerous organisations have now set up virtual volunteering as part of their volunteering portfolio.[7] In the arena of cultural heritage, UNESCO has used online volunteering in order to support its World Heritage Forest programme, which works to strengthen the conservation of forests at World Heritage Sites. During the International Year of Forests in 2011, 22 online volunteers from 11 countries supported the programme. The volunteers contributed to the 'State of World Heritage Forests' report and contributed to databases related to World Heritage forests (United Nations Volunteers, 2011: 28).

It has gained prominence in the heritage arena from the middle of the first decade of the 2000s as a consequence of the crowdsourcing phenomenon. This is a mechanism that allows organisations that have a project that can be conducted online to call for volunteers to undertake elements of the work. This can range from correction and transcription, contextualisation, complementing collections, classification, co-curation and crowdfunding (Oomen and Aroyo, 2010).

The importance of crowdsourcing to heritage organisations is the access to a global pool of volunteers. For example, the 'Valley of the Khans' project allows volunteers to search satellite images of Mongolia in order to locate the tomb of Genghis Khan and other archaeological sites. Between January 2010 and March 2012, over 53,000 volunteers had processed over 917,000 images.

Of course, putting digital heritage-related materials online is not a neutral process. Computer literacy, access to hardware and internet connections limit the number of people who can engage with the internet in a meaningful way. Moreover, crowdsourcing creates self-selected groups, of people with specific interests and technological proficiency (Oomen and Aroyo, 2010).

Volunteering together – domestic and international

The Committee for International Voluntary Service (CIVS) and the UNESCO World Heritage Centre (WHC) initiated the World Heritage Volunteers concept in 2007, as a response to a growing interest by young people to get involved with the promotion and preservation of World Heritage. The programme aims to create and strengthen synergies between local and international volunteers that come together at project level and in essence work together beyond territories and boundaries. Table 19.2 outlines the programmes growth from 2007 to 2013. As evidenced, the 2012 programme of projects was almost double the size of the 2011 programme. Whilst overall volunteer figures are available, the number of local versus international volunteers is less clear. The information available is insufficiently detailed year on year and also lacks consistency.[8]

In the World Heritage Volunteer 2012 report, the breakdown of details regarding the programme offers further details, as shown in Table 19.3. As can be seen, the programme is fairly evenly distributed across the five regions.

Table 19.2 World Heritage Volunteer Programme, 2007–2013

Year	No. of projects	No. of countries	No. of volunteers	Phase of project
2007	0	0	0	Concept developed
2008	12	10	153	Pilot phase
2009	11	10	143	Pilot phase
2010	27		367	Flagship initiative
2011	28	17	400	Flagship initiative
2012	50	25	800	Established programme
2013				Call is open for involvement

Source: World Heritage Volunteer Website and Reports (2008, 2009, 2010, 2011, 2012). Available at: http://whc.unesco.org/en/activities/574/.

Table 19.3 World Heritage Volunteer Programme, 2012

Region	Countries	Youth organisations	Projects	Sites
Asia	5	9	11	10
Africa	6	7	9	8
Arab states	2	3	4	4
Latin America	4	6	14	8
Europe	8	10	12	10
Total	25	35	50	40

Source: World Heritage Volunteer Website and Report (2012). Available at: http://whc.unesco.org/en/activities/574/.

Volunteer good practice crossing borders

At a European level, Da Milano *et al.* (2009) edited the European handbook on volunteers in museums and cultural heritage, which was the result of a two-year project funded by the European Commission. The report offers case studies on volunteering from Austria, Italy, Slovenia and the United Kingdom. The handbook offers good practice advice on a number of topics: working with volunteers; volunteers as citizens; developing volunteer involvement; guidelines for coordinators of museums; the recruitment of volunteers; volunteering as a route to employment; and training volunteers. This list is not exhaustive but gives an insight into the nuances at country level. More importantly though, this handbook was written in order for best practice in individual countries to cross over country boundaries within the European Union in order to facilitate greater levels of understanding of volunteering in cultural heritage.

Conclusions

Volunteering in its various guises is a global phenomenon. However, there is no definitive definition and no systematic data set of worldwide volunteerism. The fragmented data sources suggest that the contribution of volunteers in cultural heritage tourism is significant, but despite this, the literature discussing volunteers in the context of cultural heritage tourism remains minimal. It is evident that the literature for volunteering in the domestic or 'home' context is more comprehensive than that of the 'away' context, but even this has a strong bias towards museums. Additionally, little is known about the extent to which volunteering in a domestic (local, regional and national) setting influences volunteering in an international context and *vice versa*, or the extent to which these boundaries are becoming blurred. What is interesting to consider is that, in the future, will the concepts of 'home' and 'away' volunteers be redundant and, therefore, will future discussions be about global volunteers? It is also evident that diaspora volunteering has the potential to be highly influential for a country's heritage and, whilst there is minimal research at present, the global impact could be substantial.

Volunteering and volunteer tourism are an increasingly important phenomenon in the cultural heritage arena. Volunteering can be an important mechanism for cultural heritage site sustainability. But while the monetary benefits of the donated labour of volunteers are often stressed, there are also other nonmonetary benefits which are equally important, including positive public relations, advocacy, education, community engagement and increased support from elected officials. Plus there is a plethora of benefits that the volunteers gain. The impact of volunteering in cultural heritage is considerably more diverse than simple labour cost savings.

Notes

1 The programme allows volunteers to combine a holiday with meaningful work experience. Volunteers can work at a National Trust property where they can learn to handle historic collections, work with archives or even help with the running of the properties. Archaeological options are also available. The working holidays can be both in the UK and abroad.
2 Mount Vernon was home to George Washington for more than 45 years from 1761, during which time he enlarged the residence and built up the property from 2,000 to nearly 8,000 acres. Today the mansion has been restored to its appearance in 1799, the last year of Washington's life. Since it first opened to the public as a visitor attraction in 1860, it is estimated that the estate has received over 80 million visitors.
3 Although machine excavators are used on archaeological sites, this is primarily to remove topsoil, in order to access the archaeological layers.
4 The Masada excavations were preceded by excavations at the Nahal Hever cave in Judea, which relied heavily on (predominantly local) volunteers (Kaminski *et al.*, 2010). These excavations provided the blueprint for the volunteer excavations at Masada.
5 Despite its relatively remote location, Masada is Israel's top paid tourist attraction.
6 www.mayaresearchprogram.org/web-content/aboutus_history.html.
7 Probably the best known outside the field of cultural heritage is the online volunteering service for the United Nations Volunteers (UNV).
8 At the time of writing, the details for the 2013 programme were unavailable; however, the call was open for interested organisations to apply.

References

Atkinson, K. (2006) 'Diggers – From paid peasants to eager volunteers', in Miller, K. E. (ed.) *I volunteered for this?! Life on an archaeological dig*, Washington: Biblical Archaeology Society, 10–17.

Bacon, E. (1971) *Archaeology: Discoveries in the 1960s*, New York: Praeger.

Barkin, D. (2001) 'Strengthening domestic tourism in Mexico: Challenges and opportunities', in Ghimire, K. (ed.) *The native tourist: Mass tourism within developing countries*, London: Earthscan, 30–54.

Basu, P. (2007) *Highland home comings: Genealogy and heritage tourism in the Scottish diaspora*, London: Routledge.

Benson, A. M. (2011) 'Volunteer tourism: Theory and practice', in Benson, A. M. (ed.) *Volunteer tourism: Theoretical frameworks and practical applications*, Abingdon: Routledge, 1–6.

Benson, A. M. and Wearing, S. (2012) 'Volunteer tourism: Commodified trend or new phenomenon?', in Moufakkir, O. and Burns, P. M. (eds.) *Controversies in tourism*, Wallingford: CABI, 242–254.

Brown, S. and Lehto, X. (2005) 'Travelling with a purpose: Understanding the motives and benefits of volunteer vacationers', *Current Issues in Tourism*, 8(6), 479–496.

Callanan, M. and Thomas, S. (2005) 'Volunteer tourism – deconstructing volunteer activities within a dynamic environment', in Novelli, M. (ed.) *Niche tourism: Contemporary issues, trends and cases*, Oxford: Elsevier Butterworth-Heinemann, 183–200.

CIRET (2012) Personal communication with Rene Baretje-Keller, President and Emeritus Member of the International Academy for the Study of Tourism. Aix En Provence: Centre International de Recherches et d'Etudes Touristiques, www.ciret-tourism.com.

Coles, T. and Timothy, D. J. (2004) *Tourism, diasporas and space*, London: Routledge.

Da Milano, C., Gibbs, K. and Sani, M. (2009) *Volunteers in museums and cultural heritage: A European handbook*, Ljubljana: Slovenian Museum Association.

Davis Smith, J. (2012) Chief Executive of Volunteering England. '2012 could be the year of the volunteer – but investment is key', *Volunteering England*, 20 April. Retrieved from www.volunteering.org.uk/aboutus/news-releases/2275-2012.

Department for Communities and Local Government (DCLG). (2010) *Citizenship survey, 2009–2010 England*, London: DCLG.

Department for Communities and Local Government (DCLG). (2011) *Citizenship Survey, 2010–2011 England*, London: DCLG.

Diaspora Volunteering Alliance (2013) 'What we do: Diaspora volunteering', *Diaspora Volunteering Alliance*. Available at www.diasporavolunteeringalliance.org/what-we-do.

Edwards, D. (2004) 'Defining field characteristics of museums and art museums: An Australian perspective', in Stebbins, R. A. and Graham, M. M. (eds.) *Volunteering as leisure/leisure as volunteering*, Wallingford: CABI, 137–150.

Edwards, D. C. (2005) 'It's mostly about me: Reasons why volunteers contribute their time to museums and art museums', *Tourism Review International*, 9: 1–11.

Edwards, D. and Graham, M. (2006) 'Museum volunteers: A discussion of challenges facing managers in the cultural and heritage sectors', *Australian Journal of Volunteering*, 11: 19–27.

English Heritage (2012) *Annual reports and accounts 2011–2012*, HC 266, London: The Stationery Office.

Erb, M. (2003) '"Uniting the bodies and cleansing the village": conflicts over local heritage in a globalizing world', *Indonesia and the Malay World*, 31: 129–139.

European Commission (2007) 'European social reality report', *Special Eurobarometer* 273.

European Year of Volunteering (EYV) 2011 Alliance (2011) *Policy agenda for volunteering in Europe, P.A.V.E.: Working towards a true legacy for EYV 2011*, Brussels: EYV 2011 Alliance.

Graham, M. (2000) 'The professionalisation of museum volunteers: An ethical dilemma', in McNamee, M., Jennings, C. and Reeves, M. (eds.) *Just leisure: Policy, ethics and professionalism*, Eastbourne: LSA, 185–210.

Graham, M. (2001) 'The role of museum volunteering in relieving social isolation', in Graham, M. and Foley, M. (eds.) *Leisure volunteering: Marginal or inclusive?*, Eastbourne: LSA Publication, 75: 57–75.

Henderson, K. A. (1981) 'Motivations and perceptions of volunteerism as a leisure activity', *Journal of Leisure Research*, 13: 208–218.

Heritage Lottery Fund (HLF). (2010) 'Assessment of the social impact of volunteering HLF-funded projects: Yr 2. Final Report: August 2010', London: HLF and BOP Consulting.

Heritage Lottery Fund (HLF). (2011) 'Assessment of the social impact of volunteering in HLF-funded projects: Yr 3. Final Report: September 2011', London: HLF and BOP Consulting.

Holmes, K. (1999) 'Changing times: Volunteering in the heritage sector 1984–1998', *Voluntary Action*, 1(2): 21–35.

Holmes, K. (2001) 'The motivation and retention of front-of-house volunteers at museums and heritage attractions', in Graham, M. and Foley, M. (eds.) *Leisure volunteering: Marginal or inclusive?*, Eastbourne: LSA Publication, 75: 95–109.

Holmes, K. and Edwards, D. (2008) 'Volunteers as hosts and guests in museums', in Lyons, K. D. and Wearing, S. (eds.) *Journeys of discovery in volunteer tourism*, Wallingford: CABI, 155–165.

Howlett, S. Machin, J. and Malmersjo, G. (2005) *Volunteering in museums, libraries and archives*, London: Institute for Volunteering Research.

Jackson, S. (2011) 'Profiling volunteer holiday leaders: A case study of National Trust working holiday leaders – socio-demographics, basic human values and functional volunteer motivations', in Benson, A. M. (ed.) *Volunteer tourism: Theory framework to practical applications*, Abingdon: Routledge, 135–156.

Jameson, J. H. (2003) 'Purveyors of the past: Education and outreach as ethical imperatives in archaeology', in Zimmerman, L. J., Vitelli, K. D. and Hollowell, J. (eds.) *Ethical issues in archaeology*, Walnut Creek: Altamira Press, 153–162.

Kaminski, J., Arnold, D. B. and Benson, A. M. (2010) 'Volunteer archaeological tourism', in Benson, A. M. (ed.) *Volunteer tourism: Theory framework to practical applications*, Abingdon: Routledge, 157–174.

Kelner, S. (2010) *Tours that bind: Diaspora, pilgrimage, and Israeli birthright tourism*, New York: New York University Press.

Kenoyer, J. M. (2008) 'Collaborative archaeological research in Pakistan and India: Patterns and processes', *The SAA Archaeological Record*, 8(3): 12–22.

McGehee, N. and Santos, C. (2005) 'Social change, discourse, and volunteer tourism', *Annals of Tourism Research*, 32(3): 760–779.

McCloskey, E. (2003) *Archaeo-volunteers: The world guide to archaeological and heritage volunteering*, Milan: Green Volunteers.

McIvor, S. and Goodlad, S. (1998) *Museum volunteers: Good practice in the management of volunteers*, London: Routledge.

Mintel (2008) *Volunteer tourism: International – September 2008*, London: Mintel.

National Trust (NT) (2012) *Going local: National Trust annual report 2011–2012*, Swindon: National Trust.

Newland, K. (2011) *Diaspora tourism*, Migration Policy Institute, Washington DC, for Diaspora Matters, Dublin, Ireland: Impress Printing Works.

Newland, K. and Taylor, C. (2010) *Heritage tourism and nostalgia trade: A diaspora niche in the development landscape*, Washington DC: Migration Policy Institute.

Oomen, J. and Aroyo, L. (2010) 'Crowdsourcing in the cultural heritage domain: Opportunities and challenges', *C&T'11: Proceedings of the 5th International Conference on Communities and Technologies*, 138–149.

Orr, N. (2006) 'Museum volunteering: Heritage as "serious leisure"', *International Journal of Heritage Studies*, 12(2): 194–210.

Osborn, J. A. (1994) 'Engaging the public', *CRM*, 17(6): 15.

Osborn, J. A. and Peters, G. (1991) 'Passport in time', *Federal Archaeology Report*, 4: 1–6.

Rosen, E. E. (2006) 'The volunteer's contribution to archaeology and vice versa', in Miller, K. E. (ed.) *I volunteered for this?! Life on an archaeological dig*, Washington: Biblical Archaeology Society, 18–20.

Scheyvens, R. (2007) 'Poor cousins no more: Valuing the development potential of domestic and diaspora tourism', *Progress in Development Studies*, 7(4): 307–325.

Stebbins, R. A. (1992) *Amateurs, professionals and serious leisure*, Montreal and Kingston: McGill-Queen's University Press.

Stebbins, R. A. (1996) 'Volunteering: A serious leisure perspective', *Nonprofit and Voluntary Sector Quarterly*, 25: 211–224.

Stebbins, R. A. (2004) 'Introduction', in Stebbins, R. A. and Graham, M. M. (eds.) *Volunteering as leisure/leisure as volunteering*, Wallingford: CABI, 1–12.

Stebbins, R. A. (2007) *Serious leisure: A perspective for our time*, New Brunswick: Transaction Publishers.

Stebbins, R. A. and Graham, M. M. (2004) *Volunteering as leisure/leisure as volunteering*, Wallingford: CABI.

Terrazas, A. (2010) *Connected through service: Diaspora volunteers and global development*, Washington, DC: Migration Policy Institute.

Timothy, D. J. (2011) *Cultural heritage and tourism: An introduction*, Bristol: Channel View Publications.

Tourism Research and Marketing (TRAM) (2008) *Volunteer tourism: A global analysis*, Arnhem: ATLAS Publications.

United Nations Volunteers (UNV). (2011) *State of the world's volunteerism report: Universal values for global well-being*, Bonn: UNV Publication.

Volunteering Australia (2011) *The latest picture of volunteering in Australia*. Available at www.volunteeringaustralia.org/Volunteering-Facts/-Statistics/-The-latest-picture-of-volunteering-in-Australia-2011.asp.

Wearing, S. L. (2001) *Volunteer tourism: Experiences that make a difference*, New York: CABI.

World Heritage Volunteer Website and Reports (2008, 2009, 2010, 2011, 2012) Available at http://whc.unesco.org/en/activities/574/.

Yadin, Y. (1966) *Masada: Herod's fortress and the Zealot's last stand*, New York: Random House.

20 Cultural heritage tourism

Future drivers and their influence

Jaime Kaminski, David Arnold and
Angela M. Benson

Introduction

This chapter will consider how external global geopolitical and socio-cultural trends may influence cultural heritage tourism over the next four decades. The late twentieth and early twenty-first centuries have been a time of rapid global change. Numerous countries, states and organizations are attempting to make sense of how the world will develop over the coming decades. These perspectives include security (MOD, 2010; NIC, 2012), economy (Ward, 2011, 2012), energy provision (IEA, 2012) and climate change (NRC, 2011) to name but a few. With such a diversity of perspectives, these different organizations have elucidated different key megatrends for the future. For example, the National Intelligence Council in the US sees the four global megatrends as individual empowerment; the diffusion of power; demographic patterns; and the growing nexus among food, water and energy in combination with climate change (NIC, 2012). In contrast, the UK's Ministry of Defence see the key global drivers of change (what they term as the 'Ring Road' issues) as being globalization, climate change, global inequality and innovation (MOD, 2010).

What is certain is that in the coming decades the world is likely to experience a number of global megatrends that will influence cultural heritage tourism and tourism more generally. In the mid- to long-term future,[1] issues such as population growth and other demographic change, climate change and other environmental impacts, economic changes, societal changes such as the growth of the middle class and technological innovation are all likely to become more prominent. This chapter will consider how cultural heritage tourism is likely to be influenced by these external megatrends from two perspectives: how principally tangible heritage assets are likely to be affected (supply) and how travel and tourism will be affected (demand). It also highlights how on a global stage cultural heritage tourism is interconnected with many different apparently unrelated systems. Some of these trends will affect tourism more generally, and influence cultural heritage tourism as a subsidiary of tourism, while others will have a direct impact on cultural heritage tourism.

Population and demographics

According to estimates by UNESCO, the world population reached seven billion in October, 2011. At the time of writing, the population is already 7.1 billion and is pushing inexorably upwards. Currently growing at a rate of around 1.15 per cent per annum, world population is projected to reach eight billion by 2025 and stabilize at just above ten billion after 2200 (UNFPA, 2011). Population growth is probably the key megatrend because it underlies so many other systems. Increases in human population will influence the economy, environment and society. This in turn will have numerous direct and indirect implications for cultural heritage and cultural heritage tourism.

Despite numerous advances in global poverty reduction, many of today's seven billion people will be destined to live lives of poverty and hardship, but increasing numbers will have the capacity and desire to travel (see 'The economy' below). All things being equal, increased population will lead to more tourist activity and, with that, cultural heritage tourism. However, simply extrapolating current demand for heritage tourism onto future population growth is problematic. As described in chapter 1, cultural heritage tourists share characteristics of disposable income and a generally higher level of education. Numerous variables ranging from economic growth to energy price fluctuations and the provision of education in growing populations will therefore influence cultural heritage tourism demand. These factors remain far more fluid and difficult to predict. Moreover, where these new tourists originate from, and wish to travel to, will also be of significance. The growth of tourism demand is likely to be driven by the growth of the middle class in the emerging economies. How these new consumers will view cultural heritage remains to be seen.

Naturally, more cultural heritage tourists will create both opportunities and challenges. Opportunities include the potential for increased economic sustainability of heritage sites and the knock-on effect for the wider economy. However, more heritage tourists may bring new challenges as the top heritage visitor attractions struggle to cope with the volume of tourists, while wear-and-tear on sites increases.

Aside from increasing the potential number of cultural heritage tourists, population influences many other systems, such as the environment (climate change and pollution) and society (urbanization, migration and conflict). All of these can have an effect on heritage tourism through the cultural heritage assets or the tourist demand. Under the umbrella of population growth, there are a number of demographic trends which will influence (heritage) tourism. The most significant of these are population aging, migration and increasing urbanization.

Population aging

Population aging is a phenomenon caused by a rise in the median age of a country's population. Fuelled by a combination of decreasing fertility and increasing life expectancy, numerous countries are moving towards a future where a higher percentage of the population than ever before is over 65 years old (UNDP, 2005: Table 5, 232–235).[2] In Europe, predictions suggest that 29.5 per cent of the European Union's population will be aged 65 years or over by 2060, compared to only 17.4 per cent in 2010 (Eurostat, 2013).[3] Overall according to the United Nations, there were 810 million people aged 60 years or over in the world in 2012 compared to 178 million in 2002 (United Nations, 2012). It is expected that an approximate demographic balance will return by the middle of the twenty-first century.

As a socio-economic phenomenon, population aging leads to a decrease in the size of the workforce and a corresponding growth of senior citizens, which can then cause an increased financial burden on those who are working. Economic growth is likely to decline in countries with an 'aging' population. However, the socio-economic outcomes of demographic change are entirely dependent on the policy environment (Libicki *et al.*, 2011).

An aging population also has implications for cultural heritage tourism. In the west there is empirical evidence that older people have a greater interest in history and culture (Nederlands Bureau voor Toerisme, 1988). The post-retirement period is often divided into two components. The 'third age' is used to describe the period between retirement and the time when an individual's physical and mental health starts to degrade. The 'fourth age' is the period when physical and mental health start to degrade and the individual requires special care and support. These have differing supply and demand implications for cultural heritage tourism.

Those in their third age can and do engage with heritage sites as tourists. For many the period of early retirement is one where travel is a component (Moscardo, 2006). The potential for a combination of good health, a body of savings to draw on, increasing interest in life-long learning and what for many are unfulfilled travel ambitions can be important drivers for tourism and engagement with cultural heritage. Older individuals are more likely to engage in cultural and heritage tourism than younger individuals. In the fourth age, physical travel may be less likely because of infirmity or the drawing down of finances. In future decades, this could reduce the cultural heritage tourism experience for some to virtual visits. ICT may be a mechanism for those in the fourth age to experience cultural heritage without travel (see chapter 17 in this volume).

Clearly the increasing aging population is a market opportunity for the heritage tourism sector (Koers *et al.*, 2012). However, there are also challenges associated with engaging the elderly as consumers of the past and heritage. The needs of the elderly are different compared to the needs of other groups. Those who do travel will have additional requirements for accessibility to sites and museums (this can include physical, sensory and interpretive requirements). These challenges will need to be met by the heritage tourism sector. Of course, many heritage tourism sites based on ancient monuments can be difficult to retrofit with accessibility devices compared to more recently constructed structures. Castles or decorated caves were never designed to be easily accessible.

On the supply side, those in their third age can contribute to the economic sustainability of cultural heritage sites. In the more developed countries where cultural heritage volunteering is more common, those in their third age may volunteer at heritage sites, thereby increasing economic sustainability (see chapter 19 in this volume). Many retirees undertake volunteering at heritage sites both to fill spare time and to provide companionship (Graham, 2001). Research by Edwards (2005) revealed that approximately 61 per cent of museum and art museum volunteers were retired. This can translate to significant numbers of third age volunteers in heritage – for example, the UK's National Trust has 6,000 staff and over 67,000 volunteers, many of whom are retired (National Trust, 2012: 2). However, as a global phenomenon, post-retirement volunteering is less well established.

Cultural heritage can contribute to a high quality of life for an aging population and the same population can help sustain cultural heritage attractions through both tourism and volunteering. Moreover, with the aging population becoming an increasingly powerful market segment, it may be that particular forms of culture (e.g. classical music in the West) are preferentially preserved (Koers *et al.*, 2012).[4]

Migration

Another demographic trend that has the potential to influence cultural heritage tourism is migration. The Industrial Revolution witnessed a huge movement of people from the countryside to towns across Europe. This was complemented by movements of people between countries and subsequently between the Old World and the New World. Migration is still a hugely important phenomenon. Globally it was estimated that there were 214 million international, and 740 million internal, migrants in 2010.[5] In total, around one in seven of the world's population are migrants (IOM, 2011). In the coming decades, migration is predicted to increase markedly driven by globalization, income differentials between countries, contrasting age profiles between richer and poorer countries and the presence of pre-established migrant networks (NIC, 2012: 23). It is estimated that international migrants could potentially reach 405 million by 2050 (IOM, 2011: 49).

Migration is a complex phenomenon that paradoxically both homogenizes cultures and simultaneously increases their diversity. Clearly this will have an effect on heritage tourism. Migration can lead to the creation of future cultural heritage assets. Without migration there would be no Amish in North America or Chinatowns in Western cities. Migration can influence the demographic composition of a country, which over the longer term can influence what is considered to be cultural heritage. The definition of cultural heritage is not static. What contemporary society considers to be culturally significant is determined by social, political and economic filters. Those filters can be influenced by demographic changes. Clearly, migration can increase the diversity of both consumers and culture providers; these in turn can stimulate local cultural heritage. Migration also creates cultural diasporas and increases the potential for diaspora volunteering and tourism, where individuals travel in order to (re)engage with their cultural heritage (see chapter 19 in this volume).

Urbanization

Despite the early origins of cities and urban life in the Near East, it was not until the late twentieth century that the balance of population has tipped in favour of urban rather than rural living. Today around half of the world's population lives in urban areas; a figure which is expected to rise to 60 per cent in the next two decades. It has been estimated that over the next 40 years the volume of urban construction needed for housing, work space and transport infrastructure could equal the entire volume of such construction to date in world history. This inconceivably huge burst of activity will be driven by rapid urbanization in Asia and Africa (NIC, 2012: 24).

Urbanization can be a threat to cultural heritage assets because of urban sprawl, pollution, infrastructure congestion and gentrification. Increasing land values in growing urban centres puts pressure on heritage sites. For example, in Singapore, pressure on space led the government to demolish many of the old areas of Chinatown. The loss of character had an influence on tourist numbers, which led the government to recreate some of the neighbourhoods (UNFPA, 2011: 83). Such losses can be compared to the demolition of much of Shanghai's unique Shikumen (stone gate) tenement housing (Zhao, 2004), the hutong lanes and siheyuan courtyard houses which once dominated Beijing's cityscape (du Cros *et al.*, 2005), or Russia's nineteenth century heritage in its leading cities (MAPS, 2007). Conversely, urbanization can generate new forms of urban architecture, art and urban culture that will become the heritage of the future. In essence one form of cultural heritage will be replaced by another, although it may not be appreciated as such at the time of construction.

The economy

In 2007, the collapse of the US sub-prime mortgage market cascaded into a global economic crisis. It did so because of the global nature of the economy. Similarly tourism and cultural heritage tourism are not isolated islands in the global economy; they are an integral (and considerable) part of it. Tourism is vulnerable to economic volatility because it relies on discretionary expenditure. Although there are many variables associated with tourism consumption, there is a tendency for a reduction in tourism expenditure in times of economic hardship. Hence, global tourism rapidly felt the impact of the financial crisis as it rippled across global economies in 2008. The result was an 8 per cent drop in international tourist arrivals in the first quarter of 2009 compared to the same period in the previous year and an overall contraction of 4.2 per cent across the year (Papatheodorou *et al.*, 2010, UNWTO, 2009). In total, international tourism arrivals saw 15 consecutive months of negative growth. However, only three years later tourist arrivals had climbed to record levels. For the first time in history, international tourist arrivals surpassed one billion (1.035 billion) in 2012, up from 996 million in 2011 (UNWTO, 2013: 1).

The short-term impact on tourism demand and its subsequent rebound was overshadowed by a more insidious longer term pressure on the cultural heritage assets in affected countries. Beginning in 2008, numerous countries in the developed world began to impose austerity measures in an attempt to reduce debt loads and stabilize faltering economies. This has had a huge impact on heritage sites. In Europe and North America, the economic downturn has featured heavily in cultural heritage politics. Cuts in funding (cf. Anon., 2013a) and subsequent job cuts were the most obvious manifestation (cf. Anon., 2013c). Culture has been a soft target for politicians looking for areas in which to make cuts. In Greece, state-funded museums have seen cuts of 20 per cent, and archaeological excavations 35 per cent. Across Europe and North America, sites have closed, reduced their opening hours or changed to trust status and are now run by volunteers, in order to compensate for the shortfall in government support. In rare instances, such as Spain's Prado museum, opening hours have been increased in order to bring in extra revenue (Kendall, 2012).

However, funding cuts and poor economic conditions do not immediately equate to diminishing visitor numbers. In the UK, 52 per cent of people questioned in the 2011–2012 'Taking Part' survey said that they had visited a museum or gallery in the last year, compared to 42 per cent when the survey began in 2005–2006. This was at a time when government funding of museums and heritage sites was reduced by 11 per cent (Anon., 2013b). Similarly during the same period, Britain's National Trust saw membership grow to more than 4 million, while visitor numbers at the Trust's pay-for-entry sites increased by 1.7 million to 19.4 million (National Trust, 2012: 4).[6] In these instances, economic uncertainties encouraged the 'staycation' effect thereby stimulating domestic mobility and cultural consumption (see chapter 18 in this volume).

Austerity measures could result in fewer heritage sites, which could mean less variety in the tourism offer; however, a restructuring of the tourist offer may not reduce visitation significantly. In many countries, a small number of heritage sites receive the majority of the visitors (a rule of thumb is that around 20 per cent of sites attract 90 per cent of the visitors). The sites which will have greater exposure to austerity measures are those with fewer visitors at the other end of the spectrum. In the long term, the reduction in choice and variety may influence cultural heritage tourism visitor patterns as visitors choose to visit countries with a broader heritage offer.

In countries where austerity measures are being enacted, the longer term implications of the loss of skilled conservators, curators and site managers will have complex and potentially negative implications for heritage tourism based around cultural heritage assets, such as museums, monuments and sites. But the exact mechanisms through which this will take place are unclear.

At the time of writing, this picture of economic uncertainty and austerity is one that permeates much of Western society. However, it is not representative of the global heritage sector or its potential for heritage tourism. While much of the West stagnates in an economic malaise, numerous economies are thriving, including the People's Republic of China, India and Brazil.[7] Here, and in many emerging economies, the potential for cultural heritage tourism is considerable.

The growth of the Chinese economy in conjunction with an increasing political interest in the country's past has seen the creation of over 1,200 museums in the last decade alone, at a rate of over 100 per year. Although China only opened its first museum in Nantong in 1905, and there were only ten museums in the country in 1928, this number had risen to 2,200 in 2001, and 3,589 at the close of 2011.[8] 2011 alone saw the opening of 349 new museums. China now has more museums than the UK (although fewer per head of population). The budget for culture has been growing year on year, while the equivalent of a billion euros has been invested in order to provide free entry to nearly 60 per cent of the country's museums (Xu and Le Guay, 2013). Moreover, China has a rich stock of heritage sites. In 2013, China had 45 sites inscribed on the World Heritage List (of which 10 are natural heritage and four are mixed), ranking third in the world after Italy and Spain (see Table 1.2 in chapter 1).[9]

These apparently positive developments have led to new issues. The enormous rush to build and capitalize on culture and heritage has led to a situation where there is a shortage of trained museologists to support the boom. Consequently, educational outreach, scholarship and overarching curatorial perspectives are absent from many institutions (Anon., 2013d). However, this is a short-term situation that will gradually redress itself as more universities supply qualified staff.

The growth in cultural heritage assets in Asia is complemented by a growth in tourist infrastructure, ranging from hotels to low-cost airlines. All of which will lay the foundation for considerable growth in cultural heritage tourism in the coming decades.

In economic terms, there is a new world order emerging. Countries which are currently labelled as 'emerging' will power global growth over the coming decades. It is predicted that, by 2050, the collective size of what are now seen as 'emerging' economies will have increased five-fold and will be larger than that of the current 'developed world'. In contrast, the aging economies of Europe will face structural and cyclical issues and so remain stable or decline. This is not to say that the West will get poorer; it is simply that most of the 'stable' economies are in the developed world where high levels of income per capita and weak demographics will act as a curb on growth (Ward, 2012).

The increasing economic power will also herald new political power. There is likely to be a gradual shift in influence away from the current developed world towards the emerging nations. This multi-polar distribution of power will ultimately have implications for the ability of the current developed economies to influence the global policy agenda (MOD, 2010: 10; Ward, 2011).[10] While such trends in global power politics may seem remote from cultural heritage and cultural heritage tourism, they are the vanguard of deeper cultural shifts. Currently, for example, much international heritage policy is heavily influenced by Western perspectives. The major global heritage organizations have their headquarters in Europe,[11] which naturally influences their outlook. For example, as of 2012, 48 per cent of World Heritage Sites were in Europe and North America (see chapter 1 in this volume). As the global power balance shifts eastwards in the coming decades, issues relating to non-Western cultural heritage will gain prominence.

Energy and the economy

Energy will be another area that will have a considerable influence on cultural heritage tourism (and tourism more generally) in the coming decades. Tourism is a significant component of global travel and is potentially vulnerable to changes in fuel price. Numerous analysts see the era of cheap and easily accessible oil supplies drawing to a close. However, the picture is complicated. It is not simply one of diminishing resources compounded by increasing demand. The last drop of oil is not going to drain from the oil well anytime soon. The predicted increase in the global economy, especially in the developing world, is estimated to lead to a 50 per cent increase in demand for fuel in the next 15–20 years. However, global fuel production is increasing, spurred on one hand by OPEC production increases and the use of horizontal drilling and hydraulic fracturing, to extract oil from shale source rock, on the other (NIC, 2012). Advances in this technology, and the huge global reserves of oil shale, are actually driving an emerging energy boom.

Fuel will undoubtedly increase in price, driven by demand, but increasing supply may moderate those rises. However, there is still a lag between shale oil reserves coming online in quantity. Hence some analysts are still predicting 'a global oil supply crunch and price spike' (Lloyds, 2012); some heritage tourism attractions are considering how potential fuel prices rises could affect their operations in scenario planning (see Chapter 18 in this volume). Fuel price increases clearly have the potential to influence travel; however, they also have more direct effects on heating and cooling costs for some cultural heritage attractions (which may not be able to benefit from effective insulation etc.).

Society

Societal changes are another area which will have a profound influence on heritage tourism. It is with individuals, communities and society more generally that cultural heritage is constructed.

The growth of the middle class

One of the most fundamental socio-economic trends in the next decades will be the growth of the middle class: 'for the first time, a majority of the world's population will not be impoverished, and the middle classes will be the most important social and economic sector in the vast majority of countries around the world' (NIC, 2012: 8). While being middle class does not immediately equate to a desire or the capacity to become tourists, it does represent a tectonic shift in global social structure. When viewed in conjunction with greater educational attainment[12] and individual empowerment, the middle classes become a huge potential reservoir of cultural heritage tourists. At the beginning of the twenty-first century, about one billion people have been responsible for three-quarters of global consumption; the expanded middle class in the developing world could add another two billion consumers. Even if a small fraction of these engage in cultural heritage tourism, this will lead to a considerable increase in visitor numbers.

However, socio-economic status needs to be matched by the availability of leisure time. As holiday entitlement increases then consumers will have the opportunity to engage in tourism. However, the relationship between leisure time and tourism is complex. Increased working hours in some parts of the world and growing unemployment is creating a dichotomy between the time poor but money rich employed, and the time rich but money poor unemployed.

Conflict

Armed conflict is a reality that will not change. The Heidelberg Institute for International Conflict Research recorded 18 wars and 25 limited wars in 2012. Another 165 conflicts were classified as violent crises. In total, 208 conflicts involved violence, giving 2012 the dubious distinction of being the year with the highest number of violent conflicts observed by the institute. The number of conflicts of all types has increased between 1945 and 2012 (HIIK, 2012). When assessing the period between 2010 and 2040, the UK's Ministry of Defence could find: 'few convincing reasons to suggest that the world will become more peaceful. Pressure on resources, climate change, population increases and the changing distribution of power are likely to result in increased instability and likelihood of armed conflict' (MOD, 2010: 14).

Armed conflict potentially has a dual impact for cultural heritage tourism. First, on the supply side it can damage or destroy the heritage tourism assets that make a region unique, including both tangible (monuments and sites) and intangible cultural heritage. The destruction of the tangible assets can be both direct and immediate, such as by shelling as in the case of the Stari Mosti Bridge, or more circuitously because of the breakdown of authority leading to abandonment, looting and other incremental damage. For example, Cambodia with its rich cultural heritage witnessed 30 years of conflict. The genocide during the Khmer Rouge regime (1975–1979) took the lives of many curators and site guardians and left numerous monuments unprotected, further compounding the depredations of military action. Similarly because of the importance of human transmission of culture, much intangible heritage was lost because so many people were consumed in the genocide. Second, conflict has a profound effect on demand as visitors naturally tend to shy away from areas of active conflict. A nascent tourism industry in Syria, with much heritage potential, has been virtually eliminated by the conflict which has blighted the country since 2011 (Anon., 2011; Cunliffe, 2012). Similarly in Egypt, a more established and robust tourism industry with a plethora of cultural heritage tourism sites saw a 37 per cent drop in arrivals between 2010 and 2011 because of the unrest of the Arab Spring. Conflict has an immediate impact on the demand for (heritage) tourism in all forms.

It is not only armed (military) conflict that has an influence on the visible evidence of the past. Breakdowns in civil order may be exploited by some to loot and vandalize cultural heritage, as seen in the Arab Spring uprisings in Egypt. Moreover, Ansar Dine, an al Qaeda-linked group, desecrated the mausolea of Sufi saints in Timbuktu, Mali, while in Djerba and northern Tunisia Salafists have vandalized Ibadite mausolea in local mosques (see chapter 6 in this volume). The lack of maintenance or abandonment of monuments and sites further exacerbates the situation.

A number of conventions explicitly consider the protection of cultural heritage in the event of war, such as the 1954 Hague Convention for the Protection of Cultural Property in the Event of Armed Conflict and its First Protocol (Clément, 1992) and the 1972 World Heritage Convention. Despite the good intentions of the signatories, the life and death reality of conflict on the battlefield and city streets makes such conventions difficult to enforce. The reality of war is that many combatants will use historic monuments and buildings, drawing them into the conflict, while other historic buildings will suffer collateral damage. In many instances, cultural heritage is deliberately targeted in armed conflict. In these cases, 'architectural annihilation' may be a mechanism for cultural eradication (Bailey, 2006; Bevan, 2006). Tactical targeting of cultural heritage sites occurs precisely because of the role of culture and heritage in identity. This is what Nemeth (2013) refers to as the 'strategic value of cultural heritage'.

Despite protestations of the 'universal value' of cultural heritage (Talley, 1995), recent conflicts in Bosnia, Afghanistan, Iraq and Syria have revealed just how vulnerable cultural heritage is during armed conflict. In the Bosnian conflict, the Sarajevo national library was burned, the Stari Most bridge in Mostar, Bosnia and Herzegovina was destroyed in 1993 (Armaly *et al.*, 2004) and the historic city of Dubrovnik in Croatia was heavily damaged in a seven-month siege (Rodwell, 2004). In Afghanistan, thousands of artefacts in the Kabul Museum were destroyed or looted (Grissmann, 2003) and the monumental Buddhas at Bamiyan were blown up by the Taliban (Manhart, 2001). In Iraq, the National Museum was looted in April 2003 (Bodganos, 2006; Breitkopf, 2007), while thousands of archaeological sites' monuments have been destroyed or looted in the absence of security across the country (Stone and Bajjaly, 2008; Wegener and Otter, 2008; Baker *et al.*, 2010). In Syria, the Crusader castle and World Heritage Site of Krak des Chevaliers was shelled and looted. In the coming decades, conflict will cast its shadow over cultural heritage tourism.

Six years after the destruction of the Bamiyan Buddhas, a similar Buddha was attacked in the Swat valley in Pakistan, twice. The first attack largely failed (Shahid Khan, reported by the BBC News Channel, 2007), but despite the early warning of intent, the authorities were unable to protect the Buddha from a second attack two months later (Musharbash, 2007). Interestingly, the destruction attracted only limited interest in the Western press, encouraging speculation of political motivation for this.

This destruction also poses some challenges within our definition of cultural heritage tourism. If 'cultural heritage tourism involves travelling to experience the current narrative of the tangible evidence of the past and its relevance today' (see chapter 1 in this volume), then the changes resulting from the wilful destruction also says something about the relevance of these monuments today. Some cultural professionals would argue that it is the destroyed state that represents the relevance today and hence that damaged monuments should not be restored, but rather stabilized in their damaged state. Others would argue that restored, the objects are more valuable in the cultural heritage tourism market. In the case of the Swat valley, some restoration has recently been undertaken, which probably implies a range of motivations, ranging from positive political and security messages to the population to cultural statements of identity.

The environment

With more people on the planet and predictions of a tripling of the global economy in the next four decades, it seems inevitable, based on current trends, that there will be an increase in the global carbon footprint. This has considerable implications for the planet and directly and indirectly for heritage and heritage tourism. According to some analysts, greenhouse gases output will need to be halved by 2050 in order to have a chance of containing long-term global warming to around two degrees Celsius. Although technically possible, this would require trillions of dollars of investment. Based on current evidence, this level of global investment in greenhouse gas mitigation seems a trifle Panglossian (Ward, 2011; IEA, 2012).

Climate change has a dual influence on heritage tourism. It can have an influence on demand. This can be because of price increases caused by climate change mitigation efforts in some countries (e.g. increased fuel taxes), or through consumers proactively reducing travel for environmental reasons (see chapter 18 in this volume).

Climate change can have both a direct and an indirect impact on the provision of cultural heritage tourism. For example, the diversion of funds to climate mitigation efforts may lead to an additional squeeze on funding for culture and heritage (cf. Rhisiart and While, 2008). More directly, climate change can impact the heritage assets themselves. Predictions in many climate models for warming temperatures, more seasonally variable precipitation and increased wind speeds could accelerate physical and chemical weathering, thereby accelerating deterioration of some cultural heritage sites and monuments (Giesen *et al.*, 2013).[13] The range of possible direct impacts caused by climate change is considerable, ranging from flooding at one extreme and desertification at the other.[14] Moreover, the physical effects on the cultural heritage may be compounded by impacts on the societies that sustain the heritage sites. In extreme cases, this could lead to the migration of such societies, reducing the protection for sites (UNESCO, 2006).

The most obvious and immediate example of the impact of climate change is in the Arctic and polar regions. If the warming trend seen in the Arctic regions continues, then it is increasingly probable that climate change will open up new territories in the Arctic, parts of Canada and Siberia. This may create new heritage tourism opportunities as heritage sites emerge from under ice, snow or permafrost, or known sites become more easily accessible. For example, the extent of summer sea-ice in Canadian arctic waters is predicted to decrease, which is likely to extend the shipping season (ACIA, 2005). This will allow cruise operations to ply their trade more easily in the fabled Northwest Passage.[15] Increased visitor numbers can put pressure on the fragile heritage sites in the region; moreover the increased accessibility to cultural tourists may have an as yet unknown effect on Inuit culture in the region.

Rising sea-level, the thawing of permafrost and storm surges have led to increased coastal erosion and threatened several Inuit villages along the Bering, Chukchi and Beaufort Sea coasts (ACIA, 2005: 1010; Eilperin, 2012). In such locations, the distinctive cultural heritage of some villages, which includes sod ancestral homes, ice cellars and cemeteries ringed with whalebones, is threatened. In Canada's Yukon Territory, the nineteenth century whalers' settlements of Ivvavik, Vuntut and Herschel on Herschel Island are deteriorating as the permafrost thaws. The historic grave markers and even coffins buried in graveyards around Pauline Cove are being destroyed in the freeze–thaw cycles. The sites have been on the World Heritage tentative list since 2004 (UNESCO, 2006).

In the relatively well-developed regions of the Arctic, such as parts of Northern Canada, Alaska and coastal Norway, tourism has a long history. Much of this is driven by nature and cruise tourism, but heritage is a growing subsidiary component. Improvements to accessibility have allowed tourism to develop in less populated and economically developed regions, creating a significant seasonal economy. For example, the number of nights spent at hotels in Greenland, whose cultural heritage tourism sector revolves around Norse history and Inuit culture, increased from 179,349 in 2002 to 236,913 in 2008, although not all of this is related to heritage tourism (Lloyds, 2012: 31). Arctic tourism has become more common, and more global.

In contrast, climate change will have different implications for the Antarctic. The climate of Antarctica is complex and, despite some slight warming in some areas, the region will remain the coldest on earth (Turner *et al.*, 2005; Bromwich *et al.*, 2012). Tourism is increasing in the Antarctic, but the continent is unusual in that there is no indigenous population to benefit (or suffer) from the natural and historic tourism in the region and there is no income derived from tourist visits, which would if available help contribute to site maintenance and management (Stonehouse and Synder, 2010: 139).

Currently, the most famous manifestations of Antarctic heritage are the preserved huts of the early twentieth century explorers (Stonehouse and Snyder 2010: 135). However, many other archaeological and historical sites exist on the Antarctic coast, including whaling and sealing camps (cf. Dibbern, 2009). These do not have the visibility or protection of the 'heroic age' explorers' camp sites (Senatore and Zarankin, 2012). Consequently, some of these sites now exhibit evidence of trampling, erosion, disturbance and damage to artefacts most probably caused by tourist visitation (Hughes, 1994: 196).

Polar tourism is certainly on the rise, and the trend looks to continue. Historical sites are a component of the tourist offer in the Antarctic, but without policy change, including responsibility for site management, effective management plans for the less well-known sites and monuments and recording of sites before visitation, the implications for the fragile cultural heritage in these regions are bleak (cf. Hughes and Davis, 1995: 250–253; Stonehouse and Snyder, 2010: 138). However, while the polar regions are the poster child for climate change, the effects can be felt globally.

Aside from climate change, the larger population will lead to increased exploitation of the environment for food production and other resources (energy sources, metals, building materials, etc.). This will lead to the discovery of new heritage sites, of which some may become tourist attractions. However, increased pressure on the environment will also lead to the destruction of both known and unknown heritage sites (cf. Jopson, 2013; McConnell, 2013).[16] Similarly, increasing economic output can lead to pollution, which can both affect heritage sites and in extreme instances be a deterrent to travel.

Technological innovation

Developments in ICTs in the last three decades have had a profound impact on society.[17] A typical computer at the beginning of the second decade of the twenty-first century has about ten million times the processing power of a computer in 1975, while the range of applications for ICT have increased hugely. This makes the job of understanding where technology is going increasingly difficult.

Networked mobile devices are already changing the way (heritage) tourists engage with their environment, while developments in visualization, natural language processing, cloud computing and big data are likely to enhance visitor experiences in a massively online world. Many developments point to a world where ICT is omnipresent. Processing power will continue to increase.[18] Non-contact interfaces (e.g. Microsoft's Kinect, Apple's Siri or Google's Project Glass) are heralding an era where computers adapt to the user and become a natural way of interacting with the environment, while the development of ultra-low power chips with the capacity to harvest energy and Near Field Communication (NFC) will put 'computable entities' everywhere. A huge number of objects (e.g. buildings, vehicles, clothes, museum objects) can become 'computable' in a 'Web of Things'. These entities will be able to interact seamlessly with themselves and the mobile devices of visitors. These visitors will be able to easily access digital objects and products from the physical world. Computers are becoming less invasive but more pervasive as they become embedded in the Web of Things, and non-contact interfaces make accessing the digital world more natural.

Clearly, with pervasive ICT the potential to disseminate cultural heritage to a wide, but targeted audience becomes far more achievable, while the sharing of heritage knowledge through networks and other fora will enhance the training and development of the cultural heritage professions. But of course the digital divide means that not everyone can engage in the digital world, while heritage organizations are often the least well positioned to support its development. The application of ICTs to cultural heritage tourism will be full of contrasts and paradoxes (see chapter 17 in this volume).

Culture and heritage is increasingly preserved and transmitted digitally. ICT provides new mechanisms to share, analyse and present cultural heritage. Moreover, new forms of heritage are being created digitally (Koers *et al.*, 2012). Just how this ephemeral digital heritage will be preserved and transmitted for future generations remains to be seen. Moreover, digital heritage is less likely to be tied to 'place'. There are of course exceptions, such as Bletchley Park in Buckinghamshire, UK, which was the site of the British code-breaking efforts in the Second World War and where the world's first programmable electronic digital computer (Colossus) was built and housed.[19] This is now a heritage attraction in its own right with the digital history providing a part of the offer. But such sites are an exception. Considering the huge impact digital technology has had on society, there are surprisingly few 'places' where digital heritage is preserved, celebrated or curated. Digital heritage does not lend itself to heritage tourism in the same way as a castle or a cathedral, but it is an integral part of heritage tourism.

ICT brings new opportunities for heritage tourism. For example, the potential to visit heritage sites remotely using virtual reality (virtual tourism). This brings with it its own paradoxes. Remote visits through digital media often allow the visitor to experience a heritage site under optimum conditions. There are no crowds to interfere with the experience, the lighting conditions are often optimal, the virtual visitor can stay as long as they like and experience this from the comfort of their own homes. There is no cost associated with travelling to the location (although there may be costs to access the digital site and indirect costs such as equipment and internet access). However, none of this mitigates the fact that this is clearly not an authentic experience. There is something about the journey and the cache of having been to a site that holds more value than just having visited 'online'. It is apparent that ICTs and the technological innovation that they bring will have a profound impact on cultural heritage tourism as it will on all areas of life.

Conclusions

We began this book with heritage tourists in the classical world. The intervening two millennia have witnessed a sea change in both the desire and the capacity to travel to see the cultural history and achievements of other cultures. Over time heritage tourism has metamorphosed from the preserve of the wealthy to a mass market phenomenon. The increase in the number of tourists has contributed to the increase in the number of heritage tourism sites and attractions, and the broadening of the scope of what is considered heritage.

This chapter has focused on how external drivers can influence mainly tangible cultural heritage; however, as is all too apparent, the definition of what constitutes cultural heritage is constantly expanding. Driven by fashion, politics, and public opinion, heritage is changing.

We can expect that new forms of heritage will become attractions in the future. For example, will preserved examples of contemporary, ephemeral street art become a future heritage tourist attraction? The increasing value of some street art by prestigious artists (e.g. Banksy in the UK) could turn this counter culture into something more mainstream. It is difficult to determine where fashion and taste will take heritage tourism on the margins. Moreover, as time progresses, more material becomes clearly identified as heritage simply by virtue of its getting older. If we were to look ahead 40 years, culture and buildings from the 1970s will be of the same antiquity as the 1930s are to us today. Heritage is constantly evolving.

It is evident that the coming decades will be a time of considerable and rapid change. Population growth, in conjunction with surges in economic growth and the development of the middle class, will lead to a rise in tourism from which cultural heritage tourism can be expected to benefit. However, the condition of some heritage assets and environments is threatened because of mass tourism, rapid urbanization, economic development, climate change, pollution and socio-political instability. Moreover, intangible cultural heritage is vulnerable to economic disruption and the homogenization of culture caused by globalization. The sustainable management of cultural heritage as a tourism resource is a major challenge for today and will continue to be long into the future.

Notes

1 In the context of this chapter, short term is defined as within five years (2018), mid-term within ten (2023) and long term is the remaining period up to 2050.
2 In Europe and other industrialized countries, this is linked in part to the aging of the post-Second World War 'baby boom' cohorts.
3 Japan is currently one of the 'greyest' countries on Earth. In 1989, only 11.6 per cent of the population was 65 years or older, but by 2003, that figure had risen to 16 per cent and this is expected to be at 26 per cent by 2015 (UNDP, 2005: 232).
4 Clearly, this is not static. What is favoured will depend on the fashions and experiences of each cohort as it ages.
5 The United Nations defines an international migrant as someone who has resided in a foreign country for more than one year regardless of the causes (UNFPA, 2011: 66).
6 As a charity, the UK's National Trust is independent of government. It relies on the support of its members, visitors, donors and partners for sustainability. As always, the national headline figures mask numerous regional variations and monthly fluctuations.
7 The BRICS countries (Brazil, Russia, India, China and South Africa) are the most obvious manifestation of fast growing, emerging economies.
8 Naturally, with a population of approximately 1,354 million in 2012, the relative number of museums per person is still relatively low, at one per 400,000. However, in the short term, there is no sign of a slowdown in the museum-building programme.
9 In 2013, India had 30 World Heritage Sites (of which six are natural), while Brazil had 19, of which seven are natural (one cultural site is shared with Argentina).
10 In November 2010, Europe conceded two seats on the executive board of the IMF in order to make way for the emerging economies.
11 UNESCO World Heritage (Paris), ICOMOS (Paris), ICOM (Paris), ICCROM (Rome).

12 In the context of the USA, Heilbrun and Gray (2001) note that education is one of the most important factors in influencing cultural participation. Similarly, Schuster (1993) has noted a correlation between art museum attendance and educational attainment in the UK and Sweden.

13 For example, flooding may damage building materials, and subsequent drying may encourage the growth of moulds and fungus. Timber and organic construction materials may be subject to increased biological infestation. Structural damage can be caused by increased storminess and wind gusts, while desertification, salt weathering and erosion can threaten cultural heritage in desert regions (UNESCO, 2006).

14 Of course, desertification may be bad for tourism but it may not necessarily be bad for heritage sites and monuments. Numerous desert heritage sites, such as the Roman forts at Qasr Bshir (Mobene) in the desert of Jordan, or Qasr ibn Wardan on the western edge of the Syrian desert, are so well preserved precisely because they are in deserts with dry atmospheres and poor accessibility.

15 A cruise on the MS Sea Adventurer in August 2013 takes visitors on a tour that includes Inuit sites, the 1920s RCMP station at Dundas Harbour, the Franklin crew graves at Beechey Island and the Hudson's Bay Company post at Fort Ross.

16 For example, Mes Aynak in Afghanistan is a 100-acre Bronze Age, Buddhist and Islamic heritage site which sits on top of huge copper reserves, the rights to which have been sold to the China Metallurgical Group (McConnell, 2013). Similarly, a new uranium deposit has been discovered in the Wellington Mountain Range in Australia. The range is home to many caves containing Aboriginal rock art, which may be threatened by the proximity of future extraction and increased visitation (cf. Jopson, 2013).

17 Of course, ICT may be the poster child of innovation but there are developments in many other technologies that will benefit cultural heritage. Everything from LED lights to nanotechnology can benefit heritage sites. For example, one year after an advanced building retrofit project, New York's iconic Empire State Building saved $2.4 million in energy costs.

18 Moore's Law (the doubling of processing power approximately every 18 months) has been driven by processor manufacturers packing more transistors into less space. However, as we are nearing physical limits, this paradigm will change. This could herald the introduction of quantum computers, which will turn Moore's Law on its head. It is no coincidence that the 2012 Nobel Prize in Physics was awarded to Serge Haroche and David J. Wineland for their work on quantum physics.

19 Bletchley Park has been a museum and tourist attraction since 1993 and is also the home of the National Museum of Computing.

References

ACIA (2005) *Arctic climate impact assessment*, Cambridge: Cambridge University Press.

Anon. (2011) 'In Syria, death of tourism most visible sign of major economic damage', *The Washington Post*, June 8.

Anon. (2013a) 'Local authority funding fell by £23m in 2011–12', *Museums Journal*, 113(1): 5.

Anon. (2013b) 'Proportion of adults visiting museums hits all-time high', *Museums Journal*, 113(1): 15.

Anon. (2013c) 'National redundancies top 400 mark since 2010', *Museums Journal*, 113(3): 7.

Anon. (2013d) 'A building boom in China', *The New York Times*, March 21.

Armaly, M., Blasi, C. and Hannah, L. (2004) 'Stari Most: Rebuilding more than a historic bridge in Mostar', *Museum International*, 56(224): 6–17.

Bailey, M. (2006) 'Antiquities are the most precious thing in Iraq, not oil. They represent the memory of the Iraqi people', *The Art Newspaper*, 15(175): 8–9.

Baker, R. W., Ismael, S. T. and Ismael, T. Y. (eds.) (2010) *Cultural cleansing in Iraq: Why museums were looted, libraries burned and academics murdered*, London: Pluto Press.

BBC News Channel (2007) *Attack on giant Pakistan Buddha*, September 12, accessed (April 2013) at http://news.bbc.co.uk/1/hi/6991058.stm.

Bevan, R. (2006) *The destruction of memory: Architecture at war*, London: Reaktion Books.

Bodganos, M. (2006) 'Casualties of war: The looting of the Iraq museum', *Museum News*, 85(2): 34–44.

Breitkopf, S. (2007) 'Lost: the looting of Iraq's antiquities', *Museum News*, 86(1): 44–51.

Bromwich, D. H., Nicolas, J. P., Monaghan, A. J., Lazzara, M. A., Keller, L. M., Weidner, G. A. and Wilson, A. B. (2012) 'Central West Antarctica among the most rapidly warming regions on Earth', *Nature Geoscience*, 6(2): 139–145.

Clément, E. (1992) 'Some recent practical experience in the implementation of the 1954 Hague Convention', *International Journal of Cultural Property*, 11: 11–25.

Cunliffe, E. (2012) *Damage to the soul: Syria's cultural heritage in conflict*, Palo Alto: Global Heritage Fund, available at http://ghn.globalheritagefund.com/uploads/documents/document_2107.pdf.

Dibbern, S. (2009) 'Fur seals, whales and tourists: A commercial history of Deception Island', *Antarctica Polar Record*, 46(203): 210–221.

du Cros, H., Bauer, T., Lo, C. and Rui, S. (2005) 'Cultural heritage assets in China as sustainable tourism products: Case studies of the Hutongs and the Huanghua section of the Great Wall', *Journal of Sustainable Tourism*, 13(2): 171–194.

Edwards, D. C. (2005) 'It's mostly about me: Reasons why volunteers contribute their time to museums and art museums', *Tourism Review International*, 9: 1–11.

Eilperin, J. (2012) 'Alaskan Arctic villages hit hard by climate change', *Washington Post*, August 5.

Eurostat (2013) *Population structure and ageing*, available online at http://epp.eurostat.ec.europa.eu/statistics_explained/index.php/Population_structure_and_ageing#Further_Eurostat_information (accessed January 21, 2013).

Giesen, M. J., Ung, A., Warke, P. A., Christgen, B., Mazel, A. D. and Graham, D. W. (2013) 'Condition assessment and preservation of open-air rock art panels during environmental change', *Journal of Cultural Heritage*, available online at doi:10.1016/j.culher.2013.01.013 (accessed March 17, 2013).

Graham, M. (2001) 'The role of museum volunteering in relieving social isolation', *Leisure Studies Association*, 75: 57–75.

Grissmann, C. (2003) 'The inventory of the Kabul Museum: Attempts at restoring order', *Museum International*, 218/219: 71–76.

Heilbrun, J. and Gray, C. M. (2001) *The economics of art and culture* (second edition), Cambridge: Cambridge University Press.

HIIK (2012) *Conflict barometer 2012*, Heidelberg: Heidelberg Institute for International Conflict Research.

Hughes, J. (1994) 'Antarctic historic sites: The tourism implications', *Annals of Tourism Research*, 21(2): 281–294.

Hughes, J. and Davis, B. (1995) 'The management of tourism at historic sites and monuments', in Jones C. M. and Johnston, M. E. (eds.) *Polar tourism: Tourism in the Arctic and Antarctic regions*, London: John Wiley and Sons, 235–255.

IEA (2012) *Energy technology perspectives 2012: Pathways to a clean energy system*, Paris: The International Energy Agency.

IOM (2011) *World migration report 2011: Communicating effectively about migration*, Geneva: International Organization for Migration.

Jopson, D. (2013) 'Australian uranium discovery threatens ancient indigenous cave art', *The Guardian*, March 8.

Kendall, G. (2012) 'Slash and burn', *Museums Journal*, 112(11): 24–28.

Koers, W., van der Giessen, A., van Weelden, M. and Becker, J. (2012) *Future of cultural heritage: Impact of external developments, Background paper to the 18 December 2012 European Policy Workshop, Brussels*, available online at http://ec.europa.eu/research/social-sciences/pdf/events-228/efp-cultural-heritage-background-paper_en.pdf (accessed February 28, 2012).

Libicki, M. C., Shatz, H. J. and Taylor, J. E. (2011) *Global demographic change and its implications for military power*, Santa Monica: RAND Corporation.

Lloyds (2012) *Arctic opening: Opportunity and risk in the high north*, London: Lloyds.

Manhart, C. (2001) 'The Afghan cultural heritage crisis: UNESCO's response to the destruction of statues in Afghanistan', *American Journal of Archaeology*, 105: 387–388.

MAPS (2007) *Moscow heritage at crisis point* (second edition), Moscow: Moscow Architecture Preservation Society.

McConnell, F. (2013) 'Afghanistan's heritage is at stake', *The Independent*, March 17.

MOD (2010) *Global strategic trends: Out to 2040*, Shrivenham: Ministry of Defence.

Moscardo, G. (2006) 'Third-age tourism', in Buhalis, D. and Costa, C. (eds.) *Tourism business frontiers: Consumers, products and industry*, Oxford: Elsevier, 30–39.

Musharbash, Y. (2007) 'The "Talibanization" of Pakistan: Islamists destroy Buddhist statue', *Spiegel Online*, accessed (April 2013) at www.spiegel.de/international/world/the-talibanization-of-pakistan-islamists-destroy-buddhist-statue-a-515958.html.

National Trust (2012) *Going local: National Trust annual report 2011/12*, London: National Trust.

Nederlands Bureau voor Toerisme (1988) *Waarom komen Buitenlanders voor vakantie naar Nederland?*, Leidschendam: NBT.

Nemeth, E. (2013) 'Alternative power: Political economy of cultural property', *Journal of International Affairs*, available online at www.rand.org/pubs/external_publications/EP51306.html (accessed February 28, 2012).

NIC (2012) *Global trends 2030: Alternative worlds*, Washington: National Intelligence Council.

NRC (2011) *Climate stabilization targets: Emissions, concentrations, and impacts over decades to millennia*, Washington: National Academies Press.

Papatheodorou, A., Rosselló, J. and Xiao, H. (2010) 'Global economic crisis and tourism: Consequences and perspectives', *Journal of Travel Research*, 49(1): 39–45.

Rhisiart, M. and While, G. (2008) *The future of the arts and culture in Wales within a global context: Trends, drivers of change and new paradigms*, Arts Council of Wales, available online at www.artscouncilofwales.org.uk/what-we-do/research/latest-research/the-futures-study (accessed January 12, 2013).

Rodwell, D. (2004) 'Dubrovnik: Pearl of the Adriatic', *World Heritage*, 38: 68–79.

Schuster, J. M. D. (1993) 'The public interest in the art museum's public', in Gubbels, T. and van Hemel, A. (eds.) *Art museums and the price of success: An international comparison*, Amsterdam: Boekmanstichting, 45–60.

Senatore, M. X. and Zarankin, A. (2012) 'Tourism and the invisible historic sites in

Antarctica', *Proceedings of the ICOMOS General Assembly Scientific Symposium*, Part III: Session Development as Tourism, 592–601, Paris: ICOMOS.

Stone, P. G. and Bajjaly J. F. (eds.) (2008) *The destruction of cultural heritage in Iraq*, Woodbridge: Boydell Press.

Stonehouse, B. and Snyder, J. M. (2010) *Polar tourism: An environmental perspective*, Bristol: Channel View Publications.

Talley, M. K. (1995) 'The old road and the mind's internal heaven: Preservation of the cultural heritage in times of armed conflict', *Museum Management and Curatorship*, 14(1): 57–64.

Turner, J., Colwell, S. R., Marshall, G. J., Lachlan-Cope, T. A., Carleton, A. M., Jones, P. D., Lagun, V., Reid, P. A. and Iagovkina, S. (2005) 'Antarctic climate change during the last 50 years', *International Journal of Climatology*, 25: 279–294.

UNDP (2005) *Human development report 2005: International cooperation at a cross-roads – aid, trade and security in an unequal world*, New York: United Nations Development Programme.

UNESCO (2006) *Predicting and managing the effects of climate change on world heritage*, Vilnius: UNESCO.

UNFPA (2011) *State of world population 2011*, New York: United Nations Population Fund.

United Nations (2012) 'Population ageing and development: Ten years after Madrid', *Population Facts*, 2012/4: 1–4.

UNWTO (2009) *UNWTO World Tourism Barometer*, 7(2), June.

UNWTO (2013) *UNWTO World Tourism Barometer*, 11(1), January.

Ward, K. (2011) *The world in 2050: Quantifying the shift in the global economy*, London: HSBC.

Ward, K. (2012) *The world in 2050: From the top 30 to the top 100*, London: HSBC.

Wegener, C. and Otter, M. (2008) 'Cultural property at war: Protecting heritage during armed conflict', *Conservation: The Getty Conservation Institute newsletter*, 23(1): 4–9.

Xu, J. and Le Guay, O. (2013) *Behind the China museum fever*, available online at www.forum-avignon.org/en/behind-china-museum-fever (accessed March 21, 2013).

Zhao, C. (2004) 'From Shikumen to new-style: A rereading of lilong housing in modern Shanghai', *The Journal of Architecture*, 9(1): 49–76.

Index

Page numbers in *italics* denote tables, those in **bold** denote figures.

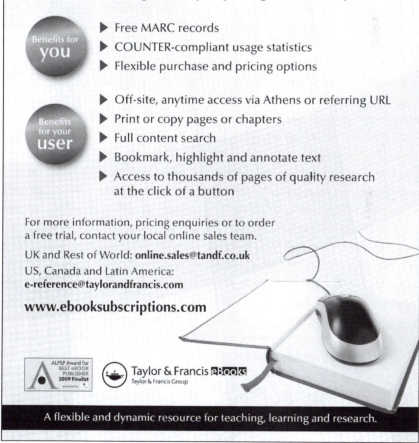